IN THE INTEREST *of*
JUSTICE

IN THE INTEREST *of*
JUSTICE

GREAT OPENING AND CLOSING ARGUMENTS
OF THE LAST 100 YEARS

JOEL J. SEIDEMANN

1e ReganBooks
Celebrating Ten Bestselling Years
An Imprint of HarperCollins*Publishers*

HarperCollins books may be purchased for educational, business, or sales promotional use. For information please write: Special Markets Department, HarperCollins Publishers Inc., 10 East 53rd Street, New York, NY 10022.

FIRST EDITION

Designed by Nancy Singer Olaguera

Printed on acid-free paper

Library of Congress Cataloging-in-Publication Data

Seidemann, Joel.
    In the interest of justice : great opening and closing arguments from the last 100 years / Joel Seidemann.—1st ed.
        p.   cm.
    Includes bibliographical references.
    ISBN 0-06-050966-X

K181.S45 2004
808.85'93554—dc22   2004051095

04 05 06 07 08 ❖/RRD 10 9 8 7 6 5 4 3 2 1

To my mother and my father,
who achieved and excelled against the odds
and whose love and encouragement gave me
the confidence to do the same

CONTENTS

ACKNOWLEDGMENTS

A PROJECT OF THIS magnitude generally cannot be successfully completed by one person alone. This book was no exception. The end product was the result of the teamwork of several gifted individuals.

The idea for a book of great courtroom speeches evolved out of my friendship with Judith Regan. I would send her brief transcripts to read, solely to amuse her. I didn't have a clue that she would read these transcripts with an eye toward coming up with a book to memorialize the brilliance of lawyers' courtroom speeches. She had the confidence in me that I could be the quarterback of such a project and made available to me the excellent editors at ReganBooks to help me achieve this goal.

My former colleague Zach Weiss—an excellent lawyer and a great friend—selflessly opened his library of transcripts to me. Beth Karas and Grace Wong of Court TV both gave me great advice about terrific cases and lawyers they had encountered in reporting cases for Court TV.

I had many helpers in gathering the cases, without whom this project would never have gotten off the ground. Josh Kotkin, Ethan Kotkin, Edan Razinovsky, Xiomara Carias-Mier all were part of the gathering, photocopying, scanning, and transcribing of the transcripts that are included in this book. Many lawyers—too numerous to mention—provided transcripts and insight on the cases that ultimately ended up in the book.

Melik Kaylan's assistance in helping me properly express and sharpen my ideas in the introductions and postscripts was invaluable.

The editors at ReganBooks, Cal Morgan and Jessica Colter, further enhanced the end product through their insightful suggestions, careful analysis, and sensible changes.

To paraphrase the junior senator from New York, "It takes a family to write a book." My family was incredibly supportive throughout this process. My brother David assisted me in reviewing the material regarding the Karen Silkwood case and in finding other material for me on the Internet. My brother Daniel recommended that I look at the opening in the Eichmann case and review the Tom Segev book *The Seventh Million*. I even put my seventy-nine-year-old father, Hans, to work reviewing materials. My wife, Yael, took all carpooling tasks away from me during this period to give me the time to complete the project. My son, Jon (aka Yonatan), was understanding when he saw me reading courtroom transcripts at his Little League games, and my daughter, Shelly, graciously accepted the fact that while I was writing this book there would be fewer trips to Leapin' Lizard.

The love and encouragement of my entire family was the driving force that helped me complete the book.

My boss, Robert M. Morgenthau, District Attorney of the Manhattan DA's office, the most prestigious prosecutor's office in the country, gave me the ability over the last twenty-two years to get up each morning and make certain that every case I handled achieved a result "in the interest of justice."

INTRODUCTION

MANY OF THE CASES in this book are famous. You have heard of them and probably formed your own opinions of them. They created quite a stir, and though, for some, their time in the limelight has passed, they have not left our consciousness and may not in our lifetime. O. J. Simpson, Al Qaeda moles, the Oklahoma City bombing—for good or ill, they entered our mental lexicon as paradigms of some principle or larger ethos. They might embody different principles to different people—indeed, each is a kind of Rorschach test through which we can discern our own worldview. Whatever that may be, they retain the power to touch a raw nerve in all of us and provoke a vivid response.

Despite overblown media impressions, most people still remain confused about what actually happened at many of the trials included in this volume. Why did O. J. win the criminal case and lose the civil one? Why did the jury acquit the cops who shot Amadou Diallo even though they fired forty-one shots at an unarmed man? Why was Sean "Puffy" Combs acquitted of all charges after that mysterious firefight at that nightclub? This book sheds light on these questions.

The first lesson herein is that events in the courtroom always differ from the media rendition. The courtroom's intense enclosed theater creates unparalleled moments of conflict and revelation, and what happens there is more human, more dramatic, more gritty than the media can convey. The truth always is. There's an old joke that best describes what the media does to reality: A mother wheels her firstborn in a stroller. When a friend compliments her on the baby's beauty, the mother replies, "You think she's pretty in real life? You should see the pictures." The media gives us the picture; in the courtroom you see real life.

This is primarily a book of great speeches by some of the best courtroom lawyers of our time, or of any time. The payoff to readers, I hope, is twofold: that they feel both the spell of a master story-teller and the sensation of being personally present at an event they've often heard about from afar. My goal is to place the reader in the jury box, face-to-face with the advocate in full flow, plying his trade, swaying a jury toward the justness of his cause.

Not all of the cases I chose are renowned or even recent. Sure, they are all highly readable and most of the attorneys are terrifically eloquent, but if that were enough, I could fill a whole other volume with different but equally entertaining examples. What is so special about the speeches compiled here? The answer may sound esoteric at first. They stand out as moments—and I'm not being mystical—in which a higher witness seems to hover in the courtroom. The courtroom seems to float in an eternal time zone, with the jury of the ages looking on. Maybe it's history being made, or the conta-gious tabloid buzz in the air, or both of those things and more. Any lawyer who has argued important cases has lived through it at least once, this sensation that the event is suddenly greater than the peo-ple involved. That ineffable feeling of transcendence is what unites the cases in this book. And in each instance the lawyers occupy center stage. Their fine-tuned awareness of the setting, of the his-toric moment, of the jury's—and often even the whole country's—mood infuses their rhetoric. At their best—as in the pages of this book—their words echo out into a wider consciousness.

The few relatively unknown cases that I feature here have that forever quality, too. Powerful and heartrending, they act as redis-covered snapshots of a haunting time. They are sentencing speeches against convicted murderers from an era when street crime held our cities under perpetual siege. In those years fear and senseless violence felt as inevitable as death and taxes. One more mindless murder, one more statistic, every day, for decades—who can differentiate them now? As part of my twenty-two years in the New York County DA's office, I have had to live through those anguished courtroom scenes of impervious killers and families in agony virtually every day, or so it seemed. This is my chance to commemorate those victims.

These extracts of opening and closing arguments can be read as intact short stories in which the lawyers unfold the events of each case in a clear, linear plotline—the best advocacy must do this anyway. To help the reader follow along, I have included an introduction and postscript to each case—the former sets the scene and the latter explains the verdict, analyzes why one side prevailed over the other, and offers an appreciation of the courtroom skills and tricks displayed by the advocates.

This is a book of classic legal dramas, ranging from the unforgettable to the unbelievable. Both conditions apply in the trial of Nazi war criminal Adolf Eichmann, represented here in the form of the famous opening statement by his Israeli prosecutor, who gives a harrowing history lesson on the most horrific crimes in history. Another case that reverberates through the decades is the so-called Scopes monkey trial from the 1920s, which pitted evolution against creationism and later became the centerpiece of the Spencer Tracy movie *Inherit the Wind*.

Sometimes, however, a trial qualifies for greatness on account not only of its high standard of advocacy but also its extreme comic appeal. The tabloid classic of celebrity sportscaster Marv Albert's prosecution for sexual assault—in which his alleged hairpiece played a critical role—is just such an instance. Another is the Bess Myerson case, one full to the brim with characters so absurd that Hollywood could never have dreamed up a zanier story. In other cases the media frenzy surrounding the proceedings—as in the Puff Daddy and Martha Stewart trials—made the courtroom feel as though it were situated in the center of the universe—if only for a few weeks or months.

I have also included three wildly unsuccessful examples of pro se advocacy, cases in which the defendants chose to argue for themselves without a lawyer. Now, that might seem a capricious choice in a book dedicated to great and moving speeches. But I would submit that these particular pro se speeches, although ultimately unsuccessful, have their own resonance. When Zacarias Moussaoui, the twentieth hijacker who never made it to the Twin Towers because he was arrested months before, makes his statement in court, we are bound to listen. It makes hypnotic reading, allowing us to eavesdrop on the self-justifying mania of a would-be Al Qaeda kamikaze. If lawyers had intervened—if Moussaoui had let them—we would not now be able to see into his mind so vividly. The same applies to the pro se speech of mass murderer Colin Ferguson, who boarded a New York commuter train with a loaded nine-millimeter semi-automatic and went on a systematic shooting spree, killing six and wounding nineteen. His eerie opening argument sounds utterly logical—except for a stray detail here and there, which, in combination, betrayed his unhinged mind. On the lighter side, Congressman James Traficant brought the same unusual flair to the courtroom that he had exhibited in his years as a congressman. Unfortunately for Mr. Traficant, his flair for the outrageous did not prevent his conviction for corruption and ultimate expulsion from the House.

Consider this book an invitation to enter the courtrooms and witness the immensely powerful and entertaining words of real-life lawyers whose brilliance shines even without the benefit of Armani suits, TV sound bites, and a dramatic soundtrack. Using anecdote, humor, sarcasm, evidence both circumstantial and direct, and every appeal to emotion they can conjure, the unforgettable opening and closing statements collected here prove one case beyond a reasonable doubt: that the great trial lawyer is a craftsman of the spoken word. Now sit back and enjoy.

1

A TALE OF TWO VERDICTS
THE O. J. SIMPSON CASE

ON THE EVENING OF June 12, 1994, Steven Schwab of Brentwood, California, was walking his dog near his home when he saw an Akita standing and barking loudly in the middle of the street, its legs and paws covered in blood. Failing to find the animal's owner, Schwab left it in the temporary care of a neighbor, Sukru Boztepe, who then took the apparently ownerless dog for a walk. Instantly, it pulled him in the direction of a walkway leading to a nearby condominium, where Mr. Boztepe made a gruesome discovery: the body of a young woman lying dead in a pool of blood, with stab wounds to her neck and a gaping slash across her throat. He immediately called the police to the scene, where they discovered the dead body of a young man with knife wounds to the neck, leg, chest, and stomach only a few feet away from the woman. The female victim was Nicole Brown Simpson, the estranged wife of former football star and sportscaster O. J. Simpson, and the young man was Ronald Goldman, whose kindness in returning a set of eyeglasses cost him his life.

This unlikely discovery in an affluent suburb of Los Angeles launched a new chapter in the annals of American legal jurisprudence, obsessing the media, dividing the country, and generating a wave of tragic pop-culture notoriety unseen since the murders of John F. Kennedy and John Lennon.

Within days of the double murder, the Los Angeles Police Department focused on Simpson as the likely killer and offered him the chance to surrender. Instead of turning himself in, he slipped out of the home of his lawyer, Robert Kardashian, and took off in his Ford Bronco, leading the police on a sixty-mile car chase involving more than twenty-five police cars. As his friend drove the getaway car, O. J. sat in the back, holding a Magnum pistol to his head and threatening to kill himself. This surreal car chase was broadcast live all over America and much of the world. It was a moment so indelible in the collective consciousness that most people still remember where they were when they watched the events on television.

O. J. Simpson was famously prosecuted twice: first in criminal court, where he was acquitted of first-degree murder charges after an eleven-month trial and less than four hours of deliberations, and then in civil court, where he was found guilty of the wrongful death of Ronald Goldman and the battery with oppression and malice of both Goldman and Nicole Brown Simpson. I have featured the opening argument in the civil case first because it offers a much clearer narrative of the night's dreadful events.

SHARON RUFO ET AL. v. ORENTHAL JAMES SIMPSON

Excerpts from Plaintiff Attorney Daniel Petrocelli's Opening Statement, October 1996

On a June evening, the twelfth of June, 1994, Nicole Brown Simpson just finished putting her ten-year-old daughter, Sydney, and her six-year-old son, Justin, to bed. She filled her bathtub with water. She lit some candles, began to get ready to take a bath and relax for the evening.

The phone rang. It was 9:40 P.M. Nicole answered. It was her mother, saying that she had left her glasses at the restaurant nearby in Brentwood, where the family had all celebrated Sydney's dance recital over dinner, just an hour before. Nicole's mother asked if Nicole could please pick up her glasses from the restaurant the next day. Nicole said, of course and hung up.

Nicole then called the restaurant and asked to speak to a

friendly young waiter there. Nicole asked this young waiter if he would be kind enough to drop her mother's glasses off. The young man obliged and said he would drop the glasses off shortly after work, on his way to meet his friend. The young man's name was Ron Goldman. He was twenty-five years old.

With the glasses in hand, Ron walked out of the restaurant to his apartment nearby, to change. He left the restaurant at 9:50 P.M. After Ron changed, he got into his girlfriend's car, parked in his garage, and drove the short distance to Nicole Brown Simpson's home at 875 South Bundy Drive in Brentwood. Ron parked the car on the side street, walked to the front of Nicole's condominium, and turned up the walkway to the front gate. Just past the front gate were steps leading to Nicole's condominium.

Ronald Goldman never made it past those steps. It was at that front gate that Ron spent the last few savage minutes of his life. It was there that his brutalized body was found next to Nicole Brown Simpson's slain body, with her mother's glasses lying next to him on the ground in an envelope. Ron Goldman's young life ended because he agreed to do a friend a favor, only to come upon her rageful killer and his.

He might have run from danger, but he did not. Ron Goldman died, ladies and gentlemen, with his eyes open. And in the last furious moment of his life, Ron saw through those open eyes the person who killed his friend Nicole. And for that reason he too, had to die. And the last person Ron Goldman saw through his open eyes was the man who took his young life away: the man who now sits in this courtroom, the defendant, Orenthal James Simpson. Ladies and gentlemen, we will prove to you that Ronald Goldman and Nicole Brown Simpson died at the hands of the defendant.

My name is Daniel Petrocelli. With me are Edward Medvene, Peter Gelblum, Yvette Molinaro, Thomas Lambert. We all represent the Estate of Ronald Goldman and Ronald's father, Fred, in this, his last fight for justice for his son.

• • •

In this trial we will present to you an extraordinary amount of evidence undeniably pointing to O. J. Simpson as the person who killed Ronald Goldman and Nicole Brown Simpson on the evening of June twelve. This evidence includes Mr. Simpson's blood leaving the scene of the murder at Nicole's condominium; his blood dripping to the ground from the fingers of his left hand; Mr. Simpson's blood on the glove he wore when he killed Ron and Nicole; Mr. Simpson's blood in his car that he used to drive from Bundy to his home at Rockingham, five minutes away; Mr. Simpson's blood on the driveway of his home; Mr. Simpson's blood inside his home; Ron's blood in Mr. Simpson's car; Nicole's blood in Mr. Simpson's car; Ron's blood on Mr. Simpson's glove; Nicole's blood on Mr. Simpson's glove; Nicole's blood on the socks in Mr. Simpson's bedroom; Mr. Simpson's own blood on his socks; Mr. Simpson's size-twelve shoe prints in the blood of Nicole, leaving the scene of the murder, exiting toward the back of the condominium; hair matching Mr. Simpson's hair in the knit cap he left behind at the scene of the murders; hair matching Mr. Simpson's hair on Ronald Goldman's shirt; strands of Nicole's hair and Ron's hair on the glove Mr. Simpson dropped on the side of his house, trying to get onto his property so no one would see him; rare carpet fibers from Mr. Simpson's Bronco found in the knit cap that he left at the scene of the murders; matching blue-black cotton fibers found on Ronald Goldman's shirt; the glove at Rockingham and Mr. Simpson's socks in the bedroom, tying all three together; cuts and bruises to Mr. Simpson's left hand during his brief but violent attacks on Ron and Nicole, cuts that to this day Mr. Simpson cannot and will not explain.

We will prove to you that Mr. Simpson has no alibi during the time when the murders were committed. He cannot identify a single person who can account for his whereabouts during the time of the murders. Not one person will take this stand and testify that he was with Mr. Simpson or spoke to Mr. Simpson during the time of these murders.

We will prove how Ron and Nicole were killed quickly and savagely. They were defenseless against a man so large, powerful, strong, armed with a six-inch knife, and in a total state of rage. Nicole had no chance to fight, and died within moments of the gaping cut to her throat. Ron tried to fight, but, trapped in a small, caged area, he was cut down swiftly.

We will prove to you that Mr. Simpson committed the murders and sped back home, just in time to drive to the airport and catch a plane that he desperately needed to catch to have any hope of an alibi. In his extreme panic and hurry, Mr. Simpson left behind a trail of incriminating evidence, starting right at the murder scene and leading right into his bedroom.

We will prove to you that Mr. Simpson was embroiled in a deeply emotional conflict with Nicole Brown Simpson after she had just ended any last attempt at reconciliation between the two. We will describe to you the rejection and pain this caused Mr. Simpson in detail, the buildup of tension, emotion, and anger between Mr. Simpson and Nicole in the last weeks and days leading up to her murder.

We will prove that Mr. Simpson killed Ronald Goldman because he would have been a witness to the rageful attack and murder of Nicole, a witness who would have testified in this trial, a young man who simply, and frankly, happened to be at the wrong place at the wrong time.

We will prove to you how Mr. Simpson's own words and actions following the murders revealed then, and still reveal today, his guilt for these deaths. You will hear Mr. Simpson on tape, just hours after the murder, unable to explain his actions during the time of the murders. You will hear him make very incriminating statements that he will now try to contradict.

We will tell you about Mr. Simpson's flight from the police when they came to arrest him and his apparent thoughts of taking his life, thoughts that are consistent only with a person who had killed and that are totally inconsistent with a man whose children had just lost their mother at the hands of a stranger. You will hear how this man came back to Los Angeles on the day after the murders and huddled with lawyers, rather than huddle with his children.

MR. BAKER:	I object, Your Honor. That's argument.
THE COURT:	Sustained.
MR. PETROCELLI:	We will reveal to you lies and deceptions in the sworn testimony of Mr. Simpson when questioned under oath for the first time about his involvement in these murders. We will prove to you that when asked all the important questions about his

involvement in these murders, O. J. Simpson could not, would not, and did not tell the truth.

And finally, ladies and gentlemen, we will show that when faced with the truth of his blood, his hair, his clothing, his gloves, his shoes, his Bronco, his rage, his motive, his words, and his actions, you will see how Mr. Simpson in this trial will resort to theories of police conspiracies, frame-ups, cover-ups and incompetence, to try to explain away all of the incriminating evidence. And we will show you that there is not one ounce of proof, and not one ounce of truth, to any of these things.

We will demonstrate to you that far from these theories born out of desperation, there is only one.

MR. BAKER: I object. "Born out of desperation" is argument.

THE COURT: Sustained.

[PETROCELLI resumes.]

We will prove to you that there is only one real and true and honest answer why all the evidence in this case points to O. J. Simpson. And that is because he is the person who killed Ronald Goldman and Nicole Brown Simpson.

I'd like to start with talking about the two victims in the case, Ronald Goldman and Nicole Brown Simpson. Ron grew up in Illinois. His parents got divorced when he was a young boy. He and his little sister, Kimberly, went to live with their father, Fred. When Ron was eighteen, Ron, Kim, Fred, and Fred's new wife, Patty, all moved to Agoura, California. Ron took to Southern California like a fish to water. He excelled at tennis; he loved to play softball. He got a job taking care of cerebral palsy patients. He was the only person at Pierce College who applied for a job helping to take care of inner-city kids to turn their lives around.

He was twenty years old when he moved out of his family's home, eventually winding up in Brentwood, where he loved the friendly atmosphere. He was a happy, outgoing, always smiling, handsome young man, who made friends quickly. He worked in odd jobs here and there to support himself. He did a little modeling, and he dreamed of opening up a restaurant. And in February of 1994, to pay the bills, he got a job at a trendy Italian restaurant called Mezzaluna, as a waiter.

He was single. He had a girlfriend; he had lots of friends; he loved his family; he was one of those people who was always there for others, and ultimately he died doing that. He was a young man, barely twenty-five years old, with his whole life ahead of him.

Nicole Brown Simpson was thirty-five years old when she was killed. She was recently divorced from her ex-husband, O. J. Simpson. She had her two children living with her, Sydney and Justin. She was a full-time devoted mother. She lived in a condominium in Brentwood.

She met Mr. Simpson at the age of eighteen, right after high school. And from that moment they were together. They lived together; they were married in 1985, and they had two children. They had a very tempestuous relationship, passionate at times, violent at other times, one of those relationships where they couldn't live with each other and they couldn't live without each other.

Nicole left Mr. Simpson in January of 1992, filed for divorce, and moved into her own apartment with her children. A year or so later, the divorce was final. After the divorce was final, she and Mr. Simpson decided they would try and reconcile, not living together, but they would start dating. This was about spring of 1993. They then spent the next year, till about three weeks before her death, trying to make this reconciliation work. Three weeks before she was killed, Nicole decided it was not working, and she ended it. One month later she was dead.

O. J. Simpson, the defendant, of course, was a celebrity football star, film actor, and sportscaster, a man who grew up poor and became rich and famous, a charismatic and a charming man, but, in the eyes of the law, a man no different from anyone else.

Now, I'd like to begin the evidence proving the murders by talking about the time when Ron and Nicole were killed. The reason for doing this is simple: After identifying when the murders occurred, we will show you that Mr. Simpson had the opportunity and the time to commit the murders.

We will show you that during this time he has no alibi. Nicole had gone to a dance recital for her daughter, went to dinner at Mezzaluna, left at around 8:30, got some ice cream with the kids, and got home before 9:00, and she put the kids to bed. She received a phone call from her mom at 9:40, asking about the glasses. Her mom asked Nicole to pick them up for her the next day. Instead of picking them up the next day, Nicole called Mezzaluna, spoke to the manager, Karen Crawford, then asked to speak to Ron Goldman and asked Mr. Goldman to bring them over.

Ron left Mezzaluna at 9:50 to go home first, change, and then deliver the glasses. Before Ron left, he spoke to his friend at the restaurant who was tending bar that night, Stewart Tanner, and he made plans with Stewart Tanner and another person to meet together after work in Marina del Rey. Ron then left the restaurant, walked a few minutes to his home, went up to his apartment, and changed out of his waiter's clothes and put on a pair of jeans, a shirt, and some new shoes. It took Ron about five minutes to get to his apartment. Ron apparently did not shave, from the autopsy pictures that we will show. He left his home and drove his girlfriend's car a short distance to Nicole's condominium. He parked on Dorothy Street, around the corner.

He walked up to Nicole's front gate. The time was sometime after ten o'clock P.M. At 10:50 P.M., fifty minutes later, a man named Louis Karpf, who lived right next door to Nicole's condominium, walked out to his mailbox on Bundy to pick up his mail, having just gotten back from the airport. He saw Nicole's dog, a very large Japanese attack dog called an Akita, out in the street, barking. In fact, the dog frightened Mr. Karpf, so he retreated back up onto his property. Then, when the dog moved away, Mr. Karpf continued to his mailbox and got his mail.

A few minutes later, another man is walking his dog from his apartment up the street and around the corner. His name is Steven Schwab. They're just citizens living in Brentwood. They have no ax to grind. Mr. Schwab came by and saw the dog, Nicole's Akita, out in the middle of the street on Bundy and Gorham. And he saw that the dog had blood on his paws, on his legs. The time was 10:55 P.M. Mr. Schwab, with his own dog, saw the dog was wandering aimlessly and barking in a very agitated way. And he decided to take the dog and go home, try to find the owner, call up the animal shelter. He got home, wasn't having any luck, and he asked a neighbor who lived in the same complex, a fellow by the name of Sukru Boztepe, if he could take care of the dog. Mr. Boztepe said sure, and he and his wife started to tend to the dog. And then they decided to take the dog out for a walk, because the dog was agitated, and maybe they could find the dog's owner. They then took the dog for a walk, and the dog pulled Mr. Boztepe on a leash which Mr. Schwab gave Mr. Boztepe in the direction of Nicole Brown Simpson's condominium. In fact, right to the sidewalk where the walkway led up to her body. The dog stopped at that point and looked down the walkway. And Mr. Boztepe saw that the dog was staring. And he then looked, and it was extremely dark, even though he was right in front of the sidewalk there. He did not see anything until the dog turned his head toward the bodies, and then Mr. Boztepe looked and saw Nicole's body laying at the bottom of the stairs in a pool of blood. Mr. Boztepe then quickly raced across the street and knocked on neighbors' doors to get somebody to call the police. And eventually the police were summoned. They arrived a little after midnight.

So we know that these murders occurred sometime after 10:00, when Ron left his apartment, and sometime before 10:50 when Mr. Karpf saw Nicole's dog out in the street. And five minutes later Mr. Schwab saw it with blood. There's another man who will testify. His name is Robert Heidstra. Mr. Heidstra is a dog lover. He has a couple of dogs. He walks them several times a day, takes the same route, knows every inch of the way. He walked his dog on this evening, two of his dogs. He left his house sometime after ten o'clock, closer to 10:15, and he walked around the corner at this point. Mr. Heidstra left his apartment around 10:15 and took this route, walking his dogs. About 10:30, 10:35, Mr. Heidstra reached this point with his two dogs, and he heard a very loud barking. He immediately recognized the dog to be Nicole's dog, because he was familiar with Nicole's dog, having walked by her condominium many times and seen the dog. The dog was barking in a very agitated way, and Mr. Heidstra was frightened that his animals might confront Nicole's dog, so he decided not to walk in front of Nicole's condominium but to take a detour. And he went this way down the alleyway. He cut down this alleyway so he wouldn't have to go by the dog. When he got to this point of the alleyway, directly opposite Nicole's condominium Mr. Heidstra heard a man, young male voice, yell, "Hey, hey, hey." Then he heard a deeper voice respond. Then he heard the other man yell, "Hey, hey." And then he heard a clanging of a gate. When he heard those sounds, it was approximately 10:35 to 10:40. He then continued his walk across the alleyway until he reached Dorothy, and he stopped and paused. He looked down the street while his dogs were doing their business, and he then saw a car pull up to this stop sign and make a right turn, and he got a crystal-clear view of that car as it approached and turned right. That car was a white utility-type or jeeplike automobile with tinted windows, like a Ford Bronco. The time was 10:40 to 10:45.

We will prove, through Mr. Heidstra's testimony and other testimony, that Mr. Heidstra heard Ronald Goldman being confronted and attacked by the defendant. The time was 10:35 to 10:40.

Now, where was Mr. Simpson at that time? Here's what we know: Mr. Simpson had driven alone to his daughter's dance recital earlier on Sunday, about five o'clock. He was not invited to dinner with the Brown family and his children. And he went home alone after the recital. They all went out to dinner at Mezzaluna Restaurant.

Mr. Simpson got to his house on Rockingham about 6:30 or seven o'clock. He was home alone that evening, ladies and gentlemen. Nobody else was in the house. His daughter, Arnel, was out for the evening, and she would not return until about 1:00, 1:30 in the morning. Mr. Simpson had a houseguest living in a guest room on the side of the house. His name was Kato Kaelin. He was there in the room passing time at 9:11 P.M., and we know this time exactly because there's a phone record. Mr. Kaelin is on the phone long-distance to San Diego to a friend when Mr. Simpson comes to his door and knocks on it. Mr. Kaelin gets off the phone. Mr. Simpson told Mr. Kaelin that he was going to the airport and needed change to tip the skycap. Mr. Kaelin said all he had was a twenty, and he gave it to Mr. Simpson. Mr. Simpson then said that he was going out to get a burger. Mr. Kaelin then asked Mr. Simpson if he could go along, and Mr. Simpson mumbled, "Okay." They then got in the car. Mr. Simpson had two automobiles: a Ford Bronco and a Bentley. He got into the Bentley that was parked in his driveway, and they drove to McDonald's. It was sometime after 9:11 P.M. They got to McDonald's, ordered the food. Mr. Simpson ate his hamburger in the car very quickly and drove back.

He got back to the house around 9:30, 9:35. How do we know that? Mr. Kaelin was not invited to eat his food with Mr. Simpson; Mr. Simpson already ate his food in the car. Mr. Kaelin got his food and walked around to the back of the house and went into his room and picked up the phone and made another long-distance phone call to the same guy in San Diego. And that call is at 9:37 P.M. So we can estimate it took a couple of minutes to get to the room from where he got out of the car. So basically, Mr. Simpson is back at Rockingham by 9:35 P.M.

Now, at 9:35 P.M. until 10:55 P.M., Mr. Simpson's whereabouts cannot be corroborated by anybody. Mr. Kaelin is the last person to see Mr. Simpson at 9:35. Mr. Simpson was not seen by anybody alive, anybody who will testify, until 10:55. One hour and twenty minutes unaccounted for. It was during this one hour and twenty minutes that the murders occurred.

Now, what happened at 10:55? Allan Park is a limousine driver who will testify. He had never driven before for Mr. Simpson. Mr. Simpson's regular driver was not available on this evening to take Mr. Simpson to the airport for a red-eye flight. Normally the driver would be there around quarter to eleven to get Mr. Simpson to the airport. Mr. Simpson had no idea that his normal driver was not going to show up and that this new person was going to show up. Mr. Park had never picked up Mr. Simpson before, and he was a bit nervous, and he wanted to be on time. He left his home at Torrance at 9:45 P.M. to get to 360 North Rockingham, where Mr. Simpson lives, in plenty of time to get Mr. Simpson to the airport.

This is Mr. Simpson's property at 360 North Rockingham. If you want to get into the house and you pull up to the gate on Ashford, you have to pick up this phone that's right outside the gate, and you call in, and it rings on the telephone inside Mr. Simpson's house on any number of phones. There's even a little light that lights up saying "gate," so anybody inside knows it's the gate. They can then press a button, and then the gate opens automatically; the person comes in and (they) press another button, and the gate closes. That's how people routinely are let into the property.

Mr. Park was given instructions by his boss, Dale St. John, to come to the property this way at this certain time and then buzz, and he'll be let in. He drove up Rockingham, and he wasn't quite sure which house was Mr. Simpson's, so he stopped and looked when he got to this area, and he saw on the curb the numbers 360. Now, that told him that this was Mr. Simpson's house, 360 North Rockingham. He stopped and paused, looking out of the driver's-side window, and visibly saw the curb and the numbers. And he did not see any cars parked there at that time. He did not see the Bronco or any other automobile near the numbers or anywhere along this curb.

Now, what time was it when Allan Park drove up? According to him, it was 10:20 P.M. Mr. Simpson will testify that he was home at 10:20 P.M., and he will further testify that his car was right here, where he claims he parked it earlier in the evening. But Allan Park will destroy that alibi.

> MR. BAKER: I object. That's argument.
>
> THE COURT: I'm going to ask you to save your argument for closing argument.

[PETROCELLI resumes.]

Allan Park will testify that when he drove up at 10:20, there was no car there. Furthermore, Park pulls around the corner at Ashford—it's about 10:25—realizes it's too early to go inside and call Mr. Simpson, so he smokes a cigarette. He then gets ready to pull into that driveway and phone in. But instead of doing that, he makes one more pass around to Rockingham, to make sure this is the right address, and he checks the curb again. It's 10:40 at this point in time, and there's no Bronco there. He sees the address, 360 North Rockingham. He pulls back around, comes back in, pulls into the driveway, gets out of the car, and then picks up the phone and calls in. No one answers the phone. It rings and it rings—two, three, four times.

Nobody answers the phone. It's 10:40 P.M. He then tried paging his boss, Dale St. John, to find out what's going on: What should I do? He didn't get an answer from his boss; he couldn't get through.

It's now about 10:45 P.M. He got back out of the car, and he rang the intercom again: second time he rang, another two, three, four times. No answer. Then gets back in the car, starts calling some people up. Finally gets hold of Dale St. John, and he makes a call to him from the cell-phone in the car, so there's a cell phone record that establishes definitively when Mr. Park got in touch with his boss. The time was 10:52. Okay. 10:52 and seventeen seconds. That call lasted until 10:55 and seventeen seconds.

Park [is] in the car, is talking to St. John at 10:52: What should I do? He's not home. Near the end of that call, he sees a man approach. He's in the car. He has a clear view. These trees do not stick out in the driveway. His front bumper is touching up against the gate. He's got his parking lights on, his headlights off, and he's looking straight ahead as he's talking to his boss, and he can see the front entranceway to Mr. Simpson's house.

All of a sudden, he sees a man approach, a male with blond hair. He didn't know who this guy is. And he indicated to his boss that he saw somebody. Continues to talk to his boss. And then, a moment later, he sees another person who he describes as large, wearing dark clothing, six feet, two hundred pounds, walking in this direction, kind of at a brisk clip. He then gets off the phone with his boss, he gets out of the car, and he rings Mr. Simpson's house again, figuring he's home. And then Mr. Simpson picks up for the first time, after he saw the figure heading toward the front door. Once the figure headed toward the front door, he saw some lighting on. He gets out of the car, and a moment later somebody answers the phone, and it's Mr. Simpson. He recognized his voice.

So we can tell from Allan Park's phone records that he saw this person entering the house at around 10:55 P.M. Mr. Simpson will admit that that was him entering the house at 10:55 P.M. We know Mr. Simpson's whereabouts cannot be tracked, beginning at 10:55, back to 9:35. That's the hour and twenty minutes that he's not accounted for.

Now, what will Mr. Simpson say about what he was doing during this time? You will hear him say that he was home the entire time. However, there's a cell-phone record that shows a call that he made from his cell phone at 10:03 P.M. to his friend, Paula Barbieri. We know he called her, but didn't make contact at 10:03 P.M.

Mr. Simpson, the next day when he came back from Chicago, told the police that the very last thing he did before he went off to Chicago, when the limousine was waiting for him, was go out to the Bronco to get his cell phone. So Mr. Simpson admitted to the police that his cell phone was in the Bronco when he left for the airport, which was after eleven o'clock. So we know that Mr. Simpson had to have been in his Bronco at 10:03 when he made that call.

Mr. Simpson will say that he was packing and rushing around during this time frame. We will show that his trip was for only one day. Mr. Simpson will say that he was lying on his bed, reading a book, starting to nod off. We will show you that he was taking a red-eye, where people usually sleep on the flight. Mr. Simpson will say that he was chipping golf balls. We will show you that it was nighttime. No one had seen him chip golf balls at nighttime. You will hear him say that he took his dog for a walk around the block during this one-hour-and-twenty-minute period. He can produce no witness who saw him taking that dog for a walk. You will hear that he was home, up in his room, but he did not answer two separate calls from Allan Park, starting at 10:40 and then again at 10:45. Mr. Park said when Mr. Simpson picked up the phone, Mr. Simpson said he had overslept, but he was taking a red-eye.

The important thing to remember is this: About this one hour and twenty minutes, there isn't anybody who can account for his whereabouts. Nobody. Mr. Kaelin was seen walking out of his room, onto the property, by Mr. Park around 10:54 P.M. The man with the blond hair that Mr. Park saw and did not recognize was Kato Kaelin. Now, why was Kaelin out there at 10:54 P.M.? Around 10:50, Mr. Kaelin was lying against the wall on his bed, talking on the telephone, and he heard some loud noises. And it shook the wall, and it even moved the picture. He thought there was an earthquake. He asked the person on the phone, Was there an earthquake? And she said she didn't feel an earthquake. He was a little frightened. He got off the phone; he got a small penlight, and he walked outside to go investigate where those sounds came from and what had happened. You will hear Mr. Kaelin's testimony about going back to that side of the house and what he saw. We will prove that was caused by Mr. Simpson returning to his property by going on the side of the house, to avoid being detected by Allan Park, who is waiting out on the street.

But you won't hear any other evidence as to what caused those noises. Evidence was found, virtually all the evidence was found in three locations: Nicole's condominium, 875 South Bundy; Mr. Simpson's Bronco, and Mr. Simpson's home, 360 North Rockingham.

Let me start with the physical evidence at Bundy. The bodies of the victims, of course, were found at 875 South Bundy. There's a walkway up to the steps, and Nicole's body was found at the bottom of the first step in the pool of blood. She was still wearing the black dress she had worn for her daughter's recital. She was barefoot. She had a watch on, and she had rings on her fingers.

Ron was found slumped against a tree a few feet from Nicole's body in a small caged-in area. It's caged because there's a fence that goes around this little dirt area and there's a big street in the middle which sort of bisects this area. And it's next to the stairs where Nicole's body was found.

Ron had a pager, and the pager was found lying on the ground next to him. Ron's keys to the car were found lying on the ground next to him. The envelope with Judy Brown's glasses was found lying on the ground next to him, obviously indicating that Ron had never gotten past the stairs with the envelope.

In between Ron's and Nicole's bodies, there was a single leather glove on the ground. There was also a dark knit cap, starting from where Nicole's body was and leading to the back of the condominiums, a long walkway that goes to the back, where there's a gate. There were shoe prints walking toward the back in blood, bloody shoe prints. There were also some shoe prints in between Nicole's body and Ron's body. All of these shoe prints are size twelve. Next to the shoe prints going toward the back of the condominium were drops of blood. To the left of the shoe prints, as though somebody had cut themselves from the left hand or the left fingers, droplets of blood, four or five. At the end of the walkway, there's a gate that goes out to the back of the house; then there were three bloodstains found on this gate.

Ron's shirt had some fibers on it and had some hair on it. The knit cap was found to have some hair on it. There were also fibers found in the knit cap.

The door to Nicole's home was open. The lights were on inside. There were candles. There was a bathroom upstairs that she used, near her bedroom. It (the bathtub) had water in it, and her children were sleeping in their beds.

None of Nicole's jewelry that she had on was taken. None of Ron's possessions was taken. Nothing inside the house was disturbed or removed. The house was not ransacked. The children were left unharmed in their bed. Expensive automobiles in the garage, one being a Ferrari, they were not taken. Everything was left intact, obviously indicating that there was no robbery here. No breaking and entry, no burglary. Nor will there be any evidence presented that there was any sexual assault upon Nicole. Her clothes were not torn, nothing was ripped.

We will prove from these facts that Nicole was the target of these murders. These murders did not occur in a convenience store or an ATM machine. They occurred at her home. We will prove that nobody knew Ron Goldman was going to be at Nicole's home except Ron Goldman, Nicole, and Karen Crawford at Mezzaluna. When Ron left at 9:50, he told Karen he was going to drop these glasses off, and he got them from Karen. And then, a half hour later or so, he's at Nicole's condo and he's killed. He went there at the last minute, unexpectedly.

The Bronco was found parked on Rockingham when the police arrived in the wee hours of the morning. It was locked, and it was parked right near this curb where it said 360. Right where Allan Park drove by and did not see a Bronco.

It had [a] little stain of blood on the outside of the door near the door handle, driver-side door, and it also had some stains of blood down at the bottom of the door. Detective Lange, Detective Phillips, Detective Vannatter, Detective Gonzalez, and others said that they could see inside the Bronco through the windows and saw blood inside as well.

When the Bronco was towed the next day to the L.A. print shed and then opened the following day, it had to be opened with a slim jim. Blood was found in various places inside on the steering wheel, on the instrument panel, on the seats, on the center console, and on the driver-side-door panel, in the area where there's a little well, where you open up the door to get out. The handle is as though a left hand or left finger was bleeding when they tried to open up the handle to get out; right in that area, there was blood found. There was also blood found on the carpet of the driver side in the shape of a shoe print.

Now, at 360 North Rockingham, there is evidence found both outside the house and inside the house. Outside the house there were blood drops outside the Bronco on the ground, and there were blood drops up the driveway. There were blood drops found inside the foyer of Mr. Simpson's house. When you open up the front door, there's a foyer; there were blood drops found on that floor. There were blood drops found in Mr. Simpson's bathroom on the floor. There were a pair of dark socks on a rug next to Mr. Simpson's bed in his bedroom. Later examination of these socks showed there were bloodstains not easily visible to the naked eye.

Outside the house, on the side of the house where Kato Kaelin heard the noises, there was a leather glove found for the right hand. The leather glove found at Bundy was for the left hand. This leather glove matched the glove at Bundy—one was right, one was left, both brown leather gloves. When this glove was examined, it was loaded with evidence. It had bloodstains on it. It had strands of hair, and it had fiber on it.

Now, let me explain how this evidence ties in to Mr. Simpson, how it identifies him. First of all, I'd like to talk for a bit about the wounds to the victims. Both victims died of knife wounds. We will call to the witness stand one of the nation's most renowned pathologists, Dr. Werner Spitz, who we hired to independently examine the photographs, autopsy reports, and make some conclusions about the autopsies done on Ron and Nicole in the nature of the wounds. You will hear he is one of the most renowned pathologists, the author of numerous authoritative works. He served on various committees, including committees investigating the assassination of

John F. Kennedy, Martin Luther King Jr. He will testify that Nicole had some superficial defensive-type wounds, not very many. She had stab wounds to the neck, and she had a gaping slash across her throat. This last wound was so deep and such a devastating cut that the blade almost hit her spinal cord. It was this last wound that caused her to bleed out massively, and she died moments later.

Ronald Goldman's wounds were also knife wounds. He had one wound that bled out onto his pants, a wound to his leg. He had a wound to the neck that severed a vein. He had two wounds to his chest below his armpits, and he had a deep wound in the abdominal area. Dr. Spitz will testify that all of the wounds to Ron and Nicole were consistent with one knife. And one assailant.

The blood testing done in this case also shows that there is a drop of blood on Ron Goldman's boot, on the bottom of the boot, which later testing revealed to be a mixture of Ron's blood and Nicole's blood. And this blood drop will show that one knife was used on both victims, hence transferring one blood to the other.

Nicole was killed at one area at the bottom of the stairs, and Ron was killed at a separate area next to the stairs. And there are some bloody footprints between Ron's body and Nicole's body, and we will prove Ron and Nicole were killed in sequence, meaning that they were not confronted and killed together at the same time. In addition, the evidence will show that there is only one set of footprints throughout the whole crime scene, all size twelve. There will be no evidence presented that anybody else that evening left any footprint.

The evidence will show that both Ron and Nicole struggled very briefly before they were killed. There was no blood on Nicole's feet. She was found laying down in a pool of blood, and there was no blood on her feet. None of her blood on her feet, meaning that she was already down when she was cut across the neck and she bled out. When she was cut on the neck, Dr. Spitz will testify that she lived no longer than about fifteen seconds or so from that point.

Dr. Spitz will explain that Ron Goldman did try to fight valiantly, but he, too, was killed quickly. He was pinned in this small caged area, taken by surprise, and he did not have room to maneuver, to defend himself, let alone fight back. His area is very small. If you try to throw a punch or get your arms up, there's not much you could do except ward off the knife blows that were being delivered one after the other, and that is why we see cuts on Ron's hands. One of the early wounds to Ron severed the aorta in the abdominal cavity. This caused an instant loss of blood pressure and an immense internal bleeding to the surrounding tissue. After this wound, Ron was rendered totally defenseless. Dr. Spitz will testify that he could have struggled about sixty seconds before collapsing to his death. It was during this struggle with Ron most likely when the glove came off and the hat came off.

Also, Mr. Simpson sustained injuries to his left hand in the nature of cuts and gouges. Dr. Spitz has examined photographs of these injuries, and he will testify that these are very likely gouges caused by the fingernails of either Ron or Nicole digging into Mr. Simpson's hand in order to try to get free.

Nicole bled outward after she was already down on the ground incapacitated, and Ron bled largely internally. Therefore the evidence does not suggest that Mr. Simpson would have been drenched with blood, nor does it suggest that he would have bruises and marks all over his body.

We will show that the struggle with Mr. Goldman was brief. The struggle with Nicole was even briefer. In a matter of minutes, both were killed.

Mr. Heidstra heard "Hey, hey, hey" around 10:35 or so. Couple of minutes later, the killings were done, and Mr. Simpson would have had plenty of time to leave the crime scene, get into his car, get back to Rockingham in time to have made the sounds that Kato Kaelin heard at 10:50 P.M. and to have been seen by Allan Park at 10:55 P.M.

The person who did this left this crime scene in an extreme hurry. They left behind all kinds of incriminating evidence. Blood drops, bloody shoe prints, a single glove, a hat.

The evidence that we will present is that Ron and Nicole struggled briefly and died quickly and that there was more than ample time for Mr. Simpson to leave there 10:35, 10:40, and even as late as 10:45 to get back to Rockingham by 10:50.

Now, with respect to the specific evidence that was found at

Bundy, starting with the hair evidence, we will call to the stand a man named Douglas Deedrick, who's an agent with the FBI, and he works in the laboratory that deals with hair and fibers. He examined the hair and fiber evidence that was found in this case. Starting with the knit cap found at Bundy, what Mr. Deedrick did is, he examined the hair found in that hat and he examined some samples of Mr. Simpson's, hair provided by Mr. Simpson, and he compared them.

Mr. Deedrick will testify that there was, in effect, a match between the two, that they shared the same microscopic characteristics—that is, Mr. Simpson's hair and the hair found in the hat at Bundy. Mr. Simpson had knit caps at that time just like the one found at Bundy. Mr. Deedrick will also testify that hair found on Ron Goldman's shirt matched Mr. Simpson's hair. He will testify that hairs found on the glove found behind the side of Mr. Simpson's house matched Nicole's hair, and other hair on it matched Ron Goldman's hair.

Mr. Deedrick will testify that he found certain rose beige fibers on the knit cap at Bundy, a particular rare type of carpet fiber that is found in very few Bronco automobiles. After comparing the fibers, the carpet fibers found in the hat to the carpet fibers in Mr. Simpson's car, they matched. They shared the same microscopic characteristics. He also examined the carpet fibers found on the Rockingham glove, and he said those carpet fibers are the same fibers as found in Mr. Simpson's car.

He also found a different kind of fiber, a blue-black cotton fiber in several different places, and it was the same blue-black cotton fiber found in these places: one, Ron Goldman's shirt; two, the glove found at Rockingham; and three, the socks in Mr. Simpson's bedroom. On the gloves, one glove was found at Bundy, one glove was found at Rockingham. Both gloves were Aris leather light, extra large, color brown. Nicole Brown Simpson, on December 18, 1990, purchased two pairs of Aris leather light gloves, extra large, color brown and color black. She purchased them at Bloomingdale's in New York City, close to where she and Mr. Simpson had an apartment. Only Bloomingdale's sold these gloves in the United States, and only two hundred pairs were sold in 1990 to 1991, when Nicole bought them in Mr. Simpson's extra-large size.

After December 18, 1990, when Nicole bought these gloves, we have pictures showing Mr. Simpson wearing both pairs of gloves. We have six photographs, somebody wearing the black gloves, somebody wearing the brown gloves. By the way, these gloves, stylewise, are made to be skintight, so that you have dexterity when you're using them. They're not big ski gloves. They're very tight-fitting gloves.

Now, we have asked Mr. Simpson to produce the gloves that he was seen wearing in the photographs, and he will not be able to present, in court, those gloves. Neither pair of them. We will prove that the gloves that he was wearing in those photographs and that Nicole bought on December 18, 1990, the brown pair, were the ones he used when he killed Ron and Nicole, leaving one at Bundy and one at Rockingham.

Let me turn to the shoe prints. We will call to the stand FBI agent William Bodziak, who is one of the country's most foremost experts in shoe-print impressions. And he will testify that these shoe prints that were left at Bundy were all the same size, size twelve, that there were no other shoe prints left behind that night. He will explain that only 9 percent of the population wears size twelve. Mr. Simpson wears size twelve. He was able to take an impression of the bloody shoe print and track down the precise type of sole that made that bloody shoe print, and it's a Silga sole, made in Italy, that is used on a shoe called a Bruno Magli shoe. It's an expensive casual shoe. It costs $160, sold in only forty stores in the United States in 1991 and 1992. So we can prove that that shoe that left a shoe print was a Bruno Magli shoe, size twelve, Lorenzo style, dark in color.

At Mr. Simpson's deposition, we asked him whether he wore those type of shoes, and his testimony is as follows on this:

Q: Did you ever buy shoes that you knew were Bruno Magli shoes?
A: No.
Q: How do you know that?
A: Because I know Bruno Magli makes shoes that look like the shoes they had in court that's involved in this case. I would have never owned those ugly-ass shoes.

Q: You thought those were ugly-ass shoes?
A: Yes.

That deposition was taken back in February 1996. A month or so later, after that deposition, a photograph appeared in the *National Enquirer* taken by a photographer named Harry Scull Jr. He's a sports photographer in Buffalo, where Mr. Simpson used to play football and go back and broadcast football games. He worked for the Associated Press in 1993, and on September 26, 1993, there was a game between the Buffalo Bills [and] the Miami Dolphins in Rich Stadium, Buffalo's stadium, and Mr. Scull, working for the AP, took photographs of lots of players, including some shots of Mr. Simpson broadcasting on the sidelines, interviewing athletes. In the past Mr. Scull had taken many pictures of Mr. Simpson. In September of 1993, one of the pictures that he took is a picture that shows Mr. Simpson in the end zone wearing a jacket, tie, shirt, belt, pants, shoes that are clearly visible, including the bottom of the shoe, the sole.

We've had those shoes [in] that picture shown to an expert who used to head the photographic and questioned-documents unit at the FBI for twenty-five years, a guy named Gerry Richards. He will testify that the photograph is authenticated. He looked at the negative, and there is no question about the photograph.

We've also had the shoes shown in that photograph that Mr. Simpson is wearing given to an expert, Mr. Bodziak, the shoe-print expert, and we've asked him to identify the shoe based on his training and knowledge, and he can positively identify that the shoe Mr. Simpson is wearing in that photograph is a Bruno Magli, Lorenzo style, size twelve, that has the Silga sole to it. That is the shoe that left the bloody shoe prints on Bundy on June 12.

Once again we've asked Mr. Simpson to produce the shoes that he has been shown wearing in that photograph taken in September 1993, just eight months or so before Nicole's death. He cannot produce them. We've asked him where are the shoes and where are the gloves that are seen in those photographs, and his answers—and we will present them to you here in court in testimony—"I gave them away." We asked him who he gave them to, his answer, he can't identify who he gave them to.

Kato Kaelin will testify that on the evening of June the 12, when he saw Mr. Simpson and went to McDonald's, Mr. Simpson was wearing a dark sweatsuit with a white zipper to it. Bear in mind also that the testimony of the hair-and-fiber expert, Douglas Deedrick, is that he found blue-black cotton fibers on various items.

At his deposition Mr. Simpson testified that he didn't recall owning any dark sweatsuit. We've asked him to produce the dark sweatsuit for us, and he has not been able to produce any dark sweatsuit, even though you will hear the testimony of Kato Kaelin that he was wearing a dark sweatsuit on the evening of June 12.

Now, the physical evidence that I've described so far at Bundy will indicate that the killer had cuts or gouges on his left hand, evidenced by the blood drops that fell to the left of the bloody shoe print. Also, we know the left glove came off, because it was dropped there, and that's probably how the left hand got injured. The Bronco had blood drops in the door, where you open up the door; on the driver's-side interior panel, there were some blood drops in that little well there, also suggesting blood on the left fingers. So the evidence will show that the killer had blood coming from his left fingers or hand.

When Mr. Simpson returned from Chicago on June 13, he had cuts on his left finger, two of his fingers. He went to the police that day and gave a statement, and one of those cuts was very noticeable and was photographed. His friend, who was at the police station with him and with him during that entire day, will testify—his name is Leroy Taft—that he saw at least two cuts on Mr. Simpson's fingers, the middle finger and the fourth finger, on June 13.

In his deposition in this case, we asked Mr. Simpson about his cuts on his left hand, and he was unable to explain exactly how he got them. His testimony in his deposition was that he cut himself in Chicago in his hotel room. After he claims to have heard the news of Nicole's death, he went into the bathroom and somehow cut himself on a drinking glass but does not remember exactly how he did it and cannot tell us how he cut himself in the bathroom in that Chicago hotel room. However, long before he gave his deposition in this case, on June 13, when he went to speak to the police at Parker Center, he told the police in a statement that he cut himself before going to

Chicago. So we have his statement on June 13 admitting that he cut himself before he went to Chicago. Now we have his testimony in this case saying he cut himself in the hotel room.

The blood evidence was tested mainly through DNA tests—highly reliable, scientific DNA tests. I want to describe what the blood tests showed. Starting with Bundy, Nicole's condominium, the blood drops to the left of the shoe print were tested, and they matched Mr. Simpson's blood. The blood found on the back gate of Nicole's condominium was tested. It matched Mr. Simpson's blood.

At Rockingham the blood on the driveway was tested. That matched Mr. Simpson's blood. The blood in his foyer was tested; that matched his blood. The blood in the bathroom was tested; that matched his blood.

There were three different kinds of bloodstains on the glove found at Rockingham. One stain matched Mr. Simpson's blood. Another stain matched Nicole's blood, and another stain matched Ron Goldman's blood. The socks found in Mr. Simpson's bedroom were tested. Two different kinds of stains were found on the socks: One matched Mr. Simpson's blood; one matched Nicole's blood. The blood in the Bronco was tested. The blood on the door panel where you open up the door matched Mr. Simpson's blood. There was blood found on the console that matched Mr. Simpson's blood. There was blood found on the panel and on the console that also matched Nicole's blood, and there was blood found there that matched Ron's blood. So you have in these three places—Bundy, Rockingham, in the Bronco—only three types of blood: Ronald Goldman's, Nicole Brown Simpson's, and O. J. Simpson's.

One other thing I'll mention about the Bronco: There was a carpet on the driver's side that had bloodstains on it. The blood was tested and found to be Nicole's blood. The blood was located in an area on the carpet where one would step into the Bronco with your foot, if you're trying to enter into the car. And there were marks in Nicole's blood in the Bronco consistent with a shoe print. And FBI agent William Bodziak will say, while there's not enough marks to make an absolute identification, that the marks that he does see on the carpet in Nicole's blood are consistent with the unique Bruno Magli sole that made the shoe print at the Bundy crime scene.

Now, the DNA tests in this case are going to be very important, because there was a lot of blood evidence. There was blood in the Bronco, at Rockingham, and at Bundy. Therefore a decision was made to have DNA tests performed on the blood found, not just at the Los Angeles Police Department's lab but also the State of California's Laboratory and one of the largest privately owned forensic laboratories in the country, Cellmark Laboratories in Maryland. All the labs agreed. All the results showed a DNA profile that matched Mr. Simpson's.

Now, the only witnesses who will be testifying . . . about doing DNA tests of the blood in this case are witnesses that we will be presenting. You will hear no testimony from any witness by the defense who did a DNA test. If they did, they're not going to testify about it. There will be no evidence contradicting any of the findings of these DNA tests.

In addition to the blood evidence, in addition to the physical evidence that points directly to Mr. Simpson, we are going to put on other evidence to show his responsibility for the murders on June 12. Among this evidence will be evidence describing Mr. Simpson's activities and his behavior after the murders. And we will prove by this evidence that he did not act and behave like an innocent man, that his behavior and his actions indicated a consciousness of guilt.

First of all, when Mr. Simpson packed that limousine, with Allan Park, driving to the airport, Kato Kaelin was present, together with Allan Park and Mr. Simpson. It was about 11:10 P.M. on June 12, and Mr. Simpson had to get to a flight. There will be testimony by Allan Park and separate testimony by Kato Kaelin that, after packing some pieces of luggage, there was a smaller dark bag out near the Bentley that Mr. Simpson insisted on picking up himself—not allowing Kaelin, who offered to pick it up and put it in the car—insisted on picking it up himself and bringing it into the car.

After Mr. Simpson returned, brought his luggage back, after all of the legal proceedings, after all of the attempts to obtain all the discovery in this case, that bag has never been seen again. There will be no witness who will bring that bag into this court. Mr. Simpson has produced some luggage that he claims he brought with him to Chicago that night, including one he claims was this bag. Kato Kaelin will testify that is not the bag he saw. Allan Park will testify that is not the bag he saw.

Mr. Simpson, on Monday, when he came back—June 13—got to Rockingham and then went down to the police station, where he gave a statement to Detectives Tom Lange and Phil Vannatter. He spoke on a tape for about thirty minutes. And this was the first time, hours after Nicole's murder, that Mr. Simpson had been questioned about what he did the night before, what his whereabouts were. Now, you'll hear that tape, or you'll have the statement read in. You will see that Mr. Simpson is unable to provide any clear explanation for what he was doing the night before. All he could say was, he was rushing and packing, and he was not able to describe with any detail what he was doing, particularly in that hour and twenty minutes.

When he was told that blood was found at Rockingham, he said he cut his finger—he must have cut his finger before going to Chicago, even though now he says he cut his finger in Chicago in the hotel room. We pressed him whether or not he saw any blood before he went to Chicago, as he told the police. And all he said in his deposition is that there was a tiny dab of blood that he saw on a pinkie one time before he got in the limousine, which he dabbed and threw the napkin away. So we will present to you direct inconsistencies in his deposition, in his police statement, about crucial events.

After he came back from the police statement, later that night, Mr. Simpson had friends over to his house, and family members. Kato Kaelin had gone to stay with a friend. He was asked to come back to Mr. Simpson's house. He got there, and he ended up in the kitchen alone with Mr. Simpson for a few moments. This is about eight or nine o'clock on the evening of June 13. Mr. Simpson then said to Mr. Kaelin, alone in the kitchen, words to this effect: "You saw me go in the house after McDonald's, didn't you?" And Kato Kaelin said, "No, I did not." Kato Kaelin's testimony is that when he came back from McDonald's, he did not see Mr. Simpson walk back into the house. Mr. Kaelin walked into the house while Mr.

Simpson stayed at the Bentley in the driveway and never moved from it. We will present this testimony to, once again, show Mr. Simpson's attempt to build an alibi.

And finally, on Friday, June 17, the police made a decision to arrest Mr. Simpson for the murders of Ron and Nicole. And Mr. Simpson was notified of this while he was staying at his friend's house, Robert Kardashian. We will present to you evidence, including the testimony of Mr. Simpson, that when he found out that he was going to be arrested, he and his boyhood friend, Allen Cowlings, got into Mr. Cowling's car and left the Kardashian home. And they took off. And in that car was not only Mr. Simpson's personal effects, including his passport, but he also had, between Cowlings and him, over $8,000 in cash, changes of clothing, of underwear, windbreaker, and other items of clothing. There was a disguise—fake goatee—and there was a loaded gun.

Now, Mr. Simpson will testify that he was suicidal because of the loss of Nicole. We will present to you evidence and prove that Mr. Simpson fled the police with Mr. Cowlings and contemplated suicide because he knew he was responsible for these murders. We will show that there is no other explanation.

Now, people always ask when there's a killing, What's the motive? And that's a good, important question. Technically, the lawsuit does not require us to prove a motive. But when there is a motive, it's important to bring out, because it helps to explain why something happened, why a person would kill another person.

In this case O. J. Simpson had a motive to kill Nicole. He had a motive to kill Ron Goldman, for the simple reason that Ron was an eyewitness to the murder of his friend, Nicole. Nicole was killed for a different reason. We will present evidence showing that in this relationship between Nicole Brown Simpson and O. J. Simpson, there was severe conflict, tension, anger, that had been building up. There had been a recent estrangement, recent rejection of Mr. Simpson. There was a history of abuse, and there was a history of rage.

After the divorce in 1992, Mr. Simpson and Nicole tried again to make their relationship work. In a month before the murders, Nicole ended it for the final time. Mr. Simpson could not accept this, was frustrated, was confused, was angry, and he retaliated. He also tried to get her back, buying her expensive gifts when she returned. And in the end there was a buildup of a lot of anger and a buildup of a lot of hostility, to the point where we will present to you a letter that Mr. Simpson sent to Nicole just six days before she was killed, threatening—putting her on notice about possible IRS violations, knowing the impact that it would have on Nicole and knowing that it would cause her to have to sell her house because of possible tax problems, and she would have to move with her two children. And, in fact, one day before her murder, on Saturday, June 11, Nicole hired a realtor and had found a place in Malibu that she was going to move to.

On the date of the murders, June 12, Mr. Simpson had flown all the way back from the East Coast. He was exhausted. He wanted to go to his daughter's recital on Sunday with the family. He was not invited to sit with the family. By "the family" I mean his wife and her mother and father and sisters. He was not invited to a celebration dinner after the recital, and he was pretty much alone, maybe for the first time in his life.

The defendant claims that he tried calling the house at 9:00 P.M. that evening, just to speak to Sydney, whom he had just seen at the recital. He said he did not say anything to Nicole. We don't know what happened in that call. But what we do know and what we can prove is that an hour later Mr. Simpson went over there in dark clothing, dark shoes, dark hat, dark gloves, with a knife, in a rage, and killed Nicole and Ron.

Mr. Simpson had time and opportunity to kill Nicole; there were severe problems in his relationship with Nicole at that time. In fact, the relationship was over. All of the physical evidence of the case points only to him and no one else. We submit to you that [the evidence in this case] establishes to a certainty that Mr. Simpson killed Ron and killed Nicole.

The evidence that we have presented to you shows a compelling case to liability against Mr. Simpson. And if you find Mr. Simpson is liable for the murders of Ron and Nicole, you'll be asked to award damages on account of his conduct.

As you know, Mr. Goldman lost his only son, and that is something that can never be returned to him. [There] can never be perfect justice, because that would mean Ron comes back and Nicole comes back. The only thing that you have in your power to do is to award damages to compensate Fred for the loss of his relationship with his son.

Now, how does one do that? You'll have Mr. Goldman take the stand, and he will testify about his relationship with his son. And then your job will be to listen to the kind of relationship that he had, make a determination as to the nature and quality of that relationship and what that loss meant to Fred. And you will be asked to award damages in an amount that could compensate him. Of course, no amount could compensate him for losing his son, but that's what we do in cases like this. At the end of this trial, I will not stand before you and presume to give you any kind of a number. You will hear Mr. Goldman talk about his son and the life they had together and the life that they will no longer have together, and it will be up to you to do what is just.

POSTSCRIPT

On February 4, 1997, the jury found for the plaintiffs in the amount of $33.5 million. Simpson moved to Florida, where by state law a home of any value and the head of a household's salary are both exempt from attachment to satisfy judgments. To date, Simpson has managed to avoid paying most of the sum, though the plaintiffs did successfully compel Simpson to auction off his sports memorabilia, including his Heisman Trophy, which sold for $230,000. Technically speaking, when a plaintiff gets a judgment against a defendant, it is the job of the plaintiff to find the money. Simpson claimed destitution even before the civil case went to the jury, and his deadbeat stature resurfaced in the news in February 2004, when he was served with a court order to hand over his earnings from recent autograph sales in St. Louis to Goldman's mother, Sharon Rufo, who claimed to have received nothing from Simpson since the decision. Simpson indignantly replied, "I will do what the law says, but outside of that, I wouldn't go out of my way to give them a dime."

No doubt Mr. Petrocelli gained insight from having reviewed the mistakes made by the prosecution in the criminal case. But that doesn't diminish the brilliance of his opening, its coherence, .its dramatic simplicity, its palpable sense of truthfulness. Most people in the legal profession—indeed most people who followed the facts objectively—would agree that this was a reasonable verdict considering the multiple sources of evidence pointing to Simpson's guilt.

Israeli comic Dan Ben-Amotz once wrote a short story entitled "There Are More Ways Than One to Kill a Joke." The same can be said about the art of storytelling. The side that must prove the case must tell a coherent story. In murder cases, though, the person who is most capable of recounting what happened—the victim—is unable to do so, making the disparate pieces of evidence provided by other sorts of witnesses critical to the final outcome. It is the job of the skillful attorney to weave those multiple strands into a compelling story. Petrocelli succeeded in telling the story of the deaths of Nicole Brown Simpson and Ronald Goldman in a simple manner, which contributed to its plausibility in the eyes of the jury, while also bolstering his apparent mastery of the facts. He sketches out vividly the victims' personalities, their fatal trajectories and last moments, but he keeps the emotionalism to a minimum. There's no need for polemics, he implies; the facts speak for themselves: the blood evidence, the shoe prints, the glove, the mask and gun in the Bronco, the timing and—not least—Simpson's damningly erratic behavior. By the end the jury believed that this is how a guilty man behaves. Petrocelli doesn't go out of his way to portray Simpson as a monster, but with short, solid strokes, he outlines a clear motive for murder. Mind you, he could have launched a strident ad hominem attack on Simpson, but Petrocelli was not interested in reigniting the dramatic chaos of the criminal trial. By restraining himself, he sent a salient subliminal message to the jury and the opposition: There's no need for dramatics if you have a strong case. By the end of the opening, the listener loses sight of the fact that there were no eyewitnesses to this crime. Petrocelli's fusion of the strands of circumstantial evidence is so seamless that you see only the end result, a story that weaves a picture of overwhelming guilt.

The Criminal Trial

The criminal trial of O. J. Simpson became the vehicle by which America would debate race relations. It was, perhaps, the most famous trial of our lifetime and the closest an American courtroom has come to a circus spectacle, demonstrating the worst possible effects of having television cameras in the courtroom. You will note that defense attorney Johnnie Cochran's summation is not a short one, even in the excerpted version below. Petrocelli, working with the criminal trial's hysteria in mind, wanted to reduce the drama and focus on the evidence. He embodied the ideal of the advocate who lets the facts do the talking. Cochran's burden was to create mirages to eclipse the facts. To do so he needed the maneuvering room of a long delivery to generate an alternative reality and put the LAPD on trial in place of his client, perhaps even to make the jury aware of the television cameras watching as he raised racial temperatures.

THE STATE OF CALIFORNIA v. ORENTHAL JAMES SIMPSON

Excerpts from Defense Attorney Johnnie Cochran's Summation, September 1995

It is a sad fact that in American society, a large number of people are murdered each year. Violence unfortunately has become a way of life in America. When this sort of tragedy does in fact happen, it becomes the business of the police to step up and take charge of the matter. A good, efficient, competent, noncorrupt police department will carefully set about the business of investigating homicides. They won't rush to judgment. They won't be bound by an obsession to win at all costs. They will set about trying to apprehend the killer and to protect the innocent from suspicion.

In this case the victims' families had an absolute right to demand exactly just that. But it was clear, unfortunately, that there was another agenda. From the very first orders issued by the LAPD brass, they were more concerned with their own images, the publicity that might be generated from this case, than they were in doing professional police work. That's why this case has become such a hallmark and that's why Mr. Simpson is the one on trial. But your verdict in this case will go far beyond the walls of Department 103 [the number assigned to Judge Ito's courtroom], because your verdict talks about justice in America, and it talks about the police and whether they're above the law, and it looks at the police perhaps as . . . they haven't been looked at very recently. Remember, I told you this is not for the naïve, the faint of heart, or the timid. The evidence shows that professional police work took a backseat right at the beginning. Untrained officers traipsed through the evidence. They delayed unconscionably routine procedures in notifying the coroners. They didn't call the criminalist out on time, and they allowed this investigation to be infected by a dishonest and corrupt detective. Because of their bungling, they ignored the obvious clues. They didn't pick up paper at the scene with prints on it. Because of their vanity, they very soon pretended to solve this crime and implicated an innocent man. They never, ever looked for anyone else. If they had done their job, as we have done, Mr. Simpson would have been eliminated early on.

This case is not about attacking the Los Angeles Police Department. We're not antipolice in making these statements. You're not antipolice. We all need the police. But what we need and what we must demand are honest, effective, nonbiased police officers. Who could demand less? Any of you say that's not what we should have?

This is a case about a rush to judgment, a case where there's been obsession to win at all costs, and, in the words of Dr. Henry Lee, "Something is wrong with the prosecution's case."

Establishing an Alibi

Apparently the prosecution, in their zeal and their obsession to win, would have you believe that Orenthal James Simpson is so amazing that he can be in two places at the same time, even though they're miles apart.

And so then the importance of the timeline. I want you to

remember these words, like the defining moment in this trial, when Mr. Darden asked Mr. Simpson to try on those gloves and the gloves didn't fit: "If it doesn't fit, you must acquit."

If you take the witnesses who stand unimpeached, you are left with dogs starting to bark at 10:35 or 10:40—and we know from the most qualified individuals, Henry Lee and Michael Baden [defense experts], this was a struggle that took from five to fifteen minutes, it's already 10:55. And remember, the thumps [on Kato Kaelin's guesthouse next to O. J. Simpson's Rockingham home] were at 10:40 or 10:45—O. J. Simpson could not be guilty. He is then entitled to an acquittal.

Let me just summarize what the prosecution has tried to tell you about their theory in this case. They try to tell you that an insanely jealous man stalks his ex-wife, stabs her and a male visitor in a murderous rage, leaves a trail of blood to his home, barely catches a plane to Chicago, in a rush to go there, leaves one glove at the murder scene and one glove behind his house.

In the defense of this case, you have heard evidence about O. J. Simpson's great life. Not only did he have a great life, he had a great day that day playing golf, comes back from being out of town all week long to go to his child's recital, goes to that recital, prepares in the evening to get something to eat, a hamburger.

He then takes a shower, barely catches his plane to Chicago, someone murders his wife and this male visitor, for reasons unknown in this trial. Others seek to implicate him as the most obvious suspect, but the investigation becomes a tragic combination of sloppy errors and cover-ups trying to achieve his conviction. Let's now turn briefly to the prosecution's timeline scenario.

When you see the people [the prosecution] tell you about mountains of evidence and oceans of evidence, their oceans soon become little streams, their mountains become molehills, when you look at the facts.

The Glove

Editor's note: The prosecution claimed that Mr. Simpson dropped that glove while trying to sneak back into his house after the murder. Mr. Cochran uses the lack of physical evidence—no blood on the shrubs where the glove was found—to suggest that the glove was planted.

Look at the glove. Now, when that glove is picked up, remember seeing any blood on the ground? No blood on that shrubbery, no blood on anything there. Where's the blood? [Detectives] Fuhrman and Vannatter will say that when they get that glove after six o'clock in the morning, it's still moist and sticky. Where's the blood on the ground? Where's the blood on the leaves around there? That glove looks as though it's been placed there.

It just doesn't fit. If it doesn't fit, you must acquit.

The Disguise

[Marcia Clark] talks about O. J. Simpson getting dressed up to go commit these murders. I was thinking last night about their theory and how it didn't make any sense. It occurred to me how they were going to tell you how O. J. Simpson was going to disguise himself. He was going to put on a knit cap and some dark clothes and get in his white Bronco, this recognizable person, and go over and kill his wife. That's what they want you to believe. That's how silly their argument is.

Let me put this knit cap on. You have seen me for a year. If I put this knit cap on, who am I? I'm still Johnnie Cochran with a knit cap. And if you looked at O. J. Simpson over there—and he has a rather large head—O. J. Simpson in a knit cap from two blocks away is still O. J. Simpson. It's no disguise. It makes no sense. It doesn't fit. If it doesn't fit, you must acquit.

The Noises Heard by Kato Kaelin

With regard to that walkway, if O. J. Simpson had been the one for whatever reason to walk into that air-conditioning, where is the hair and trace? Where is the fiber? Where is the blood? They want to tell you about his fingers bleeding one minute, and it stops bleeding, and in Miss Clark's scenario he bleeds, it coagulates, stops bleeding, and then it starts bleeding again, because that is convenient for their theory. You know, as I listened to both of them, I wanted to call them "Doctor." Dr. Clark told you, "Well, gee, look at that blood drop. That cut is not big enough for a blood drop." She is not a doctor. How does she know that? Dr. Darden [Assistant District Attorney Christopher Darden] speculates on and on. This isn't imagination. This is real life. This isn't anything for *Murder, She Wrote*. If they tried to sell this story to *Murder, She Wrote* they would send it back and say it is unbelievable.

Consider everything that Mr. Simpson would had to have done in a very short time under their timeline. He would have had to drive over to Bundy in this limited time frame where there is not enough time, kill two athletic people in a struggle that takes five to fifteen minutes, walk slowly from the scene, return to the scene, supposedly looking for a missing hat and glove and poking around, go back to this alley a second time, drive more than five minutes to Rockingham, where nobody hears him or sees him, either stop along the way to hide these bloody clothes and knives or take them in the house with you, where they are still hoisted by their own petard because there is no blood, there is no trace, there is no nothing. It doesn't fit.

Return to the Glove

Editor's note: The prosecution asked O. J. Simpson to try on the gloves found at Rockingham and Bundy, which did not appear to fit. Below, Mr. Cochran addresses the failed courtroom demonstration.

Let's look at some other things that don't fit in this case. Perhaps the single most defining moment in this trial is the day they thought they would conduct this experiment on these gloves. They had this big buildup with Mr. Rubin [prosecution witness, former vice president of the glove manufacturer Isotoner, who testified that gloves would shrink if they got wet], who had been out of the business for years—he had been in marketing even when he was there—but they were going to try to demonstrate to you that these were the killer's gloves and these gloves would fit Mr. Simpson. That vision is indelibly imprinted in each and every one of your minds of how Mr. Simpson walked over here and stood before you and you saw four simple words: "The gloves didn't fit."

And all their strategy started changing after that. Rubin was called back here more than all their witnesses. Their case from that day forward was slipping away from them, and they knew it, and they could never recapture it. We may all live to be a hundred years old, and I hope we do, but you will always remember those gloves—when Darden asked him to try them on, [they] didn't fit. They know they didn't fit, and no matter what they do, they can't make them fit. It doesn't make any difference. They could talk about shrinkage.

But we did something even better, didn't we? We brought a man who won the Dondero [John Dondero Award for excellence in forensics] Award, Dr. Herb MacDonell, who did an experiment on these Aris Light gloves. And what did he say? Put as much blood as you can on them. They don't shrink. It doesn't work. They have the power of the state. They could have done their own demonstration. They didn't, because you know he is right. We didn't just stand up here and speculate as to what might be. They could have called witnesses. They didn't. We called the witness to prove beyond any doubt those gloves don't shrink. The gloves didn't fit Mr. Simpson because he is not the killer.

Miss Clark said the other day, "Well, gee, these gloves had been thawed and they had been frozen." Those gloves were measured on June 21, 1994 [and] were basically the same size now as they were (on) June 21, so that won't work.

Remember that each of the glove photographs [was] taken or pictures of Mr. Simpson were taken in the winter [reference to the sports photographer who captured O. J. Simpson at a Bills game wearing Aris Light leather gloves]. And you know Mr. Simpson was living in New York generally from August through January when he is at football season and working for NBC Sports. Generally in Southern California you don't wear winter dress gloves. . . . You don't go skiing in Aris Light gloves. And you remember that the police, in searching Mr. Simpson's house, you remember Detective Lange. They searched O. J. Simpson's house for gloves, for shoes, for clothes. Found one brown glove that does not fit. . . .

Sympathy

You are to do your job devoid of sympathy or passion or emotion, and I daresay you are very intelligent people. It is very hard for any of us to sit here and have to look at photographs of dead bodies, people who did not deserve to die. This case is about who committed these crimes. You understand this case is not about trying to appeal to your emotion. This case is about the facts and whether these facts establish guilt or innocence beyond a reasonable doubt.

Dismissing the Claim That Simpson Was Enraged

And then [Mr. Darden] goes into this make-believe fantasy world where he is going to tell you on June 12 he is going to conjure up this rage [in O. J. Simpson]. June 12. Very interesting date, isn't it? It is wonderful that we live in the age of videotape, because it tells you about who O. J. Simpson [is]. A picture is worth a thousand words, so let me show you this video. This is for Chris Darden.

You will recognize some of the people in this videotape after a while. Mr. Simpson kissing Denise Brown, Judith Brown, Louis Brown. Talking to a friend. That is his son Justin who he kisses, smiling and happily waving. You see that with your own eyes. How does that comport with this tortured, twisted reasoning that he was angry in some kind of a jealous rage? Did he look like he was [in] a jealous rage to you? Your eyes aren't lying to you when you see that. Thank heaven we have videotape. And we know in this city how important videotapes can be when people don't want to believe things even when they see on it videotapes, and you saw that yourself. [An allusion to the Rodney King tape, the infamous beating of Mr. King by Los Angeles police officers. Via this maneuver, Cochran transforms the case into a referendum on the Los Angeles Police Department.]

When somebody tries to tell you there was some kind of jealous rage on June 12, look at O. J. Simpson interacting with the Brown family and everyone else. It doesn't fit. It doesn't make any sense. He isn't brooding. He is not angry. He kisses these family members. He is laughing and joking. He is playing with his son Justin. Those are the facts, not what I made up. These are items that don't fit.

Even after that video, like any proud papa, you know what O. J. Simpson did? Took a photograph with his daughter. Let's look at this photograph for a minute, if you want to see how he looks while he is in this murderous rage, while this fuse is going on. Where is the fuse now, Mr. Darden? Look at that look on his face, like any proud papa. Who wouldn't be proud of her? She has the flowers apparently he went out and bought for her. We had no way of knowing that Chris Darden someday would try to make you believe that that man was in a murderous rage at that time and that we would bring forward that same picture so you would see it with your own eyes.

So thank heaven again for the visual. A photograph is worth a thousand words. So he [Darden] can speak a thousand words, I could show you one photograph and that video. What it does is, [it] puts the lie to this theory about some kind of murderous rage.

The Theory of a Hired Assassin

In the words of Shakespeare, they [the prosecutors] are hoist by their own petard. They talk about these incidents involving Nicole and Mr. O. J. Simpson. Every time they would have an argument, everybody would know about it; whether it was in '89 or in '93, everybody would know about it because it would be loud. It certainly doesn't make it right, but they were loud arguments, and everybody knew about it. What kind of characteristic is that in this case? This is a case about stealth. This is a case about somebody who is a professional assassin who kills these two people.

We look at other things that don't fit. We know that there was this terrific struggle involving primarily Mr. Goldman as he fought for his life. Why no bruises on Mr. Simpson's body? Admittedly there was a violent struggle involving two very fit adults. Let's look briefly at the bruises on Mr. Goldman's hands. We had a large bruise on the knuckle [that], according to Dr. Baden and others, is consistent with Mr. Goldman's fight that he put up for his life. He struck something, probably a person at that point, but Miss Clark and the others can't even admit that. The prosecutors said, "Oh, no, he must have been flailing back; he must have hit his hand against the tree."

If you fought for five to fifteen minutes in an area like that, both parties would have a lot of bruises and marks on them, wouldn't they? Mr. Goldman did, and I bet you his perpetrator does.

These socks that all of a sudden appear in that video at the foot of his [O.J.'s] bed, were being worn by Mr. O. J. Simpson. Well, ladies and gentlemen, when you see these socks, what do you think the dirt and dust was on these socks, now? Where was the dirt that was thrown up and moved around on these socks? You're not going to see any dirt, because those socks weren't there. You see that dirt?

Common sense would tell you there would be bruises and nicks and marks on all the perpetrators. With the heavy foliage there, with the fence and the trees, you would expect scratches on everyone. Whereas Mr. Goldman has more than thirty stab wounds, you would expect this struggle [of] five to fifteen minutes to have left that, but there is nothing like that on Mr. Simpson's body.

Miss Clark says O. J. Simpson was a football player, and he has to run through the line, and he has the killer instinct. Isn't that really stretching it, ladies and gentlemen? O. J. Simpson hasn't played football for fifteen years. That man is forty-six years old now. But she doesn't know much about sports, does she? Because a running back avoids trying to be hit. The problem with them—they don't block, they always run, they try to get out of the way, so he is not looking for contact. He gets tackled, but running backs don't try to run over anybody. Only maybe [football great] Jim Brown. The rest of them run out of bounds.

The Fingerprints

One thing about blood spots, you can never tell generally how old they are. Another thing that doesn't fit, the fingerprints. We called Gilbert Aguilar. He's the fingerprint expert. He examined and dusted and found seventeen latent prints that he was able to lift at Bundy, the crime scene—the gate, the fence, the front door. He was able to identify eight of the prints after comparing the known exemplars of the police officers, people you might expect around there. But there were nine identifiable prints that were never identified.

Are those the prints of the real killers? We will never know. They have not found those prints.

The Melting Ice Cream

If there were ice cream that was still melting or partially melted at 12:40 when [Police Officer Robert] Riske saw it—and that's Riske's testimony, partially melted ice cream at 12:40—if they don't bother picking up—that ice cream is [there] when you go down those steps, and it's on that little banister there as you're going out in the garage. Might mean that Nicole Brown Simpson went down there and was letting somebody out who had been there earlier that evening. We'll never know. When they saw all those candles lit around the bathtub and water in the bathtub, they didn't bother to check. They were too worried about how they would look notifying and worrying about the press. They said the ice cream wasn't important, but they had an ice-cream-melting test.

I asked Lange about this again. It was Ben & Jerry's ice cream, remember that? It melted in an hour and fifteen minutes. It should be totally melted by that time frame. If you extrapolate backward, if Riske finds the ice cream at 12:40 and it's partially melted, let's give him the benefit of the doubt and let's say it all had melted. If you went back an hour and fifteen minutes, that's 11:25. Now, if the children are asleep, Nicole is the one eating ice cream. That's another bit of evidence. When you cannot, because of negligence and incompetence, determine the cause of death, you have to look at other things. Isn't that reasonable? We think that is important.

The Socks Found at Simpson's Rockingham Estate

So those are the socks. No dirt, no soil, no berries. Nobody sees any blood until August 4. All these miraculous things start happening, and then we find out it has EDTA (Chemical preservative used to store blood samples; it prevents blood samples from coagulating; Mr. Cochran suggests that blood on sock was taken from blood sample given by O.J. and placed on socks.) in it. Is it planted along with that back gate? How would it be on there? Why didn't they see the blood before that? There's a big fight here. Where is the dirt? Why would Mr. Simpson have on [this] kind of socks with a sweat outfit? You don't have to be from the fashion police to know that you wear [this] kind of socks with a suit. You don't wear [this] kind of socks with a sweat outfit.

Doesn't it make sense to you that those socks were in that hamper from Saturday night when Mr. Simpson went to that formal event? [This] kind of socks is what you wear with your tuxedo when he was dressed with those other ladies. They went and took it out of the hamper and staged it there, and you see what happened. It's posed there.

The Blood Found on the Bronco's Console

How do you stand up here and talk about an ocean of evidence? This is a tiny trickle of a stream. This Bronco is particularly troubling. Less than seven-tenths of that drop of blood is what's in that alleged console. Dr. Baden says the perpetrator would be covered with blood. Your common sense tells you the perpetrator would be covered with blood, [after a] five- to fifteen-minute struggle of this dimension. And so it just doesn't fit. Something is wrong. How does anyone drive away in that car with bloody clothes with no blood there on the seats, no blood anyplace else? Every police officer who came in talked about how bloody this scene was. It doesn't make any sense. They can't explain it because Mr. Simpson was not in that car and didn't commit these murders.

The Mark Fuhrman Tapes

Editor's note: Between 1985 and 1994, Laura McKinny hired Mark Fuhrman as a consultant for a screenplay and novel on women in law enforcement. Over the course of their meetings, McKinny tape-recorded Furhman using the word "nigger" about forty-one times. She was brought in to testify about these tapes.

Let's take Miss Laura McKinny, in all accounts a nice and gentle lady who didn't want to be here. I had to go all the way to the North Carolina Court of Appeals to get these tapes. She has proof about what she says. She has the conversations on tape. When Mr. Darden is questioning her, remember her famous response: "Why are we having this adversarial conversation? Why do I detect this negativity? I'm just here to tell the truth. Aren't you in a search for truth, Mr. Prosecutor?"

They went on to ask, "Well, why didn't you stop him from using this so-called n word?"

She said, "I was in a journalistic mode. I didn't try to stop him from using that word any more than I try to stop him from talking about cover-ups where male police officers have no respect for women police officers because they don't cover up the misdeeds." She is credible, don't you think?

Mr. Darden said something very interesting today. He said, "I'm just the messenger." Now, how many times have you heard that: "I'm the messenger. Don't blame me, I'm just doing my job"? There's no way out. He's a fine lawyer, but he can't hide behind just being a messenger. Well, whose message is he sending? Who is he representing in this message? He's a man of integrity. That statement is not going to fly. He's not any messenger. He's the prosecutor with all the power of the state of California in this case. We're not going to turn the Constitution on its head in this case. If you can't trust the messengers, watch out for their messages. . . .

In 1985, Mark Fuhrman responded to a call on Rockingham. Mark Fuhrman is a lying, perjuring, genocidal racist, and from that moment on, anytime he could get O. J. Simpson, he would do it. That's when it started, in '85.

If you cannot trust the messenger, you can't trust the message. When Fuhrman gets on the witness stand and says, "I haven't used this n word for ten years," you think Phillips [Detective Ron Philips, Fuhrman's partner] knows he's lying? Some of you probably knew he was lying. It took those tapes to make [believers of] those of you who didn't believe these kinds of things . . . take place. Didn't he have an obligation to come forward under those circumstances? If Fuhrman speaks so candidly to this lady that he met in a restaurant in West L.A., you think he talks like that to the guys on the force? That's the way he talks. That's the way he is. Nobody came forward to reveal this. We revealed it for you.

This whole thing about the police and what they've done in this case is extremely painful to us. All we want is a good and honest police force, where people are treated fairly no matter what part of the city they're in. Then we come to Detective Mark Fuhrman. This man is an unspeakable disgrace. He's been unmasked for the whole world for what he is, and that's hopefully positive. His misdeeds go far beyond this case, because he speaks of culture that's not tolerable in America. Well, it's not the case of Mark Fuhrman. Mark Fuhrman is not in custody. That's the man who they're trying to put away [O.J.] with witnesses like this, a corrupt police officer who is a liar and a perjurer.

They [the prosecutors] were talking yesterday in their argument about, "Well, gee, you think he would commit a felony?" What do you think it was when he was asked the questions by F. Lee Bailey about whether he ever used the n word in ten years and he swore to tell the truth and he lied and others knew he lied. Lee Bailey asked this man whether or not he ever met Kathleen Bell. Of course he lied about that. "Never met this woman. I don't recognize her." Boy, and he sounded really convincing, didn't he?

Then Bailey says, "Have you used that word, referring to the n word, in the past ten years?"

"Not that I recall, no."

"You mean, if you call someone a nigger, you had forgotten it?"

"I'm not sure I can answer the question the way it's phrased, sir."

And then [Bailey] pins him down. "I want you to assume that perhaps at some time since 1985 or '86, you addressed a member of the African-American race as a nigger. Is it possible that you have forgotten that act on your part?"

Answer: "No, it's not possible."

"Are you therefore saying that you have not used that word in the past ten years, Detective Fuhrman?"

Answer: "Yes, that is what I'm saying."

Question: "And you say under oath that you have not addressed any black person as a nigger or spoken about black people as niggers in the past ten years, Detective Fuhrman?"

"That's what I'm saying, sir."

"So that anyone who comes to this court and quotes you as using that word in dealing with African-Americans would be a liar, would they not, Detective Fuhrman?"

"Yes, they would."

"All of them, correct?"

"All of them."

That's what he told you under oath in this case. Did he lie under oath? Did this key prosecution witness lie under oath? And they tell you it's not important. This is the man who was off this case shortly after two o'clock in the morning, right after he got on it. This is the man who didn't want to be off this case. This is the man, when they're ringing the doorbell at Ashford, who goes for a walk. And he describes how he's strolling. Here's what he says:

> I was just strolling along looking at the house. Maybe I could see some movement inside. I was just walking while the other three detectives were down there.

He's the one who says the Bronco was parked askew, and he sees some spot on the door. He makes all of the discoveries. He's got to be the big man, because he's had it in for O. J. because of his views since '85. This is the man who climbs over the fence. He's the guy who goes in and talks to Kato Kaelin while the other detectives are talking to the family. He's the guy looking at shoes and looking for suspects.

He's worried about bodies or suspects or whatever. He doesn't even take out his gun. He goes around the side of the house, and, lo and behold, he claims he finds this glove, and he says the glove is still moist and sticky. Under their theory, at 10:40, 10:45, that glove is dropped. It's now after six o'clock. So what is that? Seven and a half hours. The testimony about drying time around here—no dew point that night. Why would it be moist and sticky unless he brought it over there and planted it there to try to make this case? And there is a Caucasian hair on that glove.

This man cannot be trusted. He is sinful to the prosecution, and for them to say he's not important is untrue, and you will not fall for it, because, as guardians of justice here, we can't let it happen.

We talked about a police department who from the very beginning was more interested in themselves and their image. We talked about socks that appeared all of a sudden that weren't there, socks where evidence was planted on them. We talked about police officers who lie with impunity. We talked about messengers where you couldn't trust the message.

In short, we talked about reasonable doubt. Something has made this country great. You can be accused in this country for crime, but that is just an accusation, and when you enter a not-guilty plea, since the beginning of the time of this country, that sets the forces in motion, and you have a trial. That is why we love what we do, an opportunity to come before the consciences of the community. You are the consciences of the community. You set the standards. You tell us what is right and wrong. You use your common sense to do that. Your verdict goes far beyond these doors of this courtroom. As Mr. Darden said, the whole world is watching and waiting for your decision in this case.

But it is not just about winning, it is about what is right. A man's life is at stake here. You promised to take the time that was necessary. I asked you when you got down to the end of the case, then you couldn't just rush through that [deliberation]?

You will give it the importance to which it is entitled. Please don't compromise your principles in rendering this decision. Don't rush to judgment. Don't compound what they've already done in this case.

Have a judgment that is well thought out, one that you can believe in the morning after this verdict. I want you to place yourself the day after you render the verdict, when you get up and you look in the mirror and you are free, no longer sequestered—you will probably look for each other, but you will be happy to be home again. Look in that mirror and say, Have I been true to my oath? Did I do the right thing? Was I naïve? Was I timid? Or was I courageous? Did I believe in the Constitution? Did I believe in justice? Did I do my part for integrity and honesty? That is the mission you are on in this journey toward justice.

Vannatter as Complicit in a Police Conspiracy

We started talking about the messengers in this case. We talked briefly about Vannatter and about all of his big lies. Lies become very important, because he is the co–lead investigator in this case. From the very beginning, he was lying to you. Vannatter took that stand, and you had a chance to again observe his demeanor, and you are smart. You have got this visceral experience, and you have got your experiences in life, and you know when somebody is lying.

And he said something really interesting: "Mr. Shapiro, Mr. O. J. Simpson was no more a suspect than you were." Who in here believed that? Did he really think we were going to believe that O. J. Simpson was no more a suspect than Robert Shapiro? You can't believe anything he says, because it goes to the core of this case. When you are lying at the beginning, you will be lying at the end.

The Book of Luke talks about if you are untruthful in small things, you should be disbelieved in big things. There is no question about that. The two of them need to be paired together, because they are twins of deception. Fuhrman and Vannatter, twins of deception, who bring you a message that you cannot trust. Vannatter, the man who carried the blood; Fuhrman, the man who found the glove.

Fuhrman tells you that Rokahr, the photographer, took this photograph after seven o'clock in the morning. And the reason he tells you that is because he wants that photograph of him pointing at the glove taken after he supposedly finds the glove at Rockingham. He says he took the photograph at Rockingham after seven o'clock A.M., after they returned from Rockingham.

They all go over to Rockingham from 5:00 to 7:00, and so it becomes very important, as we look at this photograph in a few minutes. Rokahr then comes here near the end of the case and says these photographs on this contact sheet are all taken while it is dark. He says he could tell the difference in a photograph taken an hour and a half before sunrise, 5:41, 5:42, and an hour and a half afterward, so then why is this big liar in the crime scene with access to the glove and the hat? Why is he down there pointing at this glove where he is walking all in the blood and everything when he wants you to believe it is seven o'clock? Now, we know it is not seven o'clock. You see that photograph up there? That is Mark Fuhrman pointing. You see the envelope, pointing under this neatly arranged cap. Glove supposedly just happened to fall right under that bush in that fashion. That is what you are asked to believe.

You recognize Fuhrman, personification of evil. He is trying to tell you this is an important piece of evidence here, and I just came back from Rockingham, and this matches the glove found over there. That is what he tells you. But he is lying again. He is lying, and that is why he is central to this case, because he hadn't even been to Rockingham at that point, and he is tracking in that blood at that point, and that becomes very important, because you remember he slips up and says "in the Bronco" at some point. You get "in that Bronco." He put a bloody footprint in that Bronco. Are his shoes size twelve? He talks about "them." Remember, there is a question he was asked about gloves, and Lee Bailey asked him about. He is talking about gloves, and he says, "them." He never explained that. Does that mean two gloves? He said, "I saw them." Is that two gloves? Why would you say "them"? He is intelligent enough to come and lie to you. So that photograph there, that seals their doom. This man who is asked to go and help O. J. Simpson and notify him and take care of the kids, this man, this perjurer, this genocidal racist, this is the man. And he says then inferentially he didn't plant the glove, and now we know about these photographs, when they were taken, and you will have that contact sheet, and you will see a photograph of Miss Nicole Brown Simpson and the last two on the roll taken at nighttime with the flash at 4:30 in the morning.

Why did they then all try to cover for this man Fuhrman? Why would this man, who is not only Los Angeles' worst nightmare but America's worst nightmare, why would they all turn their heads and try to cover for [him]? Why would you do that if you are sworn to uphold the law? There is something about corruption. There is something about a rotten apple that will ultimately infect the entire barrel.

We live in a society where many people are apathetic, and that is why all of us, to a person, in this courtroom, have thanked you from the bottom of our hearts. Because you know what? You haven't been apathetic. You are the ones who made a commitment toward justice, and it is a painful commitment, but you've got to see it through. Your commitment, your courage, is much greater than these police officers'. This man could have been off the force long ago if they had done their job, but they didn't do their job. People looked the other way. People didn't have the courage. One of the things that has made this country so great is people's willingness to stand up and say that is wrong. I'm not going to be part of the cover-up. That is what I'm asking you to do. Stop this cover-up. If you don't stop it, then who? Do you think the police department is going to stop it? Do you think the DA's office is going to stop it? Do you think we can stop it by ourselves? It has to be stopped by you.

If you grow up in this country, you know there are Fuhrmans out there. You learn early on in your life that you are not going to be naïve, that you love your country, but you know it is not perfect, so you understand that, so it is no surprise to me, but I don't take any pride in it. But for some of you, you are finding out the other side of life: Things aren't always as they seem. It is not just rhetoric, it is the actions of people, it is the lack of courage, and it is a lack of integrity at high places.

Credibility doesn't attach to a title or position; it attaches to the person, so the person who may have a job where he makes two dollars an hour can have more integrity than the highest person. It is something from within. It is in your heart. It is what the Lord has put there.

Now, they [the prosecutors] want to distance themselves. These same people say, "Oh, he is not important," but the Rokahr photograph puts the lie to that. He is very important. And what becomes so important when we talk about these two twin demons of evil, Vannatter and Fuhrman, is the jury instruction that [says], "a witness whose testimony is willfully false in one material part of his testimony is to be distrusted in others. You may reject the whole testimony of a witness who willfully has testified falsely to a material point unless from all the evidence you believe the probability of truth favors his testimony in other particulars."

When you go back in the jury room, some of you may want to say, "Well, gee, you know, boys will be boys. This is just like police talk." That is not acceptable as the consciences of this community. That is why we have this, because nobody has had the courage to say it is wrong. You are empowered to say, "We are not going to take that anymore."

You may reject the whole testimony. You can then wipe out everything that Fuhrman told you, including the glove and all the things that he recovered with the glove. That is why they are so worried. That is why when people say Fuhrman is not central, they are wearing [blinders]. They have lost their objectivity.

Mobilizing the Jury to Use Their Verdict to Police the Police

Who then polices the police? You police the police, by your verdict. You are the ones to send the message. Nobody else is going to do it in this society. They don't have the courage. They have a bunch of people running around with no courage to do what is right, except individual citizens. You are the ones in war who are on the front line. These people set policies, these people talk all this stuff; you implement it. You are the people. You are what makes America so great, and don't you forget it.

And so understand how this happened. It is part of a culture of getting away with things. It is part of . . . looking the other way. We determine the rules as we go along. Nobody is going to question us. We are the LAPD. And so you take these two twins of deception, and if you wipe out their testimony, the prosecutors realize their case then is in serious trouble. It is not about them winning; it is about justice being done. They have other cases. This is this man's one life that is entrusted to you.

When we talked about this evidence being compromised, contaminated, and corrupted, some people didn't believe that. Have we proved that it was compromised, contaminated, and corrupted?

When you heard Fuhrman [say] he hadn't used the n word, . . . you probably thought, Well, he is lying; we know that is not true. That is just part of it. That is not the part that bothers us on the defense. I live in America. I understand. I know about slights every day of my life. But I want to tell you about what is troubling, what is frightening, what is chilling about that Kathleen Bell letter.

You will recall that God is good, and He always brings you a way to see light when there is a lot of darkness around, and just through chance this lady had tried to reach Shapiro's office, couldn't reach it, and in July of 1994, she sent this fax to my office, and my wonderful staff got that letter to me early on. And this is one you just couldn't pass up. She wasn't a fan of O. J. Simpson. What does she say? "I'm writing to you in regard to a story I saw on the news last night. I thought it ridiculous that the Simpson defense team would even suggest that there might be racial motivation involved in the trial against Mr. Simpson."

You can't fault people for being naïve, but once they know, if they continue to be naïve, then you can fault them. Don't ever say again in this county or in this country that you don't know things like this exist. Don't pretend to be naïve anymore. Don't turn your heads. Stand up, show some integrity.

"And so I then glanced up at the television. I was quite shocked to see that Officer Fuhrman was a man that I had the misfortune of meeting. You may have received the message from your answering service last night that I called to say that Mr. Fuhrman may be more of a racist than you could even imagine. Between 1985 and 1986, I worked as a real-estate agent in Redondo Beach. At the time my office was located above a marine recruiting center off of Pacific Coast Highway. On occasion I would stop in to say hello to the two marines working there. I saw Mr. Fuhrman there a couple of times. I remember him distinctly because of his height and build.

"While speaking to the men, I learned that Mr. Fuhrman was a police officer in Westwood." Isn't that interesting? Just exactly the place where Laura McKinny met him. "He said that he had been in a special division of the marines. Officer Fuhrman says that when he sees a 'nigger,' as he called it, driving with a white woman, he would pull them over. I asked what if he didn't have a reason, and he said that he would find one. I looked at the two marines to see if they knew he was joking, but it became obvious to me that he was very serious."

If he sees an African-American with a white woman, he would stop them. If he didn't have a reason, he would make up one. This man will lie to set you up. He would do anything to set you up, because of the hatred he has in his heart. People could have views but keep them to themselves, but when they have power over you, that is when racism becomes insidious. He has power.

A police officer in the street is the single most powerful figure in the criminal-justice system. He can take your life. Unlike [with] the Supreme Court, you don't have to go through all these appeals. He can do it right there and justify it. And that is why this has to be rooted out, in the LAPD and everyplace. Make up a reason because he made a judgment. That is what happened in this case. They made a judgment. Everything else after that is going to point toward O. J. Simpson. They didn't want to look at anybody else.

Mr. Darden asked, Who did this crime? That is their job as the police. They turned down our offers for help. But that is the prosecution's job. The judge says we don't have that job. We would love to help do that. Who do you think wants to find these murderers more than Mr. Simpson? But that is not our job; it is their job. And when they don't talk to anybody else, when they rush to judgment in their obsession to win, that is why this became a problem. This man had the power to carry out his racist views and that is what is so troubling. That is chilling.

If that wasn't enough, the thing that really gets you is she goes on to say, "Officer Fuhrman went on to say that he would like nothing more than to see all niggers gathered together and killed. He said something about burning them or bombing them. I was too shaken to remember the exact words he used. However, I do remember that what he said was probably the most horrible thing I had ever heard someone say. What frightened me even more was that he was a police officer sworn to uphold the law."

And now we have it. There was another man, not too long ago in the world, who had those same views, who wanted to burn people, who had racist views and ultimately had power over people in this country.

People didn't care. People said he was just crazy, he is just a half-baked painter. They didn't do anything about it. This man, this scourge, became one of the worst people in the history of this world, Adolf Hitler, because people didn't care or didn't try to stop him. He had the power over his racism and his antireligion. Nobody wanted to stop him, and it ended up in World War II.

And so Fuhrman wants to take all black people now and burn them or bomb them. That is genocidal racism. Is that ethnic purity? We are paying this man's salary to espouse these views? Do you think he only told Kathleen Bell, whom he just had met? Do you think he talked to his partners about it? Do you think commanders knew about it? Do you think everybody knew about it and turned their heads? Nobody did anything about it.

Things happen for a reason in your life. Maybe there is a reason why you were selected. There is something in your character that helps you understand this is wrong. Maybe you are the right people at the right time at the right place to say, "No more, we are not going to have this." What they've done to our client is wrong. O. J. Simpson is entitled to an acquittal. You can't trust the message.

It is not just African-Americans; it is white people who would associate or deign to go out with a black man or marry one. You are free in America to love whoever you want, so it infects all of us, doesn't it, this one rotten apple, and yet they cover for him.

And then there was Natalie Singer. Barely knew this man. He was dating her roommate. This man is an indiscriminate racist. He talks so bad that she didn't want him back in the house. What does he say to her in her presence? "The only good nigger is a dead nigger." You probably all heard that expression sometime in your background, and that is tremendously offensive.

This happened to come to light, but I would be pretty frightened if the majority of people in this country acted like this behind closed doors. Because what you do in the dark is going to come to the light. Remember that. That is what this case is about.

This is this man who is out there protecting and serving. That is Mark Fuhrman. And he is paired in this case with Phil Vannatter. They are both beacons that you look at and look to as the messengers that you must look through and pass. They are both people who have shown that they lie, will lie, did lie on the stand under oath.

This really is a case about a rush to judgment, an obsession to win, at all costs, a willingness to distort, twist, theorize in any fashion to try to get you to vote guilty in this case where it is not warranted, that these metaphors about an ocean of evidence or a mountain of evidence [are] little more than a tiny stream that points equally toward innocence, that any mountain has long ago been reduced to little more than a molehill under an avalanche of lies and complexity and conspiracy.

As great as America is, we have not yet reached the point where there is equality in rights or equality of opportunity. There are still the Mark Fuhrmans in this country, who hate and are yet embraced by people in power. But you and I, fighting for freedom and ideals and for justice for all, must continue to fight to expose hate and genocidal racism and these tendencies. We then become the guardians of the Constitution, for if we as the people don't continue to hold a mirror up to the face of America and say, "This is what you promised; this is what you delivered," if you don't speak out, if you don't stand up, if you don't do what's right, this kind of conduct will continue on forever, and we will never have an ideal society, one that lives out the true meaning of the creed of the Constitution or of life, liberty, and justice for all.

This is a case about an innocent man wrongfully accused. Soon it will be your turn. You have the keys to his future. You have the evidence by which you can acquit this man. You have not only the patience but the integrity and the courage to do the right thing. We believe you will do the right thing, and the right thing is to find this man not guilty on both of these charges.

Why Kato the Dog Did Not Bark

Kato, the dog, was purchased by O. J. Simpson after the other dog died. He let his son have the dog. They named the dog after Kato who is now living with O. J. Simpson. That dog knows O. J. Simpson. It is his dog. He bought the dog. If O. J. Simpson had been the one there that night, that dog would have followed him out the back gate. He wouldn't be going out the front. Those paw prints wouldn't be going out that way and down the sidewalk. That is common sense.

[O. J. Simpson] was always there for the kids. If it meant coming back from Chicago, he came home. He came home because his little girl was having a concert. That is the kind of dad he is. And somebody has to stand up for him. People don't want you to stand up for him. People can't stand the truth, but they are going to hear truth in here. There is one place you can't take away somebody's voice, and that is in the courtroom. This is a good and decent man who loves his family, who loves his kids. None of us are perfect, but he is a man who went a long way. Raised primarily by his mother. You know what he did with his life. He had a good life, a wonderful life.

He is not going to give all that up, try and kill somebody with a knife.

Can you imagine that a man who loves his children so much is going to go over, kill his ex-wife, kill their mother and leave her so that the children could come downstairs and find her? That defies credulity.

So forgive me if I speak out for O. J. Simpson, if I'm so presumptuous as to believe the Constitution means that [defendants] are presumed to be innocent until you make the decision. Nobody outside here has a vote. You have that vote, thank heaven. These narrow-minded people, thank heaven they don't have a vote.

The Fate of the Children

It doesn't fit; you must acquit. Something is wrong with the prosecution's case, and your common sense is never going to let you fall for it. O. J. Simpson was at home getting ready for his trip. He had no problem with his ex-wife. He had gone to this concert. She had gotten tickets for him. Nobody has come in here and said they had any argument that day. There is no fight. They talked earlier, made arrangements for the tickets.

He went to the concert. You saw him at the concert. You traced his steps that day and what he did, and then he went on to Chicago and came back immediately, and everything he did was consistent with innocence. This case is a tragedy for everybody, for certainly the victims and their families, for the Simpson family—and they are victims, too, because they lost the ex-daughter-in-law—for the defendant. He has been in custody since June of 1994 for a crime that he didn't commit.

Someone has taken these children's mother. I certainly hope that your decision doesn't take their father and that justice is finally achieved in this case.

Johnnie Cochran's Biblical Plea: A False Witness Shall Not Go Unpunished

In times like these, we often turn to the Bible for some answers. I happen to really like the Book of Proverbs, and it talks a lot about false witnesses. It says that a false witness shall not be unpunished and he that speaketh lies shall not escape. There was Mark Fuhrman acting like a choirboy, making you believe he was the best witness that walked in here, generally applauded for his wonderful performance. It turns out he was the biggest liar in this courtroom, for the Bible had already told us the answer: that a false witness shall not be unpunished and he that speaketh lies shall not escape.

In that same book, it tells us that a faithful witness will not lie but a false witness will utter lies. Finally in Proverbs it says that he that speaketh the truth showeth the forthrightfulness but a false witness shows deceit. So when we are talking about truth and lies and conspiracies and cover-ups, you know when things are at the darkest, there is always light the next day. In all of our lives, you have the capacity to transform O. J. Simpson's dark yesterday into [a] bright tomorrow. You have that power in your hands.

It is now up to you. We are going to pass this baton to you soon. You will do the right thing. You have made a commitment for justice. I will someday go on to other cases, no doubt as will Miss Clark and Mr. Darden. Judge Ito will try another case someday, I hope, but this is O. J. Simpson's one day in court. By your decision you control his very life in your hands. Treat it carefully. Treat it fairly. Don't be part of this continuing cover-up. Do the right thing, remembering that if it doesn't fit, you must acquit; that if these messengers have lied to you, you can't trust their message; that this has been a search for truth. Thank you for your attention. God bless you.

POSTSCRIPT

O. J. Simpson was acquitted of all charges in less than four hours of deliberation. To some this was proof that our criminal-justice system was a total failure. To others it was a vindication of our criminal-justice system. Perhaps, prosecutor Marcia Clark believed that the ten women on the jury would sympathize with Nicole Brown Simpson as a female victim. In the end it seemed that race, and not gender, carried the day.

Johnnie Cochran no doubt sought to find enough racism in the case to impel the jury's rejection of the overwhelming evidence of guilt. The jury may have been predisposed to acquittal in the first place, but Cochran cleverly furnished them with a plausible reason to vote with their prejudices: Mark Fuhrman. Then, to ensure that evidence provided by Detective Vannatter would not convict Simpson, Mr. Cochran used the racism brush broadly to include Vannatter, dubbing Fuhrman and Vannatter "twins of deception." Whether this claim had any real merit did not change its impact on the jurors.

Successful lawyers win cases by convincing the jury that the issues that help their side look good are intrinsically important to the decision. Mr. Cochran claimed repeatedly—almost as a refrain—that the key issue was the failure of the glove to fit Simpson's hands. Gradually he was able to put the LAPD on trial in place of his client—no matter that his argument often stood in stark contradiction to the facts. For example, Mr. Cochran implied that the one glove found at Rockingham was planted there by the police. Yet he could not explain the inconsistency this implied: If the police had framed O. J. Simpson by leaving the glove there, they might have chosen a glove that fit him.

Mr. Cochran's summation was a great example of a multibarreled approach to creating reasonable doubt. By nitpicking every stray detail offered by the police and distracting the jury with irrelevant issues, he created a drizzle of doubt in the jurors' minds.

His passion, it seemed, masked his faulty reasoning. Still, Mr. Cochran took a major risk by propping his defense against such a dodgy argument. He argued, famously, that the prosecution's timeline was wrong, since his experts said that the murder took as much as fifteen minutes—a long time for a killer to operate in the open. Mr. Cochran also argued that since no one had heard arguing or shouting, as had been the case in past domestic disputes between O. J. and Nicole, the real killer must have been a professional assassin. But would a professional assassin use a knife? Would a professional assassin take up to fifteen minutes to do the killing? Would a professional assassin leave his wool cap and glove on the scene?

Defense attorneys often assert that the fingerprints lifted from the crime scene are those of the real murderer. The law does not require the prosecution to prove the defendant's guilt in any particular manner. Some cases are solved by confessions, others by eyewitness testimony. Some are solved by fingerprints. Jurors have unrealistic views of how often fingerprints solve cases. Mr. Cochran took advantage of a jury's expectations, bred by years of TV shows, that fingerprints are crucial to murder cases. Yet had O. J. Simpson's fingerprints been found, Mr Cochran would easily have argued that his client had often visited Nicole Simpson's house and innocently touched surfaces. Or perhaps that the police had somehow framed Mr. Simpson again.

Yet how does one explain the notorious difference in verdict between the two trials, civil and criminal? What does it mean about the juries, the lawyers involved, about the justice system itself? A full answer to such questions could fill an entire book, but a few useful observations can still dispel much of the fog. In the criminal case, the State of California was required to prove its case "beyond a reasonable doubt" and the jury had to agree unanimously on the verdict. Furthermore, the defendant had the right not to incriminate himself, not to testify or produce evidence. As in all criminal cases, the scales of justice were weighted in the defendant's favor. In contrast, the civil plaintiff had to prove the defendant's guilt only by a preponderance of the evidence to nine out of twelve jurors. Perhaps most crucial to the O. J. Simpson case, the civil plaintiff had the right to ask Simpson to produce evidence—the Bruno Magli shoes, the gloves, the bag that he took with him to Chicago—which he ultimately could not provide. In the criminal proceeding, however, the procedures are much more heavily structured to the rights of the accused: It was within Simpson's rights to refuse to talk to the police about shoes or gloves or even to refuse to take the stand.

It is impossible to say what would have happened if Mark Fuhrman had played no part in the case. It is equally impossible to say what would have happened had the prosecution, of its own volition, decided not to call Mark Fuhrman and have the case go to the jury without the glove found at Rockingham. Certainly the result could not have been less favorable.

Then the all-important difference: the composition of the juries. The civil case's jury was composed of six men and six women, made up of nine whites, one Hispanic, one Asian, and one Asian-black. The criminal jury was composed of ten women and two men, of whom two were white, one Hispanic, and nine black. The two juries had radically different views of race in America: In Los Angeles the black community had a deep-seated negative view of police conduct in general. Would the verdict have been different if the civil jury heard the criminal case instead?

2

CELEBRITY CRIME IN THE SPOTLIGHT

MARV ALBERT AND SEAN "PUFF DADDY" COMBS ON TRIAL

WHEN A DEFENDANT IS a celebrity, a slew of arguments are available to both defense and prosecution, rather like standard countermoves in a chess game. The prosecution argues that fame itself should not immunize a person who breaks the law. Conversely, the defense argues that the defendant has been singled out for being famous, introducing a financial motive behind the victim's claims (after all, if the prosecution launches a successful criminal case, the recovery of civil damages from the guilty party becomes that much easier).

MARV'S BEDROOM SECRETS ... OR NIGHTMARES?
COMMONWEALTH OF VIRGINIA v. MARV ALBERT

Marv Albert, the New York Knicks and NBC announcer, faced sodomy and assault charges in Virginia, brought against him by his former girlfriend. Both the defense and the prosecution played on the celebrity issue. While the defense portrayed Albert's accuser as emotionally troubled and financially desperate, the prosecution accused Albert of implicitly abusing his celebrity influence by behaving brutally and egomaniacally to the plaintiff.

Excerpts of the two opening statements are set out below.

Excerpts from the Opening Statement of Prosecutor Richard Trodden

On February 12 a coarse and a crude abuse of a human being took place at the hands of that man. And it took place and was accomplished by his physical domination of a forty-one-year-old woman who had been his friend; a woman who had been his lover; a woman who he knew for ten years; a woman who had cared for him. But it was a woman whose human dignity he chose to ignore on this night in his egocentric quest for sexual gratification. This trial is going to be the first time that Vanessa Perhach will tell her tale in public of what this man did to her. Ms. Perhach has known the defendant since about 1986.

At that time Ms. Perhach was living in Miami. She was undergoing the stress and the beginnings of the breakup of a marriage. She had two children. And she began to try to get herself back on her feet by seeking employment. She found employment at the Airport Hilton in Miami.

She was working as a telephone operator when she met the defendant in '86, and the relationship took off rapidly. And make no mistake about it, it was a sexual relationship from almost the very beginning. But it was not an intense relationship. It was a relationship that would be marked by periods of absence of two to three months, because of the nature of the defendant's work. He would frequently fly into her town, to announce a game, and there would be a meeting.

There were constant telephone calls between the two. And Ms. Perhach will tell you at the outset she was enamored of the defendant back in '86. And she'll tell you he was a thoughtful, caring person. She liked him. He made intelligent conversation.

He took her to a world that was different from her drab existence. She enjoyed that. Over the years their relationship continued in this episodic way of every two or three months. And, quite candidly, their sexual relationship during this period of time was, . . . for want of a better word, "conventional."

But as time passed, the defendant desired a different kind of sexual activity. And he began to talk to the victim about, "let's be a little bit more creative. Let's engage in some scenarios." And he began to ask her, "Is it possible that we could participate in a three-some?"—where three individuals would participate in sexual activity together. And Ms. Perhach will tell you that indeed they did that, once in Los Angeles with a consenting and participating woman, once in Miami with a consenting and participating man.

Ms. Perhach will tell you that the last time she engaged in a threesome with the defendant was about 1990–1991. Around that period of time, she was getting on her feet. Her marriage was indeed ending. And she was looking to relocate with her children.

The defendant even solicited her and said, "Look, why don't you come to New York. I'll get your kids in private school up here." But Ms. Perhach was by 1991 a bit sadder, a bit wiser, and she said, "No, I can't go up to New York. What if he throws me out? I'll be stuck up there, and it won't be my place." So she brought her children and moved to this area, and she got a job with a hotel here. The defendant calls her on a fairly regular basis, and they meet periodically every couple of months. But many times he begins fantasy sex, as it were, on the telephone.

And the fantasy sex generally centers [on] participating in a three-some with another male and around undergarments and ladies' underwear. Sometimes when they had encounters, the defendant would ask her to bring extra underwear for him to wear to play out scenarios, and it was frequently a precursor to some sexual activity.

But as the years passed, human nature being what it is, sexual fires tend to ebb a little bit. Their relationship, as it got closer to February of 1997, was not as intense as it had been before. As a matter of fact, in 1996 she may have seen the defendant maybe three times. And she'll tell you that not all the time did [they] have a sexual relationship. [They] had known each other for ten years. "Sometimes, believe it or not," she'll tell you, "I would go to his room and we would talk about our kids, about the experience of divorce that we had," about things that they shared in common. So at all times it was not sexual. But there was a constant refrain, which was the talking about, "Let's do threesomes," and particularly threesomes with males.

The context of these meetings is that the defendant was a sports announcer, and he would frequently come to this area to do sports announcing. And so consequently their encounters were generally after he had finished his sports announcing for the day, and it would be late after he would get to his hotel. Their contacts were always at his hotel when he was visiting, and it was usually late in the evening.

On February 12, a couple days before the defendant called Ms. Perhach and he said, "I'm coming to announce, the Knicks-Bullets game. Do you want some tickets?" And he frequently would ask her did she want some tickets, would her daughter want some tickets to the game. And he said, "Do you think you can get a threesome?"

Well, this was not completely unusual. She had heard this request before. But he seemed to be a bit more insistent about it. Even before he left New York, he called her again and he said, "What's your schedule going to be? We're going to get together this night. Can you get a threesome?"

She was generally parrying these requests. She was not all that excited about threesomes, and she kept kind of putting him off. But he kept being insistent about it. He called her again that day, about 1:30, this time on her cell phone as she's shopping, again trying to make arrangements for, "When are we going to meet? Got somebody to take the tickets? And, oh, by the way, do you have somebody for the three-some?" And, again there's this great interest in the threesome.

In the afternoon she called him to talk about picking up tickets and making arrangements for these tickets, and again the subject matter came up. He called her one last time from the arena, saying, "Hey, do you have somebody lined up? Keep trying to get somebody." She kept saying, "I don't have anybody right now." "Well, keep trying."

About 11:38 she left her home, and she's on her way to visit the defendant after the game, as she had planned to do. She calls him up on her cell phone in her car, saying, "I'm about ten minutes away," and, again the subject is brought up one last time. But this time there's a bit more insistence for this threesome. She says no. She goes up to his hotel room. It's about midnight. Knocks on the door. He opens it, says, "Ah, I see you have nobody. Come in. You look great. How you been doing?"

They sit down . . . on the sofa, and they do what old friends do. They talk about their families, they talk about their children, they talk about their love lives. And they do what they have done many times in the past, they get comfortable. And she'll tell you she was not going to be surprised if there was going to be sexual activity that night. It happened many times. She quite frankly liked the defendant. There was nothing she didn't like about him. So she would take off her shoes, sat on the sofa. Eventually she may have taken off another article of clothing, whether it was his tie or her blouse, I'm not quite sure.

And he says, "Hey, wait a minute. I want to show you a tape." And he leaves, and he goes in the bedroom, and he comes back with a pornographic tape. And he puts the tape into the tape player, and they sat and they begin to watch a pornographic tape.

And this is a pornographic tape of three individuals having sex, two males and a female. As they watch this tape, temperatures rise a little bit, the victim takes off her pants at the defendant's request, the defendant begins a little heavy petting of the victim, a little massaging of himself, and it's this tape that is playing, and the victim will tell you she wasn't quite sure this was the right approach for her that night. Things didn't feel quite right. Things were a little different. But it was clear where it was probably headed. It was [headed] to the bedroom.

She goes to the bathroom, brushes her teeth. And by this time she has removed her pants. She is wearing her panties and a camisole and a pair of socks. And she goes into the bathroom, thinks for a minute, and she puts on a robe. She began to feel she had put on a little weight, she was a little self-conscious. She comes out of the bathroom, and Marv Albert is in the bedroom. He said, "Hey, what are you wearing a robe for? I've seen you plenty of times before." She takes off the robe.

He grabs her by the arms, and he throws her on the bed, and he says to her, "You've been a bad girl. You didn't bring anybody for me." As a matter of fact, when they were watching that pornographic movie, he looked at her and said, "If you had brought somebody, that's what we could be doing." But he grabs her, and he throws her on the bed, and he jumps on her back. She is shocked. He then begins to bite her back. The first bite is complete shock. But as she realizes what is going on, she says, "Stop, it hurts." But he did not stop. He continued to bite her on her back in a painful way. In fact, he mocked her. He said, "Aw, come on, you know you like this." She said, "Stop, it hurts."

You'll see photos of the bites, and you'll hear about DNA evidence that shows that his saliva is there at the site of the bites. He slides off of her back, and there is a brief conversation about whether vaginal intercourse should be taking place. And she says, "Hey, I'm not on the pill. You don't want to get me pregnant." And he then grabs her hair and starts to pull her head down to his genital area.

She's engaged in oral sex with this man many times before. And if things had gone right this night, she probably would have engaged in oral sex with him that night. But after he had assaulted her and bit her on the back, she was damned if she was going to do it. And she clenched her teeth and was not going to open her mouth.

He grabbed her mouth and squeezed it until it opened, and then he shoved his penis inside of her mouth. Prior to doing that, he had removed her panties—when they had had that discussion about whether there was going to be vaginal sex, the panties came off. As he had his penis in her mouth, he forced her head up and down, until he ejaculated. She spat out the semen in the panties that were lying on the bed. After he ejaculated, he fell back into the bed and was spent.

She began to get up, shocked, dazed, and began to gather her items together. She took the panties and put them in her pocket. Then she put them in her purse, gathered her things, and said, "I'm leaving." He said, "What, so soon?" She walked out of that hotel room. She went down to her car, which was parked on the street, absolutely stunned, looked for a police vehicle in the neighborhood, started up her car, and started driving to look for a police car.

She pulled over about a block away and called 911 and told the police what had happened. Officer Hanula responded to the place where she had placed the phone call, and there she was, leaning out of the side of her car, gagging and retching into a pool of liquid outside of her car, wincing as she felt her back. It was a crude use of a human being. And the evidence will show that it was done by this man for one purpose. He wanted a scenario that night. And the dignity of a human being that was with him did not matter. She was his property, and that's a crime.

Excerpts from the Opening Statement of
Defense Attorney Roy Black

It has been unrelenting publicity in this case for some five months now. Mr. Trodden says that their story has not come out. I disagree with what he says. But whatever it may be, the first time that Marv Albert's side of what happened on February 12 will be heard here today.

There has been an unrelenting campaign of publicity in this case, all because of his status of being on television. And he has never been able to tell his side of what happened, until today.

We intend to show that what happened on the night of February 12 is far different than what Mr. Trodden says. This is not a woman who was abused, who was taken advantage of, who was violated in any way; that everything that happened that night was consensual, just as it had been for the ten and a half years of their relationship. That what happened that night was the same as what happened every other night when Marv and Vanessa got together in various cities throughout this land. That nobody was forced to do anything that they didn't want to do. And that it was purely consensual.

The only difference is that, based upon things that were going on in 1996 and 1997 in the life of Vanessa Perhach, . . . she had become unbalanced, vindictive, and wanting to get revenge against Marv Albert, and this is her revenge. And we will see it play out in this particular courtroom for the next couple of days. But one thing I want to tell you about is that you're going to hear matters about sexual conduct, some of which you may not agree with, some of which may offend you in some way.

The purpose of this trial is to search for the truth of what happened on February 12. It's not here to sell newspapers or television stories or to titillate the public or sell tabloid newspapers. Anything that comes in about [the] sexual conduct of these two people is only worthwhile if it illuminates what went on that particular night. If it just comes in to horrify people or to titillate people, it is totally inappropriate.

Anything that we bring into this case that deals with sex is only to explain the relationship between Marv and Vanessa Perhach and what happened on the early-morning hours of February 12, 1997, and only that.

Let me tell you a little bit about Marv Albert. I think all of you have heard something about this case. But let me tell you who he is, so you will know him when you are listening to this case. This is a middle-aged man, who has lived the American dream. When he was growing up in Brooklyn, and his father, Max, [who] is here, owns a grocery store in Brooklyn. [Marv] started working at the grocery store. And early in his life, the one thing that he wanted to be was a sportscaster. As a child he got a tape recorder. He used to watch television and turn the sound off and practice calling games. This was his desire in life. This is a young man who is not averse to work.

At fourteen years old, he went to work for the Brooklyn Dodgers, doing everything from running errands to delivering mail to sweeping the floors to going up on the roof of their building and changing the scoreboard during games. When he went to school, he took journalism and started to work on the radio. He went to school at Syracuse University and soon got opportunities in the radio and news and calling minor-league baseball games. And then he got a very big break in his life. He was asked to do a New York Knicks game, because the regular announcer was snowed in somewhere.

And Marv then started in on doing this kind of work and has not stopped ever since. He has called all the New York Knick games for thirty years. He has been on NBC for twenty-three years, doing the NBA finals, the NFL games.

He wrote an autobiography, the title of which is, *I'd Love To, But I Have a Game.* And that sort of sums up his life. Here is a man who . . . Friday, Saturday, and Sunday works for NFL football, preparing and calling the games.

On Monday through Thursday, he calls the New York Knick games. If he has one time when he has a free hour or two, he calls the New York Ranger games during that. He works seven days a week. At one time he was not only doing that but doing the six and eleven o'clock news at the same time, running back and forth from one event to the other. And as a man who is on the road two hundred days a year, [he is] consumed by his career. And part of the reason he's here today is because he's a celebrity. He's well known. And certainly some people think that he's well-off.

Marv Albert met Vanessa Perhach in 1986. You will see he's even preserved the sign-in registration form that he filled out to check in to the Miami Airport Hilton, where she worked at the front desk. You will hear that Vanessa Perhach is a person who collects celebrities. That when Marv came in, she called up his room and ended up stopping by, allegedly doing the rounds of the hotel, and they had sex that night. That she would brag about the celebrities that she had relationships with, people like Peter Jennings, who's on the ABC News to sports figures, to other people who are with NBC, anyone who she thinks is . . . a celebrity. She would brag to people about her relationship with them.

And she did that with Marv Albert, telling her friends that she was going to end up marrying him, that he was going to get her a lot of money, that the next time they would see her, she would be driving a fancy car and would have a lot of jewelry. And she built up this relationship that she had with Marv into something that she considered to be the most important thing in her life.

They would meet in hotel rooms throughout this country. Certainly in Miami, in Baltimore, in Virginia, here in Arlington, in Los Angeles, many times in New York, [in the] Washington-Baltimore area.

Mr. Trodden says that there were times when there would not be sex. Well, Ms. Perhach gave a statement to the police in which she was asked specifically, "Whenever you visited with him, did you always have sex?" "Yes." First there would be the phone conversation, but yes, they had sex each and every time that they met in hotel rooms, usually late at night, usually after Marv had called a game, and it was all consensual. Everything that they did together was consensual, just as it was in the early-morning hours of February 12.

You may not like it, but when you look at this, this is a relationship that was built on sex. That was the relationship between the two of them. Every time they would get together, they would have sex. Every time they talked on the telephone, they talked about sex. They would have what is called phone sex. Or they would talk about their fantasies over the phone, each one telling each other various things about their sex life.

This went on sometimes as many as three times a week, and they would meet in these various cities, and she would fly in to meet Marv late at night in these hotel rooms. And no doubt there were times that they acted out these various fantasies, not always things that you or I or other people may agree with, but this was the relationship between the two of them. And you will hear that things like biting and other kinds of sexual activity would occur, just as it occurred on the early-morning hours of February 12 in the Ritz-Carlton.

Now, things did change, as it got to 1996 and 1997. Things changed in Vanessa Perhach's life. And things changed in Marv Albert's life. In Marv Albert's life at the end of 1996, at the beginning of 1997, he was thinking of getting engaged to another woman. And this was communicated to Vanessa Perhach. At the same time, Vanessa Perhach's life was being somewhat difficult. You will hear that when she gets into a relationship and this relationship starts to disintegrate or starts to break up, she does things that are sometimes self-destructive, sometimes destructive to other people. At this time in 1996, she was having a relationship with a police officer named Peter McGrath. That relationship was also falling apart at the same time her relationship with Marv Albert was falling apart.

With Peter McGrath her acting-out was somewhat different than it was with Marv Albert. She threatened to kill him, threatened to kill his dog. At this period of time—when her life is falling apart, she is losing McGrath, not only making threats to him about killing him, his dog, and any woman he's with if she ever finds him—at the same time, she is doing things like filling her mouth full of pills and making believe that she's committing suicide. And then, when McGrath leaves, she spits them out.

She sees Marv in October of 1996, in Baltimore, and they have sexual relations. That's when some of these problems start to come about between them. She begins to realize that whatever relationship she has with Marv is now disintegrating, the same as it's disintegrating with McGrath. She's committed to a mental hospital in December of 1996, right after this meeting with Marv in Baltimore in October of 1996, on one of these suicide attempts. She's released from the hospital, and it's only . . . a month and a half later that this event occurs that we are here to decide for the next week or so as to what went on.

You will find that she had lost her job at the Hilton at the same period of time because of—

MR. TRODDEN: Your Honor, I object.
THE COURT: Objection sustained.

Well, you will hear that she was heavily in debt and unemployed, that her life was sort of in extremis all at this period of time, at the end of 1996, right up to and through February of 1997, all of which bears on what her state of mind is and bears on the desperate measures she was taking.

Marv Albert comes to town on February 11 to call a game in the evening. It is true that there are conversations between Marv and Vanessa during the day, in which they talk about sex and what kinds of sex they're going to do, just as they've done hundreds of times before.

Just as every other time, they agree to meet in Marv's hotel room late at night. She goes and drives to his hotel room at sometime around midnight on the end of February 11, beginning of February 12 of this year. That she leaves her sixteen-year-old daughter at home by herself on a school night in order to go out and meet Marv in his hotel room, just as she's done throughout this country, in Miami; Los Angeles; Baltimore; Washington; and yes, Arlington, Virginia; and New York City.

That when she goes up to the room and meets Marv, there's absolutely no anger between them whatsoever. That they greet each other and they sit on the couch and talk about things like their children, their past events in their lives. She talks to him about decorating her house, about what she's doing while she's unemployed, what kind of job she wants to do. It is a perfectly natural, calm conversation between two adults, just as they've had before in the past.

There comes a time when they start taking their clothes off. That Marv takes off his shirt and pants. And in fact they discuss what his underwear looks like. And Vanessa says that "I thought he had gray-looking Calvin Klein underwear on." She begins to take off her clothes, her blouse, her pants. In fact, her pants are so tight that she tells Marv to stop taking them off, and she removes her pants.

Marv then says, "Let's go into the bedroom and go to bed." She says, "Well, first I'm going to go to the bathroom," and she goes into the bathroom and she takes out her toothbrush and brushes her teeth prior to going into the bedroom. When she leaves the bathroom, she goes into the bedroom and gets into bed with Marv. She will admit all of these things. But where things change is when they are in bed. And the reason they change is because Vanessa Perhach has it in her mind that night that she's going to make an accusation against Marv Albert.

She asks him to bite her on the back, and he does so. And, by the way, you know, there are people who get involved in biting and there are people who may not. But for this relationship that is something that's acceptable. You will see in evidence the photographs of these bite marks. There is no breaking of the skin. There is no scraping, as you have in some type of an aggressive bite mark. There's no blood. There's no gashes. It's true you can see teeth marks, but this is not aggressive biting that one does in a fight or to inflict harm upon somebody or to cause somebody deliberately pain. This is more like biting [as] part of a sexual activity.

They then—ironically, Mr. Trodden didn't mention to you, after the biting, Marv begins to pull off her panties, and she said, "Stop, it's hurting . . . me the way you're doing it." And he says, "Okay." And then he takes them off a lot more gently. This man who allegedly has assaulted her by biting her on the back, causing her pain, is now taking her panties off gently, because he originally pulled them too hard.

She then says, "Well, I don't want to have sexual intercourse, because I don't have any birth control, and I'm at the end of my menstrual period." So this madman, this man who's assaulting her, who's biting her back, says, "Okay, if you don't want to, that's fine." This man who's a rapist says, "Okay, that's fine." And then they have oral sex.

One of the strangest parts of this case is, after they have oral sex, Vanessa Perhach says in her police statement that she looked around, found her underwear, opened them up, and spit the semen into the crotch of the underwear. And she said, "I spit it on my underwear, because I wasn't going to grab a sheet and take it with me."

She's collecting evidence. This woman who has now been traumatized, who's in shock, is now collecting evidence. And this statement is full of half-truths. Some truth but some lies. She then goes into the bathroom, and after she goes into the bathroom, she goes back into the bedroom, after this alleged assault, where Marv Albert is.

Then Marv goes into the bathroom. And while he's in the bathroom, she stays there, this woman who's alleged to have been assaulted and is in shock and is traumatized. And then, when Marv comes out of the bathroom, they sit there and talk about things like their children and redecorating her house. And [the police] even ask her, "Well, did Marv know that he traumatized you"? She says, "Well, how would he know that?" "Did Marv show anything that he knew that you were upset?" "No, he didn't show anything. Why would he?" This is what she says in her police statement.

She does not run out of this hotel room. And you will hear there are phones all over the place. When you go into the bathroom, you can lock the doors and call security. You can call 911. None of these things are done. And then, when they are outside after this in the living room and continuing to talk about such things like that, they even kiss and hug good-bye. And then she leaves, and she tells later at the hospital that the alleged event occurred at 12:30. The first call to 911 occurs at 1:44 A.M., an hour and fourteen minutes later. And she leaves. When she leaves the hotel room, she doesn't go to the front desk of the hotel.

She doesn't go to the security people. She doesn't tell the people out in the car park or the people in security in the hotel. And she's worked security in hotels. So she knows how easy it is to call the police from a place like that. But she goes somewhere for some period of time and then after that makes a complaint about Marv and pulls out the panties that she spit the semen into the crotch of . . . and gives that to the police as her evidence of this alleged assault.

And that's basically what happened between the two of them on that night. Marv Albert has always been a gentleman with her, and she will admit that. He doesn't use swear words. Their alleged motive for this is that she didn't bring a man with her. And she'll tell you that he's been asking for this for seven years. So after seven years, I guess he finally got mad enough to bite her on the back because she hasn't done it.

None of these things, ladies and gentlemen, fit together. And I think when you listen to this evidence and you see what happened, [you will see] that because of things going on in her life, because of the way things are falling apart in these relationships, the way it's falling apart in the relationship with Marv Albert, that Vanessa Perhach did things and has made a false accusation against him.

You will see that Marv Albert did nothing with Vanessa Perhach other than what had been done many, many times before and [in] many, many different places. It was all consensual. There was no forcible sodomy. There was no forcing of oral sex. Any type of biting was done voluntarily and consensually. And it was simply not a crime. And hopefully in this country, being successful and being a celebrity and being well known is not enough to convict you of a crime.

POSTSCRIPT

Marv Albert pleaded guilty to a misdemeanor charge of assault and battery on September 25, 1998. The felony sodomy charge was dropped. On October 24, 1998, he received a twelve-month suspended sentence with a court order to get counseling, which stipulated that the charges against him would be expunged from his record were he to stay out of trouble during that period.

Albert's guilty plea was apparently motivated by a surprise prosecution witness, one Patricia Masten, who had worked as a liason for the Hyatt's VIP guests. She testified that she first met Mr. Albert when he traveled with the Knicks in the early 1990s and stayed at the Hyatt. Masten described two separate nonconsensual biting sessions with Albert. The first occurred in Miami in 1993, when Albert invited her to a Knicks team party. When she arrived, no one was there but him. Albert asked her questions about oral sex and threesomes and bit her on the lip. She pushed Albert away and fled the hotel room. Then, in 1994, Albert called her again when he was staying at a Hyatt hotel in Dallas. He apologized for the prior incident and asked her to come to his room to help him send a fax. When she got to the room, he came out wearing panties and a garter belt. According to Masten, he pushed her head toward his crotch and bit her on the side of the neck. Masten tried to push Albert off of her and, in so doing, accidentally lifted his hairpiece and raised it off of his head (Marv Albert denied Ms. Masten's accusations in their entirety and even offered to call his hairdresser to testify that pulling his wig off was impossible.)

Roy Black moved to exclude this testimony as highly prejudicial, but Judge Kendrick permitted it as showing a pattern of behavior. Albert's guilty plea was understandable in view of the testimony that could be admitted. Even if Marv Albert was acquitted—which, with Ms. Masten's testimony, was no longer a certainty—he would have to suffer more adverse publicity in the process.

Entrenched cultural prejudices, potentially harbored by any jury in America, acted as an invisible minefield on both sides of this case. Any famous person may have fans or detractors who bring their feelings into the jury room. Many jurors may feel that relationships with celebrities automatically invite an abuse of power. Some will blame the celebrity; others will fault the victim for inviting the abuse. The victim in this case was accused of collecting celebrities. Peter Jennings denied ever meeting Vanessa Perhach. If her allegations were true, it would show that the victim was strangely attracted to follically challenged broadcasters who perhaps possessed bad hairpieces. These no-holds-barred tactics, in which both sides of the lawsuit air each other's dirty laundry, is a phenomenon of the last thirty years. It was a strange case, with the two opposing sides in total agreement about most of the lurid facts but disagreeing on the critical matter of consent: Did the biting and sodomy occur with the victim's consent? The defense argued that Marv and the victim had engaged in similar sexual escapades in the past, so consent was inbuilt.

A prosecutor might call Albert's defense an "accommodation" defense. Marv Albert and Vanessa Perhach knew each other for several years. DNA tests showed that the saliva at the site of the bite marks on the victim belonged to the defendant. The defense could not therefore argue that the victim was never bitten, or that someone other than Marv Albert had done it. Hence, the strategy followed by defense counsel Roy Black "accommodated," or accepted, the harsh facts of the bite-mark evidence while painting an innocent explanation of it.

In some ways both sides had to incorporate a strategic concession up front. For the defense, Mr. Black understood it was unwise for him to dispute the physical DNA evidence, since it came from experts whose credibility he couldn't easily shake. Unlike Vanessa Perhach, they had no reason to lie. He left it alone.

Mr. Trodden was equally up front with the jury about the nature and duration of the relationship—a bond lasting over ten years. He couldn't deny that the plaintiff might easily have consented to having relations that night had Mr. Albert not forced it upon her first. Mr. Trodden might have tried to downplay their intimacy, to make the assault appear more egregious, but the strategy was risky, and he might have lost his plausibility entirely. So Mr. Trodden's theme was that Marv Albert committed this crime because of his "egocentric quest for sexual gratification."

The one danger that a prosecutor faces in cases in which the conflicting parties know each other so intimately is that the defendant often knows more about the victim than the prosecutor does. Put off by the prospect of losing as much dignity in the courtroom as the defendant may, the victim does not necessarily share all the details of her life with the prosecutor. All the disturbing negative information about Perhach that came out from the defense did not make the prosecution's job any easier.

Much of Roy Black's opening consisted of portraying Marv Albert's life positively and attacking the credibility and character of the victim. Mr. Black went through a number of predictable maneuvers. He dealt with the issue of celebrity by showing that Marv Albert became famous through hard work. He also made the standard point that the defendant's fame was the main impetus for the accusation. His genuine shrewdness came into play when he argued that the comfortable atmosphere after the alleged attack was inconsistent with the prosecution's claim that the victim was traumatized. This included a postattack conversation about her family. He also argued brilliantly that the victim, in spitting the semen into her panties, acted very suspiciously. It looked as though she was collecting evidence against Marv Albert.

You will note how Roy Black referred to Marv Albert's eighty-one-year-old father, who was present in the courtroom. Often lawyers use human props to make their clients look more presentable. In a rape case, you may see a female attorney sitting next to the accused and softly touching his shoulder as she pretends to discuss legal strategy quietly with him, all done in the presence of the jury. The hidden message to the jury is "This guy who is accused of rape is not dangerous." It's a little gruesome here, of course, that the defendant's octogenarian father had to witness the events. One can only hope he was so deaf or mercifully senile as to be impervious to the goings-on.

PUFF DADDY AT THE SHOOT-OUT: *THE PEOPLE OF THE STATE OF NEW YORK* v. *SEAN COMBS, JAMAL BARROW AND ANTHONY JONES*

On December 27, 1999, a scuffle at Club New York in Manhattan resulted in three innocent bystanders being shot. By the end of the night, famous rapper and producer Sean "Puff Daddy" Combs, movie star Jennifer Lopez, and sidekicks Jamal Barrows and Anthony Jones found themselves under arrest.

Media scrutiny quickly mounted to a frenzy. With the O. J. Simpson chaos always in mind, here was a test not just of the lawyers but of the system's ability to handle an intense blend of celebrity and racial pressures. As other cases in this book also show, this case demonstrates just how warped an explanation the media offers of real-life events; a well-presented court argument in a carefully ordered trial can show what really happened.

The excerpted opening statements of Asstistant District Attorney Matthew Bogdanos and defense attorney Benjamin Brafman are set out below.

Excerpts from the Opening Statement of Assistant District Attorney Matthew Bogdanos

On Sunday evening, December 26, 1999, a thirty-year-old mother of two, Natania Reuben, was getting dressed to go to a party. At the same time in a different place across town, twenty-seven-year-old Julius Jones was also getting dressed to go to a party. At the same time in a different state, Robert Thompson, a forty-year-old engineer from Connecticut, was getting dressed to go to a party. Each of them [was] looking forward with some enthusiasm to a Sunday-night party at Club New York, a club on Forty-third Street between Seventh and Eighth Avenues. Each of those three [was] looking forward to seeing their friends [and to] making new friends.

By the time that evening was over, two of those people were in a hospital, seriously injured. By the time that evening was over, Natania Reuben had a bullet in her face. She was shot in the face. By the time the evening was over, she had a bullet in her head that fragmented into eight different pieces. By the time that evening was over, pieces of the bullet fragment were so close to her spine that they couldn't remove seven from her. By the time that evening was over, Julius Jones lay in a hospital gurney first at St. Claire's and then St. Vincent's. He had a bullet in the shoulder, nerve damage in the shoulder, bullets along [the] cervical spine. It is in his shoulder today. They can't take it out. Before that evening is over, Robert Thompson had a graze on top of the right shoulder. All three were shot.

How did three such disparate strangers suffer such similar fates? Under the laws of New York, it is my duty to tell you and then show you how that happened. As an assistant district attorney, it is my job and my honor.

Let me introduce to you the parties. You have Sean Combs, a music-industry executive; you have Anthony Jones, a security guard. You have Mr. Barrow, one of the rapper employees of Sean Combs. You will hear witnesses refer to Mr. Combs alternately as Puffy, Puff, Puff Daddy. Mr. Barrow will be referred to as Shyne, and Mr. Jones as Wolf.

Wardel Fenderson, nickname Woody, is a forty-two-year-old divorced father. He is a professional driver. In the fall of 1999, Mr. Fenderson took a weekend job. He had a full-time Monday-to-Friday job. He needed the money, and he was willing to work seven days a week. Mr. Fenderson began driving for Sean Combs on the weekend.

Mr. Combs, on the late afternoon/early evening, Sunday the

twenty-sixth, decided that he wanted to go into the city to the Sunday-night party. And the plan is for Mr. Bill Williamson to get Wardel Fenderson. They called him up: "Hey, Wardel, man, your Christmas is over, sorry. You got to work today." "Sure, no problem, I understand."

Mr. Combs and Miss Lopez hire a limousine from Hampton's Limo out in the Hamptons, and about ten-thirty they leave the Hamptons, arriving at the studio on Forty-fourth at about midnight. Mr. Combs and Miss Lopez begin socializing. Mr. Fenderson is just sitting in the Lincoln Navigator front seat. He's the driver; he's getting paid to drive Mr. Combs wherever Mr. Combs tells him to go. At that point Paul Offord [one of Combs's security guards] comes over to the Lincoln Navigator [and] tells Mr. Fenderson to get out of the driver's seat, go take a walk for a few minutes. Mr. Fenderson doesn't question him. It seemed strange, but he walks away.

Combs first leased the car in November of '98. It was a normal standard Lincoln Navigator. Mr. Combs added some aftermarket items, if you will. And [one] aftermarket item in particular was a trap, a secret place, a stash, a hidden compartment. In fact, in order to open it, you will hear you had to turn a radio on, turn the front, the left and right temperature controls clockwise and counterclockwise, hit the rear-window defogger, and then manipulate one of the levers on the front driver's seat. All of this has to obviously be done [by someone] seated in the driver's seat. This trap, you will learn, just happens to hold two guns.

Mr. Fenderson gets back into the car, and he continues to wait for his instructions from the defendant. And while he's sitting there, Mr. Combs gets in the back of the Lincoln Navigator. There's no conversation, there's no talking. Mr. Fenderson is just sitting in the driver's seat. Mr. Combs gets in the back.

We're into Monday morning, December 27. Something catches Mr. Fenderson's eye. There's a movement, a gleam, so he very carefully looks over his right shoulder, and what he sees shocks him. He sees a gun in Mr. Combs's hand. He sees Mr. Combs handling a black semiautomatic pistol. He will tell you he can't believe it.

This guy is a multimillionaire—that's Puffy Daddy—he's got security surrounding him, and he's got a gun. It gets worse. The gun . . .

Mr. Combs is handling is pointed directly at Mr. Fenderson. His first concern is if that goes off, even accidentally, "it's aimed right at me." Mr. Fenderson says nothing to the boss, not a word. It's his boss. He needs the job. That's Puff Daddy. At that point he sees Mr. Combs place the gun into his front waistband.

Minutes later they decide that they're going to go to Club New York. Initially they're going to have Mr. Fenderson and the limousine driver drive Mr. Combs and his entourage around the corner to Club New York, but the traffic is just too bad. So Mr. Combs decides to walk.

Mr. Combs has Leonard Howard [another of Combs's security guards] and Miss Lopez and Mr. Combs walk to Club New York while Mr. Fenderson and the driver of the limousine follow them. So they get to the front of the club now. When they get to the front of the club, Mr. Combs meets up with other members of his entourage, Anthony Jones [and] Jamal Barrow. They all go into the club.

At the two landings before the second set of doors, there are people whose job it is to search. They search everyone who goes in the club that night. Not quite. They don't search everyone. They search almost everyone. You see, you don't search Sean Combs. Sean Combs never can get searched. Anthony Jones, when he's with Sean Combs doesn't get searched. Jamal Barrow, when he's with Sean Combs, doesn't get searched.

They walk right by the searchers on that first landing and the searchers on the second landing, and no one lays a glove on them. So now they're inside the club. So the evening progresses. There's partying, there's drinking, and there's dancing. Mr. Combs was dancing during the course of the evening. Mr. Combs was drinking during the course of the evening. He was doing everything you would expect someone going to a club to do. Nothing terribly unusual about the evening's events up until about two-thirty. More crowded than usual, but just a normal Sunday night, everyone having a good time. Mr. Combs decides it's time to leave. So he notifies his security. There are hundreds of people in the club. Mr. Combs tells Mr. Howard that in fact it's time to leave. Mr. Howard calls to Mr. Fenderson on the Navigator phone and says, "Okay, Time to go. So start pulling up."

About half an hour before that, it had been so crowded in the club that the police actually were called to that location for crowd control. It was so crowded that the police actually told the owner of the club and the front security you couldn't let anyone else in the club anymore until other people left. So there was police presence on the block related to the crowd control.

Down the block there's a DWI checkpoint, and several people are actually arrested. Again totally unrelated to the shooting. It's now about two forty-five in the morning. Mr. Combs is leaving. The three defendants plus several security personnel [are] leaving in a single file from this VIP section through the dance floor. It is very congested. Fifty to sixty people in an area about the size of a jury box.

The witnesses will tell you that they're accustomed to being pushed and shoved when celebrities leave and enter a club, and they have no hard feelings about that. They will tell you they're accustomed to Mr. Combs when he enters and leaves a club. This had an edge to it. This was more violent, more aggressive than they were accustomed to in the past.

Mr. Combs is saying good night, shaking hands, high-fiving people. People are being pushed and shoved, and finally Mr. Combs thumps into a gentleman standing at the bar and knocks his drink on him. It's a gentleman who is not awed by celebrities, who doesn't think the fact that you have a lot of money means you can push me over and knock my drink on me and the bar. A gentleman who doesn't care who Puff Daddy is. So this individual turns around and actually without first realizing who it was shoves an elbow back into defendant Combs. So they begin arguing [and] cursing at each other. And the crowd of fifty to sixty people is everywhere. While the argument's getting worse and worse, security starts responding or starts moving over.

Many of the security personnel there were working there for the first time. There's a lot of pushing. There's a lot of shoving. There's a lot of cursing. The words are, "Fuck you, you're Puff Daddy, you ain't shit! You ain't got money. What's money? What did that mean, money? Who me? Do you know who I am? What are you doing? You're pushing me." More and more testosterone is in that pushing-and-shoving argument, talking about who's got more money, talking about who's tougher, who's not so tough. And who's a fake and who's real. And it gets more and more heated. Mr. Jones doesn't like the way his employer is being disrespected.

So Mr. Jones throws a punch at one of the individuals, and now it is pushing and shoving and security trying to get in the middle. Security actually pulls Mr. Barrow out of that melee. Security turns to Mr. Combs and Mr. Jones and says, "Get out of here. It's not worth it. Leave." Mr. Jones says, "Nah, we ain't leaving. We're staying right here." And so they stay right there. At that point someone throws a big stack of money in Mr. Combs's face. Now you've got money flying around, twenties, fifties, hundreds flying in all directions.

Now you've got people reaching and grabbing for money. It's just about then when it's more than Mr. Barrow can stand, the man for whom he works being disrespected like that. So Mr. Barrow pulls out a loaded nine-millimeter semiautomatic handgun.

In the crowd of several hundred people, he begins firing, trying to murder the man who disrespected his boss. Again, as fate would have it, he misses entirely his intended murder victim. Hits three completely innocent bystanders who just happened to be there. Mistakenly thinking they could have a good time and it would be safe because everybody gets searched at the door.

While Mr. Combs is surrounded by security—and many of them very big, very tall—while he's there being shielded by that security, while he's there being shielded by Mr. Jones, while he's there being shielded by everyone looking or almost everyone looking at Mr. Barrow pulling out his gun and firing, Sean Combs pulled out his gun in that club. Almost everybody was shielded. Almost everybody was looking at Mr. Barrow, but not quite everyone.

You will hear from the witnesses who saw Sean Combs pull out his nine-millimeter semiautomatic handgun how he fired a shot straight up. There's no indication that Mr. Combs aimed it at any particular individual. That was Mr. Barrow's weapon. People saw the muzzle flash, the flash that comes out of the front of the barrel of a gun when it's fired. [I]t appears Mr. Barrow fired three times and Mr. Combs once.

Miss Reuben is then hit in the face, and she's struck in the right side of the nose. The bullet fragments into eight different pieces. The largest piece lodges in the back of her head near her spine, and that's ultimately taken out by emergency service at St. Vincent's. They were concerned, since it was so close to her spine and so close to her throat, that she would choke to death on the bullet. The other fragments remain in her head, still in the left and right cheekbone area.

Mr. Thompson's struck in the right shoulder. It's a graze wound. And then there's a third bullet that actually matches Jamal Barrow's gun, and it is found near the VIP stage that's off to the left. So you've got Jamal Barrow firing once in this direction and hitting Julius Jones. Second time generally straight, hitting Miss Reuben and Mr. Thompson, and then a third toward the VIP area, and that's recovered later. And immediately above defendant Combs is a bullet hole from the ceiling. The bullet's not recovered. It's a ricochet, but it's a bullet hole right in the ceiling right above. It's tested with a presumptive test for the presence of lead. It's a test you'll hear indicates that it was [made by] a bullet.

Mr. Barrow takes that gun, puts it in his waistband, and runs out the front door. Mr. Combs and Mr. Jones also run out the front door, fleeing right behind Mr. Barrow. Then they get out onto the street. It isn't until Mr. Combs gets to the Lincoln Navigator outside that he realizes that he's actually fled the club without Miss Lopez. So someone has to go back in and get Miss Lopez.

Mr. Barrow's got the gun in his waistband, and sure enough, as he runs out of the club, he runs right into two rookie cops. Two kids, probably between the two of them they don't shave every day. He runs right into them. Here they are, just out there for crowd control. They've got three years on the police department total. Their job is making sure that the cars don't get stuck by people double- and triple-parking and making sure that the club isn't overcrowded.

They see the gun sitting in his waistband. They grab Mr. Barrow, they put him on the hood of the limousine that Mr. Combs and Miss Lopez came in. They . . . handcuff him, and they recover that gun from his waistband, and they unload the gun. It's got a bullet in the chamber, ready to fire. You touch that trigger, it's going to fire. Mr. Barrow is taken to the precinct, and the gun is taken into evidence.

As they get in the Lincoln Navigator, Mr. Fenderson is in the front seat. Mr. Jones gets in the front right seat. Miss Lopez gets in the rear left, and Mr. Combs the rear right.

Mr. Combs looks down the block, he sees Jamal Barrow—Shyne—getting arrested, and he comments out loud, "They got Shyne" or "They got Jamal."

Crime-scene detectives are coming to the club, trying as best they can to gather whatever evidence is not destroyed by this stampede, and they're able to recover two spent nine-millimeter shells. There are two discharged shells found generally where Mr. Barrow was firing. Both of those shells are matched ballistically to the defendant's gun. Also, that bullet that was recovered in the dance floor, that's matched ballistically to Barrow's gun.

Now, let me go back to the Navigator. As soon as the four of them get in the car, immediately Combs and Jones scream, "Go! Get out of here, leave!" Mr. Fenderson leaves. Although there are now police everywhere, police are barricading the street, marked police cars, lights, sirens, the defendants tell Mr. Fenderson, "No, no, no. Don't run to the police. Get out of here, away, get away from the police!" And the reason, the evidence will show you why they did that: They got two loaded nine-millimeter semiautomatic Smith & Wesson Model 915 guns in the car. While they're screaming at Mr. Fenderson, "Go! Leave, get out of here!" Miss Lopez screams out, "I saw Shyne bust off in the air," or "Saw him bust off" [shoot the gun in the air].

The police had begun to blockade the corner of Forty-third and Eighth, but they left an out. There's a narrow area on the right-hand side where [Fenderson] can slip through. His boss tells him to go; he goes. His right two tires went up on the curb as he was fleeing. He turns right on Eighth Avenue, fleeing from the police officers.

While this is happening Mr. Combs and Mr. Jones are screaming at him, "Open the stash place! Get the trap! Open it, open it!" Mr. Fenderson doesn't know what they're talking about. "I'm sorry, I'm your weekend guy, I don't know about the trap. No one told me how to open it. I don't know how to open it."

"Open the stash place!" Mr. Jones, in the front seat, is frantically trying to reach and work controls and pushing buttons, and he grabs the steering wheel with one hand, and he has a second gun in his hand while he's doing this. And he's frantically saying, "Open the stash place!"

Mr. Combs is doing the same in the back: "Open the stash place!" After they turn right on Eighth Avenue from Forty-third and Forty-fourth Street, defendant Combs's window, the rear right window of the Navigator, opens. They speed up Eighth Avenue. Sergeant Jack Konstandinidis sees the Navigator coming at him down Forty-third make a right-hand turn, and it is obviously to him suspicious that a car is fleeing the scene. Sergeant Konstandinidis decides to chase [the car] up Eighth Avenue. He has to do a K-turn in order to follow [them] up Eighth Avenue.

He loses sight of the Navigator between Forty-third and Forty-fourth. Sergeant Konstandinidis sees the Navigator up Eighth Avenue going through red light after red light and red light. He decides he's going to chase. He chases them, and while this is happening, Mr. Fenderson is being told "Keep going, don't stop."

Meanwhile again and again they're repeating, "Where's the stash place?" Mr. Fenderson sees the police are chasing him. He pulls over. They pull over behind him. He says, "They're pulling me over, I'm stopping." Defendant Combs says, "No, you're not. Keep going."

Defendant Jones says: "No, you're not. Keep driving." So he keeps driving. Finally, at Fifty-fourth Street after they had run 11 red lights, . . . a marked police car comes out of Fifty-fourth, cuts across Eighth Avenue, and in effect stops the Navigator from going any further, and Mr. Fenderson turns to them and says: "That's it, I'm stopping. I'm not going anymore."

So now the Navigator is pulled over, all four are in the exact same position. Sergeant Konstandinidis's gun [is] drawn. He screams out, "Driver, out of the car!" Sergeant Konstandinidis is taking each of them out. Mr. Jones is the last one out of the car. And when Mr. Jones is taken out last, where his feet had been in front of the front right passenger seat, about half under and half out, is a loaded nine-millimeter semiautomatic pistol, Smith & Wesson Model 915. Immediately all four are arrested.

If you have a gun in the car, not physically on somebody, but on the floor or the seat, New York State law treats that as if it's everybody's gun. The sergeant explained to them that if no one admits to the ownership, if no one admits possession of the gun, it's their gun. Everybody gets arrested for the gun. So Mr. Combs asked him if that's accurate. Sergeant Konstandinidis informs him that that is an accurate statement of the law, and Mr. Combs there on the street says, "Okay, deal, deal," as if he is in a boardroom. "I'll get you the owner of the gun." Mr. Combs . . . at that moment begins formulating a plan. He begins to decide who is going to take the rap for that one remaining gun. Who is going to say, "It's my gun"?

When they get to the desk of the Midtown North Precinct, the three male defendants are lined up together in front of the desk, Mr. Combs leans over to Mr. Fenderson, whispers in his ears so that no one else could hear, "Take the gun, say it's yours. I will give you fifty thousand dollars."

Mr. Fenderson looks at him, stunned. Mr. Fenderson, who's never been convicted, never been in trouble. Mr. Fenderson, who is in handcuffs. Mr. Fenderson doesn't know what he did wrong. Mr. Fenderson, forty-two-year-old father of two, with two jobs, sitting in front of the desk, petrified, frightened beyond explanation, . . . is being told by Puff Daddy, "Fifty thousand dollars. Take the gun."

At that point Mr. Jones leans over and says, "Take it. He is good for it. You will be part of the family if you take it."

They were taken back to the holding cell. It's a small jail cell that temporarily keeps prisoners on their way to court. Mr. Fenderson and Mr. Jones are put in the same holding cell, and then begins a relentless unremitting barrage: "Take the gun, say it's yours. Do it now, I'll give you fifty thousand dollars. I'll take care of everything. I'll pay your bail. I'll pay for your lawyer. You don't have to worry, you'll be one of us. You will be one of a family now. Take the gun. I can't go to jail. I'm Puff Daddy. Miss Lopez can't go to jail."

What about Mr. Jones? He can't either, because he is a predicate felon [a person with a prior felony conviction. The minimum sentence for a prior felon with a gun is five years].

"You've got to take the gun. Do it." Mr. Jones says, "Come on.

I'm a predicate. I'll do time for the gun. I can't take my gun. You got to take it. You have never been arrested. The worst you will get is probation. You won't do time."

Mr. Combs said, "Take my ring as collateral." He was wearing a pinkie ring, a gift from Miss Lopez the prior birthday. "Take this ring. You don't believe me. I'm good for the money. This ring is worth several hundred thousand dollars." It's actually not. Mr. Combs says, "It's all right, fifty thousand dollars, you will be one of us. I'll take care of everything, but you got to do it now, you got to do it now. He said that again and again, twenty times."

To his lasting shame, Mr. Fenderson says, "I'll do it." And at that moment the defendant is guilty of bribery. So Mr. Fenderson calls one of the police officers over to the bars of the holding cell, and by now Mr. Combs is in the holding cell. Wardel Fenderson says to the officer, "It's my gun."

The police officer said, "Hold it. Wait a second. You have all been arrested. The DA has got to sort it out now." Mr. Fenderson repeats it to a second officer at the insistence of Mr. Combs and Mr. Jones. He says it's his gun. It isn't until several hours later that finally they are put in separate holding cells. And it is at that point Mr. Fenderson will tell you that he reflects there for the first time on what he has done.

It is at that point Mr. Fenderson thinks about his daughters, his family. It is at that time, Mr. Fenderson will tell you, he can't commit the crime. He tells the police officer when he was alone and Mr. Combs and Mr. Jones [were] not there. He says, "I can't do this. I'm not taking the rap for these guys. It's not my gun."

The officer says, "All right. I'll tell it to the DA." All four of them are brought down to criminal court for arraignment. They get arraigned, and bail is set for Mr. Fenderson—ten thousand dollars. He didn't have ten thousand dollars.

Mr. Combs was good for his word. If he says he is going to take care of you, he takes care of you. Mr. Combs paid his bail. Mr. Fenderson doesn't have money for a lawyer. Mr. Combs got him a lawyer, and so at arraignment Mr. Fenderson stood there before a judge along with the others in the presence of the other defendants and had Mr. Combs's lawyer and Mr. Combs's bail money, and he walks out. All three of them are released on bail that night.

Mr. Jones and Mr. Fenderson get in a limousine along with a lawyer, and they drive uptown to the precinct to get their property that had been taken. Again in the car Jones is unrelenting: "Okay, we have a deal. He kept his end of the bargain, you keep yours. We got to do it soon, got to do it now, set it up tomorrow. Don't worry about a thing. Everything will be taken care of."

On the twenty-eighth, Jones called him twice to say, "Okay, let's meet with Combs's lawyer, Harvey Slovis. Let's get it done. You're going to take the gun. We'll get you fifty." Mr. Fenderson for the first time tells Jones, "No, I'm not going to do it. I am not going to lie. I am not going to commit a crime."

Jones tells him, "You're sure?" He says, "Yes, I'm sure." "In that case you are going to have to tell Puffy yourself." So Mr. Jones calls him back the second time and says, "You have got to pay your own bail now and get yourself a lawyer."

Later on in the day, there was a meeting set up [in] Mr. Combs's house at Park Avenue. Mr. Fenderson doesn't go. He is afraid. Mr. Combs calls him again to set it up. He says, "Yes, we'll do it tomorrow."

On December 29, Mr. Fenderson is scheduled to see Mr. Combs [at] his house, but he is afraid. He doesn't want to go alone. So he calls a friend of his up and asks his friend if he will drive him there, and [the friend] agrees to wait outside the apartment. [Fenderson tells] this friend, "If I am not out in fifteen minutes, check with the doorman to see what's happening. If I am not out in an hour, call the police."

Mr. Fenderson goes inside and tells Mr. Combs, "I can't lie. I can't commit a crime. I'm sorry, I can' t say the gun is mine." He then goes to get his own lawyer. Mr. Combs continues to call Mr. Fenderson. You will hear a voice-mail message from defendant Combs; clearly it is cryptic, but its import is clear:

"Hey, yo it's P." This is Mr. Combs. "I'm just thinkin' bout you, dog. I know you probably going through a lot of shit. Um—calling to let you know I'm there for you. Um—just hit me on, hit me on my cell, 'cause I am just concerned that news you hit me with earlier really fucked me up, and I just wanna make you feel, like comfortable, you know what I'm saying? Make your family feel comfortable, that you know, that you know everything gonna be a'right. All right, so just hit me. It's Puff. I'm on my cell, or hit me at the house. You ain't gotta see me or nothing. Just at least hit me back, though, a'right? Peace."

After he gets his lawyer, Mr. Fenderson [and] his attorney come into the district attorney's office, and once they come into the district attorney's office, Mr. Fenderson tells exactly what happened. Mr. Fenderson is warned by me, under oath in the grand jury, that "if there is one shred of evidence that connects you in any way to the gun found in the car, you will be prosecuted to the fullest extent of the law." He is told that if he lies in any way, shape, or form about the smallest of details, he will be prosecuted to the fullest extent of the law.

Mr. Combs's right rear window went down between Forty-third and Forty-fourth. George Pappas [is] sitting in a car, George Pappas, a regular working stiff, a nine-to-five guy sitting in the car drinking coffee. He drives for an escort agency. He is sitting there at about three o'clock, parked on Eighth Avenue between Forty-third [and] Forty-fourth, sipping his coffee. He sees this Navigator fly by. He sees the right rear window open. He sees a hand throw something out. That something hits his front bumper, and then a few moments later he sees one police car after another chasing or at least going up Eighth Avenue. He gets out of the car, and he sees a nine-millimeter semi-automatic Smith & Wesson Model 915 on the ground.

One of his first instincts was just to leave it there, but he will tell you that no one should leave a gun on the street where a kid can find it. So he picks it up. He did not turn it in to the police that night. He didn't want to get involved. He was somewhat embarrassed that he drives for an escort agency. So he puts the gun in his car, and he decides that he is going to call his boss and give it to his boss, Anthony Nastasi. Mr. Nastasi has a friend working for the FBI.

So Mr. Pappas calls him up. He says, "Tony, you're not going to believe this. I got a gun. I don't want to leave it on the street, but I want nothing to do with it. Please come get it." Mr. Pappas gives Mr. Nastasi that loaded nine-millimeter gun, still wrapped in the towel. Now, Mr. Nastasi immediately calls Special Agent Pat Kern up to inform him that he has got a gun.

Pat Kern goes out with Police Officer Andrew Varga to get the gun. They pick up the gun, and it is the exact same gun as was found in the car, Smith & Wesson, nine-millimeter, semiautomatic black Model 915, stainless-steel magazine.

The district attorney's office does not present charges to the grand jury as to either Miss Lopez or Mr. Fenderson, but charges are presented as to the three defendants before you, and they are indicted.

Mr. Barrow is indicted for attempted murder and assault in the first and second degrees He is also charged with possession of that nine-millimeter. Defendant Jones is charged with possessing a single gun, the gun that was found at his feet. Mr. Combs is charged with the loaded gun that was thrown out his window, and he is charged with the loaded gun that was found at the feet of his employee. Mr. Combs is also charged with criminal possession of a weapon with the intent to use it unlawfully. This charge encompasses all of his conduct during the course of the night, from his putting the gun in his waistband before going into the club to his pulling the gun out in the crowded club and his firing the shot at the ceiling in the club.

Finally, each of those two defendants Mr. Jones and Mr. Combs are charged with bribery, for offering or agreeing to confer upon Mr. Fenderson a benefit, namely $50,000 in order to get him to say that the gun was his. Some of the witnesses have prior criminal convictions themselves. Some of the witnesses, have pending criminal cases themselves. Mr. Nastasi has a pending criminal case in Las Vegas.

[Mr. Fenderson] has been promised nothing for his testimony. Nothing. You will hear that Mr. Fenderson was not charged. He has promised to tell the truth. Each of the shooting victims will testify. They will tell you what they saw, what they heard, what they felt, how they were injured. Each of the shooting victims will tell you that, as is their constitutional right in this country, they filed a lawsuit. They were injured, they incurred expenses, medical treatment, rehabilitation, loss of earnings from their jobs, and they filed a lawsuit against the people responsible for shooting them, responsible for putting them in the hospital. And Mr. Fenderson will tell you how he as well has filed a lawsuit, as is his right, for what the defendants did to him, for threatening him, for the emotional distress of what they did to him in the car during the chase.

I shall return before you in several weeks, and I shall ask you to do justice—evenhanded justice, Shakespeare calls it. I will ask you to find Jamal Barrow guilty for what he did in that club, shooting that gun in that club at those people. For Mr. Jones, I will ask you to return a verdict of guilty for what he did: having that gun, attempting to use it unlawfully, attempting to bribe Mr. Fenderson. And Sean Combs, I will ask you to return a verdict of guilty no matter who he is, because of the crimes he committed, and I will ask you to do this, for one reason and one reason alone—because they are.

Excerpts from the Opening Statement of
Defense Attorney Benjamin Brafman

[Mr. Combs stands]

Ladies and gentlemen, this is Sean "Puff Daddy." You can call him Sean, you can call him Mr. Combs, you can call him Puff Daddy, or even just plain call him Puffy, but what you cannot do in this case, you cannot call him guilty, because from the facts, from the evidence, from the law, you will conclude that he is not guilty. It's that simple. [Mr. Combs sits down.]

On December 27, 1999, Mr. Combs did not possess a weapon, either before going to Club New York or after Club New York or inside of Club New York. He did not try and bribe anyone. He is not guilty. It's that simple. And when this case is over, you are all going to conclude that Mr. Bogdanos was wrong in what he outlined the evidence will prove and that Mr. Brafman was right in what he told you the evidence would be.

My name is Benjamin Brafman. This young man is Johnnie Cochran, and together we have the privilege of representing Sean Combs. He has been wrongly accused. Now, I am not Johnnie Cochran. If you have trouble distinguishing me and Mr. Cochran, let me make it easy: I always wear a pin on my collar, so when you see the guy with the pin, it's Mr. Brafman.

This case is not about us. It is not about Mr. Bogdanos. It's not about personalities. It's about the way a trial should proceed. If you're trying to do justice and if you're trying to be fair, and in this case it's really quite simple: As to Mr. Combs, Mr. Bogdanos does not have credible evidence that Mr. Combs committed any crime during the period in question. When this case is done, you are going to conclude that Mr. Combs is not guilty, and that is the only verdict that the law will allow as to Mr. Combs.

Keep in mind that there are three separate people on trial in this case. When I stand, when Mr. Cochran stands, we represent Sean Combs and only Sean Combs. This morning Mr. Bogdanos tried very cleverly and very skillfully with a great deal of experience to paint with a broad brush, using the word "defendants." Well, there are three separate people on trial. And you will be required to render three separate verdicts as to each defendant separately, and in this case, on the crimes that Mr. Combs is charged with, you will return a verdict of not guilty.

When one of us chooses not to speak, that, too, is a statement far more eloquent, being made on behalf of Mr. Combs, because much of the evidence in this case will not involve Mr. Combs, even though he has been the centerpiece of Mr. Bogdanos's opening statement this morning.

Many of the witnesses called by the district attorney will have no evidence whatsoever to offer against Mr. Combs. Most of the witnesses called by the district attorney will help to exonerate Mr. Combs, so please keep in mind Mr. Combs is not charged with shooting anybody. And the reason I repeat it is because when you were questioned, many of you, based on what you heard in the media, presumed that Mr. Combs was involved in shooting someone, and he has never even been accused of shooting anyone, and that statement, more eloquently than anything else I could ever do, must tell you how important it is that you not allow what happens outside the courtroom to influence your decision in this case, that you not allow the tidbits of gossip that sells papers to enter this courtroom, and you gave us your oath that you would do that. Mr. Combs does not want an advantage because he is a superstar, but he is not entitled to a disadvantage either, and the disadvantage of superstar, in this case, he is saddled with. You will conclude from the evidence that the police and the prosecutors presumed guilt and then started to go back and fill in to make the pieces fit.

Within twenty minutes of Mr. Combs's arriving at the precinct, a media frenzy was created, and the police did not treat this case with care. When all of the evidence comes out, you will see that what happened here was a rush to judgment, and now Mr. Bogdanos is stuck with this case.

You are in for a battle. All you got to do is sit back and make yourselves comfortable. This isn't simply a defendant standing up and saying, "I am not guilty." This case is about prosecutors and police acting on a presumption of guilt, when the overwhelming evidence will demonstrate without question that Mr. Combs was not guilty, and that Mr. Combs should not even have been charged in this case, and that there is no evidence that Mr. Bogdanos could even produce in this case, to satisfy his burden of proving guilt beyond a reasonable doubt, because Mr. Combs is not guilty. You will conclude that this was a starstruck selective prosecution of a superstar, and this case is about fame and money, not truth and honesty and a search for justice.

Part of the problem with this case [is that] you have an experienced, articulate assistant district attorney who just laid out an opening statement which suggested that Mr. Combs was guilty of certain crimes. Two problems. One: Nothing Mr. Bogdanos says is evidence. Second problem is that even in his opening statement, he suggested things that the evidence will show to be inaccurate.

Let me give you a perfect example. He said to you that everyone else gets searched at this club, except Puff Daddy. Well, that's not true from the evidence. His own witnesses will confirm beyond question that that night was chaos, that they had many new security guards, that people got into the club, and, clearly, people besides Mr. Combs did not get searched. The district attorney and the police never bothered about it, because they are not superstars, but you will hear that one of those people pulled a weapon. You will hear that one of those people [was] threatening "to put a cap in Mr. Combs' ass [shoot him]."

Mr. Bogdanos suggested that Mr. Combs, for much of the night, was doing nothing unusual, just dancing and drinking, which is nothing unusual in a club. What he fails to tell you is that every single witness, even his own witnesses, will tell you that Mr. Combs's dancing was quite unusual. It was quite vigorous, it was quite entertaining. And it was substantially inconsistent with the activities of a person [who] has a weapon tucked in his waistband, because what Mr. Bogdanos didn't tell you about the dancing is that witness after witness will tell you that, at various points in the evening, Mr. Combs was on top of a table with his hands raised over his head, with a bottle of champagne and a glass of champagne, and they were able to see his waist.

There was never a gun. People will tell you that they hugged Sean to wish him happy New Year and merry Christmas and that they felt no weapon. Dozens of people will tell you that, at the time of the shooting, they were there and that Mr. Combs did not have a weapon, that he never pulled out a weapon, that he never fired a weapon.

How is it that if there is a gun thrown out the window and half of the New York City Police Department is chasing this car up Eighth Avenue, how come none of the police officers saw this gun that supposedly came out the window. [Mr. Bogdanos] said, "Well, the first car had to make a K-turn, and by the time it got around, the Navigator was ahead. That's great, except the Eighth Avenue man, the "working stiff," will tell you that at the time the weapon came out the window, police cars were five, ten, or twenty feet behind the Navigator, and the sergeant driving that car, a trained police officer, [who] was supposed to be able to observe, did not see a weapon come out of the window. Mr. Bogdanos told you that Mr. Combs is surrounded by enormous security guards. He describes them as six-four, six-five, 275 pounds. They were surrounding him.

Well, those security guards will be called as witnesses. None of them saw Mr. Combs with a gun. Some of them threw him to the ground the moment they heard guns fired and covered him with their body. People with impeccable background, not promised by law enforcement for favors, not suing for millions of dollars. People whose only motive is to tell the truth to help exonerate an innocent man.

Mr. Bogdanos will suggest, "Well, maybe at the second that Mr. Combs held a gun, maybe they were looking this way, maybe they were looking that way." It does not work, and when this case is over, you will be shaking your heads in dismay. You will conclude beyond question that this was a selective prosecution from jump street, and it got worse until today. Now it gets better, because now Sean "Puff Daddy" Combs gets his day in court, not before a prosecutor, not before a police officer—before you, the community.

Ladies and gentlemen, Mr. Bogdanos said to you that there were fifty or sixty people around the incident in a space the size of the jury box. Think of the chaos, think of the bedlam, and he says to you, "Nobody could see everything."

If there were fifty or sixty or a hundred people in this confined space, if that works for us, it's got to work for his witnesses. If he suggests that the security guards who threw Mr. Combs to the ground and covered him with their bodies missed something, then how can you rely completely, beyond a reasonable doubt, on one or two people who have hundreds of dollars to gain, who suggests to you that they think Mr. Combs had a gun?

We have a prosecutor's opening statement sometimes described as a map, a map so that the jury can follow from point A to point B, where the prosecutor wants to be. If this opening statement was a map and you're supposed to use it to get you from New York in the East to California in the West, first you would have ended up in Canada, then you would have ended up in Florida, and ultimately you would drown in the ocean of sea of reasonable doubts.

If you compare the prosecutor's opening statement to the introductory preface in a book, and if you read the jacket cover in Barnes & Noble and say, "This looks kind of interesting. I think I'll buy the book," when you read the whole story, you would recognize that the preface just told a completely different story. That the author had a bias. That the person who wrote the preface was not the author. That the person who wrote the preface gave a view of the facts that [was] completely fictional, and that even if the rest of the work is fiction, it's two different fictions.

You just heard the opening statement from Matthew Bogdanos, who's an assistant district attorney, and the law gives him the right and the privilege to stand up and say that he represents the people of the state of New York. So throughout this trial you're going to hear statements like "the People call their next witness," "the People offer the following exhibit." The People. He's not the People. We're all the People, and Mr. Combs is one of the People. And in this case what you have to understand from jump street is that Mr. Bogdanos is an advocate.

He's a lawyer. He represents the People, but you're the people who are going to make the judgments in this case, not him. And then you as the People of the State of New York will ultimately stand up and say, "We the people on this jury find Mr. Combs not guilty." He's an advocate just like us. And he's going to try very hard to win. And when you listen to all of the evidence, when you review all of the facts, if you are patient, if you really keep an open mind until the end of this trial as you promised you would do, you're going to find he tried too hard to win. And if you want something too badly, sometimes it affects your judgment. Sometimes it causes you to gloss over those facts that don't support your position.

This case is not only not supported by the evidence, but it doesn't make any sense whatsoever. First of all, Mr. Bogdanos will have you believe that Mr. Combs, one of the biggest superstars in America, who everybody immediately recognizes, pulled out a gun in front of five hundred people when he had an armed guard with him who was licensed to carry a weapon, who was hired to be his personal bodyguard. That, you will conclude at the end of this case, is just stupid. And the reason five hundred people did not see Sean Combs with a gun is because he didn't have a gun. You will conclude that never in a million years would Mr. Combs, who the entire world knows is running record companies and running recording studios and running fashion lines, never in a million years, with so much to lose and nothing to gain, would [he] do what Mr. Bogdanos claims he did in the presence of five hundred people.

When you listen to the chronology of events, you will understand that Mr. Combs went to this club not to shoot, not to fight, but between Christmas and New Year's, he went to this high-profile party that everyone knew attracted African-American stars from the recording industry and ordinary African-American citizens who just wanted to have a good time, and that he went there not to carry a weapon but to carry champagne. He went there not to fight but to dance. And that the argument that ultimately was initiated was not initiated by Mr. Combs but was initiated by others, and all Mr. Combs wanted to do was get out of this place, and the security guards who escorted him will tell you that.

What happened in this case is sort of like what happens when there's a final sale at a huge department store. It's advertised. People run in, and they grab bargains. Then they get home, and they realize it's damaged goods, and after careful inspection they realize that they didn't get a bargain, because what they got is something that's either no good or damaged or not what it's cracked up to be. That's what happened in this case. Maybe it created a frenzy at the precinct, the case that got a life of its own as headlines stream, charges flew. Now we're here, and he's stuck with damaged goods, and [what] he fails to understand, or what you must understand, is that generally speaking, . . . a final sale [has] a no-return policy. You inspect before you buy, and when you're buying into someone else's life, you better inspect carefully. Buying a sweater that has a hole in it is a whole lot different than buying a case that turns out to have a hundred holes in it. That sweater you can throw away. What do you do for someone who's been wrongly accused of a crime? The only thing you can do is find them not guilty.

> **Editor's note:** Mr. Brafman now comments about the fact that Mr. Bogdanos is sitting at counsel table alone, whereas there are several lawyers at the defense table.

Let me mention one other cosmetic aspect of this case which is not relevant. Mr. Bogdanos sits here alone. He's part of the six-hundred-member office, sitting here alone. Great. You watch the amount of witnesses who are police officers who work for him, who investigated for him, who examined evidence, who interrogated or interviewed witnesses, who did scientific tests, who helped in every aspect bring this case against Sean "Puff Daddy" Combs, and you know what? Not one police officer will provide testimony that is damaging to Mr. Combs. To the contrary. Some of the best evidence for Mr. Combs comes from the army of police officers. Not one police officer will tell you that any of the weapons are tied to Mr. Combs—no fingerprints, no forensic evidence, nothing whatsoever, despite pulling out all stops to try and make this case. Not one police officer will tell you that Mr. Combs did anything wrong. None.

Your verdict is not only going to be easy when you say, "Mr. Combs you're not guilty." You're going to feel good about it, because you're going to conclude that, despite the media prejudging him, despite the police prejudging him, despite the district attorney selectively presenting evidence, that you had the courage and the integrity to stand up and say no. It's not the kind of evidence we want as a jury before you can ask us to make him a convicted felon. Not in the year 2001 in the United States of America. Whether he be a homeless man or a superstar. The rules are the same. All we want are the same rules.

Let's start about witnesses and lawsuits. If you get injured, you have a constitutional right to bring a lawsuit against the party who injured you. But you do not have a right to commit or perpetrate a fraud. If you do that, even if you're a victim, [I] or Mr. Cochran [has] a right to inquire to test your motive. Is your lawsuit consistent with the proof? You decide.

One thing I will tell you: None of the witnesses who tell you that Mr. Combs did not have a gun have anything to gain from these proceedings. Most of them have never met him. Most of them have no connection to him. They're not employees. Many of them are not even fans. They were there; they saw. They will tell you the truth.

Is Mr. Fenderson an evil man for filing a lawsuit? No, Mr. Fenderson is a simple man with a simple plan. Not everybody is evil in this case. And the plan is, "How do I, Wardel, capitalize on this case? How do I, Wardel, just a 'working stiff,' get a huge payday from a case, even though I don't deserve a nickel?" See, let me start with his lawsuit. He's suing Mr. Combs for $5 million. He was not inside Club New York. He was not shot. He was not injured. Nobody laid a glove on him. You know why he wants $5 million? He's going to tell you because for the twenty seconds that he was in the Lincoln Navigator, he was damaged psychologically to the tune of $5 million. Does he have a constitutional right to sue? Yes. He does not have a right to perpetrate a fraud. Most important from Mr. Fenderson is that his biggest fraud is his willingness to lie, and the way you're going to figure that out is, without us having to call any witnesses, just from Mr. Fenderson himself, who will strike you on direct examination as a soft-spoken, basically decent guy who unfortunately never tells the same story twice. And what he's banking on—and I use the word "banking" only purposefully—is the current. Puff Daddy, rap star, gun, car chase, Navigator, Jennifer Lopez. Buzzwords. What he's banking on is if you convict Sean, he scores even if he has no injuries. But what he hasn't banked on is you or me. Not on our watch, ladies and gentlemen. Your watch, my watch, Mr. Cochran's watch.

When Mr. Fenderson is finished testifying, you will conclude that he was a simple man with a simple plan and the plan is going to go up in smoke. I don't know if you ever saw the movie *A Simple Plan,* but in the movie *A Simple Plan,* a bunch of working guys get together to do something that they know starting out is wrong, and their basic, fundamental decency is what screws them. And they begin to lie, and they begin to kill, and they begin to torture each other, because their simple plan turns out to be an unmitigated disaster. I don't believe for a second that you should conclude that Mr. Fenderson got up in the morning and decided that he was going to become involved in a major case. Absolutely not. But when he saw that he was involved and he saw that he was criminally prosecuted for a crime that he didn't want to fess up to or that he didn't believe he committed, what was the out?

The out is, sue Puff Daddy. I claim I got bribed even though there is not a penny exchanged, and that helps me because they're so eager to prosecute Puff, and they don't have any evidence, that they embrace me. They dismiss my charges. They assume I'm telling the truth about the bribe. I sue. If Bogdanos wins I, Wardel, march all the way to the bank.

The people who were shot have a constitutional right to sue? Yes. But the ones who are suing Mr. Combs for hundreds of millions of dollars will tell you themselves that he did not shoot them, that he did not cause their injury. Nevertheless, he's the big pocket.

So Natania Reuben, $150 million. Julius Jones, $700 million. Mr. Thompson for a graze wound, $100 million. Why? Because this case is about fame, and it's about money, and it's about opportunists.

But you've got to be patient. This does not happen like in the movies, [or on TV] where there's a twenty-minute proceeding, then you go to a commercial, then you go to verdict, then you go to commercial, then everybody is finished.

Look at yourselves when you go into the jury room. What do you have in common? Nothing. You're all different races, different ages, different educational backgrounds, different jobs or careers, different family circumstances. You come from different parts of the community. You don't have any anything that jumps off the page at you as being in common with each other except one thing. You said to both sides, "I can be fair. I can apply the law. I can allow this case to be decided on the facts and the law and not on the hype."

How does a superstar find himself in this position where he's accused of a crime that he tells you he did not commit? It happened because he is a superstar. Don't you understand, ladies and gentlemen? Mr. Bogdanos talks about people getting searched, and of course Puff Daddy doesn't have to wait in line. A privilege that he has as a celebrity, but you know what the evidence will show? That Puff Daddy would not be here if he was John Q. Public, and that, [I] submit, is not a fair trade-off, between getting in a club without waiting on line, and being on trial and fighting for your life and career for a crime you did not commit.

Mr. Fenderson will tell you that he admitted at the precinct that the gun in the Navigator was his, twice, to separate officers. Mr. Bogdanos will tell you he later changed his mind. He didn't think it was such a good idea. [They] dismissed the case against Mr. Fenderson in return for what? In return for testifying against Mr. Combs. Why? What in that moment caused Mr. Bogdanos and the police to believe Fenderson, the only person who admitted that the gun was his. You know why? Because prosecuting Wardel Fenderson is just another case. So you trade a Wardel, against whom at that moment they have the strongest evidence, and you indict Puff Daddy, against whom you have no evidence at that time. This has been a starstruck case from the beginning.

You're in a car—constructive possession according to Mr. Bogdanos means that everybody in the car is responsible for the weapon. Well, Jennifer Lopez was not charged. I'm not suggesting that she should have been charged, because she's a citizen in this case as [is] Puff Daddy, but why cut her out and prosecute Mr. Combs? You're going to find the mind-set of this prosecution is weapons and a rap singer. That works. Maybe a jury will make that leap without evidence.

The press is certainly eating it up. Jennifer Lopez, that's a kind of reach. Let's cut her loose. We already have the superstar. We don't need to mess up this case, and we don't need to reach even further than we're reaching, because if you reach too far, you push the envelope too far, eventually it falls off the table.

Why is [Fenderson's] word accepted by them at a time when he's just another guy in the car? Because he is just Wardel Fenderson? It's not a starstruck case if you indict the driver. And if you want him to be your witness, [haven't] you got to give him something? Why can't you let the charges stand and let a jury like you decide if he's telling the truth? Because Fenderson wanted out, and he knew that the way to get out was to give them Sean Combs.

Mr. Bogdanos told you that there is a tape that was saved on Mr. Fenderson's answering machine at home. Well, ladies and gentlemen, on behalf of Mr. Combs, we thank the good Lord that that tape was saved. No amount of sarcasm or cynicism used to read the conversation by Mr. Bogdanos gets him out of the mess Fenderson has already created, because what you're going to find is, the story Fenderson tells is just all over the place.

According to Mr. Bogdanos, the tape means the following: When Mr. Combs says, "Yo, man, what you told me yesterday blew me away, and I just want to tell your family that everything's going to be all right," Mr. Bogdanos implies by that that they were talking about the bribe and the meeting when Mr. Fenderson told him that he's not going to take the money and told Mr. Combs that the bribe is over. Well, the problem he has is that Mr. Fenderson has already testified under oath in connection with that conversation. And he will tell you, because now he's stuck with this statement, and if he deviates from it I'm going to put it in his face, and when he previously testified under oath, what he said was the reference to Mr. Combs's saying, "What you told me yesterday had nothing to do with the bribe. It had reference about me, Wardel, having told Sean that I lost my job."

That message on the machine is Mr. Combs returning the call. [Fenderson] calls Mr. Combs to tell [him] that he lost his day job, his driving job for Mr. Mark something. That's what he calls to complain. Ask yourselves this: Why [call] the guy who tried to bribe you? Who you're afraid to go visit, according to Mr. Bogdanos. Who you're afraid to tell, and you go and you tell him. Why [are] you calling him three days later to tell Puff Daddy that you lost your job if you're not all about money? Because from the very beginning, what you're going to find with Wardel Fenderson is that's what he was. All about money.

That he saw in Combs his way out and that any conversation that pertained to money was not initiated by Mr. Combs. There is not one person who'll be able to corroborate that suggestion. It's not initiated by Mr. Combs; it's Fenderson seeing a payday. "Plan A, I take the weapon. Plan B, I sue him. Plan C, I get my charges dismissed. And what do I do in case somebody talks about money [is] tell them it was a bribe offer." Even according to Fenderson, this bribe offer was over in twenty minutes. According to Fenderson, he tells you he rejects it. Then why is he calling Sean Combs days after to tell him that he lost his job?

[Mr. Bogdanos] refers to Mr. Combs's conversations with the police shortly after the car was stopped, and in words or substance, Mr. Bogdanos suggests to you that this is when Mr. Combs was already beginning to formulate the plan. Mr. Combs repeatedly asked them why all four of the people in the car were being arrested. When told by the police that the four were being arrested because no one would admit to the gun, Mr. Combs asked the officer, "What would happen if someone admitted to the gun?"

Mr. Combs asked [the police] whether Miss Lopez and he would have to be arrested if someone admits to the gun. Let me ask you a question. What's wrong with that? You're in a car that you don't know has a weapon. The police stop you, they're arresting you. They don't find any weapon on you. They're taking you in. They're taking the person you love dearly in, who also did not have a weapon. Isn't that a normal conversation you would have with a police officer? I don't have a gun. If the person who admits to having the gun says it's his gun, do you have to take us all in? Do I have to be publicly humiliated? Do I have to watch my career and her career be on the front page of every tabloid in the world? What's wrong with that conversation? It's consistent with someone who has an innocent state of mind. Seeking to inquire. And it explains why, at the precinct, Mr. Combs would have conversations with Mr. Fenderson.

Mr. Bogdanos says the chase up Eighth Avenue is evidence. Of what? They're not running away from the police. They're running away from people in the club, [from what they] perceived to be an attempted assassination of Mr. Combs. And that the club security threw them into the Navigator and said, "Get away, get away." And at the time they rounded Eighth Avenue, they didn't know if the people who were involved in the shooting were following. Eventually the police cars caused them to stop. But where are they going? Think about one thing, because you're not supposed to leave your common sense at home. You're Puff Daddy. You're Jennifer Lopez. You've been involved in an incident in a club in front of five hundred people. All of them know who you are. You're an icon. Everyone knows you. Where you going? To Peru? Are you just getting away temporarily from a dangerous situation until things can be sorted out? Is that so hard to understand?

Wait till you hear the testimony of the club security people, not our security people, who throw him into the car and say, "Get away, get away," because no one knew what was really going on at that time. Mr. Combs is in a state of shock, according to the club security guards, with his hands against the wall, with glaze on his face, thinking he had been shot. You can't just take a piece. Did you think that Miss Lopez and Mr. Combs did not believe that at some point that evening there was going to be inquiry [by] the police? You were witnesses, you were in a club, there was a shooting, you've been identified by four hundred people. Did you think they were just going to take off, go to the moon and leave their careers and hundreds of millions of dollars of companies here? This isn't someone robbing a bank and fleeing anonymously so that they don't get involved. They knew they were involved. But what they wanted was safety, and instead of creating a safe environment, the police did what unfortunately they did in this case. They arrested first and asked questions later.

What Mr. Bogdanos needs to do in order to win this trial against Mr. Combs is try and force a square peg into a round hole. You can't do it. It's physically impossible to put a square peg in a round hole if you shave it and you carve it and you cut it and you trim it and eventually you push it hard, it will go into the round hole—then it's no longer a square. And if you listen to the truth and you see how the truth has been shaved and altered and amended and changed to fit the theory of this case by witnesses with a lot to gain from a conviction, you will conclude at the end of the day that the People's case against Mr. Combs is not truth. It's a perversion of the truth.

The most important thing I remember from law school [is] the words "Maybe does not cut it in a criminal case." And all Mr. Bogdanos has to offer you are "maybes." Maybe Fenderson is lying 'cause he wants to get rich, or maybe Fenderson just wanted his case dismissed. Or maybe Fenderson is just frightened about going through the process and trusting people like you to decide that he's not guilty. Maybe the person on Eighth Avenue who claims he found a gun is, like Mr. Bogdanos suggested, just a working stiff, working nine to five. He's not. He glossed over it. At night what this guy does is, he works for a prostitution agency driving hookers all over the city. He's a criminal. The man he works for is a criminal. And what does the Eighth Avenue man do with this weapon when he finds it? "I don't want to leave it on the streets because maybe children could get it."

There are two hundred police officers within thirty feet. "No, I don't want to give it to them, God forbid." Who does he give it to? Does he give it to a safe person? He gives it to Anthony Nastasi, who's a criminal, a professional informant who runs the prostitution agency.

Maybe a gun went out the window, and maybe it didn't. And maybe this guy is a liar, and maybe he's not. But nothing about that gun is tied to Mr. Combs. Nothing about that gun is tied to the shooting. No ballistic evidence, no forensic evidence. No fingerprint evidence, and the biggest problem he's got with that gun is, Wardel Fenderson, who is the driver who's now his star witness, doesn't say that a gun went out the window. That part Mr. Bogdanos left out. Wardel Fenderson, the man who's driving the car, does not confirm that a gun went out the window. And remember, it's winter. If you are speeding in a car that a window opens and opens far enough for a hand to be able to put a nine-millimeter out, everybody in that car, I submit, would feel a blast of cold air.

Wardel Fenderson isn't with the program. Wardel Fenderson only knows certain parts of the case that he can finesse. He is not going into a program area where he knows he's going to get beaten up by the cross-examination, by "the engine of truth" that cross-examination is often called.

Maybe the two or three witnesses that will tell you that Mr. Combs had a gun are telling the absolute truth and nothing but the truth, despite the fact that [they tell] you that Mr. Combs was surrounded by enormous security guards so that nobody could see what he did and what he didn't do. Maybe they're just opportunists. Maybe the twenty people who were with him, who were holding him, who threw him to the ground, who carried him from the club, maybe they're lying, maybe they're telling the truth. Maybe Mr. Fenderson was offered money, or maybe he wanted money and it wasn't paid. Remember, not one penny goes to Wardel Fenderson.

You promised that you would be fair. Let me tell you up front and in person what does pose a concern. The current. A strong current can sweep away facts and logic and reason and make you drown even if you wouldn't drown without the current being a factor. And . . . the current rages through this case. And anyone who suggests otherwise is simply being naïve. But you gave us your word, and we took you at your word. We trusted you with only one important concern: that you would not allow this case to be decided on the current, that you would not allow this case to be decided on publicity, or media, or hype. And this case, ladies and gentlemen, if you level the playing field and you simply ignore the outside forces that have purposely sought to undermine Mr. Combs's right to a fair trial simply to increase circulation, you will conclude that he is not guilty.

Whether you are a fan is not relevant. Whether you like rap or hip-hop or rock 'n' roll or jazz or the Beatles or Lawrence Welk or Mozart is not relevant. What's relevant is, can Mr. Bogdanos bring you reliable, consistent, fair, honest evidence of proof beyond a reasonable doubt? And as to Sean Combs, he can't. The reason he spends so much time talking about the quote "victims" close quote is because if you focus on them, maybe you'll convict someone who's not guilty.

Well, Mr. Combs is not charged with shooting anyone. So when someone comes in, if you conclude by the time they leave the stand that they are indeed an innocent bystander, that's a factor you may consider, but it's got nothing to do with the case against Sean Combs, because he did not cause their injury. And in fairness you must constantly throughout these proceedings keep that in mind.

First of all, if I raised my voice this morning, I don't apologize. I don't do it as a sign of disrespect. When you've seen the facts in this case, then you're going to understand. And then, when the case is over, you're going to raise your voices as through your foreperson you stand up and you say, "Sean Combs, you're not guilty. Sean Combs, the evidence as to you is not there." The credible reliable evidence carries only one verdict: a verdict of not guilty.

Ladies and gentlemen, you will learn that Mr. Combs is a world-class recording artist and extraordinarily successful producer of rap music. It's not rap music in a way it's about rap, a bum rap, a false accusation. You'll conclude that Mr. Combs is a world-recognized genius in the hip-hop music industry. The case is not hip-hop. The only hip-hopping you're going to see is Mr. Bogdanos trying to hip-hop around the inconsistent theories in this case of reasonable doubts.

And you're also going to hear Mr. Combs is a force in the fashion industry, that he has his own fashion company, his own fashion line, Sean John—fashions that are eminently successful. This case is not about fashion, but there has been fashioning in this case. The evidence has been fashioned. There has been designing in this case. Witnesses have designed in their own mind how to tell a story that gives us access to deep pocket.

You will conclude [that] the case against Sean Combs is a bad case. Sit back and let the trial happen. Just be comfortable. We'll do our work, you'll do your work, and at the end of the day, you will conclude that Mr. Combs, Sean, Puff Daddy, Combs—whatever you want to refer to him—you'll conclude that he is not guilty. When you go back into the jury room, look at each other, and you'll see what we see. A group of honest citizens who gave us their words that could sit in trial in a case where one of the people on trial is a superstar with headlines screaming all over the city and really decide this case just on the facts.

We have an awesome responsibility. Yours is more awesome. You are sitting in judgment in a case where, at the end of the trial, you will conclude [that] a man has been falsely accused of [a] serious felony. You asked for it. You could have been excused. You said you would be fair. We trusted you then, and at the end of the case, we will trust in your verdict. And in this case we trust that your verdict will be a verdict of not guilty.

POSTSCRIPT

Jamal Barrow was convicted of assault and other charges. Sean Combs and Anthony Jones were both acquitted.

On paper the case seemed heavily weighted against Combs, not least because New York law permits a jury to convict all persons in a car with a gun inside it as guilty of possession. Yet in reality the prosecution faced an uphill task; historically, jurors disagree with that law, making such cases difficult to prove. Furthermore, the situation offered the jury an easy out—namely, to convict the shooter alone. The prosecutor faced the added bad luck that the gun was recovered by a driver for an escort agency, not a model citizen. Finally, underlying social forces favored the defendant. Here, again, was a famous African-American who could hint at racial persecution as a motive behind the prosecution's case; Johnnie Cochran's very presence made the point tacitly, but clearly.

A courtroom has a quiet, dignified atmosphere far removed from the drama of the crime scene. To succeed in presenting his case, prosecutor Bogdanos conjured up the horrors at Club New York by telling a vivid story that appealed to the jurors' empathy.

By starting off about the normality of the victims' lives before the shooting, he tacitly communicated that their unfortunate fates could have been any of ours.

If the scales of Lady Justice tipped in favor of the prosecution at the end of Mr. Bogdanos's opening, then Benjamin Brafman managed to tip the scales back to the middle with his argument. Rightly concerned that the evidence against the other defendants would help convict Mr. Combs, he repeatedly spoke of three separate verdicts to prod the jury into differentiating them.

Keep in mind that at this juncture in any trial, none of the testimony has yet been heard or witnesses seen. Mr. Brafman knows that Fenderson is the prosecution's linchpin witness. He must demolish the witness but cannot blacken him with heavy language, because there is the danger that, when Fenderson appears in the flesh, he might come across as sympathetic, which would result in Mr. Brafman's losing credibility with the jury. His demolition job, then, had to be subtle but decisive. And indeed it was. Wardel Fenderson's motives were impugned with a simple statement of reality: He had filed a civil suit against Combs (a criminal conviction first would make civil damages easy for him to get), and the district attorney dropped charges in return for his testimony. Mr. Brafman could not accuse Fenderson of heinous villainy in the opening. What if he turned out to look totally decent? And, anyway, parts of his testimony would help the defense—Fenderson didn't see Puff Daddy throw a gun out the window—so he had to seem partially credible.

Mr. Brafman argued that Puff Daddy was in court only because of his fame. But then he added that twist—that Puff Daddy had not really "fled" from the crime scene; there would be no point in doing so, since he would be recognized wherever he went. Everyone knew he was at the club. And a final, seemingly minor, point that displayed Mr. Brafman's hyperacuteness—he was concerned that Mr. Bogdanos's sitting alone at the DA's table would engender sympathy for the prosecution. He swiftly dealt with that concern by saying that Bogdanos had six hundred colleagues and numerous cops working for him.

• • •

The pay and publicity associated with celebrity cases means that they tend to attract the best legal talent and generate the finest courtroom advocacy. The Marv Albert and Sean "Puffy" Combs trials bear that out; although either of the two could have lost their cases outright or, like O. J. Simpson, won pyrrhic victories at the expense of their reputations, they both prevailed despite adverse circumstances. Celebrity cases are difficult to predict inside and outside the courtroom, because jurors have deep-seated opinions of the celebrity on trial. Any lawyer able to navigate these waters and deliver his client safely beyond harm's reach has earned his keep.

3

THE GREEN BERET DOCTOR OF DEATH

THE UNITED STATES OF AMERICA v. JEFFREY MACDONALD

> First, do no harm.
> —*The Hippocratic Oath*

ON FEBRUARY 17, 1970, the family of Green Beret doctor Jeffrey MacDonald was brutally murdered in their home in Fort Bragg, North Carolina. From that day on, this case has fascinated the American public. This was the definitive serpent-in-paradise story that burned holes into stereotypical images of the American dream. A Princeton graduate, Dr. MacDonald married his high-school sweetheart, Colette, and had enlisted in the Green Berets. By all accounts, Dr. MacDonald and his wife were happily married. Anyone prosecuting the case had the unenviable task of forcing the jury to believe the impossible: How could a telegenic leading man and popular physician like Dr. MacDonald commit such atrocities? What more could he want out of life than he already had?

In the morning hours of the day his family was murdered, Dr. MacDonald called the police to his home, where they found Colette—pregnant at the time—dead in the bedroom with a fractured skull and numerous stab wounds. Their five-year-old daughter,

Kimberly, was found dead in her bedroom with similar injuries, and their infant daughter, Kristen, was dead of wounds from a knife and ice pick. Dr. MacDonald sustained several injuries also, including a contusion to the left side of his face, four punctate-type injuries [prick marks], and an injury to his right side that caused a potentially life-threatening collapse of his lung.

Dr. MacDonald's version of the events went as follows: His wife returned home from a psychology course at a local college and went to sleep. Dr. MacDonald was watching Johnny Carson on television in the living room when he was awakened by his wife's call of, "Jeff, Jeff, Jeff, why are they doing this to me?" and his daughter Kimberly shouting "Daddy, Daddy, Daddy."

According to Dr. MacDonald, he got up and was confronted in his living room by four strangers—three men, one of whom was black, and a woman in a floppy hat—wearing sheets and carrying candles. One man knocked him over with a club that looked like a baseball bat, and the other two men thrust a knife and ice pick at him. The woman was chanting, "Acid is groovy, kill the pig." MacDonald claimed that his blue pajama top was torn and pulled over his head during the struggle. He claimed that he fell unconscious after the attack ended.

Dr. MacDonald's story was called into question by much of the physical evidence. Although he described a fierce struggle with the intruders in his living room, the Valentine's Day cards from his children still stood upright on a counter in that room. In addition, an *Esquire* magazine found in Dr. MacDonald's house after the murders contained an article entitled "Does Witchcraft Lurk in California?" which mentioned the words "acid" and "pig," the same words MacDonald attributed to the female intruder. The word "PIG" was written in Colette's blood over the headboard in her bedroom. There were pieces of latex found in the master bedroom, containing type-A blood (Colette MacDonald's blood).

There was simply no physical evidence to back up Dr. MacDonald's story. Although the intruders had allegedly ripped his pajama top, there were no blue threads found in the living room. There were, however, more than fifty blue threads found in the master bedroom—including one under the headboard—and blue-black pajama fibers found underneath Kimberly's bedcovers where she lay dead. MacDonald claimed he took his ripped blue pajama top and placed it on top of Colette to keep her warm. The blue pajama top had Colette's blood on it, but the FBI determined that the blood got on the pajama top before the top was cut, something clearly inconsistent with MacDonald's version that the pajama top was ripped first by the intruders. MacDonald claimed to have checked on Kimberly only after he placed the pajama top on Colette. There was no reasonable explanation for the pajama threads under Kimberly's covers if MacDonald was no longer wearing the pajama top.

An ice pick caused many of the wounds. MacDonald claimed that he did not have an ice pick in the house. However, Mildred Kassab, his mother-in-law, said she saw one in the house. The murder weapon—a club—was found outside the back door to the apartment, with two blue pajama threads on it in addition to Colette's blood. MacDonald claimed that he never went outside the apartment or saw the club, let alone touched it. Finally, FBI forensic experts determined that wood grain from the club was of the identical growth ring, grain size, and composition as a part of Kimberly's bed, and paint samples from both matched as well.

The military conducted an Article 32 hearing to determine whether MacDonald should be court-martialed for murdering his wife and children. Initially, the Kassabs thought it highly unlikely that MacDonald had committed the murders, which certainly contributed to the military's dismissing all charges against him. However, they became skeptical when MacDonald later appeared on *The Dick Cavett Show* and claimed to have sustained twenty-three stab wounds, injuries they never saw when they visited him in the hospital after the murders. Mr. Fred Kassab read the thirteen volumes of transcripts of the Article 32 hearing and, based on the evidence, came to believe that MacDonald did in fact murder his stepdaughter and grandchildren. He petitioned the army and the Department of Justice to reopen the case. In July 1974, charges were brought against MacDonald, who had moved to California, where he was a popular emergency-room physician with a new life and numerous friends. MacDonald finally stood trial in 1979.

Excerpts from the Summation of Prosecutors Brian Murtagh and James Blackburn

MR. MURTAGH: I would like to thank all of you personally for your patience and attention throughout this long and well-fought trial. You have all spent your summer performing your civic duty in what was far from a pleasant task.

This case is a tragedy for both sides no matter what happens. If the defendant is convicted, as we hope, or if he is acquitted, society loses either way. If he is convicted, society loses an excellent doctor. If he is acquitted, society loses in that someone [who] we believe we have proven beyond a reasonable doubt committed an atrocious crime goes free. There are no losers and winners in this case. It just doesn't come down that way.

Mr. Smith [one of the defense attorneys] started out in his opening statement quite eloquently [talking] about duty, and it was a moving poem that he recited. He talked about the duty of the prosecution to prove this case beyond a reasonable doubt. He also talked about the duty of the court as the giver of law and the duty of the jury, perhaps the most difficult duty of all, as the finders of fact and the final arbiter of credibility.

Mr. Smith recited a poem which went something to the effect of "I dreamed that life was beauty and I awoke and found that life was duty." I wish that we could have discharged our duty to Colette, Kimberly, and Kristen MacDonald, whom I must say we stand here representing, by presenting nothing but pictures of a perfect family life, of a perfect marriage, of a perfect husband and wife, but that was not our duty.

Our duty was to take you through a tour of a slaughterhouse, not a slaughterhouse for the defendant but certainly a slaughterhouse for Colette, Kimberly, and Kristen. It was our duty to show you many pieces of physical evidence, much of it grotesque, and to put these bits and pieces of the jigsaw puzzle together.

Obviously, we couldn't bring the eyewitnesses to testify, because the eyewitnesses were murdered. As Mr. Blackburn told you in opening statement, things, objects and bloodstains don't lie. They tell the story. It is not an emotional story, but it is a logical story.

The defendant tried to obliterate or to account for or to disassociate himself [from] all the physical or trace evidence connecting him to the commission of the crime. While this case is anything but simple to judge, it does boil down to one simple concept. It is a concept for which juries were invented and for which they have evolved: that is, to determine credibility, who is telling the truth and who is lying.

Is the story told by the defendant and his injuries or lack thereof credible? Does it ring true? Does it in light of all the circumstances make you say, " I believe him," or is the story told by the crime scene, the physical evidence, the bloodstains, the pajama top, the sheet, does it leave you a little uneasy, and does it on further reflection make you say to yourself, "No way. Impossible. Incredible. I don't believe it."

Has the defendant lied about the alleged struggle with the intruders? There were actually two struggles: one between the defendant and Colette, which started in the master bedroom and moved to Kristen's room. That struggle ended with Colette unconscious in Kristen's bedroom.

The other struggle started immediately [after the crime] and continues this day in this courtroom: that is, [the struggle] to make Jeffrey MacDonald's story of the murders fit the physical evidence. It is his effort to provide an innocent explanation consistent with his innocence for the presence of his wife's blood type on his pajama top and to account for his own injuries or lack thereof and make them consistent with the injuries inflicted on the victims.

Milton once said, if I may paraphrase, "Truth and falsity shall grapple in the courtroom and truth shall prevail." Well, that is the poet's view and not a prosecutor's. Let me share with you a prosecutor's view of that verse. Truth and falsity have indeed grappled in the courtroom at least daily, and truth shall prevail, maybe, but only if the jury decides the issues on the basis of the evidence.

[The defendant] is not on trial for being a bad doctor. Truth will prevail, but only if the jury requires the government to prove each and every element of the offense beyond a reasonable doubt but not beyond any doubt whatsoever, because, as Judge Franklin Dupree instructed you during jury selection, very few things are capable of proof to an absolute certainty.

Mr. Segal [another defense attorney] has sought very capably to try everybody but the defendant. The CID [military police] and the FBI agents are not on trial, nor is the army, the Special Forces, or the Justice Department. Nor are the Kassabs on trial.

Truth will prevail only if the jury, in conformity with its oath, makes no distinction as the law requires between circumstantial and direct evidence. The defense has done its utmost to confuse the issues and to play upon your emotions.

The government's case, stripped to its essentials, consists of the crime, the physical evidence, the defendant's story voluntarily told, the conflict between the story and the physical evidence. We submit [that this] was a fabrication of the evidence, and [we] ask you to find his guilt.

The defendant has chosen to relate his version of the events. He has also chosen to explain all the physical evidence [and] to discredit the investigators [and] the experts and to offer massive amounts of character evidence. But character evidence is really one-sided in this case because the only character witness who could have shown the other side of the crime was Colette, and Colette was murdered.

Besides, because we contend that the physical evidence connects the defendant as the only possible criminal actor, it is immaterial and irrelevant to require the government to prove by evidence of bad character that he was the type of individual who could have committed the crime.

For example, the footprint. You have heard the testimony of Mr. Hilyard Medlin (Army lab technician), who identified the defendant's footprint exiting from Kristen's bedroom. You have also heard the defendant admit on the witness stand under oath that [it] was probably his footprint.

Character evidence doesn't add anything to that. If you find that that footprint could only have been made during the commission of the crime, between the time when Colette was in the north bedroom, as we contend the physical evidence shows, and the time she wound up on the floor of the master bedroom, it doesn't matter. We are not required to prove the defendant was the type of person who could have left a footprint. The footprint—the evidence—speaks for itself.

I believe that you will not let the defendant go free if despite your belief that the physical evidence identified him as the perpetrator beyond a reasonable doubt because [military police investigator] Bill Ivory did not send the feather to the Smithsonian to find out what kind of bird it came from or that he failed to interview the cat or because the medic moved the flowerpot.

• • •

MR. BLACKBURN: What about the defendant's injuries? There has been a tremendous amount of testimony about the defendant's injuries. It is undisputed from both sides that at least he had a contusion on the left side of his face or head that was nonbleeding, and that it could have caused unconsciousness.

Dr. Merrill Bronstein [staff surgeon at Fort Bragg who saw Dr. MacDonald in hospital] stated that unconsciousness could not have come from bleeding wounds. Dr. Severt Jacobson [Green Beret neurosurgeon who treated Jeffrey MacDonald in the emergency room] said that he had four punctate injuries in this area [indicating the left pectoral area] sort of in a line—one, two, three, four close together—I think he used a fork or something like that when he testified as to what it might have been made with, in his opinion.

He had an injury to the right side which caused the pneumothorax [collapsed lung]. Think for a moment of the testimony of the government's doctors and even on cross-examination, the defendant's doctor, who stated that it was a treatable medical injury, and that in his opinion any injury inflicted to the chest is potentially fatal. Recall the testimony of Dr. Frank Gemma [Dr. Gemma treated MacDonald's pneumothorax by inserting chest tubes] who said that if you got proper medical treatment, the insertion of a chest tube and the chest tube worked properly, that there was very little—almost no risk of it developing into a tension pneumothorax.

Well, I am not going to stand here today and argue for long over whether a pneumothorax is or is not potentially life-threatening or not life-threatening. That could go on all day long. Even if the government concedes, which we do not, that that was a potentially life-threatening wound [at] that point, how many did [Dr. MacDonald] get, compared and contrasted with the number his family got? One.

How many ice-pick wounds did Dr. Bronstein say he saw in Jeffrey MacDonald's chest? None. How many ice-pick wounds did Mike Newman, the first person who washed up the defendant, say he saw in MacDonald's chest? None. How many ice-pick wounds did Frank Gemma say he saw? He said that he didn't observe any.

Now, I am not trying to suggest in of itself that because the defendant was not killed, he is, therefore, guilty of the slaughter of his family. I don't think that is sufficient evidence. I am not saying that. I am saying that when you compare and contrast his injuries to their injuries with the other physical evidence that we have, it certainly should raise in your mind the question as to why he was not hurt worse.

The coloring, according to the government's doctors of the defendant, was good. His condition, according to their testimony, was good. He walked to the funeral. He was out of the hospital in seven or eight days. In seven or eight days, Kimberly, Colette, and Kristen went to Long Island to be buried.

Now, we heard a lot of testimony during the defense's case about drug abuse. We even heard yesterday from Dr. Jerry Hughes [doctor who worked with Dr. MacDonald at Fort Bragg]. We heard Major Williams [medical service corps officer who sponsored Dr. MacDonald at Fort Bragg] talk at length about all the people that had grudges, perhaps, against the defendant. He said when he heard that the defendant's family had been killed, "My God, the drug people have gotten him."

They were concerned that perhaps MacDonald was a fink, because there was no privilege between a doctor and a drug patient at Fort Bragg. Okay, we see all of that. If that be true, ladies and gentlemen, let me ask you some questions. Why, if they had a grudge against the defendant, didn't they kill him? Why, if they came there for wanton destruction, didn't they kill everybody—particularly one who could identify them? Why do you kill a two-and-a-half and a five-year-old and don't kill the strongest person who can hurt you back? Why did the intruders leave the defendant alive?

There was, in fact, a life-and-death struggle in the house that night. There were at least two white people involved in it. There wasn't a black person involved. There was only one white male and one white female. The white female was Colette MacDonald, and the white male was her husband, Jeffrey MacDonald. Some of the injuries that Jeffrey MacDonald sustained could well have been inflicted by his wife, Colette. We know from the evidence, ladies and gentlemen, that she fought mighty hard before she died. You don't get both of your arms broken by standing there waiting to be killed. You don't get all the injuries she got just standing there waiting to be killed.

We know from the autopsies that it wasn't sex abuse. We know from the testimony of Bill Ivory [army Criminal Investigation Division agent] it was not vandalism. The house did not look ransacked. The clothes in the closet were still hanging. The furniture was not taken. Of course, the defendant stated, some rings were taken. We have only his word that those rings were there the night the murders occurred.

Think for a moment what you need to make the defendant's story concerning the intruders and what happened to him make sense. First of all, you need three sheets, which were left outside the house. You need some candles—at least three. You need a white hat according to his story, a dark hat according to Mr. Beasley [Prince Everett Beasley, a Fayetteville, NC, cop who said he saw Helena Stoeckley, the night before the murders, wearing a floppy hat]. You need some boots. You need a feather. You need a club other than the one right here [indicating the club recovered by the police]—perhaps like a baseball bat. You need a motive for them. Randomness? If it was randomness—if it was, why didn't they kill him? If it was because of drugs, why didn't they kill him? If it was vandalism, why didn't they take something? If it was sex, why didn't they do something? Why were syringes and medicine left in the MacDonald apartment?

Ladies and gentlemen, the defendant's theory of defense in this case has been like this: "I tell a story, and you are to trust me. I am telling the truth. I loved my family. I loved Colette. I loved Kimberly and Kristen. Trust me. I couldn't have done this. I could not have done this. There has been a lot of character testimony [i.e., character witnesses]. They say I can't do this; and therefore, because I am not the type of person, I couldn't do that."

If we convince you by the evidence that he did it, we don't have to show you that he is the sort of person that could have done it.

The defendant, by all the evidence, is an outstanding doctor. I don't think anybody could dispute that. In 1970 he had a lot to live for. His wife, Colette, had a lot to live for. She had a dream, according to his testimony, of a farm in Connecticut with children, animals, and cats and dogs and horses. The children had a dream, too. They wanted to grow up. They wanted to be alive. They didn't get that chance. The defendant wanted to continue his career as a doctor. You heard Dr. Hughes yesterday talk about the defendant's airplane, his boat, his car, his medical kits, and the money it must take to buy those things—you can't have those things, ladies and gentlemen, if you are in jail. If we are correct and the defendant did what we claim he did—if he could murder his family, think for a moment what he would do on the witness stand to save his life and his career.

We were talking about the defendant's story of the intruders. When you take all seven weeks that you all have been here, and all these charts, and all this testimony, and all the bench conferences, and you pour them all out the window, you are left with two things, and it is those two things on which I suggest that you have got to make a decision. It boils down to two things. One is the defendant's story and his credibility that it is true. If you believe it is true, if you believe everything he said, then your task is relatively simple. You will acquit him.

If, on the other hand, you contrast that with the physical evidence and somehow it doesn't wash, it doesn't make sense, then you have got a little bit more of a difficult task and it might take you a little longer. When you compare and contrast his story versus the government's story—testing the credibility of the government's case as well, as I think you should—you have got to come down on one side or the other, because the evidence in this case, if it shows nothing else, it does show that what he said and what the physical evidence says are not reconcilable and that they are diametrically opposed.

Editor's note: Mr. Blackburn responds to defense claims about mistakes made by the police.

If you believe that because military policeman Richard Tevere picked up the telephone on which no prints were later found, if you believe that a broken flowerpot [was] picked up by a medic, if you believe that some clothes in the hall [were] put on the sofa by Officer Joe Graebner, if you believe that Officer Shaw in picking up the glasses and looking for a fleck of blood—interestingly enough, found to be consistent with the same blood type as that of Kristen—if you believe that these things—along with letting the garbage can be emptied before they looked into it—if you think that all of those things are so important and so bad that you have got no choice but to acquit the defendant, then I think you ought to do it—smoke a cigarette and do it.

If you believe that because the film moved when a truck or something went by and some of the prints had to be retaken two months later—and as they were, by maybe not as nice a camera as the defense had but the only one that the government at that time had at the CID—if you believe that that entitles the defendant to an acquittal, then acquit him.

None of those mistakes change what is here. We aren't asking you to convict the defendant on what might have been. We are asking you to convict the defendant on what is here—not what is not here, not what we didn't find, but what we did find.

What about his story? Let's take the defendant's story, and let's go through the crime scene and see how it fits with the physical evidence. First of all, he said that some intruders met him in the living room . . . there was one, two, three, four. The girl was number four, and she is the one that might have had the candle.

The black [man that MacDonald alleged was one of the hippies] had the club, but [MacDonald] said on cross that it was probably not this club. It was round like a bat, and he didn't think it was this club. He said that the first time he ever saw this club was the sixth of April, 1970 [the date of MacDonald's tape-recorded interrogation by army CID investigators] Isn't that interesting when you compare the testimony of the government experts that this was, in fact, the murder weapon used on Colette and Kimberly certainly, or a murder weapon, and that it did come from the house—once part of the piece of wood that formed a bed slat in Kimberly's room—but he didn't see it until the sixth of April, 1970.

How many threads—purple, blue, yellow, green, any color—were found in the living room? You heard Officer Ivory and Mr. Medlin say that they went through the nap of the carpet in the living room. How many threads, yarns, and fibers did they find? Not a single one. How much blood, where he says he was struck with a sharp blade, was found in the living room, on the sofa, on the wall, on the floor, on the table, on the glasses, on the *Esquire* magazine, on anything that matched his blood type? None.

How many splinters were found in the living room that matched anything? None. But we know that splinters were found in Kristen's room, Kimberly's room, and the master bedroom. Now, on cross-examination, I asked the defendant about the [lack of his own type-B] blood if the jury should find, as I have just told you, [that his blood was not found in the living room] did he have an explanation for that? He said, "Well, it is obvious that the wound did not bleed too much." Well, perhaps that makes sense, until you remember, ladies and gentlemen, that by his testimony he believed, although there is a question mark, but he believes that he did not go to the hall bathroom until number six—he did six things. He goes to the master bedroom and then to the kids' room and then to the hallway and then somewhere else before he goes back to the hall bathroom and washes off his hands for the first time. His hands were bloody, according to his own testimony.

He had touched three dead people who had bled a lot. You recall his testimony on both direct and cross: "I saw a lot of blood." Well, then, why is the blood in the bathroom sink, according to the government testimony, that of type B, which matches his, rather than type A, type AB, or O, which matches his family? That is all right, until you think for a moment that if the wounds didn't bleed too much over here [in the living room], how come he bled a lot more over here [in the bathroom, fifteen minutes later]? You know he said that he lay unconscious, for how long he did not know right there. How much blood of type B was found on his pajama top, which he said was under his wrists? Very little.

Ladies and gentlemen, the reason and the explanation why there is no type-B blood in the living room, why there are no splinters in the living room, why there are no threads and yarns is really a very easy answer. What you can infer from the evidence is: One, the pajama top wasn't torn then; two, a club did not splinter there; three, nobody bled there; and, four, you can infer from the evidence that no struggle took place there.

Now, I am not about to suggest that the burden of proof ever shifts to the defendant, because it doesn't. It stays with us. You recall on Friday that we asked a lot of questions that, if the jury should find this and that, did he have an explanation of that? You recall essentially his testimony: "It would be pure conjecture," or "No," or " I can't recall." Perhaps he does not have to explain, but think for a moment: If you were on trial for your life and the only thing that made your story perhaps not believable was the inconsistency of the physical evidence, don't you think if you could explain it, you would? Don't you think for one moment if you were on that stand and somebody asked you a question like I asked Dr. MacDonald and you could tell me, "Mr. Blackburn, you are an idiot. Here is the answer. Bam," doesn't it make sense that you would do that?

Let's go to the master bedroom. There were over sixty purple cotton sewing threads, which matched identically in composition, color, and texture to the blue pajama top, over eighteen blue polyester yarns matching the pajama top, and at least one blue-black sewing thread matching that top. What does that suggest to you? They got there because that is where the top was torn.

Now, what does the defendant say about that? He doesn't know where the top was torn. It could have been torn here or it could have been torn in the master bedroom. We asked, "Did you hear any ripping sounds when you were in the master bedroom?" and he said, "No." I asked him if he had an explanation for why there were no threads in the living room. He said, "Well, it would suggest to me that perhaps it was not torn there. It was pulled over my head."

Now, if the pajama top was pulled over his head, what were all these four people doing while it was being pulled over his head? Was the guy with the club standing there waiting until MacDonald got it around his wrists before he could bash him again, because it is not fair to hit a guy when he is down? What was the guy with the ice pick or knife doing? Again, waiting—didn't want to hit him in the back? He was going to hit from the front—you know, it is a coward that hits in the back. They weren't very courageous when they hit Kristen from the back, were they?

You have heard the testimony of Paul Stombaugh [FBI fiber and hair expert] who stated that, with respect to the pajama top, it was torn, in his opinion, down the front. It was a V-neck. It was torn in the front, you know, while the person was stationary tearing it like that, or as the person turned away. Isn't it interesting, ladies and gentlemen, that the defendant has four little marks right here in a line? You can infer from the evidence that Colette MacDonald pulled that pajama top with her four fingers and ripped it down the front, and it was torn in the master bedroom. That is where those cuts, or scratches, or punctate marks came from.

What about the type-A blood that Paul Stombaugh testified was on the pajama top before it was torn? Did you hear defendant's experts say that there wasn't type-A blood on the pajama top before it was torn? Did you hear that? Huh-uh. Don't you know if they could have had an expert here from somewhere, they would have had to have said that, because, ladies and gentlemen, the defendant's story is that he placed the pajama top on Colette after she was dead. There is not one whit of evidence to suggest that after it was placed on Colette's body, it was then taken up and ripped.

All of the evidence [from the defense] suggests that, however it was ripped, it was ripped before and not after it was placed on top of the chest of Colette MacDonald. Well, what does that suggest to you? It suggests that Colette MacDonald bled on that pajama top before it was torn in three places. If you should find that from the evidence, I suggest she bled while she was alive and engaged in a struggle with whoever was wearing that blue pajama top before—not after—it was torn.

We asked the defendant if he had an explanation for that, and he said not to his knowledge. Don't you know that if he could have explained it, he would have explained it? We even know that Kimberly's AB blood type was on the pajama top. How did it get on there? If you believe the defendant's story that on the first visit to the bedroom, he took it off and put it on her body and then went to check Kimberly and then he perhaps got Kimberly's blood on it [it still makes no sense]. He did not see Kimberly until he had the pajama top off. How does the AB blood walk from Kimberly's room over here to the master bedroom and get on the pajama top? We asked him that question, and his response was, "It would be pure conjecture." He also testified that in 1970 he did not know the blood types of his family.

We know that the pajama top, at least, was placed on Colette's chest. That is one thing with which the government and the defendant are in agreement. Why? The reason the pajama top was placed on the top of Colette's chest was because it already had type-A blood on it [Colette's blood type], and he had to have an explanation that would sound reasonable as to why that type-A blood was on it.

We know that Mr. Smith [Wade Smith, one of MacDonald's two lawyers] talked at great length and very eloquently about how the government couldn't tell you "maybe," it couldn't tell you "possibly," it couldn't tell you "could have"—that wasn't good enough. We had the burden of proof beyond a reasonable doubt. We had to tell you that "it did." Ladies and gentlemen, if we have proved anything to you it is that this club was the murder weapon—used to strike Colette and Kimberly. We know it had their blood type on it—type A and AB. We know that splinters from it matched identically in three bedrooms. We know that one splinter in excess of three inches long fits identically into this piece of wood and had A-type blood on it. I don't know what more we can show you about that club. That is not "maybe." That is not "possibly." That is not "can."

How did the threads and the yarns from the pajama top, matching the blue pajama top, get on Kimberly's bed on top—underneath the sheet—fourteen of them, fourteen blue-purple cotton sewing threads and at least five blue polyester yarns. The pajama top was already off. Now, we asked the defendant about that, and, as I recall his testimony, he said, well, it was sticking to his arms. We asked him if he got on the bed and he said, "No." We asked him if his arms were moist, and he said that he didn't know. Was there blood on him? "Surely." If you believe that that is where they came from, fine. We suggest that they came from the blue pajama top itself, as Kimberly MacDonald was carried back into that room with that torn pajama top and placed in that bed.

We know that pieces of latex were found and torn and some with type-A blood in the master bedroom. How did they get there? We asked the defendant about it, and he said, "Not that I can recall," "No," or "No explanation." Again, while he has no legal responsibility to explain, don't you know that if he could have, he most certainly would have?

We know that Medlin stated that somebody wrote the word "Pig" in type-A blood on the headboard over where Colette Mac-Donald slept. We know that a blue thread or purple thread was found in that area matching the pajama top. We know that there is a good possibility from the evidence that those surgical gloves matched those in the house, but even if you should find that they didn't—where did they come from, and what were they doing there? Isn't it interesting, ladies and gentlemen, that droplets of type-B blood—that of the defendant—is found in the kitchen near the cabinet where surgical gloves were kept? Looking at this chart, you can see that he didn't go there until number thirteen [this is the defendant's chronology of what he did during the incident]—drops of blood at number thirteen—but at number one, where he was cut according to his story, there wasn't any.

The defendant we do not contend inflicted all of his injuries—not by any stretch. You know the contusion on his head—remember the hairbrush in the master bedroom. I think you can infer that this defendant with his medical knowledge—knowing that MPs [military police] would soon be on the way—very likely inflicted one—not all, but one—injury in the bathroom, and that is where the B-type blood came from, and that was close to the end, and that is why B-type blood was not found in the kitchen until number thirteen.

Perhaps the most telling thing of all, ladies and gentlemen: You come back to two pieces—you could throw the whole shooting match away, except for two pieces of evidence. I think you could just hold on to two—these two [holding up the club and pajama top]. Why are they so important?

Well, you remember, he said that he hadn't seen this [the club] until April 6, 1970 [the date of his tape-recorded statement with army investigators], and he didn't think this was the club that he was hit with. The club, the knives, and the ice pick were outside the door. He didn't go outside the door, but he went to it. They had A and AB blood on it and some threads which matched—or some yarns which matched the throw rug in the master bedroom. They had two little purple threads on them matching identically in composition with these. This sounds sort of minor, really, until you think about something. How did they get there? If he never touched them, if he never saw them, if the pajama top was not taken off of his body in the hall or the living room until this club was out the door, how in the name of all that is reasonable did they walk out the door and get on the club and stick to it? There is an explanation, and that is that this club was not outside the back door until after—not before—that pajama top dropped threads and yarns and blood to the floor, and as it fell on the floor, it picked up the threads and picked up the yarns with the blood, and it was thrown out the door.

What does it all mean? How could this have happened? We know that the defendant was a good doctor. We know that his family loved him. We know that from the valentine cards. We know that from the card that he read from the witness stand shortly before the end of direct examination, that Colette loved him very much.

What the defense tried to do was to prove the defendant's love and character through Colette and not from himself. We know that the defendant had been unfaithful in his marriage. [The defendant himself admitted at the Article 32 hearing that he had infrequent affairs while married to Colette. There was some evidence to suggest that MacDonald had an affair in his military quarters during the period of time that the Article 32 proceeding was taking place.] We know that he had worked the weekend before; he was perhaps tired.

We know that there was a minor problem of Kristen coming to the bed. According to his story, he went to bed late that night and found that the bed was wet. I am not by any stretch of the imagination suggesting that the slaughter took place over any one thing. You can infer from the evidence that a fight developed in the master bedroom between Colette and the defendant—a struggle—an altercation. We know that Colette was bruised—perhaps she was struck.

You know those words—you heard them in Wade Smith's opening

argument—"Daddy, Daddy, Daddy, Daddy." Those words were said, but not from fear of intruders, but I think that you can infer from the evidence that they were said as Kimberly came to the master bedroom to find out what was going on from her father and mother. We know that she was there. We know that her blood was found on the sheet, on the floor, and in the hall—or at least her blood type.

You can infer from the evidence, ladies and gentlemen, that the defendant in one tragic, brief moment—so brief—lost control and came back with that club, and as he did, he struck Kimberly and struck his wife—perhaps not originally trying to hit Kimberly—perhaps she walked into the club.

At that point, ladies and gentlemen, the future is at stake. It may be too late at that point to undo that which is done. You know how hard it is to unring the bell. You know the words "Jeff, Jeff, Jeff, why are they doing this to me?" Think how close that is to "Jeff, Jeff, Jeff, why are you doing this to me?"

You can find from the evidence, again, things had simply gone beyond repair. You can't go back and make the family happy again, drink liquor, and watch Johnny Carson.

An Old Hickory paring knife was located, and Colette Mac-Donald was stabbed sixteen times, and Kimberly was stabbed in the neck at least eight to ten times.

You remember the *Esquire* magazine and the words in it—the Manson-type murders and the multiplicity of weapons equaling the multiplicity of people. An ice pick was obtained—you know from Mildred Kassab and Pamela Kalin [the MacDonald baby-sitter] that they had seen an ice pick at the MacDonald residence, and even though the defendant said he did not recognize it, we suggest that it was there and that you could find that from the evidence. That was taken, and Kristen was stabbed superficially with the ice pick after she had already been stabbed with the knife.

The surgical gloves were then taken and used to write the word "pig" on the headboard. The self-infliction of one injury was made [i.e., Dr. MacDonald cuts himself in the chest, collapsing his right lung], the story was concocted, the MPs were called, and he lay down next to his wife to wait for help. That help came, and this confusion began as they tried to get him to the hospital. Who created so much of that confusion [when both the MPs and CID came to the crime scene]? Who created the red herring of going to look for the intruders? The defendant did.

Ladies and gentlemen, we have not presented an emotional case. We have presented a reasonable and sometimes boring, tedious, and logical case. We have given you the explanation that we believe to be true for how all this got where it did and what it means.

You know, the defendant had a lot of nice character testimony, and I am sure that each of you, if you were accused with a crime, would have the same. Don't ever forget that perhaps the greatest crime of all was committed two thousand years ago. And the night before Christ was betrayed, Judas Iscariot would have had twelve of the best character witnesses this world has ever known to have said he couldn't have done it, but you know that he did.

Ladies and gentlemen, if in the future, after this case is over, if in your jury deliberations you should think again of this case, I ask you to think and remember Colette, Kimberly, and Kristen. They would have liked to have been here. They have been dead for almost ten years. That is right now around thirty-four hundred or thirty-five hundred days and nights that you have had and I have had and the defendant has had that they haven't. They would have liked to have had that. If in the future you should cry a tear, cry one for them. If in the future you should say a prayer, say one for them. If in the future you should light a candle, light one for them.

We ask for nothing in the name of persecution. We ask for nothing in the name of harassment. We ask for nothing in the name of what is wrong—nothing—but, God, we ask for everything in the name of what is right and in the name of what is just. That is why we are here. We ask for everything in the name of truth. We ask you, ladies and gentlemen, that this horribly tragic and horribly sad—as it is because you know that you have seen Mrs. Kassab [Colette's mother] and you have seen Mrs. MacDonald [the defendant's mother], and it is sad for both of them—both of them were grandmothers, not just one—it is sad for the defendant—but it is sad most of all for those who paid the highest price of all with their lives—and we ask you, ladies and gentlemen, to return a verdict of guilty as to clubbing and stabbing Colette, guilty of clubbing and stabbing Kimberly, and guilty perhaps most of all for stabbing little Kristen.

You remember—I am sure you have heard it many times, part of the third chapter of Ecclesiastes: There is a time for everything under the heavens—a time to be born and a time to die. Surely God did not intend on the seventeenth of February, 1970, for Colette, Kimberly, and Kristen MacDonald to die. It is time, ladies and gentlemen—it is so late in the day—it is time that someone speak for justice and truth and return a verdict of guilty against this man.

Finally, ladies and gentlemen, I want to say in closing that this is a difficult case, not because the evidence is difficult, but it is difficult because of the people involved—the Kassabs, who have been injured and will be injured the rest of their lives regardless of your verdict. Mrs. MacDonald, who has been injured and will be injured the rest of her life regardless of your verdict; their friends will suffer the same fate and, I guess, the defendant himself.

You know, I am sure it is very sad for everybody who knew these people to look at those photographs. I think it is very sad for people who knew these people to look at pictures of kids playing, of Halloween and Christmas. I wish more than you that we could have shown you that kind of picture. I wish more than you that we weren't here. I wish more than you know that I did not think the evidence pointed to the defendant. I think the supreme tragedy in this whole thing really is, if our evidence is correct and the defendant did it, which we believe he did, think for a moment of the last minutes of Colette, Kimberly, and Kristen when they realized they were going to die and they realized for the first and last time who it was that was going to make them die. It is incredible. It is unbelievable, as Wade [Smith said]. You wouldn't think it. People have said, "He is not that kind of guy," but, ladies and gentlemen, people do strange things, man's inhumanity to man—but we think he did it. For that, we are sorry. For that, you have an awesome burden and responsibility. You have to decide beginning tomorrow what the evidence is and what your verdict will be. We believe strongly—as strongly as we don't want to believe—that he did it and he is guilty of count one of first-degree murder, of count two of first-degree murder, and count three of first-degree murder, and I ask you to so find.

POSTSCRIPT

Jeffrey MacDonald was convicted of all counts and is currently serving three life terms in prison. The verdict itself was eminently reasonable in view of the physical evidence's stark contrast to MacDonald's story. Dr. MacDonald was foolish enough to give too many details in his version, details that could be checked and used to destroy his credibility. The blood types of his children and the location of the numerous pajama fibers, for example, simply contradicted his narrative sequence.

Yet, whatever the evidence, prosecuting Dr. MacDonald was a difficult task because it went against the grain of so many cultural assumptions. Even for those who believed that he was guilty on the evidence, there was the manifest contradiction that an altruistic man would throw away his whole life in a matter of minutes. A good-looking, middle-class, Princeton-educated doctor surrounded by a nice mother and good friends—many of whom turned up to the trial—did not commit this sort of crime, no matter what the evidence says. In many murder cases in the United States, no one shows up in court for the defendant. An audience of supporters is a form of subliminal advertising to a jury that, in this case, says, "This man is not a triple murderer." To enhance that advantage, Dr. MacDonald had character witnesses testify at trial on his behalf. After all, this man was in a profession of healers, and, furthermore, there was no discernible motive. He had a happy life. Why would he throw it away? It was a difficult matter for any jury to convict. The prosecution overcame these difficulties and convinced the jury to decide the case based on the evidence alone. Some of the jurors on MacDonald's jury cried when they rendered the verdict, including a juror who was an ex–Green Beret.

The prosecution faced a challenge even in the practicalities of the case. Because there were no eyewitnesses besides the defendant, the case against him was based solely upon physical evidence. Granted that most of these facts contradicted everything he said about how the murder occurred, the fact remained that MacDonald had suffered some serious injuries that lent credence to his story. In fact, one mentally unstable local drug addict, Helena Stoeckley, allegedly confessed to the murders. When she ultimately testified at MacDonald's trial, however, she denied participation in the crimes. The prosecution was faced with mistakes made by the police in investigating the crimes. There is no such thing as a perfect investigation. This case was no exception.

Despite these case weaknesses, the prosecution had in its favor the tragic scenario of three totally blameless victims and a crime scene horrifying enough to give any juror nightmares. In the end, the emotional currents on both sides neutralized each other and, in the skillful hands of prosecutors James Blackburn and Brian Murtagh, the impartial physical facts clinched the difference.

Cases built on physical evidence are often stronger than eyewitness cases. Eyewitnesses can lie or be mistaken, and their credibility can be shaken—which is precisely what happened to MacDonald, the only eyewitness in the case. Why does the statement of a guilty party hurt him, even if the statement says "I didn't do the crime"? Because, inevitably, there are flaws in it that the prosecution identifies and holds up to the jury. Without such a statement, the prosecution cannot minutely pick apart the defendant's scenario. In a criminal case, remember that the defense does not need to prove innocence or offer a convincing story. It can simply exert all its force on attacking the prosecution's hypotheses and creating a reasonable doubt. In effect, MacDonald acted as his own worst enemy by speaking up, helping Mr. Blackburn and Mr. Murtagh's case by giving them a story to compare to the physical evidence.

4

WHEN CRIMINALS CRAVE THE LIMELIGHT

THREE DEFENDANTS DEFEND THEMSELVES

THERE'S A FAMOUS SAYING about pro se defenses: "A lawyer who represents himself has a fool for a client." If a lawyer, who has legal training, cannot effectively represent himself, then how can a defendant, untrained in substantive law and evidence, have any hope of success? This is similar to a person with no medical training operating on himself. Any good lawyer knows that pro se defenses have inbuilt structural disadvantages. At its most basic, arguing one's own innocence just appears so much more self-serving and less impartial to a jury. Motivated by the wrong impulse—to have a moment in the limelight, rather than to save themselves—defendants who decide to represent themselves in criminal cases usually shoot themselves in the foot and lose it all. The late Judge Harold Rothwax, admonishing a pro se candidate about the dangers of representing himself, leafed through the accused's rather lengthy criminal record and tartly commented, "I realize you have extensive experience in the criminal-justice system. However, unfortunately for you, your role has been limited to that of defendant."

THE LONG ISLAND RAIL ROAD SHOOTING:
PEOPLE OF THE STATE OF NEW YORK v.
COLIN FERGUSON

On December 7, 1993, Colin Ferguson, a Jamaican immigrant, boarded a Long Island Rail Road commuter train with a loaded nine-millimeter pistol. After the train passed the Merillon Avenue station, he started shooting at the passengers, killing six people and injuring nineteen others. Ferguson was subdued by three of the train's passengers, but only after he had finished discharging his second clip.

The police recovered from Ferguson a bag containing another two fully loaded clips and approximately ninety additional rounds of ammunition. They also removed several notes from Ferguson's person, which suggested his motivation behind the massacre: anger over what he perceived as racism at Adelphi University and a Workmen's Compensation board, the faulty running of the transit system, and his embarrassment by someone named Mr. Su. One of Ferguson's notes read, "New York City has been spared because of my respect for David [David Dinkins, New York City's first African-American mayor]. Nassau County is the venue." Ferguson also wrote, "Those filthy swine who live at 226 Martense Street, Brooklyn [Ferguson's residence] are not my friends. Once they hear of this they will loot all the evidence in my room such as documents and tapes. I hate them with a passion." When the police questioned Ferguson about the notes, he told them that he did not care about the people on the train and only wanted to know how many he had killed.

Firearms records revealed that Ferguson bought the murder weapon in California in the spring of 1993. The police executed a search warrant on Ferguson's home and found a pad of paper that, according to forensic testing, matched the notes found in his possession at the murder scene. Finally, several of the surviving passengers on that LIRR identified Ferguson at his trial. Not promising odds for Mr. Ferguson, who chose to defend himself.

Excerpts from the Opening Statement of Colin Ferguson

What you just heard was Mr. Peck [the prosecutor] reading from an instrument called an indictment. This is simply an instrument which brings the defendant in to court to face trial. It is not in any way an admission of guilt by the defendant. It is not in any way confirmation of guilt by the defendant, but simply charges brought against the defendant by way of a grand jury.

We're here today because on December 7, 1993, Colin Ferguson was charged with the murders of six people, and the wounding of nineteen others, during a shooting which occurred on the Long Island Rail Road commuter train. There are ninety-three counts to that indictment. Ninety-three counts only because it matches the year, 1993. Had it been 1925, it would have been twenty-five counts. This is a case of stereotyped victimization of a black man and subsequent conspiracy to destroy him. Nothing more.

In criminal cases the prosecution, having the burden of proof, presents evidence first. It is only thereafter that the defendant will have a chance to present anything. Mr. Ferguson, the defendant in this case, does not contest the fact that he was a passenger on the train, the 5:33, on December 7, 1993. That fact, however, is not the issue in this case. Even though there were numerous injuries, there were deaths on the train, that is not the issue in this case. The issue in this case is whether Mr. Ferguson did the shooting. In other words, did Mr. Ferguson take a gun and board a train and shoot passengers he did not know and for absolutely no reason? Please remember that the defendant, Mr. Ferguson, does not have to prove anything in this case. It is the prosecution that has the burden of proof beyond a reasonable doubt that Colin Ferguson committed the crimes by shooting people on the train.

The evidence will show that Colin Ferguson was, in fact, a well-meaning passenger on the train transporting to a safe haven a firearm which, in fact, he purchased legally. At the time that Mr. Ferguson was on the train, like any other passenger, he dozed off, having the weapon in a bag. At that point someone opened the bag, took the weapon out of the bag, and proceeded to shoot. It is at that point that Mr. Ferguson was awakened by the gunfire himself and, amidst the confusion, sought to run for cover like any other person on that train.

We have seen numerous cases, and this is no different, in which it is so seemingly automatic for a white person to accuse a black person of committing a crime. We saw this in the incident in which a white female in North Carolina murdered her two children and blames a black man [a reference to the case of Susan Smith, who killed her two children by driving her car into a lake and attempted to blame it on an alleged black carjacker. At that point all hostilities are pointed to the black community, pointed toward every single black individual therein.

We have seen also the case in Boston, in which a white male murders his wife, murders his children, and reports to the police officers that a black man entered the house and murdered his children, murdered his wife [a reference to the case of Charles Stuart, who killed his pregnant wife and blamed it on a black man]. So we have a scenario where the police officers are coming to black communities looking for black men, only for this man to confess at a later date that, in fact, he did this. No different than the case in North Carolina. Even in Long Island here, the incident—

MR. PECK: Objection.

MR. FERGUSON: —where a black man . . .

THE COURT: Mr. Ferguson, there's an objection, which is sustained.

Mr. Ferguson, being black, was thereafter targeted as a suspect, only too normal for someone of Mr. Ferguson's race to be automatically a culprit, and this is precisely why I asked you during jury-selection process whether or not you felt that blacks were more likely to commit a crime. I believed all of you indicated that you did not think so, that you could be fair.

This is yet another stereotype, victimization and subsequent conspiracy, and you will see that this particular conspiracy is more wide-ranging once we get into police headquarters. Federal, state, and county [law enforcement] officials, once they discovered who Ferguson is, once they ran an identification check on Mr. Ferguson to find out that, in fact, the Immigration and Naturalization Service, along with a number of other agencies, had been targeting Ferguson for quite a number of years.

What happened before and during the incident? Mr. Ferguson, owning a legally purchased gun, realized that the safest place for it was not at his place of abode in Brooklyn. In fact, it was not a safe place, because the tenants of the house could not be trusted to stay out of his room.

The fact [is] that he had all intentions to return to California, to resume the kind of work that he had been accustomed to doing, and that he needed a weapon for protection.

He could not go back to California, for a number of reasons, and decided that he had to transfer the weapon to [a] safe haven: The only place that he could transport the weapon after deciding on whether to throw it in the ocean at Coney Island and get rid of it because it's not something that Mr. Ferguson would have wanted to get in the hands of anyone else.

Mr. Ferguson moved to take it to persons who he knew very long periods of time in Westbury. We are talking about an individual in Westbury, who you will come to know later, who Mr. Ferguson lived with as a tenant. Trusted that person, a person who was responsible, had a wife and two children which Mr. Ferguson knew personally. Or else another person in Westbury which also presented himself as an option for Mr. Ferguson in which the husband of that particular person was a New York City corrections officer, a person living in Westbury where Mr. Ferguson lived, who was also of his nationality, Jamaican born.

Mr. Ferguson felt these were responsible people that he had known over a period of time, [and he took the weapon] to them rather than having it in a place of his abode that was not safe, he elected to do so.

And on the train Mr. Ferguson himself had to run for cover to protect himself. Total confusion. It was sometime after that confusion that Mr. Ferguson felt force being applied to him, after which he was handcuffed and led away. The evidence will also show, once at police headquarters, Mr. Ferguson was identified and targeted as a person whom a number of government agencies—state and county agencies—were targeting, and thus was made a political prisoner. As such, Mr. Ferguson expects the evidence to show that he did not fire a gun and is simply a victim of a shooting on the train like any other victim on the train and very unfortunate that anyone was hurt on the train.

As you heard earlier, there were numerous injuries. There were several deaths, something which is quite unfortunate. However, I'm here to show that Mr. Ferguson was in no way involved in the shooting of anyone.

Mr. Peck spoke of notes. Mr. Peck spoke of statements. The evidence will show that, in fact, Mr. Ferguson did not sign any statements of admission to anything. You will see that these are notes that were normally written by anyone else. And you will also see photographs of the scene as it was at the time, and not an indication of someone's guilt or innocence.

Evidence will also show that Mr. Ferguson, even after the incident, was made a scapegoat in a political campaign for the office of governor of the state of New York. So Mr. Ferguson continued to be the victim beyond the day of December 7, 1993.

I therefore ask you ladies and gentlemen, to withhold your judgment until you have heard all the evidence in the case and I'm confident you will render a verdict in favor of Mr. Ferguson.

I'm absolutely sure the prosecution will not be able to prove beyond a reasonable doubt that Mr. Ferguson committed a crime. I expect that after you have deliberated and carefully weighed the evidence in this case, you will return the only possible verdict. That is a verdict of not guilty.

POSTSCRIPT

Colin Ferguson was convicted of all ninety-three counts in the indictment and received a sentence of two hundred years to life.

In reality, Ferguson did not do a terrible job of arguing his case; he was rational and eloquent much of the time, except for the fact that he repeatedly referred to himself in the third person. Mr. Ferguson was originally represented by famous civil-rights lawyers William Kunstler and Ronald Kuby, who suggested that he interpose a defense of mental illness that was caused by oppression in our racist society. Because he could deny neither being on the train nor owning the gun used during the murders, Ferguson created an accommodation defense that conceded these two facts but denied his being the actual shooter.

Naturally, Ferguson could not admit writing the notes found on his person. They revealed the mind of a man with strong motivations to carry out the shooting. Mr. Peck, the prosecutor, spoke little of the motive for the massacre in his argument. He said at the end of his opening, "You may have some questions about the reasons why, and I'll develop that a little bit later, the next time I see you in summation." But the jury did not have to wait for Mr. Peck. Ferguson himself inadvertently gave it away. He began by saying that it was all a conspiracy against him because he was black. He seemed to believe there was a monumental, coordinated plot against him by the INS and other government agencies. His neighbors in his apartment building were always in his room watching him. He couldn't return to California either. Unwittingly, he gave the motive for the crime: *I am a stark, raving lunatic.* And if anyone had any doubts, he let you know in the beginning of the opening, when he said that there were ninety-three counts of the indictment because it was 1993. If it had been 1925, there would have been twenty-five counts of the indictment. Once the jury heard this, they could conclude that he was a deranged and paranoid individual. Mr. Ferguson unwittingly did the prosecutor's job of establishing a motive for his senseless and unfathomable crime.

THE MIND OF AL QAEDA: *UNITED STATES OF AMERICA* v. *ZACARIAS MOUSSAOUI*

For the new generation, September 11, 2001, will be like November 22, 1963, the day President John F. Kennedy was assassinated: All Americans will remember where they were and what they were doing. Nineteen hijackers succeeded in toppling the Twin Towers and doing significant damage to the Pentagon. Moussaoui, a French-born Moroccan Islamic radical, came to the United States in February 2001 and took flight lessons in Oklahoma and Minnesota. His flight instructors became suspicious because Moussaoui wanted to learn how to fly but had no interest in learning how to take off or land. They informed the FBI, who, in a rare act of prescience, arrested him on August 17, 2001, and held him on immigration charges.

In December 2001, Moussaoui was indicted and charged with being part of Al Qaeda. The following transcript sets out a court proceeding in federal district court in which Moussaoui reads a letter to the court, trying to fire his lawyers and go pro se.

Excerpts from the Court Proceeding

MR. DUNHAM: Good morning, Your Honor. Frank Dunham, the federal public defender.

THE DEFENDANT: Ma'am. I am sorry to note they are not anymore my lawyer.

THE COURT: Mr. Moussaoui, before you say anything, you have a right to speak in court, and I want to advise you that anything you say may be used against you by the government in the prosecution of its case. Do you understand that, sir?

THE DEFENDANT: Zacarias Moussaoui [Arabic spoken]. In the name of Allah, I, Zacarias Moussaoui, today the twenty-second of April, 2002, after being prevented for a long time to mount an effective defense by overly oppressive condition of confinement, take the control of my defense by entering a pro se defense set for presentation in order to mount a significant defense of the life that Allah, the most masterful, has granted to me. I, slave of Allah, Zacarias Moussaoui, reject completely the imposition of the U.S. so-called appointed lawyer Dunham, Zerkin, MacMahon, and denounce their misconduct and their intentional ineffective assistance.

I, slave of Allah, Zacarias Moussaoui, will engage action against the U.S. Department of so-called Justice for very serious misconduct. I, slave of Allah, Zacarias Moussaoui, have the intention in the shortest time practically possible to hire my own chosen Muslim lawyer to assist me in matters of procedure and understanding of the U.S. law. [Arabic spoken.]

In the name of Allah, O you who believe, take not as your Bitanah, adviser, consultant, friend, those outside of your religion, pagan, Jew, Christian, and hypocrites, since they will not fail to do their best to corrupt you. They desire to harm you severely. Hatred has already appeared from their mouth. But what their breast conceals is far worse. Indeed, we have made plain to you the Ayat, the proof, the evidence, the verse, if you understand. Koran, Sura Al-i-Imran, Number 3, Ayat 118. Under the cover of assistance of the defense counsel, the legal version of humanitarian assistance, the United States are orchestrating my sending to the safe haven, Bosnia style. What they have done is a sophisticated version of the Troy horse or the kiss of death. They imposed the dream team. Greed, fame, and vanity is their motivation. Their game is deception. Their slogan is no scruple. So what to do? Then fight in the cause of Allah. No doubt they are spending millions of their *haram*, evil money, to kill me.

I will not entertain the illusion that a U.S. District Judge Leonie Brinkema is an honest broker. Reality tells me that this judge is here as a field general, entrusted with the mission to get this matter over quickly. Every general has a commander in chief, and I know how much the U.S. commander in chief wants me to be over quickly. As Allah say, "O you who believe, when you meet those who disbelieve in the battlefield, never turn your back to them."

I will not make your day by giving any excuse

to your marshal to assault me in court, but be sure that I do not fear you. As Allah say, "It is only Satan that suggested to you fear of his friends. So fear them not, but fear Allah if you are true believer." Surah Al-i-Imran, Number 3, Ayat 175.

My experience tells me that the U.S. will not hesitate to have a trial without me. After all, they only need me for the gas chamber. But Allah is my witness. Nobody will ever represent me, Inshallah, because *suicide is forbidden in Islam* [emphasis added].

I pray to Allah for the return of Andalusia, Spain, to the Muslim and the liberation of Ceuta and Medilla. I pray to Allah for the return of India to the Muslims and to the liberation of Kashimir. I pray to Allah the severe in punishment for the destruction of the Jewish people and states and for the liberation [of] Palestine by the Muslim, for the Muslim. I pray to Allah, the protector, for the destruction of Russia and the return of the Islamic Emirates of Chechnia. I pray to Allah, the powerful, for the return of the Islamic Emirates of Afghanistan and the destruction of the United States of America.

I want a Muslim lawyer. [The court-appointed attorney] cannot send his female investigator to Muslim country. And I know that people who could have provided vital evidence for me will never speak to a non-Muslim, because they have the same kind of understanding in life than me.

We [the court-appointed lawyers and I] have in this case [a] very different approach. *And it's impossible to have two teams trying the same case, because they want to try by jury. And me, I want to try by a judge* [emphasis added]. Because all the information and the complexity of the case make it very difficult for a simple person to comprehend in a very short time, and a judge, you have to collate information and be able to understand concepts very quickly, and this is not very easy for a simple person. The only person who can grasp this kind of thing is maybe a judge, okay? I was reading the transcript of embassy bombing in my cell, and I discovered that the government just overwhelmed the court of information, and the people just naturally lose track of what has been said. At the end they are lost. The judge can see through the trick of the government and will be able to assess the validity of the argument.

THE COURT: Even if you have come to the decision that you want to waive the jury, the United States, if they want a trial by jury, has an absolute right to request that. And the court can waive a jury only if both sides agree, all right?

THE DEFENDANT: By the way, I'm born in France. I have a master's degree in international business. I'm fully acquainted with Western system of justice, okay? I never live in the Middle East country or in Arabic Country, okay? The conception that I'm completely ignorant of the rule of Western system of justice and Anglo-Saxon, because I live in London, it's not correct. What you were proposing, in fact, is impractical, and you will damage my defense and ultimately my chance to live.

THE COURT: All right. Mr. Moussaoui, we're going to have a psychiatrist checking you over in the cell. And I'll make my final decision about whether I'm permitting you to proceed pro se based upon that report.

POSTSCRIPT

This is, perhaps, an even better example of a moderately intelligent person so deluded as to believe that he is smart enough to represent himself. Note the differences between Moussaoui and John Walker Lindh, the nineteen-year-old American who was caught in Afghanistan in the same building where a Taliban mob killed CIA operative Johnny Spann. Lindh was represented by a team of shrewd lawyers led by James Brosnahan. The lawyers fashioned an elaborate thesis in which they portrayed Lindh as a starry-eyed and misguided American teenager in search of himself, who could just as easily have boarded a plane to Club Med Martinique but instead made some wrong decisions and ended up in Yemen, Pakistan, and Afghanistan. Moussaoui might have mustered a tenuous defense claiming that he was merely taking lessons to learn flying and got caught in the web of anti-Muslim paranoia pervading the country. But any hope of floating that or any other halfway plausible scenario instantly faded when Moussaoui started his speech with, "I, Slave of Allah. . . ." To begin with, Moussaoui let it be known that he wanted a Muslim lawyer and that Christian, pagan, Jewish, or other infidel lawyers "will not fail to do their best to corrupt you." By the time Moussaoui finished giving his speech, with his acute distrust of unbelievers and Americans, he betrayed his religious fanaticism and virtually convicted himself as an Al Qaeda activist. One could imagine the prosecution quickly turning to Judge Brinkema and pleading, "Can we mark this individual down as Exhibit One for the prosecution?"

Now, in fairness to Moussaoui, I should note that a person who wanted to commit suicide by flying a plane into a building may not balk at committing legal suicide by representing himself in the courtroom. Yet it was curious to observe how this extreme Islamist claimed that suicide is forbidden in Islam.

Among the many mines that Moussaoui set off—one of the common dangers of acting pro se—was his unabashed insult against the court. He told Judge Brinkema that she was the "field general entrusted with the mission to get this matter over quickly." It is always foolhardy to insult the referee. While this can happen to a lawyer in the heat of battle, it is never a good strategy. Then, to cap this off at the end of the court proceeding, Moussaoui said that he wanted his trial to be conducted by a judge. Should the judge who decides on his guilt, on his fate, or indeed on how he is tried, be a field general of the enemy?

THE TRIUMPH OF THE ANTS: *UNITED STATES OF AMERICA* v. *CONGRESSMAN JAMES TRAFICANT*

The trial of Ohio congressman James Traficant, who was charged with ten counts of bribery, tax evasion, and racketeering, is one of the most entertaining political-corruption trials in history. The gravamen of the charges was that Congressman Traficant required some members of his staff to kick back portions of their salary and perform work on his boat and farm (including shoveling manure), and also that he filed false tax returns and sought to persuade his staff to lie under oath and destroy evidence. Traficant was additionally charged with receiving free labor and materials from construction businesses in exchange for his intervention on their behalf before federal regulators.

Traficant decided to represent himself, although he was not a lawyer. His defense was that the government had a twenty-year vendetta against him that began in 1983, when he was acquitted in a federal racketeering trial that charged him with taking $163,000 while serving as sheriff of Mahoning County in Ohio.

For those who were unfamiliar with Congressman's Traficant antics, they got a small taste of what the ten-week trial would be like when the congressman, at his arraignment in Youngstown, Ohio, pleaded not guilty "by reason of sanity." Judge Leslie Wells warned Congressman Traficant, "I expect you to behave yourself. This trial is not going to be a donnybrook."

Following are excerpts from the court proceedings, quoting both Congressman Traficant and Assistant United States Attorney Craig Morford.

Excerpts from the Closing Statement of
Assistant U.S. Attorney Craig Morford

"[T]he evidence in this case [has established] that Congressman Traficant used his official actions for personal profit, first by paying certain employees high salaries and then having those employees make kickbacks to him; second, by having congressional staff members do work at his farm and on his boat; and third, by seeking and obtaining thousands of dollars' worth of free construction work, farm supplies, farm chores, boat repairs, and cash from businessmen who were seeking constituent services, which are official acts from his office.

Congressman Traficant has asserted that he is a courageous, compassionate, outspoken congressman who worked hard to create jobs for his constituents. But if you think about the issue . . . under the charges that we filed in this case, they are not [about] whether Congressman Traficant was good or effective. Those things are not relevant to this case, for Congressman Traficant is not charged with being an ineffective Congressman.

He's accused [of] doing things that were corrupt, whether he was effective or not. He's charged with using his official actions to obtain personal gain. And the law, as Judge Wells told you on Friday, is very clear. A federal official cannot accept things of value in return for his official actions as a federal official, period. There's no question about that. The law is clear.

He can't use his position to feather his own nest. He can't use his public office as a trough to feed his selfish appetite.

His duty is to serve the public interest, not his personal desires. His office is a public trust. It's not a gravy train. And his staff members are public servants; they're not his personal servants. And that's why, if Congressman Traficant wanted to put an addition on his farmhouse, if he wanted to have a crew of people come out and bale his hay, if he wanted to have his boat repaired, he needed to do what every other American has to do. He needed to go out and hire workers, and he needed to pay them for the full value of their work, just like everyone else has to do.

You see, a Congressman can't ask for tips; he's not a waiter who can stand around with his hand out because he performed good service for someone. We don't allow our public officials to do that.

He's not allowed to use his official duties to obtain things of personal value, no matter who he is, no matter how powerful his office is, no matter how effective he is, regardless of his party affiliation, regardless of his voting record, no matter how much bacon he brought home to his home district, no matter how great an athlete he was, and regardless of his sense of humor and his personal charisma or anything else.

The law is still the law, and no man is above the law, including the man who makes the law.

Excerpts from the Summation of Congressman Traficant

Traficant Asks a Favor

THE COURT:	(to Congressman Traficant) Thirty minutes, Counselor.
CONGRESSMAN TRAFFICANT:	That's all I have left?
THE COURT:	Nope, that's what you've gotten to now.
CONGRESSMAN TRAFFICANT:	You mean I have an hour. Hooray!
THE COURT:	Well, you asked.
CONGRESSMAN TRAFFICANT:	Don't take any more of my time. And you didn't interrupt Mr. Morford.
THE COURT:	He didn't ask us to be his timekeeper.

Traficant Attacks the IRS

I love America. I bend over backward for our military. I fight for Transportation, General Services Administration. In fact, I authorized that new courtroom you're moving into. And I lost the postal workers. Many of them are getting screwed.

But you know what, when an agency comes before the United States Congress and says, "If you change the burden of proof and change the seizure laws in the IRS, you take away the only leverage to collect taxes." And they say, "What's that?" And they said, "Fear. If the taxpayers don't fear us, the deadbeats will get over."

Now, we changed those laws, and do you know what? We went from 10,067 seizures of homes to 51 in the whole country when the IRS had to prove it in court.

Does the IRS like me? Hates my guts. Do I like them? I'd like to break their damn necks. I have a bill right now that would abolish the Sixteenth Amendment [the right of Congress to tax] and get them out to get a real job and exempt everybody up to the poverty level.

> THE COURT: Congressman, these folks have to deal with the evidence in the case.

Traficant Attacks the Prosecution's Use of Informants

[The FBI] talked to Mr. Sinclair (Alan Sinclair; the prosecution charged Traficant with hiring Sinclair and getting $2,500 per month kickbacks from him) about kickbacks, and he stood up and said, "I'll have no part of it, helping you get Jim Traficant." Does that sound like a guy who fears me? And then, one week later, he signs a proffer [a cooperation agreement to help the prosecution]. I don't blame him. I don't blame Sinclair, I don't blame Sabatine, I don't blame Buccis [all government cooperating witnesses]. They're trying to save their asphalt.

Traficant Demands Fingerprint Evidence

Fingerprints are routinely found on cash from bank robberies, betting parlors, and illegal activities. Fingerprints can even be lifted from dead bodies. The larger the volume of documents, the more likely a print can be identified. Many thousands of dollars in cash, it would almost be impossible to fail to recognize one print. And the more the documents, the impossibility of having not one print is almost unheard of.

Traficant Dismisses Circumstantial Evidence

I want you to imagine I'm an artist. I've got an easel. I've got ten different colors of oil paint on that easel. And I take that brush, and I'm painting and painting, and I'm trying to put it together. I'm trying to put it together, and I'm desperately frustrated with it.

So I go to Mickey D's. I go to McDonald's, and I get those little plastic condiment cups, about three-quarters of an inch high, about an inch in circumference, and I take them back with me, and I put ten different colors of oil paint in those ten cups. And I take them, and I throw them on the canvas and see what sticks.

Now, here is what I can tell you: If you in your heart believe that they have proven beyond a reasonable doubt my guilt, find me guilty. But I want to tell you something: When you start taking down the burden of proof and you start putting people in jail for circumstantial evidence predicated on what someone said without being corroborated, you have taken the Constitution and you started to shred it.

Mr. Tough Guy

I've stood right here, I'm ready. I made up my mind. I will not take their bullshit. Excuse my mouth, but that's it. Now, you hurt my family, you don't just hurt me. I mean, where does it end? Where do we call an end to this? . . .

I've been a real pain in the ascot. I don't know if you were in the room when I threw the box. If you were, I apologize.

I don't totally understand our courts, and I don't want to know them, and I hope to God you never do either. But you are the court now, you are the trier of last resort. You're the one who makes the decision.

Assistant U.S. Attorney Responds to the Congressman's Attacks on the Government

Congressman Traficant spent an hour and a half, and he talked about everything under the sun except for one thing: the actual evidence and documents and testimony in this case, as far as what people actually said.

He talked about freedoms being eroded and the IRS is bad and the FBI is bad and the government is bad. Who's he? He is the government. He's a U.S. congressman, one of the 435 most powerful men in this country. If the government is so bad, what's he doing for eighteen years?

The Prosecutor Answers the Fingerprint Argument

Congressman Traficant talked an awful lot about [the fact] that there's no fingerprints. We told you that right up front. Joe Bushner [FBI Special Agent] testified very early in this case. And what did he tell you? The documents that matter—the money, the burned envelopes—there were no fingerprints at all. And he explained to you why that is, and it makes perfect sense. It's very difficult to get fingerprints from paper documents, because paper tends to absorb the very things that leave fingerprints. Sometimes you get them, sometimes you don't.

But with all those bills, there are no fingerprints. Not just not Congressman Traficant's, none at all.

And think about this: Congressman Traficant's own handwritten notes that some of his employees looked at and said, "That's clearly his handwriting," those didn't even have his fingerprints on them, and you know he touched them.

The Prosecutor Responds to Traficant's Attack on the Cooperators

You know, there's an old saying: "Tell me who you're running with, and I'll know what you're up to." He's the one that chose to run with these people, these felons, these crooks, as he describes them.

POSTSCRIPT

Not surprisingly, Congressman Traficant was convicted of all ten counts against him. He was sentenced to eight years in prison and a $150,000 fine. Judge Leslie Wells told the unrepentant Congressman:

> You cast yourself as a folk hero, the champion of the people and a voice for the average guy. You did a lot of good, but the good you have done does not excuse your crimes. . . . You were howling you were going to fight as a junkyard dog, and you did. You fought like a junkyard dog to protect your junkyard of deceit and corruption. . . . You sneered at

the entire calling of public service with your remarks. Using the national and local media, you attacked [government institutions]. You apparently think you are above the law. You have descended into rantings and ravings and spewing your venom. Your deceit, your distortions, and your intimidations are your weapons. . . . The truth is rarely in you. Your drumbeat is the drumbeat of the big lie, an old tactic . . . [that] if you tell a lie often enough, people will believe it. Some people believe you because you have shock and entertainment value. Others believe you because it suits their predisposition to believe conspiracy theories. [The] honorable and conscientious men and women of the jury were not fooled. You didn't distract them.

On July 25, 2002, the House of Representatives, by a vote of 420–1, voted to expel Congressman Traficant. Gary Condit, the California Democrat who had an affair with murdered intern Chandra Levy, was the only vote in Traficant's favor.

At the beginning of the trial, the prosecutor had his work cut out for him. He was prosecuting a popular congressman who had served his community for eighteen years and was perceived by many constituents as the friend of the average joe. To counter this, the government presented testimonial evidence from cooperating witnesses with deals. They also presented evidence from other witnesses who had not pleaded guilty to bribery and did not have cooperation agreements promising leniency. Finally, the prosecution had stacks of documentary evidence to corroborate all of its witnesses.

Congressman Traficant used a lawyer's trick: "If you don't have the law on your side, you argue the facts. If you don't have the facts on your side, you argue the law. If you have neither on your side, you talk about the weather." Congressman Traficant spoke about the IRS and the FBI. This attempt at distracting the jury from seeing the mountain's worth of evidence against him ultimately failed.

5

STREET-CRIME SORROWS

SENTENCING SPEECHES FOR FORGOTTEN VICTIMS

IN ORDER TO MAINTAIN the objectivity of the jury, judges are rarely given the opportunity to make speeches during the trial. Once the jury has spoken, however, judges can express their views publicly in the form of sentencing speeches, which allow them to justify the sentences they will hand down. Similarly, interested parties, such as next of kin, are given the opportunity to speak out in the courtroom prior to sentencing, in order to influence the judge's ruling.

Each of the sentencing speeches below comes from 1980s New York City, a period in which crime tortured both the streets and our collective consciousness. In the first instance, a judge eloquently defends his reasoning; in the other, two grief-stricken family members communicate the depth of their loss. These excerpts are powerful examples of a form of courtroom dialogue rarely heard by the general public, but they are without doubt some of the most moving and heartfelt words spoken by anyone in the courtroom.

THE MURDER OF A NOBLE SON OF A NOBLE HOUSE: *THE PEOPLE OF THE STATE OF NEW YORK V. JUAN SANTANA*

On July 7, 1988, Juan Santana went on a crime rampage, robbing one man at gunpoint, and shooting two others, one of whom was killed, the other seriously injured. The bleeding victim, Ernest Davis, ran past the apartment of his neighbor, Alphonso Deal, a New York State court officer. Deal went into his apartment, retrieved his gun and badge, and then went out onto the street in search of Davis's attacker. Minutes later one of Davis's friends pointed out the defendant, who was approaching the men, as the shooter. In response, Santana ran behind a nearby car and pointed his gun at Deal, who responded by identifying himself as a peace officer and ordering the defendant to drop his gun. After a tense standoff, Santana appeared to comply and walked out from behind the car. But as Deal approached the defendant with his gun drawn, Santana reached, pulled out his pistol, and fatally shot Deal in the chest.

The jury convicted Santana of murder in the second degree, robbery in the first degree, as well as assault in the first degree.

Excerpts from the Sentencing Speech of Judge Edwin Torres

I should like, if I may, to discuss the victim, Alphonso Barclay Deal. I do not propose to eulogize him today or anoint him as a paragon, but he was so extraordinary a person, both in character and lineage that I feel constrained, as never before, to at least render tribute to the man and what he stood for. Let this record, cold though it be, speak for him in the years to come.

The deceased's father, also named Alphonso Deal, was a Pennsylvania state representative and before that a member of the Philadelphia Police Department and one of the founders of the Guardian Civic League, an organization of black police officers. The deceased's mother, Ponsie Hillman, is assistant treasurer of the United Federation of Teachers. Both parents were pioneers and lifelong activists with the NAACP. The elder Alphonso Deal serv[ed] as president and chairman of the Pennsylvania State NAACP. When he died in 1987, the streets of Philadelphia were closed for his funeral route.

The list of achievements on the part of the Deal family, too numerous to detail, is so rich that I do not stray far from the mark in saying that the emergence of black America in the twentieth century is attributable, in no small measure, to the efforts and commitment of such families.

Alphonso Barclay Deal, the deceased in this case, was a fruit worthy of this illustrious tree. A senior New York State Supreme Court clerk, a lifelong member of the NAACP, an active member of the Tribune Society, a founding member of the New York State Commission on Minorities, he was also an accomplished flutist and artist. His neighborhood activities, again, like [those of] his father, too plentiful to enumerate, were at the core of his being. His immersion in the community was total. In a word, he cared, and for that he paid the ultimate price at the hands of the defendant. So it is all fitting and proper to say that Alphonso Deal was a special person, and attention must be paid to the manner of his passing and that of all the vast host of murder victims this society is harvesting. And from this seat, my vantage point, the parade of woe seems endless. In the late 1950s, when I started in the Homicide Bureau of the district attorney's office, an annual body count of five hundred [New York City murder rate] was deemed appalling and unacceptable. We are now approaching two thousand murder victims a year in New York City. The rain of bitter, scalding tears shed by their loved ones could fill vats and flood the streets. Perhaps, in our commendable quest for that elusive quarry, the innocent accused, for perfection in an imperfect world, e.g., our criminal-justice system, we have honed and refined our laws to the point where they are no longer adequate to the needs of our society.

Matthew Byrne, Everett Hatcher, Robert Machate, Alphonso Deal were peace officers all and, yes, heroes, who died in the performance of their duties, giving to us the last beat of their hearts. Their ranks are being decimated. I do not intend to make this a bully pulpit for capital punishment, but some reassessment of our legal structure is in order, that is clear. And the oncoming decade of the nineties, given the incredible monetary and firepower the criminal hierarchies are amassing, is it to be greeted with the same degree of hand-wringing helplessness?

Mr. Brian O'Donohue [the prosecutor] has delineated the facts in the case, so I shall not dwell upon them, save to say that the deceased, Alphonso Deal, showed uncommon valor, what the generals call "two o'clock in the morning" courage, as when the enemy has penetrated your perimeter and all is in panic, a few good men will rise to the occasion. Alphonso Deal was of that mettle. He entered his home, retrieved his badge and his revolver, and went out to confront the aggressor. He knew Santana was on a rampage, that he had shot and wounded Ernest Davis. Deal never flinched, never faltered. He stood his ground, the width of Convent Avenue, across from Santana. He exhorted Santana, at least ten times according to the eyewitness Scott Dillard, "Peace officer, drop the gun!" Deal played it by the book, displaying the restraint, compassion, and humanity characteristic of him, in affording Santana every opportunity to resolve the matter peaceably. That was his undoing. Santana, true to his calling, feigned surrender, slipped his pistol into his waistband, and raised his shoulders high. As Deal approached, Santana shot him through the heart at point-blank, powder-burn range [within twenty-four inches of the victim]. The mortally wounded Deal got off four shots, all striking Santana. But the fates, in all their perversity, conspired that Alphonso Deal should expire, and we are left with Juan Santana, violent predicate felon, hale and hearty.

So here you stand, Mr. Santana, no stranger to our system, having been around the block four previous times, including a four-year stint upstate for robbery. And repentance and contrition do not appear to be your strong suit, at least as evinced thus far. I am sure they will make an appearance when you commence your petitions upstate after today [the defendant's application to parole for early release]. But your passivity and calm exterior belie the violence of your history, Santana, and the uninitiated, the strangers to our system, would be vexed by the "why" of it all. They might ponder the gravitational pull of the moon on the night in question, or the socioeconomic forces, or maybe you just had a bad day. Perhaps.

But you don't give a tinker's dam for any of this twaddle, Santana, again true to your calling; you're a bottom-line guy; you want to know the "what" of it all. I agree. We understand one another, Santana. What you did, what are you going to get for it? That is the business between us.

What you did was snuff out more than the life of the noble son of a noble house; you snuffed out a legacy. And for that vile, intentional murder [and the robbery of Teddy Laracuente] I sentence you to forty-five years to life. And I recommend, for whatever it is worth, that the defendant never be paroled.

I have indulged myself this, for me, unprecedented lengthy record because the case treats issues which are truly heartfelt on my part, and if, addressing them, I waxed simplistic or demagogic, such was not my intent, and if I dwelt more on the victim than I did on the defendant, such in this instance was my bent.

And to the family, friends, and colleagues of the late Alphonso Barclay Deal, may I impart my belated condolences. You were privileged to have a man of quality in your midst. We are all transients, but it is doubly hard when a man is cut down before his time. Perhaps you can derive comfort from the thought that, when and if Alphonso Senior and Alphonso Junior meet again, and I pray they do, in the great beyond, be assured there will be a hearty "Well done, son" forthcoming.

MURDER OF A HEALER: *THE PEOPLE OF THE STATE OF NEW YORK V. DARRYL WHITLEY*

Our justice system has been rightly concerned with developing rules to ensure a fair verdict. Before anyone is deprived of liberty, the utmost is done to guarantee a fair trial and just result. Naturally, this goal requires a priority of focus on defendants' rights. But what becomes of the forgotten victims? You will learn what it is like for their relatives, who must carry on after the devastation wrought by the criminal's acts. You will learn this through the speeches of the widow and father of Dr. John Chase Wood, who was senselessly mugged and shot dead by two robbers only blocks from Columbia Presbyterian Hospital, where he worked as a surgeon. As Dr. Wood lay dying in the street, he told an eyewitness, "My wife is pregnant. Tell my wife and baby I love them." His colleagues, surgeons at the hospital, cried under their surgical masks because they could not save his life.

The trial took place in February 2001, more than twenty years after the murder. Had it not been for the immense skill and perseverance of New York Police Department homicide detective Gerry Giorgio and Manhattan Assistant District Attorney Warren J. Murray Jr., who discovered evidence in the form of admissions made by the defendant to his former neighborhood friends, this case would have remained unsolved forever.

Excerpts from the Sentencing Speech of Dr. John Wood Sr.

On being informed of the opportunity to speak before this court, I was seized with trepidation, but I knew it should be done. Initially, I considered just speaking my heart and mind as thoughts surfaced, but realized [that] sadness and anxiety might confuse my thinking and lead me to stray. Therefore, I put down a guiding outline to keep me on course. Nonetheless, it is with considerable difficulty that as Dr. John C. Wood Jr.'s dad, . . . I stand before you as a stranger, and one of the victims of extensive collateral damage; but I would ask for your forbearance in permitting me to express a few observations and feelings relating to the murder of our firstborn son on one of your more beautiful New York streets that should be open to the safe passage and pleasure of all citizens, whether they be springtime lovers strolling at dusk, a lone walker, a mother with carriage and child, or a young physician/surgeon returning from night duty at a revered medical center after a hurried visit to his apartment to check on his pregnant wife, who was having some distress.

Surely I would be remiss if I were to fail even in their absence to express appreciation to the members of the jury for their citizen sacrifice, for taking time from their jobs, indeed taking [a] slice of their lives to do their duty with serious intent and integrity, when a copout might have been less stressful, even if dead wrong. And I would be remiss not to thank all the officers of the court for providing for justice.

Appreciation from our family is voiced to the DA's office, and specifically to assistant DAs Joel Seidemann and James Golding, and colleagues, including Warren Murray, for their professional and meticulous work, representing the people, the valid citizens of the County of New York, in the quest for and indeed the demand for justice. And a deep appreciation goes to Detective Giorgio and his colleagues for skill and informed persistence over all these many years, when a lesser man might have given way to fatigue or discouragement. Detective Giorgio received accolades but also slings and arrows along the way; and although [they are] remote from the courtroom, I would like to [express] gratitude to the medical family of the Columbia Presbyterian Medical Center and College of Physicians and Surgeons, for intangible and tangible support to our son John's wife and their son.

Permit me, please, a few moments to relate, only in part, the extent of the human damage wrought by the senseless murder of a fine young physician member of the Medical Center family, devoted to healing and preserving life. It is simply not possible to describe the disbelief and despair that visited [me] upon my arrival at Columbia Medical Center's emergency room, and being guided to a side room, empty except for a cold metal gurney.

There was my dead boy, cold lips, pale skin, lifeless, and gone. His murder was just too much for his mother, now seriously ill, to bear; and she became essentially dysfunctional for about five years, during which time our marital bonds were tested time and time again, as I routinely hid behind an eighteen-hour workday.

Our daughter very nearly lost her capacity to continue in her postgraduate studies. John's two brothers developed their own coping skills that are only now eroding. Our old, inviting farm-type home, the site of regular family gatherings at Thanksgiving and Christmas, became a symbol of loss, a symbol of death of the family member who was a catalyst for family love, loved by all and loving in return.

We are on a more even keel now, but the old joy is gone. Make no mistake, the talking heads are misinformed. There is no closure subsequent to the murder of your child, only a slow acceptance of the fact of it. Note that these comments don't even touch on the serious, permanent damage done to our murdered son's newborn male child, now twenty, or to his mother, Diana.

Let me speak to the matter of justice, not as an academic authority but from the perspective of considerable thought on the matter, and whatever wisdom or insight is gained in seventy-six years, and also from some contact with both victims and criminals, as a physician. There is no perfect justice, but it behooves us as individuals and as members of a community of whatever size to attempt to define, seek, and promote justice to the best of our ability.

Justice is a linchpin in a worthy society, justice for all. Every citizen is responsible for supporting justice. To the extent that we turn our back or fail to respond when we witness or become aware of a crime, to that same extent, we lose a portion of our own humanity. We become diminished, and when [such crimes are] multiplied, the very fabric of our society of whatever level, block, community, city, county, state, or nation, is threatened with fraying and unraveling.

If a person falls or is knocked down and we fail to assist, we are diminished. If a fellow citizen is murdered and we fail to respond because of fear, lethargy, or simply because it is more comfortable not to get involved, we lose value, and in time put ourselves at risk. If we lack guts, bullies will beat us.

Perhaps we should avoid the term "vengeance" in the Old Testament sense of "an eye for an eye, a tooth for a tooth, a life for a life," but until some greater insight comes, it is appropriate to try to match the severity of punishment to the severity of the crime.

Not all criminals are alike. Some guilty of petty crime will right themselves and become productive citizens. Some violent criminals are truly deranged, driven by phantom voices, delusions, and hallucinations, and these require special consideration.

But I would submit to you that most career criminals are not insane and are not driven to prey on the weak, infirm, or unsuspecting by having grown up in a poor household, but rather are an amoral subset of humanity, lacking conscience, psychopaths who conclude that crime pays and is a good deal easier than getting up every day and doing a job; it is easier to take from others than to give of themselves.

They may set out to rob, not expressly to kill, but they are prepared to kill, and kill they will, with about as much thought or care as exercised in downing a beer at the local bar or playing macho in bragging on a street corner of a conquest. They are not brave, but they are bullies.

These individuals may fake reform to the well-intentioned social worker, but they rarely change. For intervention to be successful, it must be inserted very early in life, not after they are successful in crime; that is to say, unpunished crime becomes addictive.

They consider the odds of beating the system good; and a few months, even a few years, of enforced incarceration means little more than a period of free room and board and a few extra pounds. They will return to predation of the innocent upon release.

Accordingly, as of now, there is no safe alternative to prolonged, if not permanent incarceration. These miscreants, destroyers of others' lives, cannot be identified by dress code, by color, by speech or accent; not by intellect or by power base; not even by gender; but [by] behavior, repeated transgressions against society.

When in a position of greater power, they may promulgate crimes against humanity: Hitler and Milosevic. You must know that Whitley and his buddy, Patrick McDowell, cowardly killers, are of this type.

It is ironic that during this trial period I descended alone in an elevator with Whitley, killer of my boy. He was quite certain that he would get away with his heinous crime, because the woman of color with her baby near the crime scene, terrified, could not clearly identify him. And, after all, cokiller McDowell beat the rap, free to rob, maim, or kill again.

Having served in uniform, and having been granted the privilege of reaching a truly senior age with whatever wisdom attends that estate, let me suggest to you that terrorists from within, rotten apples in our own mix, permitted to fester and contaminate, pose a greater danger to our nation over time than do foreign terrorists. And I believe this to be so even in the face of the horrific events of September 11.

Thus, all the considerable efforts of the People to achieve justice in the murder of a single individual are, at the end of the day, worth it. In closing, permit me to read to you two small poems written to my boy, if I can do it. And I don't think I can.

THE COURT: Dr. Wood, would you like to submit those
               to the Court instead?

DR. JOHN WOOD SR.:   Yes.

Ode to a Dead Son
    Young gracious healer dead
    By Saturday Night Special
    In the backyard of
    This place of healing
    Where his father also tread.
    Skilled colleagues could not see
    To stem the leak in time.

Everything inverted, inside out
Yes, it is my son!
Cold lips, pale skin, and all.
Oh God, attend an ancient plea
Although it can't be done
Take me, give back my boy
My work is largely done
Where his has just begun.
Oh death, here is thy sting.

Please Forward
    Come home.
    It doesn't matter when
    The door's unlocked.
    And kitchen light left on.
    Coke's in supply and cooky stock refreshed.
    Your room is spruced,
    With blanket folded down.
    So come on home.
    Compose a while or two.
    Or play your solo horn.
    Grunge coat is on the hook
    To walk the fields and wood,
    Space for your private thoughts,
    Alone; the old Lab's gone now.

    Do come on home.
    And rest here for a while.
    If not this locust time,
    Thanksgiving, or when the wreath is hung,
    Or next spring to share the budding,
    When bird-song fills the air.
    Just so you come sometime.

    The light's on in the kitchen,
    And will ever be so.

Excerpts from the Sentencing Speech of Dr. Diana Wood

Like my father-in-law, I also had a lot of anxiety and sadness about coming to talk here. And I wasn't quite sure what I was going to say, and I was advised to write it down. And I just have not been able. So you're probably going to get a more muddled talking than what my father-in-law said.

When I asked the probation officer what I was supposed to say, he said, "Tell them how this has changed your life." And what I have to say is that there isn't anything that it hasn't changed in my life. I'm a middle-aged woman now. It's twenty years ago that this happened, and I was twenty-three; I was married for five months and barely knew my husband, much less his family. I was newly pregnant.

It seemed like a nightmare that this happened. It just doesn't seem to happen to other people. And I'm glad I haven't known anybody else that it's happened to. My son, who's now twenty—he's a sophomore in college—has never had a father.

I went through a period of time when I thought that Mr. Whitley and Mr. McDowell couldn't really be blamed for what they had done because they obviously didn't value life, and maybe that was because their lives weren't valued and they didn't know what they were doing, as far as what kind of person he was, because John was one of those people that just . . . he just shone.

There was something about him; there weren't any people that disliked him, and people were drawn to him. And he was talented in many, many ways. He's the only person I knew who could calm me down when I got upset, by just being loving and kind.

I don't know if it was by coincidence, or one of God's plans, but I met my second husband, and we had a long-distance relationship for several months; and then he decided to move up to Massachusetts [with me]. And the day he moved up to Massachusetts, I got a call from the *New York Times* saying that the arrests had been made. And my entire second marriage has been colored, overshadowed by this trial, and retrial, and grand jury, and now this, which has gone on for seven years or more. And it just is not fair; it's not fair to my family.

Johnny [her son] was happy when my two younger children

were born, because he felt finally that he had a family that was more than just me. And he's felt really, really abandoned.

One thing I know is that after twenty years, perhaps people had forgotten what John was like as a person; that he was a person that had a family, a future, a wife, a child, parents, and that we lived in the neighborhood. We didn't live in the high-rises; we lived in the neighborhood. We took care of the people in the neighborhood.

He's the only person in the hospital, that I knew, that knew all of the people on the housekeeping staff, knew all of the aides, went to visit the page operators, so he could know who he was talking to. And all of those people were so kind to me afterward. I didn't know them, but they all knew who I was, and they all greeted me. They were just very loving and kind. The people at Columbia gave me an opportunity to become a physician, and through their support I continued to have a career as a physician, and to be able to provide to my children what my husband should have been able to provide, or at least both of us together. There were times when I wished Detective Jerry Giorgio had not been so dogged in his pursuit, because having to come and face this every time has been very, very hard. And even today I didn't want to come, because no matter what, I still don't have John. And that's all I wanted. It's very hard to see your family here, Darryl [defendant Whitley], because I don't want to deprive them of what my son has been deprived of forever.

6

AN UPHILL BATTLE

THE CASE AGAINST
THE SUBWAY VIGILANTE

IN THE EDGY PHYSICAL menace of violent crime pervading New York in the 1980s, even aggressive panhandling felt like outright robbery. Many New Yorkers felt that law enforcement was losing the battle against violent crime and that the courts seemed to favor criminals. The public perception was that predators, when arrested, reappeared on the streets too easily. With little effective police protection, the public felt outraged and betrayed. To many, the prosecution of Bernhard Goetz seemed another example of the state's taking the wrong side.

The case of thirty-six-year-old Bernhard Goetz, who shot four African-American teenagers in December 1984, became a forum for a national debate on race and crime in America. Nicknamed the "Subway Vigilante" by the tabloids, Goetz was, at least on the surface, an average man who used a gun to ward off a posse of apparent muggers, an innocent victim who chose to fight back. However, as the details of the event became clear, his actions—and persona—came under fire.

There was no great ingenuity involved in Goetz's claim of self-defense. The real challenge fell to the prosecutor, Gregory Waples, who not only had to deal with how popular opinion had likely prejudiced the jury against the prosecution but convince jurors to take the side of three proven criminals over that of a seemingly law-abiding man with a clean record.

THE PEOPLE OF THE STATE OF NEW YORK v. BERNHARD GOETZ

Excerpts from the Opening Statement of Prosecutor Gregory Waples

At first, December 22, 1984, seemed like a day much like any other day to the twenty passengers who were seated in the seventh car of a ten-car express train. The train had begun this particular journey at White Plains Road in the Bronx at 12:30 P.M., and about 1:40 P.M. this grimy, graffiti-smeared car was lurching and swaying in the noisy and peculiar rhythm that is most unique to the New York City subway system as the train holed underground from Fourteenth Street station toward its next stop at Chamber Street.

Most of the passengers in that car were preoccupied with their own affairs, minding an infant child, reading, dozing, or contemplating a holiday season. Suddenly, however, that day that had begun so ordinarily turned into a nightmare. Suddenly every passenger on that train was jolted by the electrifying and terrifying spectacle of Bernhard Goetz standing on his feet, firing shots in every direction from a gun he was holding in his hand.

In a brief convulsion of violence, the defendant deliberately shot and seriously wounded four young men who had been riding on that train long before he boarded that car. He also fired a fifth shot, which missed its intended human target, struck the metal wall of the subway car, and then ricocheted about the car's interior. Providence alone prevented any of the many innocent men, women, and children from being killed or seriously injured by the defendant's wild shooting.

By the defendant's own admission, tape-recorded admissions that will be played for you at this trial, at least two of the four young men whom he shot were trying to run away when he gunned them down. In fact, you will hear from medical evidence in this case that two of the four young men whom the defendant shot were shot in their backs, one squarely in the center of the back as he tried to flee, another shot under the shoulder blade by a shot that traveled laterally across his body.

By far the most severely injured of all of the four wounded youths was a nineteen-year-old by the name of Darrell Cabey. The evidence will show that the defendant fired two separate shots at Darrell Cabey. That same evidence will show, beyond the slightest shadow of a doubt, that when the defendant fired the second of these shots at Cabey, Darrell Cabey was sitting down on the subway seat, much like you are sitting in your jury seats now, absolutely helpless and doing absolutely nothing to threaten Bernhard Goetz.

Shockingly, you will hear the defendant admit [that] before this last shot was fired at the seated and helpless Darrell Cabey, the defendant advanced on him as he was sitting in the seat and said, "You look all right, here's another."

The bullet which actually did strike Darrell Cabey caused massive injuries to his body; it severed his spinal cord. As a consequence, since December 22, 1984, Darrell Cabey has been paralyzed from above his waist down and can look forward to the rest of his life, if that's the best way to characterize it, living in a wheelchair.

Now, during the voir dire [jury selection] you heard Mr. Slotnick [Barry Slotnick, Goetz's attorney] constantly refer to the people as "hoodlums." But the resort to pejorative characterizations—shock words, really—cannot paper over the fact, which will be proved largely through the defendant's own tape-recorded admissions, which you will hear, that the shooting of Darrell Cabey was little more than a cold-blooded attempted execution and is [as] far from being a legitimate act of self-defense as heaven is from hell.

You're probably wondering why these four young men were so deliberately and so savagely shot on December 22 and why all of the innocent men, women, and children in that subway car were subjected to the terrorism of the defendant's reckless gunplay.

Although you have not yet heard a single witness testify in this case, each of you has some opinion as to the root causes of this tragedy. We know from the voir dire that you folks have not been living on Mars for the last two years [and] that each of you has seen, read, or heard accounts of this case from friends, from the media, from the people you work with. For whatever reason, be it right or wrong, this case has touched a raw nerve of the American anatomy. For whatever reason, this case has not become simply a media sensation but something of a cultural phenomenon.

Now, it's not my aim or purpose to debunk myths that cling . . . like moss to the branches of [a] tree; this is, after all, a court of law, not a court of public opinion. But it surely is my responsibility, as the prosecutor representing the state in this case, to peel away the layers of misconception that may tend to obscure the truth, so that the jury, the sole and exclusive judges of the facts in this case, can really understand what happened in this subway car on December 22.

The public at large need not be concerned with nice things like the truth. The public at large can believe whatever it wishes, whatever is expedient, whatever conforms to its preconceived attitudes about the shootings.

The facts that will be presented are your raw materials. Logic, the law, and your common sense are the tools that you will use to shape the evidence into a fair and just verdict. Concentrate on the facts in this case. Forget about the headlines that scream from our tabloids. Ignore the noisy and dogmatic opinions of those persons who simply have not troubled to learn or do not care where the truth lies.

Pay no heed to those persons who, through appeals to your heart rather than your heads, seek to divert your attention from the central issue in this case, the issue of whether the law will exonerate the defendant, who, in the name of self-defense, shoots people in the back who are trying to run away and fires—"You look okay, here's another"—[a] fifth shot at the seated and helpless Darrell Cabey.

The evidence will demonstrate that while the defendant has claimed that this subway shooting was a legitimate act of self-defense, the truth is much more vulgar and infinitely more complex. You must confront the reality that these shootings were totally unnecessary, vicious, and even sadistic acts of violence undertaken not by a typical New Yorker but by an emotionally troubled individual.

Mr. Cabey will not testify, because while he was in the hospital fighting for his life, struggling to recover from the gunshot wound the defendant inflicted, which paralyzed him for life, he suffered a respiratory arrest. Darrell Cabey actually stopped breathing while in the hospital and was deprived of oxygen. Mr. Cabey plunged into a deep coma, and while in that state he suffered irreversible brain damage.

You will hear testimony from the other three individuals the defendant shot, persons who have recovered from their wounds. You will also hear testimony from a number of innocent bystanders who, as fate will have it, simply happened to be in that subway car on December 22, when the gunfire erupted.

Most importantly, you will hear two lengthy tape-recorded statements that the defendant made in New Hampshire shortly after he surrendered, nine days after the shooting. These tapes will be graphic and horrifying depictions explaining, in excruciating detail, exactly how the defendant shot these four men in succession.

These tapes will prove so incriminating that you will be able to forget about virtually all of the other evidence in the case and simply find the defendant guilty on the basis of his own words. Thus you can totally ignore, if you wish, the testimony of one or more or any or all the young men who were shot by Mr. Goetz.

These tapes will provide you with rich insight into not just how but why the subway shootings took place [and] will open a window through which you can peer into the defendant's mind. They will reveal a very troubled man with a passionate but very twisted and self-righteous sense of right and wrong.

Indeed these tapes will make it clear, almost as a revelation, that when the defendant gunned down these four men, he was acting not to protect himself from a robbery or an assault but offensively and aggressively, with a deliberate and cold-blooded intention, to kill or cripple the men he was shooting at. You will hear the defendant say that when he fired his gun, he "wanted to kill those guys, to make them suffer in any way that I could."

Listening to these hours of tapes, you will come to realize that Troy Canty, Barry Allen, James Ramseur, Darrell Cabey were shot not so much for what they did in the subway on December 22, 1984—for even by the defendant's version, they did very little. Instead you will come to realize that these four young men were really shot because in the defendant's mind they were the kind of people he hated with a ferocious and all-consuming passion. Quite simply, the evidence will show that on December 22, 1984, for no legally sufficient reason, the defendant decided that Troy Canty, Barry Allen, James Ramseur, and Darrell Cabey deserved to die.

And so on that busy Saturday afternoon, in front of half a carload of subway passengers, the defendant tried to kill those four young men, not because it was necessary as an act of self-defense [but] because, according to the defendant's twisted sense of values, this was right and this was just.

Who are Troy Canty, Barry Allen, James Ramseur, and Darrell Cabey? Although the defendant tries to tar them with a single brush, in fact these four young individuals are separate human beings such as you sixteen persons [twelve jurors, four alternates]. All these young men were unemployed. They lived with their families, who were themselves poor. They were high-school dropouts; they used drugs, some occasionally, others almost as a matter of life's routine. Prior to these shootings, some of them had been convicted on a number of occasions of petty offenses, and since the shootings two of them have been sent to prison for more serious crimes.

In short, while these four men had not been dealt a very good hand in this game of life, in all candor . . . they had not labored particularly diligently to overcome the disadvantages of the life in which they were born, and in all probability you folks will discover during the course of the trial that you have little in common with these four young men. Their lifestyle is totally alien to anything you have experienced in any point of your life. And this clash of values will present you, the jury, with a real personal challenge, because just as it is your constitutional duty to accord Mr. Goetz a fair trial, so, too, is it your duty as jurors in this case to accord any witness[es] a fair hearing when they come to the witness stand.

I don't mean to suggest, folks, that you must accept uncritically any testimony that is given by any witness from this witness stand. But I do presume that each of you will listen to each witness with an open mind, even a witness that you may loathe, and reserve judgment on that witness until all of the evidence is in.

If you conclude [that] the defendant overstepped the boundaries of reasonable and legitimate self-defense, you will not simply shrug your shoulders and say, irrespective of how criminal the defendant's conduct may have been, "Well, these persons deserved what they got, and that's the end of the matter."

After all, at least as I remember in this democracy, the most loathsome man has the same right to live as the best, and, at least, in theory, the law protects everyone from unlawful violence regardless of his character.

The evidence will show that on the morning of December 22, 1984, Troy Canty, Barry Allen, James Ramseur, and Darrell Cabey, who are all acquainted with each other but who are not close friends, came together more by chance than by preconceived plan. Troy Canty and Barry Allen lived in the same building in [a] housing project, and that Saturday they decided to travel from the Bronx down to Manhattan to make some easy money breaking into video machines and stealing the quarters from the coin boxes. Troy Canty and Barry Allen were particularly adept at this, because they have done it for many years, almost a daily basis. This pastime was also attractive because it had low legal risks. Both Allen and Canty had been arrested on many occasions for breaking into these video machines. They never spent more than sixty days in jail for this kind of larceny.

In the projects they met up with Darrell Cabey and James Ramseur, who decided to go along with the two on this day.

The only tool that is needed to pry open the coin box of these video machines is an ordinary screwdriver, and this group had three of those that morning before they set off for lower Manhattan.

At 149th Street and Grand Concourse, this group of four boarded a downtown train. During the thirty-minute ride to lower Manhattan, where they intended to debark from the train and search out video machines from which to steal the quarters, this group of four was more or less monopolizing the rear quarter of the subway car, talking boisterously, loudly, engaging in horseplay. Undoubtedly, some passengers may have seemed annoyed by the rowdy behavior of these teenagers, but that's all it was, an annoyance to more genteel sensibilities, until 4:00 P.M., that is, when Bernhard Goetz boarded this train at Fourteenth Street.

The defendant was a self-employed electronics technician who lived on Fourteenth Street. This particular Saturday afternoon, he became frustrated with an electronics project he was working on at home and decided to go to lower Manhattan and visit some friends to share a pre-Christmas drink.

The defendant, however, was not your average subway passenger. This defendant is something of an enigma, a contradiction, a man who on the inside is quite different from what he appears to be on the outside. For beneath this quiet and simple and scientific, aloof exterior that you have seen in court for the past several weeks lies the real and very complex Bernhard Goetz. He is an incendiary mixture of raw nervous tension, of incredibly rigid opinion, and of explosive, self-righteous anger.

Bernhard Goetz was a tormented man, an emotional powder keg one spark away from a violent explosion, and, greatly adding to the danger that this walking powder keg would reach his flash point and explode, was the fact that on this particular day the defendant armed himself with a loaded, illegal, unlicensed handgun that he kept with him in his apartment, one of three handguns, illegal, unlicensed, that he kept in his apartment.

The defendant, in early 1981, was mugged as he was entering the Canal Street subway station in lower Manhattan and thereafter, ostensibly for reasons of self-defense, he began to carry an illegal firearm. Indeed, the evidence will show [that] the defendant's attachment to this gun developed into some kind of strange obsession that ultimately came to dominate this man's life.

According to the defendant, although he felt safe traveling [to] New Jersey or Connecticut or upstate New York without the pistol, he could not set one foot outside of [his] apartment [in] New York City without having an illegal handgun, strapped to a holster, on his waist.

The defendant himself came to feel that when he went out in New York, even in the coldest days in the winter, he could not wear gloves on his hands, because "if you wear gloves, you can't get to the gun."

As a consequence of his mugging incident in 1981, the defendant acquired what can only be called fanatical contempt for the criminal-justice system in New York City and the treatment that the criminal-justice system accords people that the defendant regards as criminals, hoodlums, and thugs. Convinced that the criminal-justice system had totally collapsed, this defendant, with moralistic and self-righteous zeal, resolved to take the law into his own hands; like a self-appointed vigilante answerable only to a higher call, this defendant determined to do on his own what he felt that the laws could not do.

After the police arrested one of three persons who mugged the defendant in 1981 and informed the defendant [that], because of a lack of evidence, they would be unable to charge him with a crime that the defendant felt was appropriate for the circumstances of this case, you will hear that the defendant actually offered to lie, so that this criminal, this person whom the defendant regarded as a hoodlum, could be charged with a crime that he felt was right and just, irrespective of what the law said. The defendant offered to do that because of his own warped vision of right and wrong. The end, getting the criminal, justified whatever means was pursued to accomplish that end.

Now, these incidents mark the first steps in the evolution of the defendant from crime victim to avenging angel. Providing real and meaningful insight to exactly why this subway shooting took place is another encounter which you will hear the defendant describe in a video-recorded statement.

This incident began one evening on Sixth Avenue, when he was walking down the street and found himself harassed and threatened by a person that the defendant described as a crazy kid on drugs. You will hear the defendant admit that, although it was totally unnecessary to do so as a matter of self-defense, he pulled his illegally possessed firearm on this person. Why? The defendant's explanation, why he pulled that gun on that hapless drug addict that night is that, to use his own words, he was "pissed." You will also hear the defendant's further explanation that this hapless drug addict, who was little more than a public nuisance, "deserved to die."

In this defendant's jaundiced mind, Troy Canty, Barry Allen, James Ramseur, and Darrell Cabey were four hoodlums who deserved to die, who the legal system would not punish. So when one of them inadvertently provided the provocation, provided the sparks, this human powder keg went off. What was this spark? What exactly drove the defendant to empty the handgun he was carrying into the bodies of four human beings on December 22?

When the train arrived, he stepped into the same car which Canty and Allen and Ramseur and Cabey had been riding when they boarded the train in the Bronx. The defendant walked by these four young men and sat down in close proximity to them. Moments after the train left Fourteenth Street, it began accelerating toward its next stop at Chambers Street. Troy Canty then did a very stupid thing, which very nearly cost him his life.

Troy Canty knew, from his considerable experience, that the safest and easiest way to obtain money from video machines was first to distract the owners into a false sense of security, by inserting coins in the machine and begin to play it in a legitimate manner. But since neither Canty nor his companions had any money this Saturday afternoon, Canty did what he had done on similar occasions in the past.

He approached the subway passenger or a pedestrian on the street for a handout.

Canty stood up from his seat, walked a few feet across the aisle to where the defendant was sitting, and stood directly in front of him and said, in a more or less normal tone of voice, "Give me five dollars" or "Can I have five dollars?"

Canty will tell you that the idea to approach the defendant was his and his alone, a spur-of-the-moment gesture, directed toward the defendant because the defendant was the nearest passenger. Canty will also tell you that Barry Allen, James Ramseur, and Darrell Cabey were in no way responsible for his decision to approach the defendant.

When Canty went over to the defendant, he had no weapon or instrument in his hands and had nothing in his pockets. In the tape-recorded statements, the defendant appears to claim that at the time Troy Canty approached him, Canty's companions also surrounded the defendant in a menacing circle.

Although, by the defendant's own admission, none of that group had any kind of weapon in their hands, although only Troy Canty spoke to the defendant, although none of these persons ever laid so much as a finger on the defendant, you will hear the defendant say [that] at that moment he became convinced that these four total strangers, for no apparent reason, were suddenly going to administer a vicious beating to him in full view of all of the other subway passengers in that car. And it was in response to this threat that the defendant drew his gun and began shooting in rapid succession at each of the four youths.

The reality is something quite a bit different. The evidence will show that at no time during this entire encounter was the defendant surrounded by a group of four persons crowding closely around him. At least two of the four young men, whom the defendant ultimately wound up shooting, never even approached the defendant, much less encircled him in a threatening manner. Before being shot, James Ramseur and Darrell Cabey remained in essentially the same position in the car that they had occupied while riding down from the Bronx.

Now, mind you, it is not the prosecution's contention that Troy Canty was acting appropriately in going up to the defendant and asking for money. It is not the prosecution's contention that the defendant had no cause to be apprehensive when he was approached on the subway and asked for money by this total stranger.

But the right to be concerned for your safety does not necessarily imply the right to lash out in very ambiguous circumstances, or to go further and to actually take the offensive and try and kill four human beings.

And indeed, this defendant knew particularly well how effective a deterrent his pistol could be, simply by drawing his pistol, because, on at least two prior occasions, the defendant had successfully repelled what he perceived to be deadly threats from individuals menacing him simply by drawing his gun and brandishing it without firing a single shot. Of all people, this defendant should have known that it was totally unnecessary to fire his gun and the bloodshed that took place was totally needless.

Avoiding bloodshed was one of the last things that this defendant had on his mind. Instead, as the defendant's own tape-recorded conversations will show, he had made up his mind to shoot these four persons and to kill them even before he fired the first bullet. You will hear him say, "My intention was to do anything

I could to hurt them. My intention was to murder them, to hurt them, to make them suffer as much as possible."

With Troy Canty still standing in front of him after asking for five dollars, the defendant stood up without any kind of resistance and drew the gun, and then, without any warning at all, fired one shot directly at Troy Canty, striking him in the chest. And as Troy Canty crumpled to the ground, you will hear the defendant admit that he realized that the other youths were then running for their own lives, having successfully defused whatever situation he felt he was imperiled by. Does the defendant stop shooting? To the contrary. After bringing down Troy Canty, the person who was actually standing in front of him and asking for money, the defendant immediately turns his sights on Barry Allen.

The defendant noticed that Allen "tried to run through the crowd, and, of course, he had nowhere to run because the crowd would stop him." Allen was shot squarely in the back, at the base of the neck.

So, after firing the first two shots at Canty and Allen, the defendant pivoted to his right and turned his attention upon James Ramseur and Darrell Cabey, who were still in the same section of the car that they had occupied for the last thirty minutes.

You will hear the defendant in his own words say that Ramseur "tried to run through the wall of the train, but he had nowhere to go."

Yet, despite the fact that James Ramseur was also trying to run for his life, the defendant pulled the trigger a third time, and that bullet ripped through Ramseur's arm, pierced his chest, and caused severe internal injuries, including loss of his spleen.

The defendant fired the last two bullets at Darrell Cabey. What happened to Darrell Cabey was positively grotesque. Cabey was holding on to the subway strap, pretending that he was not with the three companions who had been shot down previously, but the defendant fired his fourth shot at Cabey, although Cabey is not looking at him. That shot in all probability misses. The defendant quickly turns his glance away from Cabey and looks at Ramseur and Allen and Canty, and determines that they're cold. That's his word, "cold."

And at that point the defendant turns his back, and this time he notices that Darrell Cabey is not standing holding on to the strap but is now sitting in one of those small seats at the end of the car. And the defendant notices that Darrell Cabey does not appear to be injured. He advanced toward where Cabey is sitting in that seat, and he says, "You look all right, here's another," before firing the fifth shot—the last shot—almost at point-blank range into Cabey.

Cabey was literally at that moment a sitting duck. One of two shots, in all likelihood that last shot—struck Darrell Cabey in the back, underneath the left shoulder blade, and traveled laterally across his body, piercing his left lung and severing his spinal cord, then damaging his right lung before coming to rest in the right side of his body. The shot that did not hit Darrell Cabey pounded into the metal wall of the subway car, then bounced around the car's interior, fortunately not striking any of the innocent passengers.

The defendant was not content to paralyze Darrell Cabey for life. Instead you will hear the defendant's explanation for not having killed Darrell Cabey: "If I were thinking a little more clearly, if I was a little more under self-control—I was so out of control—I would have put the barrel of the gun against his forehead and fired."

You will hear the defendant complain about running out of bullets: "If I had had more bullets, I would have shot them again and again and again." You will hear the defendant describe, as the smoke began to clear in the subway car, this burning rage [that] propelled him toward one final act of sadistic vengeance.

You will hear the defendant describe how this burning rage actually caused him to reach into his pockets for a set of keys he carried, because at that moment it was the defendant's intention to gouge Troy Canty's eyes out with that set of keys, to torture this wounded individual some more.

Fortunately, that ultimate act of mayhem never took place, because almost as quickly as it set on, this rage began to subside, and at that point, with bodies strewn all over the subway car, with two people lying wounded with bullets in the back and one person paralyzed for life, the defendant's survival instinct took over. He ran away. Not just from the subway car but from New York City. Even before the blood was dry in the subway car, the defendant was renting an automobile, and later that Saturday afternoon, he drove up to New England. In an attempt to conceal his involvement in this crime, he burned the clothing he was wearing that day and broke up the gun that he had used to shoot these four individuals and discarded it in the woods.

A few days later, the defendant returned to New York City to take care of some personal business. The defendant knew he was involved in the subway shooting, and, concerned that the police would come to his apartment and find additional illegal handguns he had concealed there in his stash, the defendant went to a downstairs neighbor, Myra Friedman, with a serious package. After giving Mrs. Friedman this package, the defendant then rented another car and returned to New England where on December 31, 1984, he walked into the Concord, New Hampshire, Police Department and announced he was the person who shot four young persons nine days previously.

Later that day the defendant made these two lengthy tape-recorded statements that will be played for you.

When [the package he gave Mrs. Friedman] was unwrapped, it was found to contain a nine-millimeter semiautomatic handgun and a .38-caliber revolver, similar to the gun that was used in the subway shootings. These were guns in addition to and separate from the weapon he used to try to kill Troy Canty, Barry Allen, James Ramseur, and Darrell Cabey.

This trial is not a referendum on crime in New York, nor are you here to pass moral judgment on the efficiency of the criminal system or on the lifestyles of any of the New York City inhabitants.

What you are here to decide is whether New York law will condone one individual walking up to another person, when he is sitting in a seat and totally helpless, and saying, "You look all right, here's another," before firing a shot point-blank that leaves that individual paralyzed for life. You are here to decide whether the idea of equal justice under the law for all people is a reality or is an empty dream.

Keep an open mind throughout this trial. Listen to all of the evidence fairly and objectively. That's all I ask of you. And if you do that, as each of you has promised to do, then I, for one, will have no cause to complain.

POSTSCRIPT

The jury acquitted Bernhard Goetz of twelve out of thirteen charges, convicting him only of possessing an unlicensed pistol. Mr. Waples could not even convince the jury to convict the defendant, at the very least, of the clearly unnecessary shooting of Darrell Cabey.

Mr. Waples gave an opening statement that had the feel of a closing statement, addressing the jury directly and trying to convey a sense of conclusion even before the first witness was called. Using his excellent powers of description, he evoked the crime scene in hopes of neutralizing the concerns of the New York City–hardened jury over what they perceived to be a wretched state of public safety and the faltering justice system. He emphasized the strongest aspect of his case, Bernard Goetz's own description of the incident in saying to the scared and helpless Darrell Cabey, before shooting him, "You look all right, here's another." Though he used ingenious strategies, Mr. Waples was pitted against what proved to be the insurmountable hurdle of popular sentiment.

During the course of the trial, James Ramseur, one of the four victims, at first refused to testify, his refusal resulting in several contempt citations by the judge. When he finally did take the stand, defense attorney Barry Slotnick asked Ramseur, "When was the last time . . . that you committed a crime against a human being?" Ramseur answered, "When was the last time you got a drug dealer off?"

Judge Crane, in sentencing Ramseur for contempt, told him, "Your conduct has played right into the hands of Mr. Goetz's lawyer. He owes you a vote of thanks. The jurors saw your contemptuous conduct. That can never be erased from their minds." As these words suggest, at the end of the day, Mr. Waples could not win this uphill battle of fighting the prevailing public opinion's revulsion with violent crime.

7

IN THE NAME OF 6 MILLION
THE TRIAL OF ADOLF EICHMANN

SS-OBERSTURMBANNFÜHRER KARL ADOLF EICHMANN (1906–62) was head of the Department for Jewish Affairs in the Gestapo from 1941 to 1945 and was chief of operations during the deportation of 3 million Jews to extermination camps. It was Eichmann who organized the Wannsee Conference of January 1942, which focused on issues related to the "final solution of the Jewish question." From this point Eichmann assumed the leading role in the deportation of European Jews to the death camps, as well as in the plunder of their personal property.

At the end of the war, Eichmann was arrested and confined to an American internment camp, but he managed to escape unrecognized. He fled to Argentina and lived under the assumed name of Ricardo Klement for ten years, until Israeli Mossad agents abducted him in 1960 to stand trial in Jerusalem. The controversial and highly publicized trial lasted from April 2 to August 14, 1961.

Below are excerpts of the opening statement of prosecutor Gideon Hausner, in which he powerfully recreates one of history's most horrific events.

THE STATE OF ISRAEL v. ADOLF EICHMANN

Excerpts from the Opening Statement of
Prosecutor Gideon Hausner

When I stand before you here, judges of Israel, to lead the prosecution of Adolf Eichmann, I am not standing alone. With me are 6 million accusers. But they cannot rise to their feet and point an accusing finger toward him who sits in the dock and cry, "I accuse," for their ashes are piled up on the hills of Auschwitz and the fields of Treblinka and are strewn in the forests of Poland. Their graves are scattered throughout the length and breadth of Europe. Their blood cries out, but their voice is not heard. Therefore I will be their spokesman, and in their name I will unfold the awesome indictment.

The history of the Jewish people is steeped in suffering and tears. Pharaoh in Egypt decided to "afflict them with their burdens" and to cast their sons into the river; Haman's decree was "to destroy, to slay, and to cause them to perish." Chmielnicki slaughtered them in multitudes; they were butchered in Petlura's pogroms.

Yet never down in the entire bloodstained road traveled by this people, never since the first days of its nationhood, has any man arisen who succeeded in dealing it such grievous blows as did Hitler's iniquitous regime and Adolf Eichmann as its executive arm for the extermination of the Jewish people. In all human history, there is no other example of a man against whom it would be possible to draw up such a bill of indictment as has been read here.

At the dawn of history, there were examples of wars of extermination, when one nation assaulted another with intent to destroy, when, in the storm of passion and battle, peoples were slaughtered, massacred, or exiled. But only in our generation has a nation attacked an entire defenseless and peaceful population, men and women, graybeards, children and infants, incarcerated them behind electrified fences, imprisoned them in concentration camps, and resolved to destroy them utterly.

Murder has been with the human race since the days when Cain killed Abel; it is no novel phenomenon. But we have had to wait till this twentieth century to witness with our own eyes a new kind of murder: not the result of the momentary ebullition of passion or the dark-ening of the soul but of a calculated decision and painstaking planning; not through the evil design of an individual but through a mighty crim-inal conspiracy involving thousands; not against one victim whom an assassin may have decided to destroy but against an entire nation.

In this trial we shall also encounter a new kind of killer, the kind that exercises his bloody craft behind a desk and only occasionally does the deed with his own hands. True, we have certain knowledge of only one incident in which Adolf Eichmann actually beat to death a Jewish boy who had dared to steal fruit from a peach tree in the yard of his Budapest home. But it was his word that put gas chambers into action; he lifted the telephone, and railroad cars left for the extermination centers. His signature it was that sealed the doom of thousands and tens of thousands. He had but to give the order, and at his command the troopers took the field to rout Jews out of their neighborhoods, to beat and torture them and chase them into ghettoes, to pin the badges of shame on their breasts, to steal their property, till finally, after torture and pillage, after everything had been wrung out of them, when even their hair had been taken, they were transported en masse to the slaughter. Even the corpses were still of value: The gold teeth were extracted and the wedding rings removed.

We shall find Eichmann describing himself as a fastidious person, a white-collar worker. To him the decree of extermination was just another written order to be executed; yet he was the one who planned, initiated, and organized, who instructed others to spill this ocean of blood and to use all the means of murder, theft, and torture.

He must bear the responsibility therefore, as if it was he who with his own hands knotted the hangman's noose, who lashed the victims into the gas chambers, who shot in the back and pushed into the open pit every single one of the millions who were slaugh-tered. Such is his responsibility in the eyes of the law, and such is his responsibility according to every standard of conscience and morality. His accomplices in the crime were neither gangsters nor men of the underworld but the leaders of the nation, including pro-fessors and scholars, robed dignitaries with academic degrees, lin-guists, men of enlightenment, the intelligentsia.

This murderous decision, taken deliberately and in cold blood, to annihilate a nation and blot it out from the face of the earth, is so shocking that one is at a loss for words to describe it. Words were created to express what man's reason can conceive and his heart can contain, and here we are dealing with actions that transcend our human grasp. Yet this is what did happen: Millions were condemned to death, not for any crime, not for anything they had done, but only because they belonged to the Jewish people.

The unprecedented crime, carried out by Europeans in the twentieth century, led to the adoption of the concept of a crime unknown to human annals even during the darkest ages—the crime of genocide.

There was only one man who had been concerned almost entirely with the Jews, whose business had been their destruction, whose place in the establishment of the iniquitous regime had been limited to them. That was Adolf Eichmann.

Men still ask themselves, and they will certainly continue to ask in days to come: How could it have happened? How was it possible in the middle of the twentieth century? We shall endeavor, however briefly, to describe the background in an attempt to explain what is perhaps altogether inexplicable by the standards of ordinary reason.

Hitler, his regime and crimes, did not come to power as a result merely of a unique combination of circumstances. It may be doubted whether, in general, there are accidents in human history, for historical processes are usually the product of many developments, like many streams flowing each in its own channel until they unite into a mighty river. They will come together only if their flow is in the same general direction.

No doubt various events contributed to the rise of Nazism: the defeat of Germany in World War I, the subsequent economic difficulties, lack of leadership and futile party divisions, fratricidal strife and disunion; all these impelled the German people, discriminated and groping, to turn its eyes toward the false prophet. But Hitler would not have been able to remain in power and to consolidate in his support all the strata of the German people, including most of the intelligentsia—to get the support of so many university professors and professional men, the civil service, and the whole army—if the road to his leadership had not already been paved. Not even the oppressive regime of the concentration camps and the atmosphere created by the terror so rapidly activated against all opposition by the hooligans of the SS and the SA are adequate alone to explain the enthusiastic and devoted support he received from the majority of the nation, unless it had been preceded by an extensive spiritual preparation.

Professor Wilhelm Roepke of the University of Marburg stated this clearly at the end of World War II: "There have been Hitlers everywhere and at all times, but it is Germany's shame that so miserable a figure could become her leader. In order to germinate, the seed of Nazism had to find a favorable soil. It found it in the German Reich and the Germans, such as they had become in their political, spiritual, economic, and social history."

Hitler did in fact liberate the hatred of the Jew which was in the hearts of large sections of the German people, intensify it, and stimulate it into greater activity. The germ of anti-Semitism was already there; he fed it with appropriate conditions and transformed it into the source of an epidemic. The Jew was pilloried as a supporter of Communism and therefore an enemy of the German people. In the same breath, he was accused of being a capitalist—and therefore an enemy of the workers. National Socialism had found an object of hostility appropriate to both halves of its name, and it set him up as a target for both national enemy and class hatred. The Jew was also a ready target through which the attention of the public could be diverted from other problems. This, too, was an age-old weapon which had been used by many anti-Semites down the ages.

A confused and blinded world was not alarmed by this campaign of hatred and the denial of human rights. It did not understand that the persecution of the Jews was only the beginning of an onslaught on the entire world. By a natural development and led by the same master feeling of hate, all the cities of England would be subjected to the same fate as bombed Coventry.

We should point out that there were in Germany tens of thousands of scientists and ecclesiastics, statesmen and authors and ordinary people, who dared to help the Jews, to raise their heads in opposition to the iniquitous regime and even to rebel against it, and among them were men whose names were famous in German science and culture. But after all is said and done, these were a small minority. The decisive majority of the German people made peace with the new regime and were phlegmatic witnesses of the most terrible crime ever perpetrated in human history. And when Goebbels, the Nazi propaganda minister, made a public bonfire of the creations of men of the spirit, Jewish and non-Jewish—the works of such men as Heinrich Heine, Thomas Mann, [Jakob] Wassermann, [Albert] Einstein, [Sigmund] Freud, Upton Sinclair, H. G. Wells, [Emile] Zola, Havelock Ellis, and scores of others—because they were "in opposition to the German spirit," he proclaimed, "Now the soul of the German people can again express itself. These flames not only illuminate the final end of an old era; they also light up the new." The majority of German intellectuals were ready to warm themselves at those bonfires and to accept as their spiritual guide the false glitter of these flames.

There is a Hebrew saying: "The wicked, even at the gate of hell, do not repent." In April 1945, at the moment of his death agonies, when the Soviet cannons were thundering in the streets of Berlin, when Hitler sat imprisoned in the cellar of the Reichskanzlei, his entire world in ruins and his country stricken, over the corpses of 6 million Jews—at that moment the Führer wrote his political last will and testament. He bequeathed to his people the injunction of eternal hatred for the Jews, and he concluded, "Above all, I enjoin the leaders of the government and the people to uphold the racial laws to the limit and to resist mercilessly the poisoner of all nations, international Jewry." Even from beyond the grave, Hitler was still trying to sow the seeds of hatred and destruction for the Jewish people.

After every manhunt, in which thousands and tens of thousands of Jews were sent to their deaths and others would manage to escape or hide, a rumor would be deliberately spread by the Nazis that this was the last operation of the kind, that the survivors would no longer be touched. And many individuals of the type that cling to any hope, those who could not or would not believe that the fate of all the Jews had indeed been sealed, or who were exhausted with hunger, misery, and suffering, would venture out of their hiding places or return from the forests, only to be captured by their persecutors in a new manhunt. The tiger played with his victims at his own sweet will.

The Accused

The accused was born in 1906 and as a child moved with his parents to Austria. In 1932 he became a member of the Nazi Party and the SS. Of course, Eichmann joined the SS and remained in the organization of his own free will.

In 1934 we meet him, with the rank of Unterscharführer, in the concentration camp at Dachau, which served as a school for all promising SS men. Dachau was the refining crucible, the school of violence and horrors, through which future Nazi leaders had to pass; it was there that they were taught the doctrine of hate, were compelled to beat prisoners and put them to death.

With the conquest of Austria in March 1938, Eichmann was sent back to the country of his childhood. At that time Nazi policy concentrated on compelling Jews to emigrate, and Eichmann devoted himself to furthering this policy with great zeal, so that after a short while his work was brought to the notice of the ministers of the Reich as the model to follow in the liquidation of the Jews. In Vienna the process was organized on the assembly-line principle: A man came into the office still a citizen, with a status in society, a job, a home, and property. After being thoroughly processed, he came out an emigrant, his property gone—in part confiscated and in part invested by government order in frozen currency of little value—his apartment registered for confiscation, no longer employed, his children no longer pupils in school, the only thing in his possession a travel certificate marked "Jude" [Jew], which granted him permission to leave Austria by a certain date, never to return.

In March 1941 we meet Eichmann as head of a section of the Gestapo concerned with Jewish affairs and the expulsion of populations. This was the office he continued to hold until the tragic end of European Jewry. But he was also [Reinhard] Heydrich's special plenipotentiary for the final "solution of the Jewish question." Eichmann was the official executor of the extermination program, with enormous authority in the Reich, which now included Austria and the Protectorate and all the occupied countries. In short, he reached out to every corner to carry out "the final solution," using the methods he found most effective, convenient and suitable to local conditions.

Adolf Eichmann will tell you that he carried out the orders of his superiors. But the conscience of the world, speaking with the voice of the International Military Tribunal [at Nuremberg], has declared that orders contrary to the principles of conscience and morality, orders that violate the essential imperatives on which human society is based and negate the basic rules without which men cannot live together, such orders constitute no defense, legal or moral. Therefore, in the light of this ruling, our own law in Israel has denied the accused the right to submit such a defense.

We shall prove to the court that he went far beyond his actual orders, that he took the initiative in extermination operations for which he had been given no orders whatsoever and carried them out only because of his devotion to his task, in which he saw his life's mission. When, in the summer of 1944, [Miklós] Horthy in Hungary did not want to cooperate with the exterminators, Eichmann managed by stealth to push through another death train from Kistarcsa to Auschwitz. He even used the cunning stratagem of convening a meeting of the leaders of Budapest Jewry at his headquarters so that they should be unable, at the last moment, to plead with Horthy for the frustration of Eichmann's designs.

Eichmann engaged in the work of slaughter not in apathy but with a clear mind, fully conscious and aware of what he was doing, and believing that it was the right and proper thing to do; that was why he acted with all his heart and soul. We shall prove that even after the downfall of the Nazi monster, when the entire world had expressed its shock and horror at what had happened, when a number of the Nazi leaders themselves had begun, in panic-stricken haste and ostensible penitence, to expose and accuse one another— even then he, Adolf Eichmann, remained faithful to his ideas and principles. He did not repent. He still believes that he did what was right and proper in destroying millions.

He knows that today it is regarded as a crime, and he will therefore be ready to give verbal and insincere expression to this view; at times he may even clothe it with a mantle of grandiloquent phrases. But we have every reason to believe that if the swastika flag were again to be raised with shouts of *Sieg heil!* if there were again to resound the hysterical screams of a Führer, if again the high-tension barbed wires of extermination centers were set up, Adolf Eichmann would rise, salute, and go back to his work of oppression and butchery.

The Final Solution of the Jewish Problem

At the beginning, when the Nazis were still sensitive to the reaction of world opinion, the solution took the form of forced emigration. Though the methods were drastic and brutal, Nazi arrogance had not yet reached the point of deciding on extermination. But when they found that it could be done, that for all practical purposes the world was silent, that circumstances were propitious— they went over to total extermination.

These two aims—the physical liquidation of the Jews by expulsion or killing and the pillage of their property—were thereafter fixed pillars in German policy. At all stages of the Holocaust, in official reports filled with shocking details of cruel killings by strangulation, burning, hanging, and unimaginable tortures, there will always be found a twin section telling of the plunder of Jewish property.

All the prophecies of that evil man [Hitler] proved baseless. The Reich that was to have lasted a thousand years collapsed like a house of cards. The "New Order" that was to have served as the basis for human civilization has become a historical byword for atrocity. The Aryan master race was thoroughly defeated by the "degenerate plutocrats" and the "inferior" Slavs. Not only was Germany driven out of the Ukrainian wheat granaries she had invaded, which the Führer had promised her as an eternal heritage, but she herself is now divided, and Bismarck's work of unification has been set at naught.

Only one single promise, the most dreadful of Germany's terrible deeds which has brought upon her eternal disgrace, was kept by Adolf Hitler. And for the execution of that promise to destroy European Jewry, he used another Adolf—Adolf Eichmann, who is on trial before you today.

In August 1941, Eichmann wrote to his Foreign Ministry that it would be advisable to prevent further emigration "in the light of preparations for the final solution of the problem" of European Jewry. That summer we shall find Eichmann in Auschwitz arranging with Rudolf Hess the various technical details and choosing the spot for the erection of the extermination apparatus.

On 25 October 1941, [Erhard] Wetzel, an official of the Ministry for the Occupied Territories, wrote that an agreement had been reached with Eichmann, to use gas chambers for the solution of the Jewish problem. Instead of the Jews' emigrating, they would be murdered. A total of 11 million Jews were to be included in the "Final Solution."

With the help of his deputies in all the countries of Europe, [Eichmann] held the Jewish people in his grip like an octopus strangling its prey. We shall see him issuing detailed directives for the implementation of the deportations to Auschwitz. We shall trace the activities of his men concerned with the supply of gas for killing Jews. Everywhere he was the official authority for murder and plunder, and all reports had to be sent to him.

Everything relating to the extermination and the preparations for it was his concern. He witnessed in Chelmno the parade of the naked Jews who had been stripped of their clothing and were waiting their turn for death by asphyxiation with gas. He looked on as gold teeth were extracted from the mouths of his dead victims. He was sent to examine the extermination activities by shooting, used by the Einsatzgruppen. He saw these groups murdering women and children. He saw those units operating against the Jews in the vicinity of Lvov, where the blood spurted from the grave "as from a spring," to use his words.

But direct murder by shooting did not satisfy him. "Our men will become sadists," he said. He had to seek a new method. This was found in the gas chambers and furnaces of the extermination centers—which he visited on a number of occasions, to examine the apparatus, to organize the transportation procedures, and to give instructions. There he also saw how corpses were burned in the open field. Now that these instruments of extermination, it seems, were functioning to his satisfaction, he concerned himself with supplying them with sacrificial victims.

Eichmann took special pains to frustrate emigration to Palestine. He had obligations on this subject, he argued to the mufti of Jerusalem, Haj Amin el Husseini, whom he had met and with whom he had established contact. El Husseini asked [Heinrich] Himmler to provide him, after the war, when he would enter Jerusalem at the head of the Axis troops, with a special adviser from Eichmann's department to help him to solve the Jewish question in the same way as it had been done in the Axis countries.

Felix Benzler, the German delegate to the Serbian puppet government, asked for directives concerning the treatment of the Serbian Jews. You will find a memorandum by Franz Rademacher, director of the appropriate section of the Foreign Ministry, containing these words: "Eichmann suggests shooting." And when Rademacher wanted to confirm this instruction and asked Eichmann again on the telephone, the accused answered, "Shoot," and cut the conversation short. Thus, with one word, he sentenced to death some ten thousand Jews. This was the man, and this was his power.

It is hardly necessary to mention that this "Jewish enemy" was a defenseless civil population, including infants, children, women, and old men. But no part of all this bloody work is so shocking and terrible as that of the million Jewish children whose blood was spilt like water throughout Europe. How they were separated by force from their mothers who tried to hide them, murdered and thrown out of trucks in the camps, torn to pieces before their mothers' eyes, their little heads smashed on the ground—these are the most terrible passages of the tale of slaughter. You will hear evidence of actions which the mind of man does not want to believe.

Those unhappy children who lived for years in fear of the beating of a rifle butt on their door; who had been sent by their parents to the woods in an attempt to save them; who had been taught to choke their tears and sighs because a weeping child would be shot on the spot; who had been ordered to deny their origins and pretend to be Christian; who saw their fathers being lashed with whips before their eyes; in front of whom "discussions" would be carried on by the German executioners as to who should be killed first—the father or the son; who went to the open graves with "Hear, O Israel" [famous

Jewish prayer affirming belief in one God] on their lips—these children and youths, who despite all the desperate measures and concealments would finally fall into the hands of their hunters, they are the very soul and innermost core of the indictment. Those Anne Franks and Justine Draengers and a million others, those unplumbed treasures of radiant youth and hope for life and achievement—they were the future of the Jewish people. He that destroyed them was seeking to destroy the Jewish people.

The Jews were to be deported as swiftly as possible and all their rights canceled. There were heartrending scenes. They would catch a Jew who had a labor card but take his children away from him, while he pleaded for permission to go with his children—but to no avail. There were SS men who caught little children and smashed their heads on the paving stones.

You will hear evidence of dogs being set onto human beings, who were bitten and torn to pieces; of SS men who would go up to people and shoot them just because they felt like doing so at the moment; of selection parades in which the weak, the old, and the children were dispatched to the extermination camps while cradle songs were played over the loudspeakers. And to move was forbidden. The slightest movement set the machine guns working.

The accused, as special commissioner for the extermination of the Jews, bears direct responsibility as the initiator and implementer of this bloodbath. We shall show proof of his initiative and his control over the ghettoes, his responsibility and his role in the setting up and the operation of the extermination camps, and the responsibility for the destruction of Polish Jewry.

In September 1942, over a hundred thousand Jews were collected together in an area called "The Pot": Thirty thousand were released for work, and the rest were sent to death camps. Listen to this account:

The Germans are transporting the surviving Jews into "The Pot." At the junction of Mila and Genscha streets, a wooden gate blocks off the whole width of the pavement. Through this gate of life and death, the crowd passes slowly in single file. Each person has to submit to a thorough search. There is a line of young, alert SS men on guard, the revolvers hanging from their uniforms. "Quicker, quicker!" they yell, accompanying their threats with lashes of the whip.

The crowd marches on in endless line, through the gate of life and death. Pale and confused figures pass by, their eyes red with fear. Men help their wives, mothers clasp their little ones. Daughters carefully guide their old mothers. Families try to keep together and cling solidly to each other. Each person holds firmly in his hands the "work card," which gives him the right to live. They hold on to this document desperately, for it is the only guarantee of their right to live and—even more important—the right of their dear ones to live.

Today is the great day. The weather is pleasant. The sun is shining brightly. Untersturmführer Handke wipes the sweat from his fat, red face. Then he wipes his neck and gets ready again for action. He lashes out again with the whip and strikes the terrified victims on their heads and faces and any other parts of the body he can reach. An energetic and aggressive officer is showing the confused people which way to go. Left—toward Stavki—is the gate of death, leading to the train that will carry them off to Malkinia and Treblinka. This is the place marked out for the women, the old, and the crippled. A gesture of the hand to the right—this is the way to life. To the right go those from whose toil and sweat some profit can still be wrung.

The bitter end of Polish Jewry came in the extermination camps to which millions were transported by order of Eichmann and his accomplices in crime.

Eichmann was a party to everything concerning Jews. He took part in the secret meeting held at the Prince Albrecht Palace in Berlin, at which Heydrich explained to the commander of the Einsatzkommandos the nature of their mission to exterminate all the Jews.

One asks oneself again and again, "How could it ever have happened?" It is almost impossible to believe that for many months, thousands of people daily, in cold blood, deliberately and of set purpose, murdered multitudes of human beings with their own hands, the numbers rising steadily until they totaled three-quarters of a million. It is difficult to accustom oneself to the idea that such beasts ever walked the face of this earth.

Murder was committed here as a matter of daily routine: After every such bloodbath, the murderers would eat a hearty meal and have a smoke and a chat about this and that. And then they were ready for the next group of victims, who had meanwhile been placed in line.

At first, people were murdered in their clothes. Later the system was changed, and the victims were ordered to undress and were left naked. Let us listen to a description of the procedure:

> The people who had got off the trucks—men, women, and children of all ages—had to undress upon the order of an SS man, who carried a riding or dog whip, and put down their clothing in fixed places, sorted according to shoes, top clothing, and underclothing. There lay a heap of shoes of about eight hundred to one thousand pairs, great piles of underlinen and clothing. Without screaming or weeping, these people undressed, stood around in family groups, kissed each other, said their farewells, and waited for a sign from another SS man, who stood near the pit, also with a whip in his hand.
>
> No complaints or pleas for mercy were heard. A family of about eight persons passed by—a man and a woman, both about fifty, with their children of about one, eight and ten and two grown-up daughters of about twenty to twenty-four. An old woman with snow-white hair was holding the one-year-old child in her arms, singing to it and tickling it. The child was cooing with delight. The couple was looking on with tears in their eyes. The father was holding the hand of a boy about ten years old and speaking to him softly; the boy was fighting his tears. The father pointed toward the sky, stroked his head, and seemed to explain something to him. At that moment the SS man at the pit shouted something to his comrade. The latter counted off about twenty persons and instructed them to go behind the pit. The pit contained about a thousand people. The executioner was an SS man who sat at the narrow opening of the trench, his feet dangling

inside. He held a machine gun on his knee and a cigarette in his mouth. The people, completely naked, descended a few steps out into the clay wall of the trench and placed their heads on the heads of those already lying there as instructed by the SS man. They lay before the dead or wounded. A few stroked those who were still alive and spoke to them softly. Then came a volley of shots. In the trench the bodies were twitching on top of the motionless bodies that lay before them. Blood was running from their necks. The next batch was already approaching. They went down into the pit, placed themselves by the earlier victims, and were shot.

The reports were received in Berlin, and Eichmann was able to keep a continuous check on the bloody work in the East, where the number of killings mounted from tens to hundreds of thousands.

A man would be faced with the choice of obtaining a work card either for his wife or for his mother. He would return home, cursing the day he married, and tell his mother that he no longer had a work card for her. This meant that she was doomed to immediate death. The mother would bless her son for his choice, present her Yiddish prayer book to her daughter-in-law, embrace her, and wish her the bliss of being spared to witness the end of the terror.

Eichmann also continued to concern himself directly with individual cases. A Jewish woman by the name of Cozzi, married to an Italian Christian, succeeded in calling the attention of the Italian authorities to her fate. The Italians requested that she be released from Riga. Eichmann replied requesting the Italian authorities to cease their interest in the woman.

At the time of Denmark's capitulation, about sixty-five hundred Jews were living there. King Christian remained the formal ruler of the state, and the Danish government continued to function. This explains why the anti-Jewish laws were not enacted, nor was the Jewish badge introduced. The king intervened personally on behalf of the Jews of his country.

The roundup [in Denmark] finally took place during the first days of October 1943. The barbarians broke into Jewish homes, seized Jews in the streets, and brought them in. But then something occurred that stunned the assassins: Most of the Jewish homes turned out to be empty. The Danish people, having prior knowledge of the murderous plot, had organized courageously and at great risk, under the very noses of the occupation authorities, an underground rescue operation, which became known as "The Miniature Dunkirk." Fishing and excursion boats and any other vessel able to float were mustered at the ports. The Jews were escorted to the coast by scouts, students, and other volunteers, put on board, and secretly transported to Sweden. In this way some six thousand Danish Jews were rescued; only a few hundred fell into the hands of Eichmann's accomplices.

When it became clear to Eichmann that this small part of his quarry had escaped his grasp, he was beside himself with rage. He had a complaint lodged against the occupation authorities, and shortly afterward he went to Copenhagen in person to ascertain what had occurred and the reasons for the failure. But it was too late. Thanks to the courage and nobility of its people, most of the Jews of Denmark were saved.

The Extermination of Hungarian Jewry: The Story of Raoul Wallenberg

Finally, in 1944, Hungary was the only country within the sphere of influence of the Reich left with a considerable Jewish population. There were about eight hundred thousand Jews living in Hungary. Eichmann was already looking forward to the extermination of Hungarian Jewry. Eichmann now became the lord of life and death, the absolute master of Hungarian Jewry.

The mass deportations began in the middle of May 1944. Naturally the Jews tried to escape, particularly to Palestine. [Eichmann] complained about the Swedish and Swiss embassies issuing the Jews papers which enabled them to emigrate from Hungary.

The main target of his venom was a young Swedish diplomat, Raoul Wallenberg, an architect by profession and a man of sterling qualities who had made the rescue of Jews his life's vocation. Wallenberg gathered around him a whole team of workers, issued passports granting the holders right of residence in Sweden, and, at the

risk of his diplomatic status and even his life, instituted rescue operations. He rented and acquired buildings, in which he housed Jews
under the protection of the Swedish flag, and assembled, at one
period, as many as forty thousand Jews. When the "death march,"
of which I shall speak later, began, Wallenberg escorted the
marchers with trucks laden with food, medical supplies, and clothing. He also tried to remove from the march anyone to whom
Swedish papers of protection could feasibly be issued. Wallenberg,
to whose credit can be counted tens of thousands of survivors, also
enrolled the support of other diplomats as well as the Red Cross.

All this was the work of one courageous man, who had the
strength to act according to his conception and belief. His deeds, like
those of King Christian of Denmark, again give rise to the somber
thought: How many could have been saved, even in the countries of
actual extermination, had there only been many others like him
among those who had the power to act, whether openly or in secret?

It is not surprising that Eichmann released a flood of anger
against this liberator. The Swedish embassy in Berlin lodged a complaint that Eichmann had told the Red Cross in Budapest he had it
in mind to shoot "the Jewish dog" Wallenberg [the member of an
aristocratic Lutheran family in Sweden].

The deportations were carried out in secret. Nothing was mentioned about them in the newspapers, and the Germans took special
measures to avoid publicity, lest the Jews of Budapest should be
alarmed. The deportees, on arrival at Auschwitz, were ordered to send
soothing postcards to their relatives. The text of the postcards was dic-
tated by the Auschwitz butchers, who instructed that an Austrian
resort, Waldsee, be designated as the place of dispatch. The postcards
stated that those transported for work were all well; they usually arrived
after their senders had been consumed in the Auschwitz furnaces.

The Camps

Eichmann made a tour with Rudolf Hess to select a suitable site
for the erection of gas installations at Auschwitz and also visited
the Treblinka and Chelmno extermination camps to examine their
effectiveness. He was satisfied with the system, which he considered

preferable to shooting. He and his section dealt with the obtaining of a gas composed of hydrogen cyanide. This gas was employed in a number of extermination camps. On Eichmann rests the direct responsibility for the operations of these fearful camps set up for the implementation of the "Final Solution."

The extermination camp Belzec was set up in the winter of 1941. When the trains arrived at Belzec, as at other camps, many of the deportees had died en route from thirst and exhaustion. I should like to quote a description of one such transport from Lvov, consisting of sixty-seven hundred people:

> The wagon doors open, and the people, to the lashings of whips, are ordered to get out. The instructions are relayed over loudspeakers; everyone is ordered to hand over clothes and belongings, crutches and spectacles as well. . . . All valuables and money are handed over at the window marked "valuables." . . . Before the entrance to the building stands a smiling SS man who declares in an ingratiating voice, "No harm will befall you. All you have to do," he says, "is to breathe in deeply. This strengthens the lungs; inhaling is necessary as a means of disinfection." He is asked what will happen to the women and replies that the men will, of course, have to work at road and housing constructions. The women, he says, will not have to work. They may, if they want, help in the kitchen or do housework. . . .
>
> For a number of men, there still flickers a lingering hope, sufficient to make them march without resistance to the death chambers. The majority knows with certainty what is to be their fate. The horrible smell that pervades everywhere reveals the truth. A woman of about forty curses the chief of the murderers, exclaiming that the blood of her children will be on his head. Wirth, an SS officer, himself strikes her in the face with five lashes of the whip and she disappears into the gas chamber. Many pray. . . . The SS men squeeze people into the chambers. The doors close. The remainder of the transport stands waiting, naked. . . . The people in the death chambers remain standing. Their weeping is heard. Twenty-five minutes pass by. Twenty-

eight minutes later, a few are still alive. After thirty-two minutes, all of them are dead. Jewish workers open the doors on the other side. The dead, having nowhere to fall, stand like pillars of basalt. Even in death, families may be seen standing pressed together, clutching hands. The blue corpses, covered with sweat and urine, babies and bodies of children, are thrown out. But there is no time! Two dozen workers occupy themselves with the mouths of the dead, opening them with iron pegs: "With gold to the left—without gold to the right." Others search in the private parts of the bodies for gold and diamonds. . . .

And now to the largest and most terrible of the extermination camps—Auschwitz, the death factory for millions, which will always be remembered in the annals of humanity as the symbol of horror and infamy.

Eichmann was in Auschwitz and saw what was being done there. He directed the operations and gave instructions which transports were to be sent to immediate extermination and which were to be kept for extermination later on. He also dealt with the tremendous pillage which continued right up to the gates of this hell. The plunder attained fantastic proportions. The looted diamonds were sold in Switzerland and, in Eichmann's words, influenced the whole of the Swiss market for precious stones.

During forty-seven days between December 1944 and January 1945, 99,922 sets of children's clothing, 192,652 sets of women's clothing, and 22,269 sets of men's clothing were dispatched.

The killings in Auschwitz were carried out by every method: shooting, hanging, and beating, but mainly in the massive gas chambers. Here, once again, we are confronted with the signboards: "washing and disinfection room." The "shower" was a flow of poison gas which the SS introduced with their own hands. The death factory operated unceasingly. The extermination of two thousand people lasted twenty-five minutes, after which the bodies were taken to one of the five giant furnaces. When there was no room in the furnaces, the bodies were burned in the open.

Here, too, hair was shorn, teeth extracted, and rings removed.

Day by day, kilograms of gold were melted down, at times as much as twelve kilograms a day. At first the victims' ashes were buried in pits, but later they were thrown into the Vistula.

At Auschwitz, medical experiments were made on human beings as if they were guinea pigs. Parts of female sex organs were cut out, or limbs were subjected to X-rays until the unfortunate creatures writhed in pain prior to their death. Men were castrated. We shall prove that in response to Eichmann's order, 150 Auschwitz prisoners were "supplied" for death in the Natzweiler camp in Germany, so that their skeletons might be sent for anthropological research at the SS Institute of Race Research [Ahnenerbe], which had requested skulls of "Jewish Communist commissars."

The methods of punishment at Auschwitz would have shamed the cruelest barbarians in history. Beating on the naked body was a comparatively light punishment. Water was poured into people's ears, fingernails extracted, and prisoners starved until they went out of their minds. In the bunker of those sentenced for punishment by starvation, a dead prisoner was found, bent over whom was a second prisoner, also dead, grasping the liver from the corpse of the first. He had died while tearing at the liver of a fellow human being. The Nazi contribution to European culture was the reintroduction of cannibalism.

The Nazis believed that their crimes would not be revealed, that their secret would remain intact. But the secret of these atrocities has been laid bare, and we must fulfill the dying injunction of an anonymous poetess who wrote, before being put to death in Auschwitz:

"There is no more hope in the white skull. / Among the barbed wire, under the ruins, / And our dust is scattered in the dust / Out of the broken jars. / Our army will go forth, skull bones and jawbones, / And bone to bone, a merciless line, / We, the hunted, the hunters, will cry out to you: / The murdered demand justice at your hands!"

A World That Has Vanished

On whose head did this venomous wrath of extermination and murder fall?

We shall prove that the Jewish people were bereaved of many millions, certainly close to 6 million people. But this meant more than the destruction of over a third of the total. It meant the extinction of those Jewish communities which represented the most important element of the nation from the point of view of inspiration and national consciousness, creative power, cultural and spiritual resources, devotion to the Jewish people and its values. There were some grounds for the Nazis' belief that if they could succeed in wiping out this part of Jewry, they would prove victorious in their battle against Jewry in general.

From the point of view of Europe, a national community was exterminated which had resided there from the second century B.C.E. as an integral part of its human landscape.

Of the 257 Nobel Prize–winners during the first fifty years of this century, thirty-four were Jews, twelve of whom were expelled by the Nazis. Here is a partial idea of the Jewish people's contribution to European culture and life—great geniuses like Albert Einstein and Sigmund Freud; Fritz Haber, the chemist; Henri Bergson, the philosopher; Paul Ehrlich and Elie Metchnikoff, biologists; Niels Bohr, physicist; Otto Warburg and Ernst Boris Chain, physiologists; thinkers like Martin Buber, writers like Emil Ludwig, Stefan Zweig, Franz Kafka, Franz Werfel, Jakob Wassermann, Max Brod, and Lion Feuchtwanger, sculptors and painters like Antokolsky, Chagall, Modigliani, and Max Liebermann; Max Reinhardt, the producer; musicians like Huberman, Rubinstein, Kreisler, and Richard Tauber.

The associations between Jewry and Germany comprise a tragic chapter in human annals. Germany was the country where Jews suffered more than in any other place. And yet the Jewish people bestowed great love and devotion on Germany. Its folk language, Yiddish, was created on the pattern of German; it carried this tongue with it to every country of the dispersion—to Poland, Russia, and across the seas. It was in German that Herzl wrote his classics of Zionism, that the proceedings of the Zionist Congresses were held, that standard works on Jewish history and philosophy were written. When World War I broke out, the German Jewish community flocked to the ranks of the German army with patriotic zeal; the aged philosopher Hermann Cohen stepped down from his university rostrum and called for a supreme effort on behalf of Germany.

In terms of the Jewish people, European Jewry on the eve of the Holocaust was the heart of the whole nation. The great majority of its spiritual guides and leaders either dwelt there or were of European origin. Here were to be found the great religious scholars, the inheritors of the great Rabbi Elijah of Vilna. It was from Europe that Rabbi Kook and the Hafetz Haim came; that the visionaries of the state, the architects of Jewish nationalism, it leaders, thinkers, and writers, emerged.

These millions who were destroyed waited for their state but were not privileged to see it. It was in these communities which were destroyed that the wonderful youth movements, imbued with national and social ideals, sprang up in the years between the wars—their members burning with faith, pure of body and heart, for whom Zion was their life breath.

Ancient communities were destroyed of which I shall mention only a few. There was the illustrious Jewry of Amsterdam, shelter of the Spanish Marranos, where Menashe ben Israel dwelt, where Baruch Spinoza lived and wrote. Gone is the Jewry of Prague with its magnificent synagogues which had been in existence since the tenth century, the city of the Maharal and the Noda Biyehuda. The Jewish community of Berlin—the home of Moses Mendelssohn and Ezriel Hildesheimer—was exterminated.

Landmarks of Jewish history have been obliterated. The heart of the Jewish people has been wounded. Adolf Eichmann knew what he was about: If he should succeed in destroying this Jewry, he would destroy the whole of Jewry. The others, he hoped, would perish or be assimilated.

By the mercy of Providence, which preserved a saving remnant, Adolf Eichmann's design was frustrated, and the intention that he cherished was not implemented to the end.

POSTSCRIPT

Adolf Eichmann was convicted of crimes against humanity, sentenced to death, and executed in Ramleh Prison on May 31, 1962.

Ordinarily, trials that are conducted in front of only judges have a different tone to them than that of jury trials. Theoretically, judges are objective automatons who are not influenced by arguments that appeal to emotion and sympathy. Why was it necessary, then, for Mr. Hausner to appeal to the judges' emotion? This, of course, was Israel's trial of the century, and the entire world was watching. The Eichmann trial was not only meant to convict one of the most evil men who walked the face of the earth but also to serve as a national education project for the citizens of the state of Israel "that would echo through the generations."*

The upcoming trial of Saddam Hussein will serve as a national education project for the citizens of Iraq, the Muslim world, and the world at large. As in the Eichmann trial, there will be little difficulty establishing Saddam's guilt of mass murder and crimes against humanity. Such a trial may record for posteirty the crimes of Saddam Hussein's brutal regime and how the "civilized" nations of the world, through indifference or economic greed, permitted this tyrant in the same century that gave us Hitler, Eichmann, and Milosevic to wreak havoc on one million innocent people.

Prime Minister David Ben-Gurion shared this view. In fact, Prosecutor Hausner consulted with him while preparing his opening statement. There were political calculations, such as not offending the German government led by Prime Minister Konrad Adenauer and damaging the countries' good relations. Every time the word "Germany" appeared in Mr. Hausner's opening, for example, Ben-Gurion substituted the word "Nazi" to signify that Israel's quarrel was only with Nazi Germany.

In every case, even in the case of genocide, lawyers seem to see the crime as less or more heinous depending upon the nature of the victim. Even Mr. Hausner does this, pointing out that the Nazis destroyed victims who possessed outstanding levels of creativity, devotion to Jewish values, and national consciousness. While this is undoubtedly true and tragic, the crime of killing 6 million people is so egregious that it is simply not meaningful to say that it is all the more awful because it included the spiritual and intellectual guides of the Jewish people. Mr. Hausner's speech exemplifies a common theme in this book: The prosecutor finds it easier to get a conviction when the victim is blameless, while the defense finds it easier to get an acquittal when the victim or government witnesses are unsavory or unlikable.

*The Seventh Million, by Tom Segev, page 336.

8

A VICTIM OF THE WAR ON CRIME

THE AMADOU DIALLO CASE

AMADOU DIALLO, A WEST African immigrant, lived and worked in New York City as a peddler. At 10:30 P.M. on February 3, 1999, he was standing in the vestibule of his Bronx apartment building when he was approached by four white plainclothes police officers who were searching for a serial rapist. During the ensuing confrontation, Mr. Diallo was shot at forty-one times by the officers and suffered nineteen gunshot wounds.

The jury was given a choice of six charges: murder in the second degree, intentional and depraved indifference, which carried potential life sentences, manslaughter in the first degree (maximum of twenty-five years), reckless endangerment, and criminally negligent homicide.

Public sentiment ran overwhelmingly against the police. Demonstrators and activists filled the streets and airwaves. The defense was faced with the nearly impossible task of justifying the violent death of a five-foot-six-inch, 150-pound, law-abiding, unarmed man, standing in the vestibule of his own building. It seemed like an open-and-shut case of police brutality. Ultimately, though, this trial demonstrates the extent to which the loud bull-horn coverage of the media so often differs from the real story as details emerge in the courtroom.

THE PEOPLE OF THE STATE OF NEW YORK v. KENNETH BOSS, SEAN CARROLL, EDWARD MCMELLON AND RICHARD MURPHY

Excerpts from the Opening Statements of Defense Attorney Bennett Epstein

I have to confess that I'm a little nervous. It's not the cameras. The cameras are here today and gone tomorrow. It is [the] twelve jurors that are really the only audience that matters. And you have Sean Carroll's fate in your hands. So I hope you will forgive me if I stand at the podium and sometimes if I appear to be reading from notes—I probably will be, because I have an awful lot to tell you, and I don't want to have to leave anything out.

Ladies and gentlemen, this is a case about five good men. One of them was named Amadou Diallo. The other four are named Sean Carroll, Kenneth Boss, Edward McMellon, and Richard Murphy.

Ladies and gentlemen, I listened to the prosecutor's opening statement, and I thought to myself that what they are trying to do, the prosecution, is to take a tragic accident and find a way to charge it as a crime, [to] make it a murder. It is not that simple. The prosecutor in doing so has left out a lot of important details. They have lost sight of the fact that in certain ways this accident was inevitable. I'm not talking about fate, but I am talking about destiny. I am talking about conditions that would make this kind of accident destined to happen and that would take good officers like Boss, Carroll, and McMellon and Murphy and put them in a no-win situation in a dimly lit vestibule.

The facts will show that four good officers are being prosecuted for something that happened while doing what we, the people, train them to do, with the weapons that we, the people, gave them, going where we, the people, wanted them and expected them to go. For, members of the jury, the proof in this case is that these four officers were sent into the breach by us.

We are going to try to put you in the shoes of these four officers, so that you can understand that situation. Members of the jury, you are going to hear about crime in the Soundview section of the Bronx, one of the most dangerous neighborhoods in New York City.

You are going to hear about robberies and rapes and drug dealing and a lot about illegal guns. You are going to hear about police officers shot and killed, including Officer Kevin Gillespie, a member of the Street Crime Unit whose locker was kept as kind of a monument about three lockers away from Sean Carroll's, and an officer named Steven McDonald, who is now a paraplegic.

You are going to hear how police officers like Sean Carroll are trained to take guns off the street in order to keep them out of the hands of criminals who prey on the citizens of Bronx County. And that means [that] those officers have to put themselves in harm's way to confront armed criminals. That means that they are trained to focus on certain signs, including a suspect's hand and body movements. That means that they are trained to try to close the gap as quickly as possible in order to attempt to seize the gun off of a real suspect, a live criminal.

But you will also learn that asking them to take such risks means that if they believe, God forbid, that they are about to be fired upon, they are trained that they don't have to wait for the glint of steel, because then it is too late, and then they wind up like Kevin Gillespie, and then they wind up like Steven McDonald.

Members of the jury, you are going to hear about how the danger to police officers from the number of illegal guns and automatic weapons that were getting into the hands of criminals caused the NYPD just a couple of years ago to switch from the standard .38 revolver, six-shot police .38 special that New York City police officers used to carry and to now require that the officers carry nine-millimeter semiautomatic pistols with sixteen shots in the magazine and the first trigger pull being a conventional trigger pull and all subsequent trigger pulls being a hair-trigger pull, and to further require that the ammunition that they carry be known as pointed full-metal-jacket ammunition, as opposed to the other kind of ammunition, which is called hollow-point bullets. It was determined by the NYPD that the full-metal-jacket ammunition went more smoothly through the gun mechanism of these new nine-millimeter automatics.

But you will also hear that this was extremely controversial because the entire sixteen-shot magazine can be fired by the average officer in less than four seconds. And, furthermore, that the full-metal-jacket ammunition tends to go through the body of someone who is shot, which leaves him standing as a threat to the officer rather than stopping the threat by bringing down the suspect. This ammunition was so controversial that after this case the police department switched the ammunition, took away the pointed full-metal jacket.

And the experts predicted—and you really don't have to be an expert to understand—that a faster gun, with more bullets and less stopping power, equals more shots.

You are going to hear that a unit known as the Street Crime Unit of the New York City Police Department was formed in order to get the illegal guns away from armed criminals, particularly in places like Soundview, where 1147 Wheeler Avenue is located. And you are going to hear how police officers like Sean Carroll were trained by the NYPD and armed by the NYPD and given the most dangerous assignment imaginable. They were sent in to protect the poorer neighborhoods, which turn out to be the high-crime neighborhoods, by taking guns off the street. And they were taught that the gun that they took off the street today could not be used against a citizen or a police officer tomorrow.

And you will hear how these officers of the Street Crime Unit and these four officers sitting in the courtroom today believed in what they were doing and thought that it was noble and thought that it was brave. And it was. You will hear how, on a regular basis, these four reasonable, good officers disarmed armed criminals, risking their lives for the citizens of places like Soundview.

Members of the jury, you are going to hear from Officer Sean Carroll. And you are going to hear about Officer Sean Carroll, that Sean Carroll is a good, decent, reasonable, honorable police officer. He is the kind of dedicated officer that you would be proud of if he were your own son or brother or if he were a member of your community.

Let me tell you a little bit about what you will learn about him. Sean is thirty-six years old. He is married for fourteen years. He has two children; a daughter, eleven and a son, seven. He is the eldest of six children. He has been working since the age of fourteen to support his family. He started working as a busboy. He attended SUNY College of Farmingdale. He studied aeronautics. He worked two jobs, one as a dispatcher at a small airport and the other as a waiter at night, and eventually he joined the naval reserve and seven years ago joined the NYPD. In approximately fourteen months in plainclothes patrol duty in the Street Crime Unit, Sean, in addition to numerous felony arrests for other crimes, took or was present and helped to take with his partners more than thirty guns off the street, sometimes actually wrestling the gun out of the hands of an armed criminal. You will learn that often that gun was a small black automatic, the weapon of choice in Bronx County. And you will learn that in all that time that he was a police officer prior to February 4, 1999, Sean Carroll fired his gun exactly once, when he was shot at—and, thank God, not shot, but shot at—eight times from a rooftop and returned the fire briefly and missed.

Members of the jury, this is what the evidence will show as the background against which this case must be judged. And the evidence will further show that the case that you are being asked to reflect upon in the warmth and safety and splendor of this courtroom took place in just a few short seconds, in the middle of the night, in the middle of the winter, in a dimly lit vestibule, in a dangerous area.

Members of the jury, the evidence will show that these police officers honestly and reasonably believed that they were confronting an armed criminal in the vestibule that night. They didn't know and they had no reason to know that they were confronting Amadou Diallo, peddler. All the hindsight and all the Monday-morning quarterbacking in the world is no substitute for being in the shoes of those four police officers.

You will hear some evidence about Amadou Diallo. Amadou Diallo, I'm sure, was loved, and I'm sure he was a terrific son. And I'm sure that his parents miss him and that they have suffered greatly.

I'm sure that to them he was a saint. But the evidence will show that he was a saint who felt compelled, for reasons best known to him but that we hope to go into, to avoid the police. And that reaction caused a chain reaction that caused this tragic event to happen.

We are going to prove to you what it was like to be in Sean Carroll's shoes that February night shortly before one o'clock in the morning. And we are also going to prove to you what was running through Sean Carroll's mind before, during, and after that tragic event. Sean had some familiarity with that area of the Bronx. He knew, for instance, that the next block over from Wheeler Avenue was Elder Avenue, a street that was so rife with drug dealing that the police department had to close it off for a year with barricades on either side of the block in order to close down the drug market and keep the citizens in that area at peace. And Sean knew that the drug dealers on Elder Avenue had felt the pressure of the police enforcement and had filtered their operations into the surrounding blocks. And Sean was also familiar with, and he carried with him when he went out on patrol, police-department bulletins about patterns of crime in the area, one of which was a serial rapist reported many times to be armed with a small black gun who was wanted for having raped fifty-two women, often African-American women who were jumped late at night as they walked home in the Forty-third Precinct, where 1147 Wheeler Avenue lies. Before Sean went out on patrol with his partners that night, he was also briefed about a series of armed robberies in the same area.

The evidence will show that a few hours earlier, while on that same patrol but before the tragic event, prior to arriving in the vicinity of 1147 Wheeler, Sean and his fellow officers stopped the person who they believed was a suspect in a homicide. They required him to identify himself, which he did. It turned out they had the wrong person. They apologized to him, and they walked away. And then eventually there came a time that they turned down Wheeler Avenue.

Eleven forty-seven Wheeler is a walk-up building with the stoop out front that has five steps going up—they are irregular steps—and a front door with a glass panel that opens to the right, and then a dimly lit vestibule, and then an inner door painted dark red with a small diamond-shaped window leading into the building itself, into the inner stairway. And on either side of the stoop, there are two platforms, one higher as you look into the building on the left and one lower as you look into the building on the right.

Mr. Diallo attracted the suspicion not only of the officers but [of] several other people on the block, because he was alternately standing out on one of the platforms and peering down the street toward Westchester Avenue and then ducking back into the building, standing on the platform peering down toward Westchester and ducking back into the building. And as the officers passed, he peeked out and looked back again. And Sean Carroll spotted this. And so began the chain reaction. The officers identified themselves with their shields out, as they are trained to do and as they do in every situation. Mr. Diallo doesn't listen to their clear orders to stop, which they are trained to give. He runs back into the vestibule. More orders to stop and to show his hands. "Show us your hands"—something the officers are trained to do for their own protection. Again Mr. Diallo does not comply. The officers pursue him with weapons drawn, as they are trained to do. He turns his back to them and runs for the inner door and tries to enter the building. He reaches into his pocket. He turns quickly toward the officers, and he extends his hand forward with a black object.

Members of the jury, we believe that the evidence will show that had Mr. Diallo stopped to answer the officers' questions, like the fellow that they had an encounter with about an hour before, the whole thing would have ended peaceably moments later and we wouldn't be here.

Now we are going to prove to you what was going through Sean Carroll's mind as he sees this reaction from Mr. Diallo and as he sees the series of events unfold and the black object coming out of Mr. Diallo's pocket toward him. His training is going through his mind. His experience is going through his mind. He is full of fear. And we will prove to you exactly what was going on in his mind, because he verbalized it. When the black object came out of Mr. Diallo's pocket in that dimly lit vestibule, he yelled, "Gun!"

Members of the jury, we are going to be spending the next several weeks analyzing what took place in the ensuing few seconds, because that's how long it took. The officers didn't stand there for several minutes firing forty-one shots into Mr. Diallo. Several seconds is all that transpired. Each of the officers fired his gun because he believed that he and his brother officers were in danger.

Mr. Diallo had taken the officers into the no-man's-land that's every police officer's nightmare. The evidence will show that Sean Carroll fired sixteen shots, scrambling for cover, because he believed he would never see his wife and children again. The evidence will show that, altogether, forty-one shots were fired in a total of a few seconds from the officers' sixteen-shot nine-millimeter weapons that were all capable of being emptied in less than four seconds. And, we believe that the fact that forty-one shots were fired indicates the fear that the officers had of being shot. The physical evidence from the scene will confirm for you that the officers fired defensively.

If you could slow down that few seconds frame by frame and view it through Sean Carroll's eyes, here is some of what you would see. You would see on the periphery one of your brother officers falling backward out of that vestibule and down on his fanny as if he had been shot from inside that vestibule. He was scrambling for cover. And you would see what turned out to be the reflection of your own muzzle shots, and you would hear what turned out to be the ricochet of your own bullets, but you didn't know it at the time, coming back at you. And you would hear the roar of your own gun echoing back at you as if somebody from inside the vestibule were firing at you. And you would see and realize that, in the horror of those few terrible seconds, more than half the shots that these officers fired missed, proving the tension that they were under, proving the fear that they were under.

You will also hear that because of this full-metal-jacket pointed ammunition, sixteen out of the nineteen shots that hit Mr. Diallo passed [clean] through nonvisceral areas of the body. What the experts had predicted would happen had come true. He remained standing, with a black object in his pocket, until that fatal final moment.

Members of the jury, the evidence will show that the officers didn't have the luxury of reflection that we have now. They didn't know that Mr. Diallo was unarmed and that he had pulled out his wallet. He didn't say to them, "Guys, I live here." It would have ended right there peaceably. He didn't keep his hands in view. It would have ended right there peaceably. If only he did, we wouldn't be here today.

Sean Carroll ran into that vestibule after he believed that the threat had ended. He ran over to Mr. Diallo and attempted to give him CPR, and he pleaded with him, "Don't die. Please, don't die."

And . . . when the superior officers came onto the scene, Sean Carroll was so traumatized and remained so traumatized to this day.

This is the person who the prosecution charges intended to kill Mr. Diallo and had a depraved indifference to human life.

Ladies and gentlemen, Mr. Diallo clearly deserved a much better fate.

And the evidence will show that Sean Carroll deserves a much better fate than being charged with a crime for being put into a situation that is every good cop's nightmare and is now his. And I hope that you will listen to the evidence and end his nightmare.

POSTSCRIPT

After more than two days of deliberations, the four police officers were acquitted of all charges. The acquittals seemed incomprehensible to anyone who knew the story only from the headlines. Yet the outcome was not shocking to most people acquainted with the details. Since the officers clearly had no motive for killing the unarmed victim, making the charges stick seemed unlikely from the start. At the time of the shooting, they were looking for a rapist accused of attacking fifty-two women. While premeditation is not an element of the specific charges of intentional or depraved-indifference murder, the officers certainly did not go to work that night planning to kill an unarmed man. At best the evidence suggested an act of negligence. The prosecution seemed to overcharge the four officers in charging murder. They might have had an easier time if they had argued criminally negligent homicide alone and not saddled themselves with a prosecution that strained their credibility as advocates.

The defense's request for a change venue from Bronx County was granted by an appellate court, which noted that extensive negative pretrial publicity—including a full-page ad in the New York Times placed by the ACLU that was highly critical of the police—made the selection of a fair and impartial jury in Bronx County "fruitless." (A defense survey found that 80 percent of the jurors in the Bronx thought that the cops were guilty, even without hearing the evidence.) There were numerous demonstrations around New York City protesting against Diallo's shooting,

including one outside the grand jury as the case was being deliberated. The appellate court transferred the case to Albany
County, New York, and the case was heard before a jury of eight
whites and four African-Americans. Needless to say, attitudes in
the Bronx differed greatly from those in Albany, and the change
of venue was perhaps the most pivotal decision in the case. After
the acquittal, Al Sharpton, who was a key figure in mobilizing the
demonstrations, blamed the unfavorable decision on the change
of venue, noting that Albany juries had never convicted a police
officer. Ironically, the demonstrations he organized had a hand in
the trial's relocation.

Defense attorney Bennett Epstein quickly dealt with the
media hoopla surrounding the case by openly referring to his
nervousness, subtly telling the jury that they, at least, must keep
their heads. The challenge—not an easy one—required him to
keep the jury focused, to prevent the drama on the streets from
infecting the courtroom, and to make sure that facts spoke louder
than emotions. Ultimately, as the details unfolded, the defense
position got stronger, and not merely because of the absence of
motive. The newly acquired semiautomatics and the full-metal-
jacket ammunition precisely explained the most dramatically
damning aspect of the case—why so many bullets were fired while
the victim remained standing.

In sentencing Isaac Jones, the rapist whom the police were
looking for when they came upon Diallo, State Supreme Court
Justice Joseph Fisch stated, "Yesterday your sister made reference to the tragedy of February 4, 1999, when the police, searching for you, saw and mistook a man bearing striking resemblance
to you. Would Amadou Diallo be alive today were it not for your
activities here in the Bronx?" At the end of the day, clearly, the
jury accepted the defense's assertion that Diallo's death was a
tragic accident.

9

A WAR OF THE WORLDVIEWS

THE STATE OF TENNESSEE
v. JOHN SCOPES

THE SCOPES MONKEY TRIAL is a fascinating example of the clash of cultural values playing itself out in the courtroom. John Scopes, a biology teacher, was being tried for teaching evolution in violation of the Butler Law, a Tennessee statute passed in 1924 that made it unlawful for any public-school teacher to teach Darwin's theory of evolution. Even though the questionable law was passed, there could be no challenge to its constitutionality until someone got arrested for violating it. By teaching evolution in the classroom, Scopes invited the charge of violating the Butler Law upon himself, thereby giving himself the opportunity to dispute its legitimacy in court.

William Jennings Bryan, three-time Democratic presidential candidate, prosecuted the case against the formidable opposition of defense attorney Clarence Darrow. The eight-day-long trial, which began on July 10, 1925, was America's definitive legal contest between the fundamentalist and secular interpretations of science. The defendant became an irrelevant actor in the process. The case was submitted to the jury without summations by either party. William Jennings Bryan delivered the summation he had prepared to reporters after the verdict.

Excerpts from the Opening Statement of
Defense Attorney Dudley Malone

Editor's note: Note that the defense does not discuss whether Scopes violated the law by teaching evolution.

The purpose of the defense will be to set before you all available facts and information from every branch of science to aid you in forming an opinion of what evolution is, and of what value to progress and comfort is the theory of evolution, for you are the judges of the law and the facts, and the defense wishes to aid you in every way to intelligent opinion.

The defense denies that it is part of any movement or conspiracy on the part of scientists to destroy the authority of Christianity or the Bible. The defense denies that any such conspiracy exists except in the mind and purpose of the evangelical leader of the prosecution. The Book of Genesis is in part a hymn, in part an allegory and work of religious interpretations written by men who believed that the earth was flat and whose authority cannot be accepted to control the teachings of science in our schools.

The narrow purpose of the defense is to establish the innocence of the defendant Scopes. The broad purpose of the defense will be to prove that the Bible is a work of religious aspiration and rules of conduct which must be kept in the field of theology. There is no more justification for imposing the conflicting views of the Bible on courses of biology than there would be for imposing the views of biologists on courses of comparative religion. Science and religion embrace two separate and distinct fields of thought and learning.

We remember that Jesus said, "Render unto Caesar the things that are Caesar's and unto God the things that are God's."

Editor's note: The issue to William Jennings Bryan was much larger than whether Scopes had violated the Tennessee law of teaching evolution in a public school.

Excerpts from the Unofficial Summation of
Willliam Jennings Bryan

Science is a magnificent force, but it is not a teacher of morals.

It can perfect machinery, but it adds no moral restraints to protect society from the misuse of the machine. It can also build gigantic intellectual ships, but it constructs no moral rudders for the control of storm-tossed human vessel. It not only fails to supply the spiritual element needed, but some of its unproven hypotheses rob the ship of its compass and thus endanger its cargo.

In war, science has proven itself an evil genius; it has made war more terrible than it ever was before. Man used to be content to slaughter his fellowmen on a single plane—the earth's surface. Science has taught him to go down into the water and shoot up from below and to go up into the clouds and shoot down from above, thus making the battlefield three times as bloody as it was before; but science does not teach brotherly love. Science has made war so hellish that civilization was about to commit suicide; and now we are told that newly discovered instruments of destruction will make the cruelties of the late war seem trivial in comparison with the cruelties of wars that may come in the future.

If civilization is to be saved from the wreckage threatened by intelligence not consecrated by love, it must be saved by the moral code of the meek and lowly Nazarene. His teachings, and His teachings, alone, can solve the problems that vex heart and perplex the world. . . .

It is for the jury to determine whether this attack upon the Christian religion shall be permitted in the public schools of Tennessee by teachers employed by the state and paid out of the public treasury. This case is no longer local; the defendant ceases to play an important part. The case has assumed the proportions of a battle-royal between unbelief that attempts to speak through so-called science and the defenders of the Christian faith, speaking through the legislators of Tennessee. It is again a choice between God and Baal; it is also a renewal of the issue in Pilate's court. . . . Again force and love meet face-to-face, and the question "What shall I do with Jesus?" must be answered. A bloody, brutal doctrine—evolution—demands, as the rabble did nineteen hundred years ago, that He be crucified. That cannot be the answer of this jury representing a Christian state and sworn to uphold the laws of Tennessee. Your answer will be heard throughout the world; it is eagerly awaited by a praying multitude. If the law is nullified, there will be rejoicing wherever God is repudiated, the savior scoffed at, and the Bible ridiculed. Every unbeliever of every kind and degree will be happy. If, on the other hand, the law is upheld and the religion of the schoolchildren protected, millions of Christians will call you blessed and, with hearts full of gratitude to God, will sing again that grand old song of triumph:

> Faith of our fathers, living still,
> In spite of dungeon, fire and sword;
> O how our hearts beat high with joy
> Whene'er we hear that glorious word—
> Faith of our fathers—Holy faith
> We will be true to thee till death!

POSTSCRIPT

John Scopes was convicted after eight minutes of deliberation and was sentenced to a one-hundred-dollar fine, which, according to R. M. Cornelius of Bryan College, William Jennings Bryan offered to pay if Scopes could not. As a simple matter of fact, he was indeed teaching evolution in the classroom in contravention of Tennessee law; there was no factual issue to be resolved in court. In 1928 his conviction was reversed by the Tennessee Supreme Court, which held that the jury, not the judge, had the power to fine John Scopes. After the reversal, the Tennessee lower court dismissed the charge, feeling that a retrial would serve no purpose. The war of the worldviews continues to this very day. A college student brought a complaint against a Texas Tech professor, Robert Dini, for requiring students to affirmatively state their belief in evolution as a condition of Professor Dini's writing a letter of recommendation. The Department of Justice dropped the investigation after Professor Dini changed his policy by agreeing to write letters of recommendation for all students who demonstrated an understanding of evolution.

10

A CONFEDERACY OF DUNCES

THE UNITED STATES OF AMERICA v. MARTHA STEWART

MARTHA STEWART'S METEORIC RISE from her humble childhood roots in Nutley, New Jersey, to a name synonymous with all that was special about home decorating and entertaining was a real-life Horatio Alger story, a testament to Stewart's own incredible drive to succeed and to the ability of any person, regardless of social status, to climb the ladder to the upper rung of American society.

In 2003, Stewart began receiving an unwelcome sort of media attention, having entered the world of corporate scandal and wrongdoing. In late December 2001, Stewart's friend Sam Waksal, CEO of a biotech company called ImClone, learned prior to the public at large that the FDA was going to reject his company's current application for approval of its cancer drug, Erbitux.

Having made the decision that he and his family should sell his ImClone stock, Waskal phoned his broker, Peter Bacanovic of Merrill Lynch—also Martha Stewart's broker—to begin the transaction. Bacanovic was on vacation but he and his young assistant Doug Faneuil spoke on the telephone. Faneuil told Bacanovic that the Waksals were trying to sell all of their ImClone stock. Baconovic instructed Doug Faneuil, to call Stewart—who was en route to Mexico at the time—in a conference call and notify her. Unable to get through, Bacanovic left her a message: "Peter

Bacanovic thinks ImClone is going to start trading downward."

When Stewart received the message, she called Merryl Lynch and spoke to Faneuil. Faneuil following Bacanovic's instructions to tell Stewart that the Waksals were selling their ImClone stock. Stewart, on learning this, instructed Faneuil to sell all four thousand shares of ImClone stock she had at Merrill Lynch, which brought in just over a quarter million dollars. While Martha Stewart was on vacation in Mexico, she told her best friend Mariana Pasternak, about her sale of the ImClone stock. She said that the Waksals were trying to sell their shares as well. According to Pasternak, Martha Stewart said, "Isn't it nice to have brokers who tell you things?"

Merrill Lynch and the SEC began to investigate the dumping of the Waksal's stock by Aliza Waksal and Martha Stewart on December 27, 2001, the day before the FDA's announcement. When ImClone publicized the bad news on December 28, 2001, its stock plummeted in value.

The focus of the investigation turned to Doug Faneuil and Peter Bacanovic. At Bacanovic's suggestion, Faneuil told Merrill Lynch investigators that Stewart had sold her stock to offset other tax gains. A few days later, Merrill Lynch investigators questioned Bacanovic, and he gave the same story.

Around one week later, Stewart and Bacanovic voluntarily underwent interviews by the SEC. Bacanovic lied and told the SEC that he personally had handled the trade, because he and Martha Stewart had agreed to sell ImClone if it ever fell to $60 per share. Stewart vouched for this story.

Four days before her SEC interview, Stewart sat at her assistant's desk and deleted Bacanovic's December 27, 2001, message, (Peter Bacanovic thinks ImClone is going to start trading downward) replacing it with the phrase "Bacanovic: ImClone." She then told her assistant, who had witnessed Stewart make the change, to "put it back." By February 4, 2002, however, Stewart told the government lawyers that she did not know if Bacanovic had even left her a message to begin with.

The SEC interviewed Peter Bacanovic a second time, this time under oath. This time he produced a worksheet to corroborate his claim that there was an agreement between Martha Stewart and Bacanovic to sell the stock if it went down to $60. The worksheet contained the notation "@ $60." The original was sent to a forensic laboratory that showed that the only entry on the worksheet that was in a different ink was the entry "@ $60." Secret Service ink expert Larry Stewart testified at the trial that he worked on two ink analysis tests. After the trial, Stewart was indicted for perjury for falsely claiming to be present when another lab worker tested the worksheet.

Martha Stewart agreed to be interviewed a second time by the SEC and in that interview said that she did not remember hearing that the Waksals were selling their stock.

Among the various charges in the indictment, Stewart and Bacanovic were charged with conspiracy to obstruct the SEC's investigation, to give false statements, and to commit perjury. They were also charged with obstruction of the SEC's investigation and making false statements to a federal official.

Below, you will find excerpts of Robert Morvillo's clever, if ultimately unsuccessful, summation.

Excerpts from the Summation of Defense Attorney Robert Morvillo
A Confederacy of Dunces

Ladies and gentlemen of the jury, the government has accused Martha Stewart of participation in a confederacy of dunces, because nobody could have done what Peter Bacanovic and Martha Stewart are alleged to have done and done it in a dumber fashion.

Let's follow the logic a little further. If two very bright, successful people like Peter Bacanovic and Martha Stewart . . . We know that they are smart people. We know that they are successful people. We know they pay attention to detail in their everyday lives. We know they have risen up the ladder from a job point of view, from an economic point of view by dint of hard work and by dint of doing things the right way. If those two people want to sit down and rig a story, wouldn't they make that story consistent on at least the major aspects of it? If you and I were conspiring to fool the government, to fool the SEC when we sat down on January 16, wouldn't we get our stories straight? Well, of course, we would. Let's see whether that's what Peter Bacanovic and Martha Stewart did. Look at the gaping inconsistencies in the recollections that they had when they testified. First, first, when did the sixty-dollar conversation take place? Now, if you and I were conspiring to create a sixty-dollar story that didn't exist, first we would create the substance; then we would say, "Hey, when did this conversation take place?" Because that's very important in the context of December 27. And then we say, where did this conversation take place? And then we say, who else should we say knew about this conversation, and things like that. But they fall down on the very first important element of this story: When did it take place? When Martha Stewart goes in and is interviewed on February 4, she says that it takes place in October or November or December. She doesn't say December 21 or December 20. When Peter Bacanovic tells the story, he says, yeah, it took place on December 20 and 21. He had the documents; he had the recollection fresh behind him. He had the ability to go and check in his file before he went and was interviewed on December 7. So what you have here is the two conspirators forgetting to tell each other the crucial element of the conspiracy. When did it take place? When did the meeting take place? When did the conversation, the key part of the conspiracy, take place?

And is that all? No. Guess what else they forget to tell each other as they sit there rigging a story? They forget to tell each other who took the order on December 27. On January 7, Peter Bacanovic tells Judy Monaghan that it was Doug Faneuil that took the order. On January 3, Doug Faneuil tells the SEC that it was Doug Faneuil that took the order. On February 4, when Martha Stewart goes and is interviewed by the SEC, she says she thought she talked to Peter Bacanovic. Now, my God. If Peter Bacanovic is saying that he talked to Doug Faneuil on January 7, and if Doug Faneuil is saying that, how was it that something as elemental as who took the order on December 27, the very key date here, is not something that meshes? So the price doesn't mesh, and who she doesn't talk to doesn't mesh.

Defining Lying

Let me read to you from the opening [statement] of [Assistant U.S. Attorney Karen] Seymour on this subject. She said that "on

December 27, Sam Waksal and his daughter Aliza Waksal were try-ing to desperately sell their shares of ImClone stock. They wanted to sell all of their stock in the company that Sam Waksal had, all of their shares in the company. Let me give you an idea of how much stock we are talking about: seven and a half million dollars' worth of ImClone stock, every last share of ImClone stock that the Waksals held." We know that's wrong, don't we? It was actually 2 percent of the stock that the Waksals held. What Ms. Seymour said was inac-curate. Do I think she was lying to you? Of course not. She is an hon-orable person. She wouldn't lie to you. She made a mistake, just like Martha Stewart may have made a mistake on the date in which she first thought the sixty-dollar conversation took place. She made a mistake; just like Heidi DeLuca [Martha Stewart's business manager] might have made a mistake on the date that she thought the con-versation with Peter Bacanovic took place. Just because somebody misspeaks, just because somebody makes an inaccurate statement, doesn't mean that they are lying, doesn't mean that they are intend-ing to deceive. Ms. Seymour wasn't intending to deceive you. She knew full well that Sam Waksal had sold only 2 percent of his shares that day. She made a mistake in confusing the fact that he had sold all of the shares at Merrill Lynch with all of his shares. She misspoke. The government is asking you to convict on similar evidence to that, because we are suggesting to you that whatever mistakes were made were good-faith mistakes, not bad-faith mistakes.

Stamping Out the Government Ink Expert

We know that Peter Bacanovic under oath recalled the conver-sation on February 13, and in his testimony before the SEC, we know that the words of sixty dollars were written on the December 21 document and in ink that is also used on another entry on that page. It is certainly another affirmative piece of evidence support-ing the notion that the sixty-dollar conversation took place.

We know that many people use more than one pen on a docu-ment. Pens roll, pens are scattered. Look over at those desks (pointing to desks in the courtroom). You will see a whole bunch of different pens on those desks. When you're talking to somebody, you pick up one pen one minute and something else happens and you get distracted, and you go back, the pen is rolled away. I actually think there is someone who eats pens in my office. They come in at night and they eat all my pens, and when I come in in the morning, they are not there anymore. I must have written with four thousand pens. What ecstasy an ink expert would have if he got a hold of one of my documents.

Mariana Pasternak's Damning Testimony

Is it possible Mariana read about the other things at a later point and, like many of us do, transferred her recollection from one date or one source to another? It's possible. We don't know. It is something that you have got to consider in evaluating Mariana Pasternak's testimony. Its message to you is, you've got to be careful about people who claim that they can recall in detail events with precision that took place such a long time ago in a context in which they were not particularly meaningful.

Look, I know you know that there are events that take place in our lives, that there are events that take place in public that capture our recollection and that we can talk to you about where we were when we heard about a certain event. Where were you on 9/11? Everybody remembers that. Where were you when President Kennedy got assassinated? Only I remember that, because I'm the only one old enough to remember that here. We remember those kinds of things. What we don't retain necessarily with precision and with detail are events which take place along the way. Everybody understands, perhaps with the exception of Doug Faneuil, that memory erodes with time. And so, in evaluating the testimony, [SEC investigator Helene] Glotzer, [FBI agent Catherine] Farmer, Faneuil, Pasternak, you have got to absolutely analyze that in the context that they are testifying about events from memory of two years old, whereas when Mr. Bacanovic was testifying on February 13 and Ms. Stewart was testifying on February 4; they were closer to the events, and therefore their recollection could be more reliable. But even on those dates, as we have seen, they made mistakes, because even thirty days is enough, because of the course of human events and course of human memory to start the erosion of memory.

That's one reason you can't put any credit in the kind of wild testimony we had from Mariana Pasternak about, "isn't it nice to have brokers who tell you things." First of all, she doesn't even tell you it was a recollection. She told you it was a recollection on direct examination. On cross-examination she told you it might not have been a recollection. It might just have been something that she thought at a time, and it's kind of in her mind, and it's floating in her mind. On redirect examination she said she really didn't have a good memory of the thing. Finally, at the end, the government, who knew about this problem all the way through, pulled out of her that it was her belief.

We don't convict people on beliefs. We convict people on recollections, and we convict people on firm recollections, on recollections that are reliable, on recollections that are credible, not belief. And if you really want to credit the testimony that it was something that was actually said during the course of that vacation, when was it said? Where was it said? What was its context? Because only then will there be some meaning to that statement. Mariana Pasternak couldn't tell you whether it was before or after the Waksal conversation. She couldn't tell you what the context was. Mariana Pasternak is a broker. She is a real-estate broker. She couldn't even tell you if you were dealing with a real-estate broker or stockbroker or some other kind of broker. She couldn't tell you any of those things. And if she can't tell you that context, you can't make any use of that statement. That statement cannot be the foundation evidence to any finding of anything on the part of, I submit to you, reasonable people.

Attacking Doug Faneuil

The best indication of [Doug Faneuil's] motivation to shade the truth just a little bit is when he was asked on cross-examination about his preparation [for his trial testimony]. You remember his direct examination. It was an absolutely terrific professional job of preparation that was done with Doug Faneuil, and it was smooth as silk. Then he was asked on cross-examination, "Did you prepare?" and he said, "Yes, I did prepare. But they didn't ask me the bulk of the questions that they asked when I was on direct examination," and that sounded pretty peculiar, that they didn't go through every single question that they were going to ask him when he testified on direct examination. That's what he said: "They didn't ask me the bulk of the questions." So on cross-examination we further said to him, "Were you surprised then? If they didn't ask you the bulk of the questions that they were going to ask you, were you surprised?" And he said, "Yeah, I was surprised at some of the questions." Now he is stuck, and he has got to go forward with it. Then we asked him, "Well, tell us. You of the prodigious memory, you of the person who remembers everything because you can remember intimately and with precision word for word a conversation that took place twenty-five months ago, tell us one of the questions that you were surprised [at] on direct examination." What was his answer? "I can't remember any as I sit here now." That pretty much sums up Doug Faneuil. Doug Faneuil carries more baggage with him than a cargo handler loading a cruise ship for an around-the-world voyage.

Keeping Martha Off the Stand

Martha Stewart did not testify in this case. You were probably looking forward to hearing from Martha Stewart. The judge is going to instruct you that you cannot take that into consideration in your deliberations. You cannot in any way, shape, or form consider the fact that she did not testify in this case in deciding whether there is sufficient or insufficient evidence of her guilt. Whatever your expectations were, whatever your disappointment may be, you cannot consider it.

Now, each and every one of you took an oath when you signed on as jurors. You took an oath that you were going to apply the law to the facts of this case. The judge is going to tell you what the law is, and she is going to tell you that you cannot take that into consideration. So I ask you to fulfill your oath, follow the judge's instruction on this, and put out of your mind whatever you feel in terms of frustration or disappointment or anger or concern about the failure of Martha Stewart to testify. The decision was made based upon the fact that you already know her testimony. She testified on February 4, she testified on April 10 (the two interviews Martha Stewart had with government lawyers and the SEC), she told the government her recollection of the events at that time. That recollection hasn't gotten any better. She is not like

Doug Faneuil and other people, who can tell you today more succinctly and more credibly what happened twenty-five months ago. Her best recollection was on February 4 and April 10, and that's why you are not permitted by law to go beyond that.

POSTSCRIPT

The court dismissed a charge of securities fraud but allowed the other charges to be submitted to the jury. Martha Stewart was convicted of all of the counts of obstructing justice and lying to investigators. She was sentenced to five months of incarceration.

The irony of the Martha Stewart verdict was that she would not have been convicted of anything had she refused to speak to SEC investigators. She could not be compelled to do so, and she did this voluntarily. That was not the decision of Robert Morvillo. If any blame could be laid on the advice given to her, it should be pointed at those who advised her to speak to SEC investigators in the first place. Of course, Ms. Stewart was not some naïve individual who had no idea what she was doing. She had been a stockbroker thirty years prior and also actually sat on the board of the NYSE. We may never know whether she was advised by lawyers not to speak to the SEC and disregarded that decision.

Contrary to the bad press that Mr. Morvillo received after the verdict, Mr. Morvillo's summation as excerpted above had many fine points. Mr. Morvillo used inconsistencies between the stories told by Ms. Stewart and Mr. Bacanovic to the SEC to label the two a "confederacy of dunces." He argued persuasively that if two bright people were trying to fool the government, they should be consistent about their stories. This argument has also been used by prosecutors to explain discrepancies in testimony between police officers (i.e., if the officers had gotten their stories together, wouldn't they be on the same page?). Of course, the alternate argument is that Stewart and Bacanovic were not very good liars and that's why there are inconsistencies.

Mr. Morvillo took the position that the jury might believe the SEC and government lawyers in relating the statements made to them by Stewart. He then claimed that some of the statements may have been mistaken, but that does not make Martha Stewart a liar. To buttress this position, he pointed out a misstatement made by prosecutor Karen Seymour in her opening statement. Mr. Morvillo most probably knew he was going to make this argument even before the trial began. He no doubt sat in the courtroom waiting for one of the prosecutors to misstate a fact so he could point to it in his closing argument.

Trials can be interesting, because the same fact can often be interpreted differently. The ink example is a good one. To the prosecution, the ink evidence is proof of a plan by Bacanovic to add the notation "@$60" after the SEC investigation began. To Mr. Morvillo this is evidence that people often use multiple pens. It was a nice touch by Mr. Morvillo to point to a table in the courtroom containing many pens to drive the point home.

After the jury verdict, the Monday-morning quarterbacks crawled out of the woodwork en masse, questioning Morvillo's decision to keep Martha Stewart off the stand. If she were to testify, the prosecution could perhaps ask her about prior bad acts that the jury had not yet learned of. She may have had to admit several facts that were in dispute. Furthermore, if one were to believe Doug Faneuil's trial testimony of Ms. Stewart's telephone manner to him, she may have blown up during cross-examination, thereby exposing herself as an unlikable person. When the defendant does not testify at a trial, the defense attorney is free to argue "reasonable doubt," and this could be twenty different versions of the event. When a defendant testifies at trial, the jury tends to weigh the prosecution's version against the defense and see which one makes more sense. It is often an advantage for the defense to be able to argue countless "reasonable doubts" rather than be stuck with the one story of the defendant. No twenty-twenty hindsight can detract from the fact that Mr. Morvillo gave a great summation.

Then why did she get convicted if the summation was so good? Well, for starters, the cultural backdrop of this case was an era of corporate corruption and corporate greed. Certainly, that did not help Martha Stewart. A second truism emerges: Very often the evidence carries the day. To paraphrase the late Judge Leff, "You have a right to a competent lawyer; you don't have the right to Houdini." Robert Morvillo could not help Martha Stewart escape from the various strands of evidence pointing to her guilt. Courtroom speeches, no matter how brilliant, can affect the result in only a small percentage of cases. Even if a lawyer gives a great speech, if he doesn't have the evidence on his side or if the cultural backdrop is heavily tilted against him, he will still probably lose the case. A great courtroom speech will help you win the cases you should win and perhaps win close cases. It will not help you win the unwinnable case.

11

An EPIC AFFAIR
BILL CLINTON
MAKES HISTORY

CONGRESSMAN HENRY HYDE, House Judiciary chairman, gave the following summation in January 1999 to members of the Senate in connection with the Senate impeachment trial of president Bill Clinton:

THE SENATE IMPEACHMENT TRIAL OF
PRESIDENT WILLIAM JEFFERSON CLINTON

One hundred thirty-six years ago, at a small military cemetery in Pennsylvania, one of Illinois's most illustrious sons asked a haunting question, whether a nation conceived in liberty and dedicated to the proposition that all men are created equal can long endure.

America is an experiment never finished; it's a work in progress. That question has to be answered by each generation for itself, just as we will have to answer whether this nation can long endure.

This controversy began with the fact that the president of the United States took an oath to tell the truth before the grand jury, just as he had on two prior occasions sworn a solemn oath to preserve, protect, and defend the Constitution and to faithfully execute the laws of the United States.

One of the most memorable aspects of this entire proceeding was the solemn occasion wherein every senator in this chamber took an oath to do impartial justice under the Constitution. Despite massive and relentless efforts to change the subject, the case before you is not about sexual misconduct, adultery. Those are private acts and are none of our business. It's not even a question of lying about sex.

The matter before this body is a question of lying under oath. This is a public act. The matter before you is a question of the premeditated, deliberate corruption of the nation's system of justice through perjury and obstruction of justice. These are public acts. And, when committed by the chief law-enforcement officer of the land, the one who appoints every United States district attorney, every federal judge, every member of the Supreme Court, they do become the concern of Congress. And that's why your judgment should rise above politics, above polling data.

This case is a test of whether what the Founding Fathers described as "sacred honor" still has meaning in our time 222 years after those two words, "sacred honor," were inscribed in our country's birth certificate, our Declaration of Independence.

Every schoolchild in the United States has an intuitive sense of the sacred honor that is one of the foundation stones of the American house of freedom, for every day in every classroom in America, our children pledge allegiance to a nation under God. That statement is not a prideful claim. It's a statement of humility. The presidency is an office of trust. Every public office is a public trust, but the office of the president is a very special public trust. The president is the trustee of the national conscience. No one owns the office of the president—the people do.

The president is elected by the people and their representatives in the electoral college. The president in his inaugural oath enters [into] a binding agreement of mutual trust and obligation with the American people.

During his first few months in office, President Clinton spoke about a new covenant in America. Let's take the president at his word that his office is a covenant, a solemn pact of mutual trust and obligation with the American people. Let's take the president seriously when he speaks of covenants, because a covenant is about promise making and promise keeping. For it's because the president has violated the oaths he has sworn that he has been impeached. The debate about impeachment during the Constitutional Convention of 1787 makes it clear that the Framers regarded impeachment and removal from office on conviction as a remedy for a fundamental betrayal of trust by the president.

The Framers had invested the presidential office with great powers. They knew that those powers could and would be abused if any president were to violate in a fundamental way the oath to faithfully execute the nation's laws. For if the president did so violate his oath of office, the covenant of trust between himself and the American people would be broken. The fundamental trust between America and the world can be broken if a presidential perjurer represents our country in world affairs. If the president calculatedly and repeatedly violates his oath, he can no longer be trusted. And because the executive plays so large a role in representing our country to the world, America can no longer be trusted.

We live in an age of increasing interdependence. The future will require an even stronger bond of trust between the president and the nation, because with increasing interdependence comes an increased necessity of trust. This is one of the basic lessons of life. Parents and children know it; husbands and wives know it; teachers and students know it.

The greater the interdependence, the greater the imperative of promise keeping. Trust, not what James Madison called the "parchment barriers of laws," is the fundamental bond between the people and their elected representatives, between those who govern and those who are governed.

Trust is the mortar that secures the foundations of the American house of freedom. And the Senate of the United States, sitting in judgment on this impeachment trial, should not ignore or dismiss the fact that that bond of trust has been broken, because the president has violated both his oath of office and the oath before his grand-jury testimony.

It's often been asked, So what? What is the harm done by this lying under oath, by this perjury? What is an oath? An oath is an asking Almighty God to witness to the truth of what you're saying. Truth telling is the heart and soul of our justice system. The answer would have been clear to those who once pledged their sacred honor to the cause of liberty. The answer would have been clear to those who crafted the world's most enduring written constitution.

No greater harm can come than [through] breaking the covenant of trust between the president and the people, for to break that covenant of trust is to dissolve the mortar that binds the foundation stones of our freedom into a secure and solid edifice. And to break the covenant of trust by violating one's oath is to do grave damage to the rule of law among us.

That none of us is above the law is a bedrock principle of democracy. To erode that bedrock is to subscribe to a "divine right of kings" theory of governance, in which those who govern are absolved from adhering to the basic moral standards to which the governed are accountable. We must never tolerate one law for the ruler and another for the ruled. If we do, we break faith with our ancestors from Bunker Hill, Lexington, Concord to Flanders Fields, Normandy, Hiroshima, Saigon, and Desert Storm.

The vote you are asked to cast is a vote about the rule of law. The rule of law is one of the great achievements of our civilization, for the alternative to the rule of law is the rule of raw power.

We here today are the heirs of three thousand years of history in which humanity slowly and painfully, and at great cost, evolved a form of politics in which law, not brute force, is the arbiter of our public destinies.

We're the heirs of the Ten Commandments and the Mosaic law, moral code for a free people, who, having been liberated from bondage, saw in law a means to avoid falling back into the habits of slaves. We're the heirs of Roman law, the first legal system [in] which peoples of different cultures, languages, races, and religions came to live together to form a political community.

We're the heirs of the Magna Carta, by which the free men of England began to break the arbitrary and unchecked power of royal absolutism. We're the heirs of 1776 and of an epic moment in human affairs when the founders of this republic pledged their lives, their fortunes, and their sacred honor to the defense of the rule of law. We're the heirs of a tragic civil war which vindicated the rule of law over the appetites of some for owning others. We're the heirs of the twentieth century's great struggles against totalitarianism, in which the rule of law was defended at immense cost against the worst tyrannies in human history.

The rule of law is no pious aspiration from a civics textbook. The rule of law is what stands between us and the arbitrary exercise of power by the state.

Lying under oath is an abuse of freedom. Obstruction of justice is a degradation of law. There are people in prison for such offenses. What in the world do we say to them about equal justice if we overlook this conduct by the president?

Some may say that this is to pitch the matter too high. The president's lie, it is said, was about a trivial matter; it was a lie to spare embarrassment about misconduct on a private occasion. The confusing of what is essentially a private matter and none of our business with lying under oath to a court and a grand jury has been only one of the distractions we've had to deal with. We can all imagine a situation in which a president might shade the truth when a great issue of national interest or national security is at stake. We've been all over that terrain.

We know the thin ice on which any of us skates when blurring the edges of the truth for what we consider a compelling, demanding public purpose. Morally serious men and women can imagine the circumstances at the far edge of the morally permissible when, with the gravest matters of national interest at stake, a president could shade the truth in order to serve the common good. But under oath for a private pleasure? In doing this, the office of the president of the United States has been debased and the justice system jeopardized. In doing this, he's broken his covenant of trust with the American people.

The Framers also knew that the office of the president could be gravely damaged if it continued to be unworthily occupied. That's why they devised the process of impeachment. If on impeachment the president is convicted, he's removed from office and the office itself suffers no permanent damage. If on impeachment the president is acquitted, the issue is resolved once and for all, and the office is similarly protected from permanent damage.

But if on impeachment the president is not convicted and removed from office despite the fact that numerous senators are convinced that he has, in the words of one proposed resolution of censure, "egregiously failed the test of his oath of office, violated the trust of the American people, and dishonored the office by which they entrusted to him," then the office of the presidency has been deeply and perhaps permanently damaged.

To fail to do so, while conceding that the president has engaged in egregious and dishonorable behavior, that [he] has broken the covenant of trust between himself and the American people, is to diminish the office of president of the United States in an unprecedented and unacceptable way.

None of us comes to this chamber today without a profound sense of our own responsibilities in life and of the many ways in which we have failed to meet those responsibilities to one degree or another. None of us comes to you claiming to be a perfect man or a perfect citizen. Just as none of you imagines yourself perfect, all of us, members of the House and Senate, know we come to this difficult task as flawed human beings under judgment. That is the way of this world—flawed human beings must, according to the rule of law, judge other flawed human beings.

But the issue before the Senate of the United States is not the question of its own members' personal moral condition, nor is the issue before the Senate the question of the personal moral condition of the members of the House of Representatives. The issue here is whether the president has violated the rule of law and thereby broken the covenant of trust with the American people. And it's not affected one way or another by the personal moral condition of any member of either House of Congress.

Senators, we of the House don't come before you today lightly. It is a disservice to the House to suggest that it has brought these articles of impeachment before you in a mean-spirited or irresponsible way. That is not true. We have brought these articles of

impeachment because we're convinced in conscience that the president of the United States committed perjury on several occasions
before a federal grand jury [and] willfully obstructed justice.

These are not trivial matters. These are not partisan matters.
These are matters of justice, the justice that each of you has taken a
solemn oath to serve in this trial. Some of us have been called Clinton haters. This impeachment trial is not a question of hating anyone. This is not a question of who we hate, it's a question of what
we love. And among the things we love are equal justice before the
law and honor in our public life.

Senators, the trial is being watched around the world. Some of
those watching, thinking themselves superior in their cynicism, wonder what it's all about. But political prisoners know that this is about
the rule of law, the great alternative to arbitrary and unchecked state
powers. The families of executed dissidents know that this is about the
rule of law, the great alternative to the lethal abuse of power by the
state. Those yearning for freedom know [that] this is about the rule of
law —the one structure by which men and women can live by their
God-given dignity and secure their God-given rights in ways that serve
the common good. If they know this, can we not know it?

If across the river in Arlington Cemetery there are American
heroes who died in defense of the rule of law, can we give less than
the full measure of our devotion to that great cause?

I wish to read you a letter I recently received:

Dear Chairman Hyde,

My name is William Preston Sommers. How are you doing? I
am a third grader at Chase Elementary School in Chicago. I'm
writing this letter because I have something to tell you. I have
thought of a punishment for the president. The punishment
should be that he should write a 100-word essay by hand. I
have to write an essay when I lie. It is bad to lie because it just
gets you in more trouble. I hate getting in trouble. It's just like
the boy who cried "wolf" and the wolf ate the boy. It is important to tell the truth. If you do not tell the truth, people do not

believe you. It is important to believe the President because he is a important person. If you cannot believe the President, who can you believe? I do not believe the President tells the truth any more right now. After he writes the essay and tells the truth, I will believe him again. William Sommers

Then there's a P.S. from his dad:

Dear Representative Hyde, I made my son William either write you a letter or an essay as a punishment for lying. Part of his defense for his lying was that the President lied. He's still having difficulty understanding why the President can lie and not be punished.

On June 6, 1994, it was the fiftieth anniversary of the American landing at Normandy, and I went ashore at Normandy and walked up to the cemetery area where, as far as the eye could see, there were white crosses, Stars of David. And the British had a bagpipe band scattered among the crucifixes, the crosses, playing "Amazing Grace" with that pierceful, mournful sound that only the bagpipe can make. And if you could keep your eyes dry, you were better than I. I walked up to one of these crosses marking a grave because I wanted to personalize the experience. I was looking for a name. But there was no name. It said, "Here lies in honored glory a comrade in arms known but to God."

How do we keep faith with that comrade in arms? Go to the Vietnam Memorial and the National Mall and press your hands against a few of the fifty-eight thousand names carved into that wall and ask yourself how we can redeem the debt we owe all those who purchased our freedom with their lives. How do we keep faith with them? I think I know. We work to make this country the kind of America they were willing to die for. That's an America where the idea of sacred honor still has the power to stir men's souls. My solitary hope is that one hundred years from today, people will look back at what we've done and say, "They kept the faith."

POSTSCRIPT

The Senate voted 55–45 against impeachment on the perjury charge and 50–50 on the obstruction-of-justice charge. The vote for the most part broke along partisan lines. It would have taken 67 guilty votes to expel Clinton from office. The vote undoubtedly reflected the viewpoint that perjury about adultery is not an impeachable offense, at least not in the cultural backdrop of a society with a 50 percent divorce rate.

12

THE SILKWOOD MYSTERY

THE ESTATE OF KAREN SILKWOOD V. KERR-McGEE CORPORATION

KAREN SILKWOOD WORKED FOR the Kerr-McGee Nuclear Company as a chemical technician in its Oklahoma plutonium plant. As an active member of her union, Silkwood began to grow concerned about the health of her fellow workers. While employed by the company in 1974, she uncovered evidence of managerial negligence in the area of plant safety. Silkwood began to raise questions about a broad spectrum of practices and safety failures, ranging from spills, leaks, and missing plutonium to such arcane details as the quality of the welds in fuel rods that power nuclear reactors. She also accused the company of deliberate wrongdoing and cover-ups—she believed that Kerr-McGee doctored the product-control X-rays that showed that their rods were adequately safe. In August 1974, Karen Silkwood had provided the Atomic Energy Commission with a detailed list of violations at the plant.

There was a mystery around Silkwood's exposure to plutonium shortly before her death. Silkwood spent her workday on November 5 processing plutonium in a glove box, a device that allows a worker to safely manipulate dangerous substances using gloves attached to an isolation chamber. That evening, the plant's monitoring equipment indicated that she was contaminated with radiation. The radiation did not, however, appear to come from Silkwood's work environment. Her gloves were found to be uncontaminated where they came in contact with her hands, and leak-free. No significant radiation was found on room surfaces, in the filters of air monitors, or in the air. Silkwood was decontaminated and performed radiation-free tasks for a few more hours. As she left the plant for the day, she tested herself again and found no contamination.

Silkwood came back to work early the next morning and discovered plutonium on her hands, right forearm, and the right side of her neck and face. Thus, Silkwood was leaving a workplace that showed no evidence of contamination, and without any contamination on her body, and returning contaminated.

Kerr-McGee physicists went to her apartment and found significant levels of plutonium in her bathroom and kitchen. Silkwood was asked how it was that there was plutonium in her apartment. She claimed that, as per the orders of her company superiors, she had taken a urine sample at her apartment. She also claimed that she'd spilled the urine and wiped off the container and the bathroom floor with a tissue. Silkwood also remembered starting to make a bologna sandwich and then changing her mind and returning the meat to the refrigerator. She claimed to have carried the bologna to the bathroom, where she put it on the bathroom seat. The package of bologna tested positive for plutonium.

Between October 22 and November 6, 1974, high levels of alpha activity—indicative of contamination—were present in four of the urine samples that Karen Silkwood took at home. Those collected at the Kerr-McGee plant contained very small amounts, if any at all.

Ms. Silkwood's opponents, including Kerr-McGee management and their sympathizers, accused her of contaminating herself to embarrass the company. Karen Silkwood's lawyers and supporters vehemently denied this. Kerr-McGee claimed that its Cimarron plant met federal guidelines and that any of the plutonium contamination must have come from elsewhere.

On November 13, 1974, Silkwood was going to deliver documents supporting her contentions of corporate wrongdoing to a *New York Times* reporter. She was later discovered dead in a ditch, after a serious car accident. The state police believed that Silkwood simply fell asleep at the wheel. According to the autopsy, Silkwood was found to have ingested Quaaludes. "The drug was removed from the U.S. market in 1984 due to its extensive misuse. Blood concentrations of the drug in fourteen persons arrested for erratic driving ranged from 2 to 12 milligrams per liter (average 6) (Graves. 1973)."* Karen Silkwood, who weighed about a hundred pounds, had 3.5 milligrams of Quaaludes per liter of blood in her system at the time of her death—almost twice the dosage for inducing drowsiness—and 50 milligrams of undissolved Quaaludes in her stomach.

However, some people found the circumstances mysterious; there was talk of dents in the back of Silkwood's car, suggesting that she may have been driven off the road. The documents she was allegedy transporting were nowhere to be found. Also confirmed was plutonium contamination, which authenticated test results taken when she was alive. At autopsy, the highest concentration of plutonium showed up in Silkwood's gastrointestinal tract, evidence that she had somehow taken plutonium by mouth prior to her death. How did that plutonium get into her gastrointestinal tract? The AEC report suggested that the most reasonable explanation for Karen Silkwood's gastrointestinal contamination was that she had done it to herself by eating plutonium. Steve Wodka, a union official, testified that Karen Silkwood had told him that she was worried that someone might have put plutonium on a sandwich she ate in the plant on November 5.

The Silkwood case became a cause célèbre among conspiracy theorists, especially during the height of the antinuclear movement. Among such people an obsessive knowledge of the minute details of her saga became commonplace, like the details of the grassy knoll and magic bullet to those obsessed with the Kennedy assassination. Karen Silkwood herself achieved a kind of posthumous heroic stature. Her struggle with Kerr-McGee and

Disposition of Toxic Drugs and Chemicals in Man, Randell Baselt, page 657.

law enforcement's inability to explain mysterious facts convinced many that this was a drama of powerful reactionary forces martyring a lone truth teller. The eventual trial of her case was a kind of longed-for theater of catharsis to all her followers.

The Silkwood estate sued Kerr-McGee. On March 6, 1979, the trial began, with Gerry Spence, the famous civil attorney from Wyoming, representing the estate of Karen Silkwood. The chief attorney for the corporation was William Paul. I have chosen to include here portions of Mr. Spence's summation to demonstrate the power of analogies, storytelling, and *schmooze* in persuading a jury.

Excerpts from the Summation of Plaintiff Attorney Gerry Spence

Every good closing argument has to start with "May it please the court, ladies and gentlemen of the jury," so let me start out that way with you. I actually thought we were going to grow old together. I thought maybe we would go down to Sun City and get us a nice complex there and sort of live out our lives. I had an image in my mind as the judge at the head of the block and then the six jurors with nice little houses beside each other. I hadn't made up my mind whether I was going to ask Mr. Paul to come down, but I didn't think this case was ever going to get over. As a matter of fact, as Mr. Paul kept calling witnesses, I got the impression that he's fallen in love with us over here and just didn't want to quit calling witnesses.

It was winter in Jackson, Wyoming, when I came here, and there was four feet of snow at Jackson. We've spent a season here together. I haven't been home to Jackson in two and a half months. And although I'm a full-fledged Oklahoman now, nevertheless I'm homesick. And I'm sure you're homesick, too. It's the longest case in Oklahoma history, and before the case is over, this is probably the most important case as well.

I've been in courtrooms for twenty-seven years, and I've been looking at juries and juries have been looking right back at me, and I have never seen a jury like this one, that was as attentive as this jury has been. When Bill Paul would get off on one of his automatic pilots over there and we'd listen to the qualifications of the [expert] witness, right down to the first bedpan that he emptied, I'd be ready to scream, and I'd look over, and, by gosh, you were listening and you were catching every word of it.

I can remember one time when we had Mr. Utnage on the stand [Mr. Utnage was a former Kerr-McGee engineer who had designed the plant, called as a witness by Kerr-McGee to demonstrate the care he took in designing the plant's contamination-control system], and he was talking about Durkee's dressing—one of my favorite dressings—and I got to think about hamburgers and Durkee's dressings. And the first thing you know, at noon, I had two hamburgers with Durkee's dressing, and then I slept all afternoon, and I think Mr. Paul did that to me on purpose.

Anybody in this case [who] claims they didn't have a fair trial— I guess I'd feel like punching them out. I've seen too much human sacrifice by this jury as you've listened so carefully.

Talk about patience, that judge up there—they say he has the patience of Job. My sense is that he'd make Job look like a raving spastic. This trial would have never gotten through with any other judge that I've ever seen, and we're lucky to have him. And I'm proud to have worked in your court, Your Honor.

I guess I'll compliment the carpet—it hasn't worn out. We've used it and used it walking up to the bench. According to my calculations, it's been 327 miles we've traveled up there. Sometimes we've tromped up there every thirty seconds.

I want to say something about my friend Mr. Paul. You know, we've all been here together a long time, and it's appropriate, after living two and half months together, that we say something about each other. I respect him. He's been a worthy adversary. He has represented his client well. That doesn't mean I won't try to point out all of the inconsistencies that he is irrevocably married to—which makes more than one inconsistency to which he's married, makes him a bigamist. But he's a fine lawyer, and I'm proud of the fact that we have worked with him.

It's the most important case of my career. I'm standing here talking to you about the most important things that I have ever said in my life. And I have a sense that I have spent a lifetime, fifty years to be exact, preparing somehow for this moment with you. I'm

proud to be here with you, and I'm awed, and I'm a little bit frightened, and I know that's hard for you to believe, because I don't look
frightened. But I've been frightened from time to time throughout
this trial. I've learned how to cover that up pretty well, but I can't
remember when Dr. George Voelz got on the stand [expert for
defense and chief scientist at Los Alamos Scientific Laboratory, one
of the world's most prestigious nuclear-research centers], and after
we [the plaintiff's lawyers] listened to his testimony [Dr. Voelz testified that, having analyzed Karen Silkwood's bones, lungs, liver, and
lymph nodes, he found that she had suffered no genetic damage and
that the level of contamination found in her system fell within
Atomic Energy Commission standards], we got together and we sat
down and said "Have we spent two and a half months here and are
we going to lose it all at this spot?" It all depends on your ability to
turn the coin over and show the truth—what's on the other side of
that matter. Can you do it? I hope you think that we did it together.

What I am setting out to do today is frightening to me. I hope I
have the intelligence, the spirit and ability and just the plain old
guts to get to you what I have to get to you. My greatest fear has
been that when I would get to this important case—I would stand
here in front of the jury and be called upon to make my final argument and I'd just open my mouth and nothing would come out. I'd
just sort of stand there and maybe just wet my pants. But I feel the
juices, and I'm going to be alright.

Your Honor, I bet you're wondering when I'm going to start my
argument?

THE COURT: Yes, I was.

I knew you were going to say that. You've given us four hours a side,
and you obviously have noted that I haven't started my argument, and
so my time doesn't start until now. Thank you, judge. It's 9:27.

You may feel a little insecure. You may be sitting here just like
me, not knowing whether you're up to doing this in a case full of
number-crunching statistics and scientific data and conflicting evidence. You are beautifully constituted to make this decision. Abra-

ham Lincoln once said, "You can fool part of the people part of the time, but you can't fool all of the people all of the time." A jury from all walks of life, with all kinds of experience, comes together as the common composite mind, and you bring with you all of your common sense. We are dealing with the most complex issue in the world. But I am bringing to you common sense.

Jurors can cut through all of the garbage that experts and lawyers and legalists like to lay down—[that] they can cut through it all with their common sense is what has permitted the judicial system to survive to this day.

The Lion That Got Away

What we're gonna talk about isn't hard. If a country lawyer from Wyoming can understand it, if I can explain it to my kids, then we all can understand it. "What's going on and who proves what?"

We talked about strict liability at the outset, and you'll hear the court tell you about "strict liability," and it simply means "If the lion got away, Kerr-McGee has to pay." It's that simple. That's the law. It came out of the English common law. Some guy brought an old lion on his ground, and he put it in a cage—and lions are dangerous—and through no fault of his own, the lion got away. The lion went out, and he ate up some people—and they sued the man. And they said, "You know, pay, it's your lion and he got away." And the man said, "But I did everything in my power. I had a good cage, had a good lock on the door. I had trained people watching the lion, and it isn't my fault that he got away."

Why should you punish him? They said, "You have to pay because it was your lion—unless the person who was hurt let the lion out himself." Unless in this case, Karen Silkwood was the one who intentionally took the plutonium out and "let the lion out," that is the only defense. Strict liability: "If the lion gets away, Kerr-McGee has to pay," unless Karen Silkwood let the lion loose. What do we have to prove? The lion gets away. We have to [prove] that. It's admitted in the evidence. They admit it was their plutonium. They admit it's in Karen Silkwood's apartment. It got away. And we have to prove that Karen Silkwood was damaged. I'm not going to labor you with the facts that prove that. It's almost an admitted fact that it got away and that she was damaged.

Does Silkwood prove how the lion got away? Mr. Paul [says] it's important to find out how the lion got away. It's important, but they have to prove how—we don't. You will hear the court say exactly this: "It is unnecessary for you to decide how plutonium escaped from the plant—how it entered the apartment—or how it caused her contamination, since it is a stipulated fact between the parties—that the plutonium in Silkwood's apartment was from the defendant's plant."

The question is, Who has to prove how the lion got away? They have to prove that Karen Silkwood carried it out. If they can't prove that by a preponderance of the evidence, they've lost. Why? Well, it's obvious. It's their lion, not Karen Silkwood's lion. It's that simple.

Damages

During the course of this trial, we petitioned the court to raise the claim from $10 million to $70 million. When we commenced this trial, we didn't know a great many things that we learned during the course of the trial. I had no idea of the things that Kerr-McGee did to living human beings who worked for them. I was never aware of the overt effort that was made by Kerr-McGee to keep from the employees the bare, clean truth of the dangers of plutonium. I didn't realize that that was the way it was in industry over, and that it was even almost encouraged and countenanced by those who were regulating Kerr-McGee.

This was a corporation of immense proportions that earned . . . $5 million a day. Seventy million dollars would represent not quite fourteen days of work, two weeks, a payday—a pay period for most folks. Seventy million dollars is only 3.5 percent of its total assets, and $10 million, which we originally asked for, was such a puny, piddling amount that it would hardly be felt [by Kerr-McGee] and [show] that the case stood for something important—it stands for punitive damages to stop willful and wanton and reckless and callous conduct by Kerr-McGee and those similarly situated—that you'll hear the court give instructions on how to stop this sort of thing in America.

The Mud Springs

There was only one legal defense. That's the defense that Karen Silkwood [had] supposedly taken this from the plant. I'll tell you a bigger defense than that—and that's getting drowned in mud springs. My favorite jurist has an old saying. He says if you want to clear up the water, you've got to get the hogs out of the spring. If you can't get the hogs out of the spring, I guarantee you can't clean up the water. During the course of this trial, you have observed a process by which you have been invited over and over again to get down into the mud springs where you can't see—where you can't understand—where things are all muddy. Getting jurors confused is not a proper part of jurisprudence—and getting people down in the mud springs is not the way to try a case.

Somebody has the responsibility as an attorney to help you understand what the issues are—to come forward and hold out their hand and say, "These are the honest issues, this is what you can rely on," because I am reliable and I'm not going to confuse you with irrelevancies and number crunching and word games and gobbledygook.

Keep out of the mud springs in your deliberations. You are not scientists, I'm not a scientist. Keep out of the mud springs. You'll be invited there. Use your common sense. You'll be invited to do some number crunching of your own. You'll be invited to play word games. You'll be invited to get into all kinds of irrelevancies.

Nuclear Energy

What is the case not about? The case is not about being against the nuclear industry. You will never hear me say that I stand here against the nuclear industry—I do not. I am not against nuclear power. The case is not about that. Please hear me: N-O. It is not about being against the development of a sound energy policy, including nuclear power in this country. But it is about responsible progress.

The Harvester-Ant Analogy

If you fly over Wyoming and look down, you'll see big round spots all over the landscape, like big polka dots all over the prairies. Those are the homes of the harvester ants. Architects study the structure of the harvester ant. They are perhaps the most interestingly wise and intelligent insect that we know of. They tried to get rid of the harvester ants, because they claim that those anthills take up a third of the state—and if they could just get rid of the harvester ant, there would be more land for grazing of the sheep. They have been trying to kill the harvester ant for a long time.

They developed an extraordinary poison and put it on bait— ants, like us, have to eat—and the ants would eat the bait. Then, in three or four days, they would stop eating. They found out what was causing them to die—and they wouldn't go near the bait.

One very enterprising young scientist made a poison that would get on their feet and would be absorbed up their legs, and they would put the poison in a round circle around the anthill, and the ant would walk across the poison and then die. Guess what the ants did? Hill after hill, without exception, they built bridges across the poison.

The next thing they did with the harvester ant to kill him was to make the male impotent, and so they put some poison on some bait that, when the male ate it, he was no longer able to reproduce. Pretty soon the harvester ant found that out and also quit eating the poison—just in the nick of time.

But they finally found a poison that would kill the harvester ant. It was a poison that did not kill him for four or five weeks after he ate it— and then one day four or five weeks after they had all eaten it, they all died. And that is how we kill the harvester ant in Wyoming today.

And in a way, ladies and gentlemen of the jury, the damages in this case are those kind of damages. [Kerr McGee has a sign that reads] "A million hours without an off-site accident." It covers up the facts that in twenty or thirty years we will be dealing with the harvester-ant syndrome.

The Paperboy Analogy

The basis of punitive damages rests upon the principle that they are allowed as punishment of the offender for the general benefit of society, both as a restraint against Kerr-McGee—so that they won't do it anymore—and a meaningful example to deter the commission of like offenses in the future. If the defendants are grossly or wantonly negligent, you may allow punitive damages and you may consider the financial worth. What is fair punishment for one isn't for another.

It is fair punishment to take a paperboy who makes five dollars a week, to take away five dollars from him for not coming home when he was supposed to or [for lying], if he lied? If one of your children lied about something that had to do with the life and health of a brother or sister, and he covered it up, and he said that the brother or sister were safe when he knew that he had exposed them to death, you might not find it unreasonable to hold him responsible for two piddling weeks' allowance in bucks, and leave fifty weeks left for him. That is what 70 million is to this corporation—two weeks—leaving fifty weeks' income. Maybe it isn't enough, but I was afraid to ask for more. You know why I was afraid? This case is so important that I'm afraid that if I stand here and ask what I really think the case is entitled to, you will laugh at me, and I can't have you thinking that I'm ridiculous, because it's important for what I'm trying to do that you find me credible. I've tried to retain my credibility with you through this trial. To my knowledge I've never stood in front of you and told you a lie. That doesn't mean I haven't ever lied, because that would be a lie. But it doesn't mean that I have never lied to a jury—because I suppose some people would say that I have—but I try not to.

The Lion Returns

We are right back where we started from. "If the lion gets away, Kerr-McGee has to pay." Mr. Paul was critical of me for not trying to explain to you how the lion got away. Do you remember his sort of accusation that somehow we failed in our obligation? "My lion got away. Why is my lion on your property?"

"It wasn't there two hours ago. It wasn't there last night." And he says, "Wait a minute, your kids don't get along with my kids. That is why my lion is on your property." And then he says, "Why did you let my lion eat you?" He says, "I accuse you, and why don't you explain it?" And I say, "But it isn't my lion. It is your lion that got away."

Now the court says—I want to put it to rest, because I don't want you jumping in mud springs on this one—"It is unnecessary for you to decide how the plutonium escaped from the plant, how it entered her apartment, or how it caused her contamination, since it is stipulated that the plutonium in Karen Silkwood's apartment was from the defendant's plant."

Mr. Paul, that is why we haven't explained how your lion got on our property. The court says it is not our obligation—it is your lion, Mr. Paul, you must explain it. It is for the defendants to prove to you, by a preponderance of the evidence, that it was Karen Silkwood who took it. Failing that proof—please hear the word "proof"—failing which proof, Kerr-McGee has to pay. The lion got away. Karen Silkwood was damaged. Does Karen Silkwood have to prove how the lion got away? The court says no. Why? Because it is their lion.

You have been listening for hours to the greatest invitation [by Mr. Paul] in the history of American jurisprudence to go dunk yourselves into mud springs.

The Case Vindicates American Values

Do you think that people should have the right to file grievances if they don't think that they have been treated fairly? Does that seem to be an important right? It seems important to me. Hundreds of thousands of American men . . . have given their lives to save those freedoms for us. His Honor sits on this bench guarding those freedoms like a prairie falcon from Kansas.

What happens if you file a grievance at Kerr-McGee? You get accused: "There is evidence in the case that you contaminated yourself." That is what he said.

Attacks on the Defense for Blaming the Victim

Mr. Paul, from his own lips, was saying to you, "She didn't appear in time—she was unreliable." Written by Dr. Charles Sternhagen—you know when he wrote that stuff about her? He wrote that stuff three days after she died—not when she was alive—but after she was dead. If there was an ugly way to interpret it, Mr. Paul did it in every case. I don't hold that against him—I want you to know that. We all have a free choice to represent the people we want to. That's his client. He has done the best he can. I'm not saying Mr. Paul is an evil man. I'm not saying the people that work there are evil people. It shows you how [far to the] bottom in the barrel they scraped for a defense in such an important case. I would have thought a lot more of them if they had come in and said, "Yes, we had a sloppy operation. We did it. We're sorry. We'll pay the damages. We'll pay the fiddler." I don't think I would be nearly so angry as when they try to slander.

Will Rogers said, "Slander is the cheapest defense going." It doesn't cost anything to slander anybody. I can slander you, and if I say it enough, somebody will start believing it. It is pretty hard to defend. You remember when you were a kid in high school and somebody said you did certain things and you didn't do it, [but] your mother accused you of something and you couldn't prove you didn't do it?

How about it when the slander is in the most important case of this century—and all the defense is a slander? How do you feel about the kind of corporation that tells Mr. Paul this is what he has to do?

The Call for the Jurors to Do Their Duty

[T]heir witness Dr. Voelz had to admit it: "Yes, we know it causes all kinds of cancer, breast cancer, cancer of the gonads. Yes, we know it causes lung cancer. Yes, the model is for people who don't have asthma." [Dr. Voelz testified about a model that was used by the Atomic Energy Commission to determine the permissible level of contamination.] Give me one little child that's got asthma—one little child exposed to the model level may have in fact received scores or maybe hundreds of times of the same amount of exposure than a child without asthma.

Can you put your stamp of approval on that? Can you pass the buck? Are you saying, "It ain't up to us"? There are only six of you in this world. There aren't any others like you—there will never be another time when there are six people like you. There will never be a judge like that one with the fortitude and decency and patience to let this case come to you. The buck stops here. There's no other place for this buck to stop. I wish that I had the power to lift this burden off your shoulders and let me take the responsibility—I'd do it. But only you can do it.

I want to talk to you about the immense tragedy in this case. I'm sure you've thought about it when you've gone home at night, but I doubt if any of you have had a chance to talk about it with each other. I would have felt that I didn't do my job if I didn't talk to you about an immense tragedy.

I see young Bill Apperson [a plant employee] at age forty or fifty. Dr. (John) Gofman [nuclear scientist and medical doctor who testified for plaintiff] says that those young men may very well die. This is a horrid secret that nobody has told us. Nobody told them. The only thing that was ever told [by Kerr-McGee] was that there was a million hours without an off-site accident.

I can hear Utnage saying to you under his oath and to those boys and girls that "there has never been a cancer caused by plutonium that we know of." I can hear that in my ears, and I can see those young men and those young women when they sat on that witness stand. I could hear the man in charge, Norwood [Wayne Norwood, Kerr-McGee's health-physics director], saying to you and to those poor boys and girls, "There has never been proven cancer from plutonium."

I look at the green book, and there was nothing there to warn them. I looked at the article on lungs from the manual, and there was nothing there but the gobbledygook, and it was the worst kind of deceit in my career that I have ever seen. I have been in courtrooms in Wyoming, little old towns in Wyoming, five thousand here—I grew up in Riverton, Wyoming, five thousand people there—I've been all over—I've been the county attorney, and eight years I was a prosecutor—and I prosecuted murderers and thieves and drunk and crazy people, and I've sued careless corporations in my life, and I have never seen a company who misrepresented to the workers that the workers were cheated out of their lives.

These people that were in charge knew about plutonium. They knew what alpha particles did. Mr. Valentine [Allen Valentine, certified health physicist from Los Alamos Laboratory, who wrote Kerr-McGee's health-physics program] had the '59 article in his hand. [Valentine used a 1959 scientific article to write the Kerr-McGee health-physics training manual.] In turn, the manual made no reference to risk of cancer from plutonium. They hid the facts, and they confused the facts, and they tried to get you in the mud springs.

You and I know what it was all about. It was about a lousy

$3.50-an-hour job. If these people knew they were going to die from cancer twenty or forty years later, would they have gone to work? The misrepresentations stole their lives. It's sickening. It's willful. It's callous. Nobody seriously contends Kerr-McGee told these people about cancer. Even the little girl that was on the stand, the one employee that they called in—they didn't dare ask her, "When you were over to the uranium plant, honey, did they tell you that plutonium caused cancer?" The question was never presented to her.

A schoolteacher, Noel [James Noel, a former Kerr-McGee lab analyst who left to become a high-school physical-science teacher], certainly a smart young man, surely he would have understood. He never heard of it. I had to ask Valentine five times before I could get him to use the word "cancer." They hid the fact.

It was a trap, surely as deadly as the worst kind of land mines. If you were in the army and your officer said to you, "Walk down that road," and that it was safe, and they knew it was full of land mines, and the only reason they told you it was safe was because that was the only way they could get you to go down the road, and that they blew you all to hell, what would your feelings be? It's that kind of misconduct that we are talking about in this case.

Now, I have a vision. It is not a dream—it is a nightmare. It came to me in the middle of the night, and I got up and wrote it down, and I want you to hear it, because I wrote it in the middle of the night about a week ago. Twenty years from now; the men are not old, some say they're just in their prime, they're looking forward to some good things. The men at that plant are good men with families that love them. They are dying like men die in a plague. Cancer, they say, probably from the plutonium plant. "He worked there as a young man. They didn't know much, about it in those days. He isn't suffering much, but it is just a tragedy." They all loved him. Nobody in top management seemed to care. Those were the days when the standards were a thousand times higher than they are today. They worked the men in respirators. [This refers to the fact that when the air was contaminated, workers at the plant were placed in respirators; although these respirators were supposed to be used in emergency situations only, the plaintiff presented evidence that Kerr-McGee required the workers to work in the respirators rather than close down the area to decontaminate.] The pipes leaked. The paint dropped from the walls. The stuff was everywhere. Nobody cared very much. Only seventy-five level-two and -three AEC violations. The place was run by good moneymen, good managers.

The company covered things up. Profits were up 83 percent in '79. No one was committed to the "low as possible" standards. Some people in the company didn't even know what it meant when they were asked what the ALAP [as low as possible] standard was. It was a joke. [Federal regulation requires that licensees "make every reasonable effort to maintain radiation exposures and releases of radioactive materials in effluents in unrestricted areas as low as is reasonably achievable."] He coughed his lungs out, he and two hundred others. They called it the Cimarron syndrome. Dr. John Gofman, Dr. Martell, Dr. Karl Morgan, the "Father of health physics" [all plaintiff expert witnesses], told them, but they called them quacks.

The children are crying. It is a horrible sight. And pale, sad faces of widows. Such a pity for strong, proud men to be this way. It is such a waste for cheap labor, $3.50 an hour for eighteen-year-olds. What training did they get? They kept the information from them, like letting an army of soldiers walk through a field of land mines without telling them, except that the explosion doesn't happen for twenty years.

I continued to write in the middle of the night. "What training?" More dangerous work than war, and yet they were told nothing. Put them in the respirators. The information was kept from them, or they wouldn't have worked. One had the oxygen cut off and gasped, and the plutonium filled the air and filled his lungs. One had the stuff spilled on him while he was welding. There wasn't room to weld and to work. Once it was a foot deep in production on the wet side, and they never shut it down. Production went on as usual. They used up one hundred gallons of paint on one spill [a reference to the plaintiff's allegation that Kerr-McGee had painted over contaminated areas of the plant, thereby sealing the contamination in holes in the cinder block]. And the plutonium cracked off the valves, the tabletops in the lunchroom, and it was in the air. Five hundred forty-three filters in five years. That's one hundred a year—one every three days. This, by their own records. Lord knows what they didn't report, what they covered up.

The training: Well it was as bad as telling children that the Kool-Aid laced with poison was good for them. A hidden danger, they never knew. Some read about plutonium and cancer in the paper for the first time during a trial called the Silkwood case—but it was too late for them. Karen Silkwood was dead; the company was trying to convince an Oklahoma jury that she contaminated herself. They took two and a half months for trial. Blamed it all on the union, on everybody else—on Karen Silkwood, on the workers, on sabotage, on the AEC. It was a sad day in the history of our country. They said the AEC was tough. Seventy-five violations later, they hadn't even been fined once.

It was worse than the days of slavery. The owners of the slaves cared about their slaves, and many of them loved their slaves. It was a time of infamy and a time of corporate dishonesty. A time when men used men like disposable commodities. It was a time when corporations were more concerned with the public image than the truth. It was a time when the government held hands with these giants and played footsie with their greatest scientists. At the disposal of the corporation, to testify, to strike down the claims of the people, and it was too late. The men are dying. The Gofmans and Morgans predicted it. They have long since passed on. But it was too late for many. They are fine men, open-faced, honest men, hardworking men who had hopes but whose lives were stolen from them for $3.50 an hour, taken under false pretenses. It was a sad time, the era between '70 and '79—they called it the Cimarron syndrome.

They are the nameless people now. One is a schoolteacher. One finally got a . . . welding certificate. One by one it is a tragedy so staggering I cannot imagine it, yet as Dr. Gofman said, "If Karen Silkwood lived, she was doomed to cancer." He could guarantee it.

What is the case about? It is a case about Karen Silkwood, who was a brave, ordinary woman who did care. She risked her life—and she lost it. She had something to tell the world, and she tried to tell the world. What was it that Karen Silkwood had to tell the world? That has been left to us to say now. It is for you, the jury, to say it for her.

I wish Karen Silkwood was standing here by me now and could say what she wanted to say. I think she would say, "Brothers and sisters, they were just eighteen- and nineteen-year-olds. They didn't understand. There wasn't any training. They kept the danger a secret. They covered it with word games and number games." And she would say, "Friends, it has to stop here in Oklahoma City today."

I'm going to tell you a simple story, about a wise old man and a smart-aleck young boy who wanted to show up the wise old man for a fool. The boy captured [a] little bird. He had the idea he would go to the wise old man with the bird in his hand and say, "What have I got in my hand?" And the old man would say, "Well, you have a bird, my son." And he would say, "Wise old man, is the bird alive or is it dead?"

The old man knew if he said, "It is dead," the little boy would open his hand and the bird would fly away. If he said, "It is alive," the boy would take the bird in his hand and crunch the life out of it and then open his hand and say, "See, it is dead."

So the boy went up to the wise old man and he said, "Wise old man, what do I have in my hand?"

The old man said, "Why, it is a bird."

He said, "Wise old man, is it alive or is it dead?"

And the wise old man said, "The bird is in your hands, my son."

POSTSCRIPT

The Kerr-McGee nuclear-fuel plants closed in 1975. The jury awarded Karen Silkwood's estate $10.5 million for personal injury and punitive damages. The Court of Appeals reversed this verdict and awarded the Silkwood estate $5,000 for the cleanup of her apartment. The Supreme Court then reversed the Court of Appeals' verdict and sent the case back to the trial court to determine the propriety of the jury's $10 million verdict of punitive damages. In 1986 the case was headed for retrial when it was settled out of court for $1.38 million.

Was the initial verdict for $10.5 million a verdict that represented the truth of what happened to Karen Silkwood? Was it merely the outcome of Gerry Spence's highly artful advocacy in depicting a greedy corporation with sloppy safety standards, oppressing underpaid workers?

Spence succeeded during the trial in convincing Judge Frank Theis to present a broad swath of evidence relating to the safety of nuclear energy, to the wisdom of the AEC standards, as well as to the entire safety record of the Kerr-McGee plutonium plant. Evidence of plant negligence by Kerr-McGee in protecting its workers from contamination was used by Spence to engender sympathy for Karen Silkwood even though neither side had eyewitness testimony to how it was that Silkwood got contaminated. William Paul, Kerr-McGee's lead attorney, pointed out in his summation that "the Court has permitted the plaintiff to bring before you evidence, bits and pieces, scattered over six long years of plant operations . . . but the case is about nine days [the period between November 5, 1974 and November 13, 1974, when Karen Silkwood died], not six years."

Mr. Spence claimed that he was not against nuclear energy. He was merely for responsible progress in the area of nuclear energy. Mr. Paul felt that the lawsuit was not a dispute between the Estate of Karen Silkwood and Kerr-McGee. He felt that people were using Karen Silkwood to advance their own platform about their views on nuclear energy and they had hijacked the lawsuit. He stated:

> I want to suggest to you that Karen Silkwood was being used, used brutally during her lifetime and that after her death she is still being used. I don't know who for certain are our real adversaries but I don't think it is Karen Silkwood. I call this to your mind about Gofman, Morgan, and Martell as a group (the three plaintiff's experts who were critical of Kerr-McGee plant safety and the AEC standards). There is a controversy raging and I wonder how much that witness stand was a witness stand and how much it was a platform. You see Dr. Martell in his testimony was asked a question "Are you having trouble getting your message through to the public?" The answer was "Yes, we are having trouble getting our message through to the public." So I ask you to think about

the difference in the witness stand and a platform. I ask you to think about the difference in witnesses like Dr. Charles Sternhagen who saw this woman and Dr. George Voelz who saw this woman, who had a reason to be here and tell you what they saw and witnesses who may have reasons to have a platform (i.e., Both doctors examined Karen Silkwood after her exposure to plutonium).

Spence's brilliant summation and equally brilliant portrayal of Silkwood displayed his excellent command of various trial techniques. He made a powerful emotional case, moving the jurors to admire and revere Silkwood while despising the greedy corporation who cared little about whether its low-paid employees came down with cancer.

Spence succeeded in demonizing and depersonalizing Kerr-McGee, which became a juror's metaphor for the greedy corporation. Mr. Paul tried to fight back. He stated:

Now, this is a trial about people. Although the defendants in our case are Kerr-McGee and Kerr-McGee Nuclear Corporation, it is a trial about people. And really, the people on trial here are Wayne Norwood, you've met him, you know him, and there hasn't been one unkind word said about him since this trial started. He was the man, he's on trial and he's passed the test I hope. But you are the judges and I hope he's passed your test. And the other Kerr-McGee people who have testified here are also on trial.

I want to start by asking you from the bottom of my heart to be fair to them. Don't get lost in the plaintiff's muddy springs and believe for one minute that this is not a trial about people. It is those people whose accountability is called into question here and I think they have passed the judgments that you're called upon to make.

This morning you heard the comment [from Mr. Spence] that the plaintiff here does not contend that any of the Kerr-McGee people are evil. That's nice to say. It says to you, "I've got no bone to pick with those men. They are not evil but still I want seventy million dollars, give or take, by way of punitive damages." Don't be fooled. It is those men who are on trial. You can't just separate out a corporation and give it a personality all its own. The personality of that corporation is the personality of those men and if those men are not evil men, neither is that company an evil company. And it's not. You know it's not.

Mr. Spence's harvester-ant analogy drove home the point of the fear of future a cancer epidemic due to the workers' exposure to plutonium. Through the use of the lion analogy, he never allowed the jury to forget that, by law, the burden of proof falls on the defendant in cases involving inherently dangerous items like plutonium. Finally Spence's personal tone was perfectly pitched; his "gift of schmooze" certainly made him a very likeable and therefore credible advocate. Whether his colorful version of martyred heroine versus merciless corporation represents the truth is still in question.

The truth of the Silkwood case may never be known. As Mr. Spence so quoted Abraham Lincoln, you can't fool all of the people all the time. That being said, almost thirty years have passed since Karen Silkwood died, yet still questions remain: How was it that Karen Silkwood could leave the plant in the evening free of plutonium and return with high readings? How did the plutonium get into Karen Silkwood's apartment? How did plutonium get into Ms. Silkwood's gastrointestinal tract? Did Quaaludes cause Karen Silkwood to drive off the road and die in a one-car accident or was she murdered? Did Ms. Silkwood have incriminating files in her possession at the time of her death and if so, what became of them?

A United States Supreme Court decision concerning the case noted that at the trial, Silkwood and Kerr-McGee lawyers stipulated that Karen Silkwood's urine samples had been spiked with insoluble plutonium, plutonium that can not be excreted by the body. Who put that plutonium in the vials?

Mr. Paul argued from these facts that Ms. Silkwood took the plutonium out of the plant to spike her urine samples and that "there is simply no way that I can think of to explain the contamination on [Karen Silkwood's] body that was there on November 7 other than it occurred while she was spiking her sample." Kerr-McGee had the burden of proof to show that Silkwood took the plutonium out of the plant and brought it to her apartment. By their verdict, the jury indicated that Kerr-McGee had not borne their burden.

Many have deified Karen Silkwood, including a core of group of activist movie stars from Meryl Streep to Kurt Russell, Ron Silver, Mike Nichols and Michael Moore who attended public celebrations in honor of her memory.

The deification of Karen Silkwood in certain circles did not extend to all of her children. In a 1999 magazine article, two of her three children expressed bitterness about the fact that she walked out on them and left them with her father and his girlfriend. Karen Silkwood asked her five-year-old daughter Kristi to watch three-year-old Michael and eighteen-month-old Dawn when she went for cigarettes and abandoned them for good. Ironically, Mr. Spence had Silkwood's children sitting in the courtroom for the opening statements.

13

CARNAGE IN OKLAHOMA

THE UNITED STATES
OF AMERICA v.
TIMOTHY McVEIGH

PRIOR TO SEPTEMBER 11, 2001, the deadliest act of terrorism in America occurred on April 19, 1995, when the Alfred R. Murrah Federal Building in Oklahoma City was bombed. Among the 168 dead and injured were nineteen children who were attending a day-care center located on the second floor. Timothy McVeigh was the first to be arrested and tried for the attack.

Excerpts from the Opening Statement of
Prosecutor Joseph Hartzler

April 19, 1995, was a beautiful day in Oklahoma City—at least it started out as a beautiful day. The sun was shining. Flowers were blooming. It was springtime in Oklahoma City. Sometime after six o'clock that morning, Tevin Garrett's mother woke him up to get him ready for the day. He was only sixteen months old. He was a toddler, and as some of you know that have experience with toddlers, he had a keen eye for mischief. He would often pull on the cord of her curling iron in the morning, pull it off the countertop until it fell down, often till it fell down on him.

That morning she picked him up and wrestled with him on her

bed before she got him dressed. She remembers this morning because that was the last morning of his life. That morning Mrs. Garrett got Tevin and her daughter ready for school, and they left the house at about seven-fifteen to go downtown to Oklahoma City. She had to be at work at eight o'clock. Tevin's sister went to kindergarten, and they dropped the little girl off at kindergarten first; and Helena Garrett and Tevin proceeded to downtown Oklahoma City.

Usually she parked a little bit distant from her building, but this day she was running a little bit late, so she decided that she would park in the Murrah Federal Building. She did not work in the Murrah Building. She wasn't even a federal employee. She worked across the street in the General Records Building. She pulled into the parking lot of the federal building, in order to make it into work on time, and she went upstairs to the second floor with Tevin, because Tevin attended the day-care center on the second floor of the federal building. When she went in, she saw that Chase and Colton Smith were already there, two-year-old and three-year-old. Dominique London was there already. He was just shy of his third birthday. So was Zack Chavez. He had already turned three.

When she turned to leave to go to her work, Tevin, as so often happens with small children, cried and clung to her, and then, as you see with children so frequently, they try to help each other. One of the little Coverdale boys, Elijah, came up to Tevin and patted him on the back and comforted him as his mother left.

As Helena Garrett left the Murrah Federal Building to go to work across the street, she could look back up at the building, and there was a wall of plate-glass windows on the second floor. You can look through those windows and see into the day-care center; and the children would run up to those windows and press their hands and faces to those windows to say good-bye to their parents. And standing on the sidewalk, it was almost as though you can reach up and touch the children there on the second floor. But none of the parents of any of the children that I just mentioned ever touched those children again while they were still alive.

At nine o'clock that morning, two things happened almost simultaneously. In the Water Resources Building, another building to the west of the Murrah Building across the street—an ordinary legal proceeding began in one of the hearing rooms; and at the same time, in front of the Murrah Building, a large Ryder truck pulled up into a vacant parking space in front of the building and parked right beneath those plate-glass windows from the day-care center.

What these two separate but almost simultaneous events have in common is that they both involved grievances of some sort. The legal proceeding had to do with water rights. It was a tape-recorded proceeding, and you will hear the tape recording of that proceeding. It was an ordinary, everyday-across-America, typical legal proceeding in which one party has a grievance and brings it into court or into a hearing to resolve it, not by violence and terror but to resolve it in the same way we are resolving matters here, by constitutional due process.

And across the street the Ryder truck was there also to resolve a grievance, but the truck wasn't there to resolve the grievance by means of due process or by any other democratic means. The truck was there to impose the will of Timothy McVeigh on the rest of America and to do so by premeditated violence and terror, by murdering innocent men, women, and children, in hopes of seeing blood flow in the streets of America.

At 9:02 that morning, two minutes after the water-rights proceeding began, a catastrophic explosion ripped the air in downtown Oklahoma City. It instantaneously demolished the entire front of the Murrah Building, brought down tons and tons of concrete and metal, dismembered people inside, and it destroyed, forever, scores and scores and scores of lives, lives of innocent Americans: clerks, secretaries, law-enforcement officers, credit-union employees, citizens applying for Social Security, and little kids.

All the children I mentioned earlier, all of them died, and more: dozens and dozens of other men, women, children, cousins, loved ones, grandparents, grandchildren, ordinary Americans going about their business. And the only reason they died, the only reason that they are no longer with us, no longer with their loved ones, is that they were in a building owned by a government that Timothy McVeigh so hated that, with premeditated intent and a well-designed plan that he had developed over months and months before the bombing, he chose to take their innocent lives to serve his twisted purpose.

In plain, simple language, it was an act of terror, violence, intended to serve [a] selfish political purpose. The man who committed this act is sitting in this courtroom behind me, and he's the one that committed those murders. After he did so, he fled the scene, and he avoided even damaging his eardrums, because he had earplugs with him.

Approximately seventy-five minutes later, about seventy-five miles north of Oklahoma City, the exact distance from Oklahoma City that you could drive in that time if you had been at the scene of the crime, he was at the mile marker that you would reach between the time of the bombing and the time he was arrested if you were driving at normal speed limit. He was arrested driving from Oklahoma City, driving toward Kansas, leaving Oklahoma City. And in his pocket at that time were a set of earplugs, the type that would be worn to protect your ears from a loud noise. And on his clothing an FBI chemist later found residue of undetonated explosives, not the kind of residue that would detonate in the course of the explosion but the kind of explosives you would have on your clothing if you had made the bomb, which is what he did.

And the T-shirt he was wearing virtually broadcast his intention. On its front was the image of Abraham Lincoln, and beneath the image was a phrase about tyrants, which is a phrase that John Wilkes Booth shouted in Ford's Theater to the audience when he murdered President Lincoln. And on the back of the T-shirt that McVeigh was wearing on the morning of the bombing, the morning that he was arrested, was this phrase: "The tree of liberty must be refreshed from time to time with the blood of patriots and tyrants." And above those words was the image of a tree. You'll see that T-shirt; you'll see the tree; you'll see the words beneath the tree; and you'll notice that instead of fruit the tree on the T-shirt bears a depiction of droplets of scarlet-red blood.

Found in the police car after McVeigh's arrest was a crumpled-up business card from a military-supply company. McVeigh had written a note on that card, and the card had McVeigh's fingerprint on it. And in McVeigh's handwriting, on this card from the military-supply company, [it] said, "TNT at $5 a stick. Need more. Call after May 1."

Inside McVeigh's car law-enforcement agents later found a large sealed envelope. It contained photocopies from magazines and from newspapers. They will give you a window into McVeigh's mind. And they'll enable you to see his intention, to know his premeditation, and to understand the twisted motive behind this deadly offense.

To give you just two examples of the material you will see, enclosed in that envelope were slips of paper bearing statements that McVeigh had clipped from books and newspapers. And one of them was a quotation from a book that McVeigh had copied. And it was a book that he had read and believed in like the Bible. The book is entitled *The Turner Diaries*. It's a fictional account of an attack on the federal government which is carried out with a truck bomb blowing up a federal building and killing hundreds of people. And the clipping that McVeigh had with him on this day of the bombing talks about the value of killing innocent people for a cause. It reads—and he highlighted this—"The real value of our attacks today lies in the psychological impact, not in the immediate casualties."

Another slip of paper that he had in that envelope in his car bears a quotation from one of our Founding Fathers who fought the British to establish democracy in America. The printed portion on that piece of paper reads, in part, "When the government fears the people, there is liberty." And hand-printed beneath those printed words, in McVeigh's handwriting, are the words "Maybe now there will be liberty."

These documents are virtually a manifesto declaring McVeigh's intention.

Everyone in this great nation has a right to think and believe, speak whatever they want. We are not prosecuting McVeigh because we don't like his thoughts or his beliefs or even his speech; we're prosecuting him because his hatred boiled into violence, and his violence took the lives of innocent men and women and children. And the reason we'll introduce evidence of his thoughts, as disclosed by those writings and others, is because they reveal his premeditation and his intent.

As McVeigh was leaving the scene moments before the explosion, a maintenance man from an apartment building in downtown Oklahoma City near the Murrah Building, about a block or so away, walked out the front door of the building to meet his wife and nephew. His nephew was a sixth-grader, sitting in the backseat of the man's red Ford Fiesta out in front of the apartment building where he worked. His wife had gone inside to get him, tell him that they were there. She walked back outside with her husband, and he was standing at the side of his car, holding the door for his wife, when the force of the bomb nearly knocked him off his feet.

At that moment he was about at least more than a city block from the front door of the Murrah Building, and he heard a whirring sound, like the propeller of a helicopter, coming toward him. He pushed his wife quickly under the car to protect her as more than 250 pounds of twisted metal came crashing down onto his car. Fortunately, it landed on the hood of his car. It crushed the car, but his wife and his nephew survived.

That huge piece of twisted metal had been at the center of the bomb. The force of the explosion had sent it whirling through the air for about two hundred yards or more. That piece of twisted metal was the rear axle of a Ryder truck. It was a Ryder truck that Timothy McVeigh had rented two days before in Kansas.

We will prove to you beyond any reasonable doubt that Timothy McVeigh destroyed the Murrah Building and killed people inside by means of a huge fertilizer bomb built inside a Ryder truck. You'll learn that the bombing was a premeditated act. It was part of a plan that McVeigh set in action long before April 19, 1995. And that's why the evidence will take so much time, because we will go back, not from the beginning of time but from a certain stage in McVeigh's life, and walk through the various details of what he was doing and how it all fit into his plan to kill people in the Murrah Building.

Timothy McVeigh grew up in upstate New York, and after high school he joined the army. He first went to Fort Benning in Georgia, and that's where he met Terry Nichols. They served in Fort Benning in the same platoon. After he and Nichols completed their basic training at Fort Benning, they were both sent to Fort Riley, in Kansas. They became friends, in part because they both shared a distaste for the federal government.

McVeigh's dislike for the federal government was revealed while he was still in the army. Even at that early time in his life, he expressed an enthusiasm for this book *The Turner Diaries*. It's a work of fiction. It follows the exploits of a group of well-armed men and women who call themselves patriots, and they seek to overthrow the federal government by use of force and violence.

In the book they make a fertilizer bomb in the back of a truck, and they detonate it in front of a federal building in downtown Washington, D.C., during business hours, and they kill hundreds of people.

Friends, acquaintances, and family members of McVeigh will testify that he carried the book with him, gave copies to them, urged them to read this book. We will show you passages from the book, and you'll see how the bombing in the book served as a blueprint for McVeigh and for his planning and execution of the bombing in Oklahoma City.

On April 19, 1993, there was another great tragedy in American history. It occurred at Waco, Texas. That's the day that many lives were lost when the Branch Davidian compound burned down. But it was more than just a tragedy to McVeigh. You'll hear testimony from McVeigh's friends that he visited Waco during the siege and that he went back after the fire and that he had already harbored a great dislike and distaste for the federal government. They imposed taxes and the Brady Bill, and there were various other reasons that he had disliked the federal government.

But the tragedy at Waco really sparked his anger, and as time passed, he became more and more and more outraged at the government, which he held responsible for the deaths at Waco. And he told people that the federal government had intentionally murdered people at Waco, they murdered the Davidians at Waco. He described the incident as the government's declaration of war against the American people. He wrote letters declaring that the government had drawn, quote, first blood, unquote, at Waco; and he predicted there would be a violent revolution against the American government. As he put it, "blood would flow in the streets."

He expected and hoped that his bombing of the Murrah Building would be the first shot in a violent, bloody revolution in this country. As his hatred of the government grew, so did his interest in a knowledge of explosives.

You'll hear that he and Terry Nichols had experimented with

small explosives on Nichols's farm in Michigan. Later McVeigh graduated to larger bombs, and you'll hear about an incident that occurred just one year before the bombing in a desert in Arizona, where he made and detonated a pipe bomb. He placed it near a large boulder in the desert, and he ran away as the pipe bomb exploded and cracked the boulder.

McVeigh also educated himself about how to build bombs, particularly truck bombs, using ammonium nitrate fertilizer and some sort of fuel oil. And we'll explain to you how you can make a bomb from fertilizer and fuel oil, and of course that's consistent with the type of destructive device that was used in Oklahoma City.

McVeigh also obtained what was really a cookbook on how to make bombs. He ordered the book through the mail in the spring of 1993, and the book is called *Homemade C4*—C4 is a type [of] explosive. This book provides essentially a step-by-step recipe as to how to put together your own fertilizer [and] fuel-based bomb. And the book even provides helpful hints as to where to acquire the various ingredients, the components. It describes how to build a powerful bomb, and it does so in simple, understandable terms. In fact, it shows how unbelievably simple it is to make a hugely powerful bomb.

Over time McVeigh's anger and hatred of the government kept growing, and in the late summer of 1994—and this is nine months before the bombing—he decided that he had had enough. He told friends that he was done distributing antigovernment propaganda and talking about the coming revolution. He said it was time to take action, and the action he wanted to take was something dramatic, something that would shake up America, he said, and would cause ordinary citizens, he thought, to engage in a violent revolution against their democratically elected government, just like *The Turner Diaries*; and, of course, just like the main character in the book, he would become the hero.

The action he selected was the bombing, and the building he selected was the federal building in Oklahoma City. And he offered two reasons for bombing—or for selecting—that particular building. First, he thought that the ATF agents, whom he blamed for the Waco tragedy, had their offices in that building. As it turns out, he was wrong, but that's what he thought. That was one of his motivations. And second, he described that building as, quote, an easy target. It was conveniently located just south of Kansas, and it had easy access. It was just a matter of blocks off of an interstate highway, Interstate 35 through Oklahoma City traveling north, and the building is designed as such that you can drive a truck up; there is an indentation at the sidewalk in front of the building. You can drive a truck right up and park a truck right there in front of the building, right there in front of the plate-glass windows that I described in front of the day-care center.

The day that he selected for the bombing also has significance. He selected April 19. Of course, first, that was the anniversary of Waco, and he wanted to, as he said, avenge death that occurred at Waco; and second, April 19, a couple of centuries ago in 1775, that's the day that the American Revolution is reported to have begun. That's the day that the opening shot was fired in Concord/Lexington. The day is known as Liberty Day.

As indicated by the materials that McVeigh carried with him, McVeigh envisioned that by bombing the building in Oklahoma City, he would bring what he thought would be liberty to this nation. Well, this was not just talk from McVeigh. He was ready for action. He knew from the literature he had how to make the bomb, and he knew how to get the ingredients. Both *The Turner Diaries* and this book *Homemade C4*, the bomb-making cookbook, told him to where to look. The best place to get ammonium nitrate fertilizer, the book said, was at a farm-supply store, and the best place to get nitro methane racing fuel, which you would mix with the fertilizer, was at a raceway.

So McVeigh engaged his friend, his army buddy Terry Nichols, in the project. Nichols, of course, shared the hatred for the federal government, and they worked together in a conspiracy. They reached this working arrangement whereby they would, together, acquire the ingredients to manufacture the bomb. And a fair amount of our evidence will be about their acquisition of the various components that were used to make the bomb that blew up the federal building in Oklahoma City.

They got four thousand pounds of ammonium nitrate fertilizer at a farm-supply store in central Kansas, where Nichols was living at the time and where McVeigh visited him. This was in the fall of 1994, at least six months before the bombing, giving you some indication of the planning that went into this process and the premeditation. They made two purchases of one ton each. The first one was made at the end of September 1994, and the second one was made the middle of October, and both purchases were made in phony names. The phony name they used was Mike Havens. We'll provide you with evidence showing that Terry Nichols used that name Havens as an alias.

We will also show you that the receipt for the first purchase, September 30, was found in Nichols's home after the bombing. Agents conducted a search of Nichols's home several days after the bombing, and they found the receipt for that first purchase of one ton of ammonium nitrate fertilizer, and on that receipt, when it was sent back to the FBI lab, were two latent fingerprints of Timothy McVeigh.

To get some of the other chemicals they needed for the bomb, McVeigh and Nichols picked up the phone book and let their fingers do the walking. They called dozens and dozens of companies and individuals in search of ingredients that they needed for the bomb. And the reason we can trace and show you so many of these calls is in part because they used a calling card to make the calls. They had obtained a calling card from a magazine called *Spotlight* magazine, and in an unsuccessful effort to avoid having the calls traced back to them, they again used a fake name. They didn't get the calling card in their own names. They used this time the name Darrell Bridges, but we'll prove to you that it was they that got, ordered, obtained, and paid for this calling card. The calling card was the type of phone card that requires you to pay in advance. It's called a debit card. The balance on the card is debited each time you make a call, and then, when you're down to a zero balance, you have to send in more money to the company to make more calls. And that's precisely what McVeigh and Nichols did, and we'll show you money orders that they sent in, and we'll prove to you that the money orders were obtained by McVeigh and Nichols; and that's why we can trace so much of their activity, at least so much of their phone-call activity, because they used the same debit card in the name of Darrell Bridges to do a lot of their business. And even though they didn't get a phone bill, as you or I would get for our home phone—they didn't get the phone bill, of course, because they were paying for these calls in advance—and even though they may have believed that by doing it that way the calls wouldn't be traceable . . . well, the phone company still needed to keep track of the calls and how much was charged so they could debit down the card.

So the phone company had records of the calls that were being made, from where to where, and how long it was, and how much it cost; and those are the records that we have that we'll present to you to prove the calls that McVeigh and Nichols were making. The debit card records reveals dozens of calls in the fall of 1994. That's when they're trying to acquire the ingredients for the bomb. The calls were made to various companies and individuals that sold or possibly could obtain the ingredients that would be used for an ammonium nitrate fertilizer bomb.

The mixture would be made and held in barrels. They called barrel companies. The mixture would use racing fuel as a most likely fuel source to mix with the ammonium nitrate. They called fuel-racing raceways. And there are various other chemicals, including anhydrous hydrazine. They called various chemical companies. For example, we will show you a copy of the Yellow Pages taken from the area in Kansas where McVeigh and Nichols were during the fall of 1994. We can compare the Yellow Pages with those records from the calling card. Going down the Yellow Pages, if you look at a page for chemical companies, you see a number of chemical companies, you see the numbers listed, and you see the number that they called on their calling card. They went down the Yellow Pages and called the companies that were on those Yellow Pages.

You'll notice that all the companies they called during that period of time, in the fall of 1994 when they were using this [calling card]—all of them have one thing in common: They all sell something you could use to make a bomb, a large ammonium nitrate fertilizer bomb.

As further evidence we'll call people who actually received the calls, and in some cases they weren't strangers on the other end of the phone. They were friends or acquaintances of McVeigh. For example, we'll call a man by the name of David Darlak. He's an old acquaintance of McVeigh. They grew up together, and they've known each other for years. Darlak received calls from McVeigh, and he remembers him. Darlak recalls that McVeigh called him trying to get racing fuel. Well, Darlak didn't ever know McVeigh to be interested in racing, and McVeigh, of course, didn't reveal that he wanted the racing fuel for something other than racing, to build a bomb—he didn't say that. He didn't reveal why he wanted the racing fuel.

Greg Pfaff is another person that received a call. Greg Pfaff is a guy that McVeigh ran into and met when they did the various gun shows. Pfaff recalls getting calls from McVeigh, and he will tell you that McVeigh asked him if Pfaff could get any det cord. Now, "det cord" is an abbreviation for detonation cord, and that's what you'll use—as you'll hear, the ammonium nitrate and fuel oil doesn't blow up by itself; you don't light a match and throw it on it and it explodes. You need some kind of detonation. Det cord would be used to facilitate the detonation of the explosion. According to Pfaff, McVeigh was so eager to get this det cord that McVeigh offered to drive across the country. Pfaff was on the East Coast. [McVeigh] offered to drive across the country to Pfaff if Pfaff could get any det cord.

You will also hear from a man named Glynn Tipton. Tipton works for a company that goes to drag races, and he was on a drag race on October 1, 1994, in central Kansas. He recalls a man that he's almost certain as McVeigh coming up to him and trying to buy large quantities of nitro methane and anhydrous hydrazine; and the books I've told you about describe those two chemicals as being part of the shopping list for making an ammonium nitrate fertilizer bomb.

All these calls are reflected on the debit card that McVeigh used, and so is a call to Mid-American Chemical Company; that's one of the companies actually that's listed in the Yellow Pages you'll see.

Linda Juhl is an employee of Mid-American Chemical Company, and she remembers getting a call in the fall of 1994 at the same time. She recalls it was from a young man in Kansas who wanted to obtain anhydrous hydrazine, one of the chemicals you can use to make ammonium nitrate fertilizer bombs. Anhydrous hydrazine is usually used as a rocket fuel, and it can seriously boost the explosion.

You'll also hear a number of calls to companies such as CP Racing and other companies that sold nitro methane. Nitro methane is a racing fuel. It, too, can be used as one of the ingredients in ammonium nitrate fuel—fuel-oil explosive devices.

We'll prove they actually acquired large quantities of explosives, getting the mixture; the fertilizer with the chemicals of nitro methane or anhydrous hydrazine or racing fuel doesn't itself cause an explosion unless you have something to detonate it with.

We'll prove to you where McVeigh and Nichols got the detonators that they needed. In short, they stole them. During the period of the fall of 1994, Nichols was living in central Kansas in a community and city called Marion, Kansas; he was working on a cattle farm there, and nearby there was a rock quarry. Now, some of you probably know rock quarries use explosives to blast the rock, and they typically store the explosive they have on site in what are referred to as magazines or secure storage lockers. The quarry that was near Nichols's home in Marion, Kansas, kept a quantity of blasting caps in locked storage facilities right there on site.

McVeigh came to visit Nichols during late September of 1994 and stayed through that first weekend of October 1994; that's the weekend when Glynn Tipton saw him at the raceway or saw somebody he believes is McVeigh at the raceway, looking for the two chemicals I just described. That's also the same weekend, on the Friday of that weekend, September 30, that they made their first purchase of one ton of ammonium nitrate fertilizer from the supply store in central Kansas. Well, it's the very same weekend that they broke into the magazine at the rock quarry and stole hundreds of blasting caps and sticks of an explosive that's known as Tovex.

The reason that we can prove that it was McVeigh and Nichols that broke into these storage units and stole the explosives is because they made essentially two mistakes: First of all, they left evidence behind at the scene of the crime; and secondly, they didn't get rid of all the loot. They left some of it in Nichols's house. The evidence that they left behind at the scene of the crime was one of the padlocks that they had drilled open. There were five padlocks that had to be drilled open to get in. Four of them were missing but one of them was left behind.

The county sheriff that came out to investigate that break-in kept that padlock. This is months before the Oklahoma City bombing, but he kept it in his evidence and provided it to the FBI after the bombing, when the connection was made between that theft and the bombing. Federal agents later searched Nichols's house after the bombing, and they found in Nichols's basement a battery-powered Makita drill and with the drill, were some drill bits, and they matched the padlock that has a hole drilled in it to open up the lock.

They went inside that hole and lock and figured out the drill-bit impressions, the tool-mark impressions, and they made tool-mark impressions also from the drill that was found—the drill bit that was found in Nichols's basement—and they matched the two. And that tool-mark expert will come in and show you that the impressions inside the lock matched the impressions made by the drill bit from Nichols's basement, so that you can conclude that drill bit drilled that lock.

The other mistake they made was that Nichols kept some of the explosives. They were found after the bombing in his basement. He had some of the blasting caps. Now, blasting caps come in a wide variety of sizes. There are different brands, and there are different delays. They come in delays from something like from 1 to 20, and all the blasting caps that were stolen from the quarry were sixty-foot No. 8 delay Primadet blasting caps.

Found in Nichols's basement after the bombing when the agents searched his basement were five blasting caps, Primadet sixty-foot No. 8 delay. Well, with this quantity of explosives or components for making a bomb, McVeigh and Nichols needed someplace to keep all of this stuff. McVeigh, during this period of time, really didn't have any home. He would stay with friends and various other places. He was just traveling around, and it would have been foolish, of course, for Nichols to have kept the stuff in his home for two reasons: first of all, it's dangerous; secondly, [imagine] if anybody found it in his home. So it's obviously traceable for him. So their solution to this is to rent private storage lockers, and that's exactly what they did.

They rented private storage lockers, but to prevent anyone who would break in and get into these storage lockers to easily trace these components to them, they again used false names. They rented three lockers in the central Kansas area near where Nichols was living at the time. And they rented all three lockers in different phony names: This time they're Shawn Rivers, Ted Parker, and Joe Kyle.

The storage lockers were paid for with cash, which is, of course, the least traceable means of payment. But we will prove through eyewitness testimony, through fingerprints, and through handwriting analysis that it was McVeigh and Nichols who rented these storage lockers in false names.

The leases on the three storage lockers began in the fall of 1994, right at the very time that they were acquiring components for the bombs, but they continued to pay the rent on these storage lockers up through the date of the bombing. When FBI agents searched the storage lockers soon after the bombings, they were all empty. Rent was paid up till then, but there was nothing in them. Of course, the components were used in Oklahoma City.

During this period when McVeigh and Nichols were acquiring the components for the bomb, McVeigh periodically drove to Arizona and visited two friends of his, Michael and Lori Fortier. He had met Michael in the army, and they had shared the same antigovernment ideas, and McVeigh had come to trust not only Michael, but he also came to trust Michael's wife, Lori.

So in the fall of 1994, he confided his plan to the Fortiers. Sitting in their living room in Kingman, Arizona, he actually drew a diagram of the bomb that he intended to build. And you'll hear that evidence from the witness stand. He outlined the box of the truck, and he drew circles for the barrels inside the truck, the barrels of fertilizer and fuel oil that he would place strategically in the truck to cause maximum damage.

Later during that same period of time, one of the times when he was in Arizona, again, fall of 1994, months ahead of the bombing, he demonstrated his design to Lori Fortier by borrowing ... her Campbell soup cans out of her cupboard and [placing] them on the floor and [showing] her the shape in which he would design the bomb inside the box of the truck. And he described it as a shape charge and explained that by putting the barrels of explosives in a particular shape, it would increase the charge in a particular direction, the direction toward the building and the plate-glass windows that I've previously described.

By the end of October 1994, McVeigh had most of ingredients he needed to build the bomb, so he was able at that time to carry out his plan. But this was still the fall of 1994. Remember, he was determined to take action when he thought it would have maximum impact, and he thought the anniversary of the tragedy at Waco would provide that kind of maximum impact. He thought that others were as angered at Waco as he was and that he could get tremendous impact, shake up the nation, by delaying his violent terrorist action until the anniversary of Waco, April 19; so he left the bomb components in the various storage lockers, and he waited till the spring.

And in late January he returned to Arizona. Again he stayed with his friends, the Fortiers, through February and March. He was really most of the time just hanging out, not doing anything. He wasn't employed. Periodically he would go to gun shows during that time. Periodically he would try to recruit Michael Fortier to participate in the bombing. And as April approached, it became clear to him that Fortier was not going to participate. That spring McVeigh was ready to put his plan into action.

He had been regularly corresponding with his sister, Jennifer, who was then living in upstate New York. And he had revealed to her his distrust and his distaste for the federal government. In fact, in the fall of 1994, he had visited her in New York. He created a file in her computer. He had marked the file "ATF read," as though he wanted them to discover this file and read it after his dramatic action.

You'll see the chilling words in that computer file. I'm going to delete the expletive. It said, "All you tyrannical m——f——ers will swing in the wind one day for your treasonous actions against the Constitution and the United States." And it concluded with these words: "Die, you spineless cowardice [sic] bastards." That was written in the fall of 1994.

By the spring of 1995, he had moved beyond words. He was ready for action. In a letter dated March 25, just three weeks before the bombing, he told his sister, Jennifer, not to send any more letters after May 1 because, quote, G men might get them.

About the same time, he sent another letter to his sister, Jennifer—this was before the bombing—in which he said, "Something big is about to happen." You'll hear from Jennifer McVeigh. You won't see that letter, because after the bombing, as she will explain, she destroyed that letter.

During this period of time, in the spring of 1994, before the bombing, while McVeigh was hanging out in Arizona, he asked Lori Fortier if he could borrow her typewriter. She let him take it for a day or so, and when he returned it, he had a phony driver's license. It was on one of the blank driver's-license forms. It had been ordered through one of those ads at the back of *Soldier of Fortune* magazine that sell phony identification kits. And McVeigh had typed on the blank form. He had made it look like it was a driver's license from North or South Dakota. He had typed in those words, the name of [the] state. And the phony name he had selected was Robert Kling.

He liked that name, he told Lori Fortier, because it reminded him of the race of characters on that TV show *Star Trek*, the Klingons. And you'll hear that name a lot in this trial, because that's the name that McVeigh used to rent the Ryder truck that he used to blow up the federal building: Robert Kling. To finish the phony driver's license, McVeigh asked to borrow Lori Fortier's iron, so he could iron on plastic lamination that came with the blank form. She was afraid he would ruin her iron, and she offered to iron it on for him. That's how it is she can tell you she saw the driver's license. She remembered the name. He handed her the Robert Kling driver's license. It had on it a small photo that McVeigh attached up in the corner in the box where the photo for a driver's license would fit. It was McVeigh's photo, of course. She ironed the lamination and gave it back to McVeigh.

During these months in early 1995, when McVeigh stayed with the Fortiers, he became more withdrawn and more unpleasant as April 19 approached. And in early April he moved out of the Fortiers' house into a local motel in Kingman, Arizona. He stayed there until April 12, 1995. You'll see those motel records. He checked out April 12, 1995, exactly one week before the bombing. He was in Arizona.

He checked out, and he was next seen in Kansas on Friday before the bombing. The bombing was on the following Wednesday. Friday before the bombing, McVeigh arrived in Kansas. Kansas, of course, is where Terry Nichols was then living, and that's where he and McVeigh had stored the bomb components in the storage lockers. The day that McVeigh arrived in Kansas was a Friday, April 14, five days before the bombing. He stopped at a Firestone service station in Junction City, Kansas. He knew that Firestone station because when he was in the service in Fort Riley, which is not far from Junction City, he had had his car serviced there before. The manager of the place, Tom Manning, remembered McVeigh.

McVeigh was there at that Firestone station, as Manning will tell you, because McVeigh said his car was burning oil. The car was in bad shape, so the manager, Manning, said he had a used car out back that he was willing to sell to McVeigh. McVeigh checked out the car and decided that he would go ahead and buy it; so he paid $250 in cash for the car and signed over the title to his car, which he had with him.

While Manning was getting the used car ready to turn over to McVeigh, he recalls that McVeigh left the Firestone station for about ten or fifteen minutes on this Friday morning. Manning provided this information the very first time he was asked whether McVeigh was there the entire time, and he remembered McVeigh left for a period of time when Manning went to get the car ready for McVeigh. During that interval of time, on Friday morning, five days before the bombing, when McVeigh left the Firestone station, a call was placed to a Ryder truck-rental agency in Junction City, Kansas. The Ryder agency in Junction City is called Elliott's Body Shop. It's listed in the Yellow Pages.

Just so you know what's coming, I've already told you the twisted rear axle that seemed to fall out of the air onto the red Fiesta of the maintenance man in the apartment building in downtown Oklahoma City—that axle traced back to a Ryder truck that had been rented two days before the bombing from Elliott's Body Shop in Junction City, Kansas. That was the truck that became the bomb.

The call I'm talking about now was made to reserve the truck. The caller said his name was Robert Kling, the same name that McVeigh had used on the phony driver's license. And the caller asked to reserve a large truck for pickup the following Monday.

That would be two days before the bombing. That call traces back to a pay phone located at a bus station in Junction City, Kansas, and that bus-station pay phone is less than a half a block from the Firestone station where McVeigh had been.

Although McVeigh had all the ingredients to build a bomb, he didn't yet have a truck. Now, in *The Turner Diaries*, the bomber steals a delivery truck in which to make their bomb; but McVeigh decided to rent his. And that's, of course, why he had the phony driver's license, and that's why he made the call to Elliott's Body Shop to reserve a truck five days before the bombing.

There's another detail about that bus-station pay-phone call that we will prove to you. Actually, there were two calls made back-to-back that morning from that outdoor pay phone. The first call went to the home of McVeigh's army buddy Terry Nichols, who was living at that time now in nearby Herington, Kansas. The next call, which started within seconds of the completion of the first call, was the one that went to Elliott's Body Shop to reserve the Ryder truck. Both calls were made on a Spotlight debit card.

For reasons that we will explain, the computer failed to record the actual customer account for the call to the Ryder truck-rental agency, but the call to Nichols's house, the first call, was charged to the calling card that McVeigh and Nichols were using. And, of course, it was McVeigh who was near that pay phone that morning, having entered into the car transaction with Manning.

Later that day McVeigh registered at a small motel in Junction City, Kansas, which is known as the Dreamland Motel. It's located about four miles up the road from the Ryder truck-rental agency. He registered there in his own name, Timothy McVeigh, and he stayed in Room 25 at the Dreamland Motel through that weekend up until Tuesday. Tuesday is now the morning of the day before the bombing. And as a result of a telephone call from the pay phone, Elliott's Body Shop, the Ryder rental place, actually reserved a large truck for Robert Kling. But they were willing to do so only if someone came in and put a deposit down on the truck the following day.

The following day, of course, was a Saturday, four days before the bombing. The only person who was working that day at Elliott's Body

Shop was the owner, Eldon Elliott. Mr. Elliott was there by himself when a young man with a military demeanor came in and said he was Robert Kling. The lighting was good. The two men stood facing each other for several minutes. There were no interruptions. The shop was not busy. They transacted business. And instead of simply making a cash deposit to reserve the truck in the name Kling, the man wanted to pay for the truck in full. He counted out several hundred dollars in cash and gave it to Elliott. It was a memorable transaction. There was some paperwork involved, and the man left. Mr. Elliott remembers this transaction, and he can identify the man. It was Timothy McVeigh.

I've already summarized ample evidence to convince you that Kling was really McVeigh, but there's still more. Although McVeigh had paid for the truck, he didn't take it with him. He said he would pick it up on Monday, April 17, two days before the bombing, after four o'clock. He was still staying at the Dreamland Motel in the same city, and that night, Saturday night, a carryout order for Chinese food from a local Chinese restaurant was made from McVeigh's room at the Dreamland Motel, a telephone call to the local Chinese restaurant ordering Chinese food; and the name used to place the order was Kling.

Now, the deliveryman who actually delivered the order had only a brief encounter with the customer. He can't identify who he gave the food to; but again the significance for us is a further association of the name Kling with McVeigh. This time, independent of anything coming from Elliott's Body Shop, independent of the call that reserved the truck, this is simply through a Kling order being delivered to McVeigh's room.

The following day was Easter Sunday. The bombing was on Wednesday following Easter in 1995. There will be no witnesses who saw McVeigh's car in Oklahoma City on Easter or thereafter. But we will provide sufficient evidence for you to conclude that McVeigh drove his car down to Oklahoma City on Easter Sunday and left it there as a getaway car for use after the bombing. For example, we will show you that McVeigh made a call that Sunday afternoon, at about three to the home of his army buddy, coconspirator Terry Nichols. He made the call from a pay phone in Herington, Kansas, just blocks away from Nichols's home.

You will see from our evidence that it's about four and a half hours from Herington, Kansas, driving to Oklahoma City. We'll show you evidence of the videotape from a surveillance camera. It actually happens to be a surveillance camera in the very same apartment building where the maintenance man came out and the truck axle fell on the front of his car. It's called the Regency Towers. They have a surveillance camera in the inside lobby. And it shoots through the inside lobby, so that you can pick up some of the activity in the street in front of the building.

From that camera we will show you five hours after McVeigh—a little more than five hours—after McVeigh made the call to Nichols's house—you can see a truck of the same features as Nichols's truck passing downtown Oklahoma City twice—passes that camera—on Sunday before the bombing. And you'll see that when McVeigh was stopped after the bombing in Oklahoma City, he had a handmade, hand-printed sign in his car. It was in his own handwriting. It said, "Please do not tow. Needs batteries and cable. Will move by April 23." There was nothing wrong with the batteries and cable when the car was stopped that day, April 19, the day of the bombing, and there was nothing wrong with the batteries and cables when Thomas Manning sold the car to McVeigh on Friday before.

As further evidence that McVeigh left his car in Oklahoma City on Easter Sunday so it would be there as a getaway car, we will prove that he needed a taxi on Monday afternoon in order to pick up the Ryder truck. Remember, when he went in on Saturday and paid the money, he didn't take the Ryder truck with him. He said he would be back after four on Monday, two days before the bombing.

Well, shortly before he was scheduled to pick up the truck, shortly before four o'clock on Monday afternoon, a call was placed from the pay phone near the Dreamland Motel. Recall that McVeigh was registered at the Dreamland in his own name. So this call was not placed from his motel phone. This call was placed from a public phone, but the public phone is just walking distance from the Dreamland Motel in the direction of Elliott's Body Shop.

We'll prove to you that it was McVeigh who made the call. The call was charged to that calling card that they had in the phony name, and it was placed to a taxicab company in Junction City. The cab company is listed in the Junction City Yellow Pages. And his call was placed on Monday after Easter. McVeigh stayed at the Dreamland Motel until Tuesday. He didn't have his car, so he needed a taxi to go to Elliott's Body Shop.

The taxicab company dispatched a cab to the location where McVeigh was by the pay phone near the Dreamland. The cab picked up one passenger, its records will show; and it drove that passenger in the direction of Elliott's Body Shop and dropped the passenger off at a McDonald's restaurant which is located about one mile from Elliott's Body Shop. The fare was $3.65, and we will prove to you that that passenger was Timothy McVeigh.

That McDonald's restaurant has a surveillance system that consists of a series of cameras inside. We will show some of the photos from those cameras on that Monday afternoon, the same Monday as the cab ride and shortly before the Ryder truck was picked up. What you will see is Timothy McVeigh on the photos taken inside the McDonald's restaurant. He was captured by the surveillance cameras. You will first see him as he approaches the counter and later as he leaves the restaurant. He spent only about eight minutes in the restaurant, and he apparently ate a McDonald's hot apple pie.

Now, McVeigh, of course, did not spend $3.65 on a taxi simply to have an apple pie at McDonald's. He took a taxi because his car was in Oklahoma City, waiting to serve as a getaway car. And that afternoon, Monday afternoon, he needed to get up to Elliott's to pick up the truck, so he took a cab and he stopped at McDonald's because it was at the intersection on the way. It's just a stopover spot.

McVeigh left McDonald's, you'll see on the video footage, at approximately four. As I said, Elliott's Body Shop is about a mile away. It's about a fifteen-minute walk. Fifteen minutes after McVeigh left McDonald's, he walked into Elliott's Body Shop and picked up the truck that he used to destroy the Murrah Building. The owner, Eldon Elliott, was again there. He recalls the transaction. Again this was not a fleeting encounter with a complete stranger. This is not like asking the cab driver or the man who delivered the Chinese food to identify the customer. Mr. Elliott had seen McVeigh two days before, and he was seeing him again on this Monday. On this occasion he wasn't simply handing over a box of Chinese food. He was giving McVeigh a valuable piece of equipment, a large Ryder truck.

He spent some time on the transaction. He walked around the truck, inspected it for damage. He filled out a damage form. And he recalls the person that he released the truck to. It was the same person who had come in on the preceding Saturday morning, the same person that paid cash on the truck. This was the second time Mr. Elliott had an opportunity to observe that man. Again the lighting was good. The two stood nearly face-to-face. The man was Timothy McVeigh.

Monday before the bombing. McVeigh was at Elliott's Body Shop. He picked up the truck. He's still in Junction City. It's two days before the bombing. There is another face that Mr. Elliott does not remember as well as he remembers McVeigh's face. It's the face of a second man that Mr. Elliott believes he saw with McVeigh on that Monday afternoon, only once, not on the first occasion. This is when McVeigh came to pick up the truck. He saw that person just for a moment, glanced at him. His business, of course, was with McVeigh. That's who he was concentrating on.

Now, whether Mr. Elliott was mistaken about the existence of another person and who that other person might possibly be, if there is such a person, doesn't change the fact that Mr. Elliott will say that this defendant rented the truck that blew up the Murrah Building.

At Elliott's Body Shop, McVeigh presented his phony driver's license in the name Robert Kling to rent the truck. And the birthday that McVeigh put on the driver's license is telling: McVeigh's real birthday is April 23. But the birthday he gave Kling was his special day, April 19, the anniversary of the fire at Waco and the date that McVeigh selected for the bombing in Oklahoma City. McVeigh also signed the rental agreement in the name Robert Kling.

Now, everyone's handwriting has certain distinctive features. That's why you can identify or recognize the handwriting of loved ones and old friends, even though sometimes you don't know why you can recognize it. And that's also why documents examiners who spend their careers examining and comparing handwriting can notice little distinctive idiosyncrasies of particular handwriting, and they can compare one document to another.

Well, with the assistance of a documents examiner who will testify for us, you will look closely at those Ryder rental documents; and together, in the courtroom, we will compare the documents, the other documents that we can prove McVeigh wrote, letters to friends, things of that sort. And you, yourself, will see the similarities. For example, on the Kling signature, you'll see that there is a little curlicue that he used to make the *K*, and you'll see a similar curlicue in other writing that we will prove was written by McVeigh.

You'll notice on the Kling documents, in the name Robert Kling, the cross stroke for the *t* is done backward. You can tell it's done backward because there is a blot of ink that starts on the backside of the *t* and tapers off on the front side of the *t*. And we'll show you other documents written by McVeigh which have that same backward cross stroke on the *t*. When you see these documents, and when you listen to the examiner, and when you compare these documents yourself, you'll conclude that Timothy McVeigh stood in Elliott's Body Shop and signed the name Robert Kling.

That Monday afternoon McVeigh drove the Ryder truck back to Dreamland Motel. You'll hear details about where he parked it when he was seen in it at the Dreamland. Now, there may be discrepancies in memories of witnesses as to the precise time and date that he was at the motel with the Ryder truck, but, completely independent of evidence from Elliott's Body Shop, there will be no doubt that McVeigh had a Ryder truck in those days before the bombing.

And our evidence will establish that the truck McVeigh had at the Dreamland was the truck that he rented at Elliott's Body Shop, because employees of Ryder Corporation searched all of their records nationwide, all of their rentals during this period of time, and there is no rental in the name Timothy McVeigh. Now, if he had rented a truck for some legitimate purpose, you would think it would be in his name. There is no rental in the name Timothy McVeigh for that period of time. That's because he rented the truck in the name Robert Kling. So my point is, there are overlapping ways, independent ways, in which we will demonstrate that Robert Kling is really Timothy McVeigh.

There are the circumstances of the telephone call from the bus station across from the Firestone where he bought his used car. There are the circumstances of him being at the McDonald's twenty minutes and leaving twenty minutes before the truck was picked up at Elliott's Body Shop. There is the eyewitness testimony of Eldon Elliott. There is the documentary and handwriting evidence. You'll see and compare the documents. And there is the fact that there was no McVeigh rental of any Ryder truck during this period of time. Between the time that McVeigh picked up the Ryder truck that Monday afternoon, and the time that the bomb was detonated early on Wednesday morning, he had plenty of time, you will learn from our explosives expert, to build a bomb in the back of a truck and drive it to Oklahoma City; and that is precisely what he did.

The Turner Diaries taught him how to mix the different ingredients, how to set up the bomb, right down to how to drill a hole between the cargo box and the cab of the truck so that he could detonate it, so that the fuse could run into the cab of the truck and he could fuse it from where he was sitting in the front of the cab. You'll hear from witness testimony that's what he said he would do. So he converted the Ryder truck from a cargo vehicle into a gigantic deadly bomb, and he drove it to Oklahoma City, and he detonated it at one of the busiest times of the day.

Bear in mind this was not three or four in the morning, when he could conceivably have detonated the bomb and possibly not have killed anyone. It was at 9:02 in the morning, when everyone was in their office, business was being conducted, and the children were in the day-care center.

The sound and the concussion of the blast rocked downtown Oklahoma City. It was as though it had been struck by an earthquake. And as McVeigh sped away from the scene of the crime, word quickly spread as to the location of the blast. No one in downtown Oklahoma City could have missed the sound. It ripped the air, shattered windows. It was a terrifying explosion. People who heard it, because of the noise, couldn't help but be concerned. Just like the shock waves of the bomb, the word spread through the city as to where it had been located. The word was, of course, it was at the federal building.

That morning Mike Weaver had driven his wife's car down to work. It had needed service, and the service station was closer to his office than to his wife's; so, as a favor, he drove her car and she drove his. He dropped their son off at junior high on his way to work, and after dropping his son off, Mike drove downtown to the service station with his wife's car. Mike's workday started at nine; and when his wife, Donna, heard the blast and then got the news that it was the Murrah Building, which was Mike's building, she rushed from her office, made her way quickly, as quickly as she could, to the Murrah Building. And on her way, she hoped against hope that maybe Mike had gotten delayed—maybe he had gotten delayed in dropping their son off, maybe he had gotten delayed at the service station, maybe he hadn't made it to work at nine. And she stopped in front of the Murrah Building and looked up. His office was gone, and she knew so was he. She was right: He was killed. She didn't have earplugs in her pocket. None of our witnesses had earplugs in their pockets that day.

The noise from the concussion from the bomb was felt throughout the city, and Helena Garrett, whose son, Tevin, was in the daycare center, she, of course, was across the street in her building. By pure coincidence she was on her way to the Murrah Building—still in her building, but she was going to move her car from the Murrah Building to her regular parking lot. When she heard the blast, she rushed outside and saw that the entire front face of the Murrah Building was missing. The plate-glass windows that the children pressed their hands and faces against were gone. The entire side of the building was gone. She ran to the scene and frantically searched the area for her son. She watched as rescue workers arrived and carried bodies of small children from the building, and she looked to see if any of them were Tevin. At one point she climbed on a pile of debris in front of the building until the rescue workers begged her to leave; and then she went home and waited. She waited for days; and when Tevin's body was found, it was taken to a funeral home. And at the funeral home, she asked to see her son, but the funeral director persuaded her not to: The body was too badly mangled. So she never saw her son again.

As she searched for her son that morning of the bombing, rescue workers searched for survivors and the bodies. And law-enforcement agents arrived to search the debris for clues as to the cause of the blast; and what they found were various parts of the Ryder truck that had blown up. The truck had blown to smithereens. And one of the pieces they found was a small piece of plywood from the side of the truck. It had yellow and red Ryder truck markings on one side of the plywood. On the other side was just plain plywood. And the piece, when it was found, was sealed in a plastic bag and shipped back to the FBI laboratory, along with all the other truck parts, pieces of debris that were found and were being sent back for examination. And the purpose of sending them back to the lab was to examine them for chemical residue, try to figure out the cause of this blast.

And the chemist who examined most of these pieces is a man by the name of Steven Burmeister. He's been with the FBI for years, and he's one of the most qualified forensic chemists in the area of explosives residue. He's spent many years studying and examining explosives residue. He's worked both at the FBI laboratory and in the private sector, and he's testified both for defendants and for the government. And when he examined these pieces of evidence that came back to the FBI lab, he was looking for clues as to the type of explosive that might be used and might have been used in the bomb. He used a microscope to examine the truck parts, and he didn't find much.

An explosion is a dynamic reaction, and Burmeister will tell you that the chemicals used in an explosive are often destroyed as part of the explosion, so you don't necessarily find bomb residue after an explosion. But Burmeister did find something: When he looked at that little piece of plywood from the side of the truck, he saw little specks under the microscope; and when he had tested those little specks, he determined their chemical makeup. The specks were crystals of ammonium nitrate, the very same chemical that McVeigh and Nichols had obtained in fifty-pound bags in the form of the fertilizer they had purchased in central Kansas months before.

You'll also hear from a chemist from Great Britain. Her name is Linda Jones, and she's also an explosives expert. She's worked numerous cases involving IRA bombs, and she has over twenty years of experience in the explosives field. She'll explain the different types of damage that can be caused by different types of bombs. She's had ample experience with ammonium nitrate–type bombs, and she knows what kind of damage they can cause. She will also explain to you why a mixture of ammonium nitrate and fuel oil or racing fuel can be detonated to create an explosion, and she'll explain it's not a complicated task. She analyzed the damage to the Murrah Building and the surrounding area, and she'll explain to you why that damage is consistent with damage caused by an ammonium nitrate–based truck bomb. She'll also explain how easy and cheap it is to make just such a bomb—so easy, in fact, it could be built by one or two people. I've already described for you the huge twisted axle that fell on the red Ford Fiesta that seemed to fly and fall out of the sky. It had been at the center of the explosion, and the force of the explosion propelled it more than two hundred yards in the air. Law-enforcement agents found it there beside the Ford Fiesta, and they traced its vehicle-identification number.

Now, many of you know that every vehicle carries a unique number stamped on various parts of the vehicle. It's referred to as the VIN, or vehicle-identification number. The agency saw the axle, located the VIN, vehicle-identification number, and called it in to find out what vehicle the axle came from and where the vehicle came from. They learned that the axle came from a large Ryder truck, and by contacting Ryder they learned that the truck had been rented two days before the bombing, from a rental agency in Junction City, Kansas. You already know the rental agency. They discovered it then: Elliott's Body Shop. That information, of course, led them to Elliott's, where they learned what I've already told you: The truck had been rented by a young man who used the name Robert Kling. Kling's address in South Dakota, of course, proved to be false. Not only was there no house at that address, the address in the listed city—there is not even an address of that sort.

The agents surveyed the area for anyone who had been seen driving a Ryder truck; and, as you know from my description of testimony related to the Dreamland Motel, they discovered that a guest at that motel had been seen days before the bombing riding in a Ryder truck, and that guest was registered in his name. It was Timothy McVeigh. That information led them to a search for McVeigh, and I've already told you much of the rest of the story.

McVeigh had been stopped and arrested in Oklahoma City on the morning of the bombing, traveling away from the city. He was arrested that morning because he didn't have a license on his car and because, when he was stopped, he had an obvious concealed weapon underneath his jacket.

He was still in custody two days later, when the federal agents tracked the VIN number, went to Elliott's, found it was Kling, went to Dreamland, discovered that Kling was McVeigh. They went to the county jail where he was being held. They took possession of the clothing he had, same clothing that he had the day of the bombing, because [the clothes] had been removed, put into storage, and he was in an orange prison jumpsuit, not wearing clothing he had on the day of the bombing.

They took those clothes and sent them to the FBI laboratory. I'm referring, of course, to the T-shirt with the image of Lincoln and the tree dripping blood on the back. And again it was Stephen Burmeister who did the examination. He conducted a chemical analysis of the clothing, and he found explosives residue on the shirt and the pants pockets and on the earplugs in the pockets, or that had been in the pockets. This residue was not ammonium nitrate. The ammonium nitrate was found at the scene of the bombing. That was on the plywood. That was explosive residue that's referred to as PETN. PETN is found in det cord, and it's a very fine powder. Det cord is sort of a narrow, hollow tubing, and when you use det cord, you often cut it. And in [the process of] cutting it open, the fine powder sifts out from inside the det cord. And it's sticky and gets all over everything. You can't really cut it without getting it on your hands and clothing. And that's the explosives residue that was found on the shirt McVeigh was wearing and on the pockets and on the earplugs that had been in his pockets.

The agents, of course, located his car. They found inside his car that manila envelope that he previously described. The papers inside there were practically a manifesto. They're almost a declaration of his terrorist intent. Some were passages in his own handwriting. Some were photocopies that he had highlighted. Many of the documents bear his fingerprints. All of them were about the right and the need to kill people who work for the federal government.

There was a passage from *The Turner Diaries*, the one I referred to earlier, that said, "The real value of our attacks today . . ." There was the quote from one of the Founding Fathers about how, when the government fears the people, there is liberty; and that's the one that had McVeigh's handwriting beneath it that said, "Maybe now there will be liberty." And there was much, much more. There were passages declaring war against the American government. There were passages calling for violence against the government because of Waco.

As you can probably tell from what I've said, there is no single witness who is going to come in here and tell the whole sad story. Our case consists of dozens of pieces of evidence put together. And those pieces will come in like bricks building a brick wall. Now, some of the bricks won't fit tightly together, because memories will be slightly different; there will undoubtedly be some unanswered questions. There always are in a case of this complexity.

But in the end we will build a solid wall of evidence against McVeigh, making your job of determining his guilt easy, I believe. You'll get a clear picture of what happened, and it won't depend on any one witness. There will be overlapping proof, and you'll be convinced beyond a reasonable doubt that he's responsible for the bombing in Oklahoma City.

We will make your job easy. We will present ample evidence to convince you beyond any reasonable doubt that Timothy McVeigh is responsible for this terrible crime. You will hear evidence in this case that McVeigh liked to consider himself a patriot, someone who could start the second American Revolution. The literature that was in his car when he was arrested included some that quoted statements from the Founding Fathers and other people who played a part in the American Revolution, people like Patrick Henry and Samuel Adams. McVeigh isolated and took these statements out of context, and he did that to justify his antigovernment violence.

Well, ladies and gentlemen, the statements of our forefathers can never be twisted to justify warfare against innocent children. Our forefathers didn't fight British women and children. They fought other soldiers. They fought them face-to-face, hand-to-hand. They didn't plant bombs and run away wearing earplugs.

POSTSCRIPT

Timothy McVeigh was convicted and executed by lethal injection on June 11, 1997.

The guilty verdict was eminently reasonable in view of the overwhelming evidence against McVeigh. This evidence, much of which was circumstantial, came from numerous different sources, many of whom did not know each other.

There was no cultural backdrop that could save Timothy McVeigh. No matter what one's political views are, most people in this country abhor the type of senseless violence McVeigh displayed in killing 168 innocent Americans. The means chosen by McVeigh were so beyond the pale in terms of American culture and politics that the verdict was in essence consistent with the political backdrop.

A jury's view of whether the prosecution met the burden of proving guilt beyond a reasonable doubt is often influenced by how they feel about the case. Is the case a waste of taxpayer money or is it an important case in the eyes of the community? Is the victim sympathetic or is he loathsome? This, of course, should not be a proper factor for a jury to use in deciding whether a case has been proved, but the justice system relies on human beings, not machines. If the victims portrayed in a case are sympathetic, a jury may require less proof than in a case in which the victim is perceived as loathsome or the issue trivial. On the other hand, if the defendant is a sympathetic figure, either because of the nature of the evidence or because he is a popular celebrity, then the burden of proof, which is "beyond a reasonable doubt" may even be increased to a bar which a prosecutor would have a hard time achieving. Obviously, in this case, the jury had sympathies that overwhelmingly favored the prosecution.

How can a prosecutor adequately describe in words the horror of the mass murder of 168 ordinary Americans? He does so by putting a human face on the victims. The number of dead is really incomprehensible. Mr. Hartzler humanized the victims by describing who they were and what they were doing immediately prior to their murder. The details of the morning routine of sixteen-month-old Tevin Garrett, which played a prominent part of Mr. Hartzler's opening statement, was not given to him on a silver platter. Mr. Hartzler undoubtedly elicited this information in interviewing Mrs. Garrett. It was Mr. Hartzler's creativity that spurred him to ask Mrs. Garrett how her baby's final hours on this earth were spent. It was Mr. Hartzler's understanding of human emotion and tragedy that caused him to make Tevin Garrett's final hours a key part of his opening statement.

Much of the evidence in the case was circumstantial. As that case shows, circumstantial evidence can be stronger than direct evidence. A witness can lie and an eyewitness can be wrong. Circumstantial evidence is often dependent upon hundreds of strands of evidence that come from people who do not know each other. That is why such cases are often more persuasive than cases involving eyewitnesses.

Mr. Hartzler skillfully weaved the strands of circumstantial evidence into a compelling story strongly pointing to McVeigh's guilt. He rendered complex scientific evidence understandable to the jurors, including enough facts to convince the jury of McVeigh's guilt, but not too many as to confuse or bore them. It was truly a masterful job by a seasoned prosecutor.

14

A MOTHER'S NIGHTMARE

AUGUSTIN BALLINAS v. *NEW YORK CITY HEALTH AND HOSPITALS CORPORATION*

MANY OF THE CASES in the preceding chapters were examples of the finest lawyers showcasing their skills in high-profile cases. Yet excellent advocacy occurs in relative anonymity across the country, in nearly empty courtrooms where gifted lawyers practice outside the glaring spotlight of the media.

Absent the involvement of celebrities, personal-injury trials take place mostly in obscurity. Yet because potentially large settlements are at stake, top lawyers often feature in them. And because the biggest awards are often obtained when the lawyer successfully appeals to the jury's sense of outrage and injustice, its desire to protect and compensate a victim, such cases often involve emotionally dramatic scenarios. This tragic case had all those elements in spades.

Augustin Ballinas was born by midwife on September 11, 1990, in the Bronx's Lincoln Hospital, which is owned and managed by New York City Health and Hospitals Corporation. Fifty-one hours before his mother, Carmen Ballinas, gave birth, her membranes ruptured, a fact that was not communicated to the pediatric staff treating the child. Testing revealed that Carmen was positive for colonized group-B streptococcus, which can cause bacterial meningitis. The baby became very sick two days after the delivery and developed bacterial meningitis from his mother's strep-B infection. Nothing could be done at that point to reverse the disastrous effects on the baby. He was released one month after his birth with severe brain damage and cerebral palsy.

Ten years old at the start of the trial, Augustin suffers from spastic and athetoid cerebral palsy. Confined to a wheelchair, he cannot speak or use his hands and is not toilet-trained.

The plaintiffs claimed that a prolonged rupture of the membranes put Carmen at risk to transfer this infection to Augustin and that a pediatrician should have been present at the time of the delivery. A pediatrician was in fact called but did not attend the delivery. In addition, although there were doctors present during the delivery, the child was delivered by a midwife.

The health of a baby at birth is measured by a score called an APGAR score, with an APGAR of ten signifying perfect health. Augutsin's APGARs were between eight and nine. The plaintiff claimed that the hospital's pediatric staff should have been monitoring Augustin for sepsis (the presence of pathogens or toxins in the blood), but that no doctor saw the baby for the first two days of the baby's life. Augustin had, in fact, exhibited symptoms of sepsis shortly after birth, though he was not treated with antibiotics until he was three days old. By then it was too late.

The hospital admitted that the fifty-one-hour history of the ruptured membrane was not communicated to the pediatricians. Nonetheless, they contended that Augustin and Carmen were closely monitored and that their medical care would not have been different had the physicians been aware of the rupture, on account of the fact that Augustin did not show symptoms until September 13, by which point treatment could not have saved him.

The plaintiff and the defendant disagreed about as to the extent of the plaintiff's retardation. The plaintiff contended that it was minor and that Augustin was aware and cognizant of his ability. The defendant contended that the plaintiff's mental retardation was more extensive. The amount of damages would depend in part on whether the jury believed that Augustin could benefit from therapy.

The court gave the jury seven questions to answer. Their answers would determine the issues of liability, causation, and damages.

Excerpts from the Summation of Plaintiff Attorney Thomas Moore

Allow me to borrow a statement made a long time ago by Edmund Burke, an Irish statesman and orator speaking in, of all places, the English parliament. Burke said, "Something has happened upon which it is difficult to speak and impossible to be silent."

Ladies and gentlemen of the jury, you have seen unfold in this courtroom events that would make Edmund Burke's words as applicable today as they were over two hundred years ago. It is not only that this child was damaged through negligence and carelessness, avoidable though it was. It is not that they had chance after chance that went begging time and time again to save him, and they did not.

As horrible and terrible as that is, what is difficult to speak upon yet impossible to remain silent is that in this courtroom—but not beginning in this courtroom, beginning as early as the events themselves— there was a deliberate, orchestrated, fraudulent effort to deprive this child of justice. That is the awful truth of this case. Carmen Ballinas carried that sacred life through those months of gestation flawlessly, lovingly, selflessly. Through the hot summer months of 1990, she carried her precious charge. Through the almost insufferable days of August of that year, as that one within her grew and grew so famously and perfectly, she heeded every direction, kept with every appointment that they scheduled for her.

And then she arrived on the doorstep of Lincoln Hospital. She presented them with a perfect baby, and God presented them with a perfect baby. Had they turned her away that fateful night of September 10 of 1990, it would have been far better than what was to happen when they welcomed her and her baby through their portal.

Did you know that next week is Bronx Week? You had to have seen that on a banner with the Bronx seal above the entrance from the Grand Concourse. And on that seal, you should be proud to know, are the words *Ne cede malis*, "Do not yield to evil." Peoples have striven, for as long as there have been peoples, against evil. And one of the greatest evils that has permeated our earth, since *Homo sapiens* first appeared, is injustice.

Ladies and gentlemen, you were told today that this child does not deserve, in essence, a penny of damages, because there's no legal responsibility resting with the City of New York. I say to you, if you follow that admonition, you would not follow that proud banner and seal of your county, and you would perpetrate an evil in the form of an injustice, as great in an individual sense as any has ever been perpetrated. What have you seen unfold in this courtroom? I told you there was a litany of errors in this case. I proved to you every single one of them. You heard in the opening statement on behalf of this fair city that they did nothing wrong, that there was no basis for these various "departures from accepted medical practice." That's what you heard less than three weeks ago. And now, in the short time since, you hear, oh, yes, of the seven departures from accepted practice that this court will ask you to decide, four of them are "conceded." Four of the seven.

The Health and Hospitals Corporation had the audacity to give the type of opening statement it gave. This is no attack on this gentleman who has the obligation to defend this Health and Hospitals Corporation. I have not personally attacked him, nor will I. But I say the opening statement in this case was unworthy of the Corporation, in light of what you have seen. And then yesterday, to hear that [Dr.] Jim Howard, [the defense expert in obstetrics nursing] had told them two to four months ago that there were various departures from accepted practice! Concession? Nonsense.

Ladies and gentlemen, to try and hold on to a ripple of credibility in an ocean of lies, they concede the obvious. But I say to you there is no truth and no credibility to the defense in this case from A to Z, from beginning to end. It was nothing but mirrors and fabrication and obfuscation, because the real truth was unavoidable. And that's what you saw unfold in this courtroom, day after day, before this Supreme Court justice and you.

Seven questions will be asked of you related to the seven claimed departures. Seven ancillary questions will also appear: Was that departure a substantial contributing factor to the injuries of Augustin Ballinas?

Since all a plaintiff has to show is one departure causally related to the damage, clearly, since they are admitting four, because to do otherwise would be preposterous, the only question is, Did it contribute, in any way, to this child's meningitis and his damage?

In a civil case, you'll ask yourselves, "What is more likely to be the case?" not "What is absolutely the case?" not "What is beyond a reasonable doubt the case?" but "What is more likely to be the case?" And you'll hear His Honor define preponderance of evidence applicable to a civil case. They take the believable evidence and divide it; on one side the plaintiff's and on the other side the defendant's. If it weighs to the slightest degree in favor of the plaintiff, favor the plaintiff.

Here are the scales, ladies and gentlemen. Put the credible evidence in favor of the plaintiff's position on one side. Where is the credible evidence to be put on the other side of that scale, the defendant's credible evidence? Oh, they spoke. Oh, they brought in witnesses. Oh, they have opinions. But credible evidence? Where was that? And where is that now, as the day of reckoning approaches?

First question—the issue of doing the culture or not doing the culture when Mrs. Ballinas first came to the hospital on September 10, 1990. [The plaintiff claimed that the hospital should have done a cervical culture on Carmen right away because her water broke; this cervical culture could have shown the presence of Beta strep B.] Dr. Bernard Nathanson [the plaintiff's expert in obstetrics nursing] was attacked in this case because he testifies a lot and he charges when he does that, but you were honored to hear a man of encyclopedic knowledge in the field of obstetrics and gynecology. As many times as I have asked him to come to court, I am proud to have presented that witness as a champion of this child's case. He jealously guarded his objectivity and would not even accept the phrase "testifying on behalf." Many witnesses accept that; he does not. That is how jealously he guards his objectivity. As a lawyer charged with the legal case of this child, if I had a Bernard Nathanson who supported the obstetrical position of the plaintiff in this case and did not put him on the witness stand for your edification, I would have no business practicing law.

Dr. Nathanson explained to you why it was so crucial to do the cervical culture right away, because of the prolonged rupture of the membranes. Despite what you heard from Jim Howard [the defendant's expert in obstetrics nursing], everybody conceded it should have been done sometime between eighteen [and] twenty-four hours after the premature rupture. Imagine somebody who has been practicing obstetrics over thirty years, as Dr. Howard claims to have done, and he doesn't know the difference between premature rupture and prolonged rupture. That is whom they brought in here, but that is just the tip of the iceberg.

The cervical culture should have been done within eighteen to twenty-four hours. It was at least thirty-two hours when Mrs. Ballinas arrived in the hospital. The world of obstetrics knows universally, now, the great risk of infection. Risk for the mother, yes, but, much more importantly, risk for the baby.

It's not just that. Even with Jim Howard, I said to him, "Wasn't it well known that even with colonization there is an increased risk of infection in this baby?" We had already heard [that] anywhere from 15 to 30 percent of women can have this colonization of Beta strep in their genital tract, and Dr. Howard agreed. And then I asked him, "But when that is coupled with prolonged rupture of membranes, doesn't the risk of infection increase dramatically?" And I gave the figure, but he didn't agree with it.

Well, he said, "I can't agree with your number, but it would certainly increase quite a bit over and above the increased risk with just colonization when there is prolonged rupture." It was explained by Dr. Nathanson because there is the increased danger of it ascending and infecting the baby, because now the protective essential of waters has been broken.

In the face of these basic principles, they admit this mother to the hospital with her baby. And they wait twenty-one hours before they take a little swab from the area of the cervix to do a culture. A half an hour after this baby was born into the world, they finally got around to it. And they tell you that was good and accepted practice in a teaching hospital in 1990? Dr. Howard said [that] in 1990 it wasn't the standard to do the culture right away. So I brought in various textbooks in obstetrics, all of them applicable to the period of 1990. All of them were copyrighted before 1990 or that year. "Dr. Howard," I asked, "is this a reasonable, authoritative work by reason of its use in the obstetrical community for people to get information and to learn from?" "No," he said. "No, you're not going to read from any of those, Moore. I'm onto that. I've been doing this stuff for thirty-five years."

Now, you even heard Dr. B. K. Rajegowda admit that under the meaning of the word "authoritative," that there were such textbooks. Not Jim Howard. Not in the history of obstetrics has there been one work written that would be considered authoritative. I thought to myself in the whole charade, Isn't it terrible to think as follows?

Here are these dedicated young people going into the medical profession, with their idealism and their passion and their desire to help, looking to learn as much as they can. They go to the medical schools. And there in those medical schools, they need certain things, don't they? They need to be nourished, so that they'll grow strong and continue to be strong, to go out and care for patients. So, obviously, on the medical-school campus there are dining rooms and cafeterias. And those same people, thankfully, want to be spiritually ready, too. So another important place on a medical-school campus is a place of worship.

Ladies and gentlemen of the jury, do any of you doubt for a second that a place of pride on medical-school campuses throughout the United States of America is the library? Is that true, Jim Howard? Or is it false?

Don't bother, lawyer, says Jim Howard. Don't bother, lawyer, working hard and staying up nights and preparing to try a case and learning the medicine and making sure that the departures were only as of the time and that nobody is going to be judged by after-acquired knowledge. That's why this stonewaller sat here, this doctor who has no other reason to be in court except, right or wrong, to try and defeat the case of an injured child. There's no question they would have gotten information much earlier had they done the culture, which should have been done. Just to highlight their lack of credibility here, if somebody does not tell the truth on one thing, they may well be lying on other things.

When would we know these cultures, and how would we know it takes forty-eight hours, so even if it's done late on the tenth, you're not going to have it until late on the twelfth. Dr. Nathanson said, yes, you're not going to get the full information for close to forty-eight hours, but you do get preliminary information. You get information that something is happening and that there is some growth, without identifying necessarily the bacteria involved.

You know what? There's living proof of that in their own record. Look at this: 9/14/90. This is 2:00 P.M., about fifteen hours after the blood culture was done. "Blood culture, gram positive." They knew fifteen hours later. Let's take a look at the cerebrospinal fluid. You know that they did not do the spinal tap until 11:00 P.M. Here it is, three short hours later. "Gram-positive diplococci," and then "Many WBCs." They knew there was bacteria in that fluid within three hours. And they knew it was gram positive, because you heard yesterday that Beta strep, group B, is a gram-positive [bacterium], and we know without doubt that Beta strep, group B, caused meningitis in this case.

Look at their record. Look at what was lost by not doing that culture when they should have done it. In the face of the double risk that this baby faced, based on the history that they had at the time, there was not a stem of reason to delay it a minute. But they did delay, as I said, almost twenty-four hours.

What happened to that culture that they took thirty-one minutes after this baby was born? The report came back on the fourteenth with Beta strep throughout. You remember the little writing at two by the resident on the thirteenth? "Cervical culture Beta strep." But it was hard to read.

Question two and all the even numbered questions are "Was that departure a substantial contributing factor in the injury to the child?" Of course, I'll deal with that in one turn.

Question three: "Was the failure to communicate from obstetrics to pediatrics that there has been fifty-one hours of prolonged rupture of membranes is this a departure from accepted standards of medical practice?" That's one of the points that were conceded the first day. It's great that the first witness, Dr. Lung Ming Wei, a director of the Department of Obstetrics, had all this difficulty with the language. These are the people that I could subpoena, the directors of Obstetrics and Pediatrics. I was waiting for somebody that didn't have a language problem who was actually involved in the care of this case to come in, but you didn't see one. Did that occur to you? Has it occurred to you that not one person—nurse, practical nurse, technician, first-year resident, second-year resident, senior, chief, or attending at Lincoln Hospital, who cared for this baby—not one was called by the defense in this case to testify about one thing. Did that occur to you? [Mr. Moore himself called the directors of Obstetrics and Pediatrics, who were hostile witnesses, to prove the negligence of the hospital.]

As Dr. Wei admitted, and as any self-respecting human being, doctor or otherwise, would have to, it was abject failure by them not to have notified Pediatrics of this cardinal point of fifty-one hours. Isn't it great, almost eleven years since it happened, the defense admits for the first time a departure from accepted practice—the first time, having opened the day before to the contrary? And you wonder: How could Moore get so serious about this and riled up? You would have to be a stone not to.

Question five: "Was it a departure not to page a pediatrician present at the delivery?" Did they really think that any self-respecting jury—you can try a case and you can deny and deny until the day of reckoning approaches, but it began when you were sworn in this case. To think that that corporation thought that maybe some jury in the Bronx in 2001 might condone the following high-risk situation! It's in the record: Pediatrics called for delivery; Pediatrics does not respond. Make no mistake; the plan was not to admit it. Do I have to tell you? If Pediatrics responded, then they would have bypassed the failure of Obstetrics to let them know, because they would have found out themselves.

Question seven: "Was it a departure not to notify Pediatrics of the temperature at 2:00 A.M. on the twelfth?" I've heard some convoluted reasoning in my life, but this one took the cake. This was one that beat the band. On the one hand, they jealously guarded, as they have a right to, the laws requiring that medical caregivers not be judged by after-occurring events. That would not be fair, of course. They jealously guard that, and then in almost the same breath, [they] said, "You know what? There was no requirement to notify Pediatrics of that temperature, because four hours later it went down."

What is going on? The basic standard, particularly in the first twenty-four hours after birth, when a mother has had prolonged rupture of the membranes, is to notify Pediatrics of any sign of maternal fever. Not that you wait an hour or two hours or three or four. Was that temperature rise a sign of infection? No, but under the risks involved, it had to be assumed to be, and that is why Pediatrics should have been notified. Then the failure of Pediatrics to come and the failure to notify of the fifty-one hours would have been overridden, because they would have had to investigate the infection in this baby, and they would have found out about his medical history.

The chart that had all this information, as this baby languished in his nursery, lay just feet away on the same floor. If this is going to be condoned as appropriate medical practice, there should be neon lights above the hospital entrance reading, "All you who enter here, beware." Another chance to have saved this baby went a-begging.

Ladies and gentlemen, remember Dr. Marcus Hermansen [the plaintiff's expert in neonatology] gave you a timeline and showed you the various events and when things should have been known and what it should have led to, in the care of this baby, and how it would have saved this baby? This is not a close case. This is not a case that needs this foundation and this edifice built before the truth can be seen. This is a case that the more you believe in medicine and the more regard you have for the practitioners of that great pursuit, the more you recognize a rotten apple at first blush.

What's the defense? Everything that medicine devised to care for a baby under these circumstances wouldn't have worked, no matter when it was done. These great things called antibiotics, whose only reason for being is to fight infection, with myriads, thank God, of success stories over the years, would have been a failure for Augustin Ballinas.

"Did they depart from accepted practice by not giving antibiotics by the evening of the twelfth? Of course they did. So many things known and more unknown that should have been known that would have led any self-respecting, halfway knowledgeable practitioner to give antibiotics, to do basically the full sepsis workup, to take the blood, to take the spinal fluid. How many babies far worse off than Augustin was at that point on the twelfth or the thirteenth or early on the fourteenth have been saved because of the great use of antibiotics? Louis Pasteur would turn in his grave.

They told you from this witness stand that it was not a departure not to give antibiotics on the twelfth, but they "conceded" departures on the thirteenth and fourteenth. They admitted departures, but claimed they just didn't cause any problem to the baby. They told you that this baby's end result would have been the very same, getting antibiotics over twenty-four hours before or maybe hours before. Same result. What's more likely, ladies and gentlemen?

Let's take the twelfth. Their own record indicated that the baby was not seen that day by one single M.D.—resident or attending. No physician saw that baby from the beginning of the day, long before light dawned, until the end of the day, long after the sun set. And September days are pretty long. How can you condone a physician not having seen this baby during that twenty-four-hour period? There is something far more telling, and you heard it touched on today already.

Obviously, there was a language barrier, because Mrs. Ballinas has never dealt in medical matters through the medium of English. She doesn't speak it at all. She did her best in this courtroom, as she did her best on September 12, 1990. She knew things were not right with her baby. He was crying too much. He was irritable. He was not feeding properly. She knew, and Dr. Rajegowda was forced to admit that you always have to listen to the mother. In essence, the mother is the neonatologist's eyes and ears.

"We're not saying she's a liar. Oh, no. She's just mistaken."

Ladies and gentlemen, you only have two choices here. You want either to believe or condemn this woman. Don't buy this "she's mistaken," please. This mother is either an unmitigated liar or she told the truth. There was a Spanish-speaking nurse arguing about these observations with an English-speaking nurse in front of Mrs. Ballinas. And in the face of what we know was going on at that hospital, they thought they had a well baby. There was no reason to be doing anything differently whatsoever. They didn't even bother getting somebody like Dr. Rajegowda who would say, yes, you have to give credence to a mother in this situation. Somebody, probably the English-speaking nurse, was of the opinion this is just an alarmist for a mother.

"Happens all the time. New mothers are very concerned about their babies. There's nothing wrong with this baby. Look at his vital signs. He's doing wonderfully."

And that was a pivotal chance lost, because, without a doubt, had they properly investigated her complaints at that time, the medical details would have been found immediately. Then this baby would have gotten a CBC [complete blood count], a lumbar puncture, and antibiotics on the twelfth.

Dr. Rajegowda was forced to admit that, had antibiotics been given on the twelfth, this baby could have been saved, and certainly the degree of damage to Augustin Ballinas's brain would have been vastly different. Obviously, this baby had a sepsis then, with almost no signs except for rather subtle ones. Antibiotics would never have allowed that Beta strep to cross the brain barrier. Meningitis never would have ensued, and this would have been a perfect baby.

The greatest vehicle for truth that's ever been implemented in a courtroom is cross-examination. The witnesses on the side of the defense fell on their faces abysmally, every one of them. I could give you chapter and verse almost endlessly about preposterous statements that were made because they were backed into them. But if they had conceded, they'd have given up. Rather than conceding the truth, they lied to a point of obvious lying, laughable at times but tragic, and more tragic if they get away with it.

Ladies and gentlemen of the jury, do you know what the awful truth of this case is? That they were almost literally paralytic at Lincoln Hospital in acting to save this baby. I hinted at it already, but do you know that it wasn't at 10:30 A.M. on the fourteenth, when everything was known, that they did a lumbar puncture. It was eleven. It almost sounds like too much to deal with, but it does bear saying. Hours, days available to them were lost, but minutes could have meant an eternity for this baby. Minutes, as Dr. Hermansen pointed out to you.

Look at this, the order for antibiotics is 10:30 A.M. but they can't give antibiotics until they do the lumbar puncture. "11:00 A.M., lumbar puncture." It's not too easy to read, but that is what it says. "11:30 A.M., IV ampicillin 40 mg and gentamicin 8.5 mg." It's there, 11:30, an hour after it was ordered, all the while these bacteria were ravaging this baby's brain. They lost another hour, one of many hours and many days.

Ladies and gentlemen of the jury, *ne cede malis*. Do not yield to evil. Do not yield to injustice. If you say that this child has been a victim of medical negligence beyond a shadow of a doubt, then Auggie, as he likes to be called, is entitled to every penny related to his damage and need. Anything less is an injustice.

Who was it who asked, "What is the last refuge of the scoundrel?" Well, I say the last refuge of the Health and Hospitals Corporation, in this case, is for you to mitigate the damages in this case and to give this child less than he's entitled to, and they have endeavored mightily to have you do that.

Where do I start to show the house of cards that they have tried to pawn off as an edifice of credibility relative to what this child is entitled to, if he's entitled to anything, which they say he isn't? By the way, they spent over an hour this morning talking about damages, and yet they still say Augustin Ballinas isn't entitled to any?

I'm going to start with Ruth Deborah Nass: "He'll live to be fifty or fifty-five. That's my testimony." I asked her, "You're a pediatric neurologist, Dr. Nass. You care for damaged children. Have you ever had one single, solitary patient who was fifty-five years old in your whole career?" Of course not. Now, experience is a great teacher. But if you don't have experience, then you've got to go to more traditional modes of learning, such as the literature. She didn't have a clue.

The article by Herbert Grossman in the *New England Journal of Medicine* ("The Life Expectancy of Profoundly Handicapped People with Mental Retardation") was particularly revealing. First off, she didn't even know he was at the University of Michigan Medical School. She probably only heard about the article the day before, when she read Dr. Martin Kremenitzer's testimony. Since he recognized it as authoritative, Nass must have figured, "Moore will probably use it on me." Ladies and gentlemen, you've got to be familiar with the medical literature. She totally and utterly misread the article. I read to you the conclusion of that article. The only conclusion in that article based on life expectancy of disabled people was, if they are severely retarded, tube-fed, and immobile, then they have an extremely short-ened life expectancy.

I went further, and I got the article three years later, by the same experts, writing in a different journal but on the same topic and with the same conclusion—severe mental retardation, immobility, and tube feeding. And, after reading those conclusions, I said to her, "Doctor, how about the article in the *Lancet*, the English coun-terpart for the *New England Journal of Medicine*? Would you find that authoritative?" "Oh, no, no, no. Sorry, Moore. Can't read from that one. That's not authoritative."

We had the same stonewalling as we had with Howard. How can they cross-examine Dr. Kremenitzer with an article, after he says it was authoritative, and have Nass come in and say, "Oh, no, it's not authoritative"? You saw what was really taking place, despite the effort at obfuscation. Dr. Kremenitzer knew the literature but had the experience that Dr. Nass does not have. He does devote about 20 percent of his time to adult neurology. He has dedicated himself to the case of the most infirm and the most disabled at his clinic, where some patients last into their eighties and nineties on feeding tubes. It just shows you that the level of care is so para-mount in terms of survivability, even in the most deprived.

Then, according to Dr. Nass, "Oh, he only needs a general prac-titioner for the rest of his life. But he's going to die at fifty-five." What is going on? You can't have it both ways. Or maybe you can have both lies coming together in a great big lie—namely, if he gets the kind of care she's advocating, maybe he will die at fifty-five.

Ladies and gentlemen, nobody told you other than what you heard right at the beginning of this trial, that this child, as strange as it sounds, is a very healthy little boy. He had one episode of pneumonia in his whole life. He was hospitalized just once after spending the first month of his life at Lincoln Hospital. Could even go in for his eye surgery on an outpatient basis.

No one knows but God when Auggie Ballinas will draw his last breath. But to reduce his life expectancy by one day based on the testi-mony you have heard in this courtroom would be a travesty. But, remember, if his life expectancy is reduced by one day or more, it is a day or days that were taken from him because of their abject negligence.

Give them a discount for their own wrongdoing! That's what they are saying. They went on and on, nitpicking, penny-pinching with this devastated child, cutting here, cutting there. I called Professor Les Seplaki, the chairman of economics at Rutgers University, to the stand to testify as an expert economist. He explained why the health-care costs provided by Nurse Sandra Gonchar grew so high over the long term. These are the costs that would be incurred with the growth rates only over the lifetime of this child. If the appropriate future, undiscounted sums are not awarded, then the adjustment required by the court cannot possibly lead to a fair and just verdict on the economic damages for Auggie Ballinas. And, I should mention, every penny of any award in this case is solely for this child and will be subject to be overseen by a court of law for the rest of his life. Every penny. Not a cent will go to his parents, his sister, or his two brothers.

I don't want to even comment about the testimony from the defense regarding therapies. They even fight that, if funds were available, Auggie should receive therapies at home so that, with his potential, the hours spent in school would be spent learning. If he's a victim of medical negligence, he needs these therapies. They tried to tell you, "Oh, he only needs two occupational therapies a week rather than three." Ladies and gentlemen, I tell you he cannot have enough. "But don't give them to him at home. Give them to him in the school. Take him out of his school time." Take this athetoid cerebral palsy child, with his potential so much greater than they are able to plumb so far. Deprive him of that, because if he receives this therapy in school, the Board of Education will pay for it. It's another discount for the Health and Hospitals Corporation.

They would urge on you that custodial care up to age twenty-one is also unnecessary. This child needs help for every single thing that he does relative to daily-living care. These parents have been incredible in their dedication to this child. But if he's entitled to care, are they supposed to be in servitude for the rest of their lives? And, what's even more telling and more important to Augustin, how about his sense of self? His sense of independence? Not wanting to be a burden on his family or on anybody else? Surely if he's a victim, he's entitled to say, figuratively, what he'll be able to think easily: "Let me be my own person. Let me pay my own way, and let me not be a burden." That's what they'd like to take away from him.

All the costs that Nurse Gonchar gave were based on her experience. You see, if you have experience, that is the great teacher. This is daily fare for her. She didn't have to make special calls on this case. She's doing it every day. I thought we were going to hear somebody other than the lawyer for the defense say that this child can get appropriate level of care that he needs for $65,000. Nurse Gonchar never said that an appropriate place for this child could be gotten for $65,000 a year. She said there are some group homes in the Bronx that charge $65,000, but the level of care that this child needs, on the average, costs $80,000. Nobody with expertise contradicted that. And then it's argued that these therapies are double-dipping, that the medical and the equipment and the supplies are included in the $80,000. Nurse Gonchar testified clearly and unequivocally that they are not included, that this is the basic cost, and all of these things are extra. With this child's warmth and love and personality and drive, he could have been anything.

They fought the neonatologist, Dr. Hermansen; the pediatric neurologist, Dr. Kremenitzer; and they fought the obstetrician, Dr. Nathanson, by bringing in experts. But when they fought Professor Seplaki [the plaintiff's expert in economic analysis] they did so through a lawyer. If they wanted to show that Professor Seplaki's methodology is wrong and not consistent with good economics, where was the expert to say it? Are they shy? Why didn't they bring in an economist, too? That nitpicking that you saw this morning is not in evidence because there is no expert testimony to support it.

But now let me get to the unkindest cut of all. Ruth Deborah Nass, M.D., of New York University Hospital and New York Hospital testified in this court of law that an IQ test called the Bailey Developmental Scale, given to Augustin in 1994, indicated an IQ of around fifty. This means that this wonderful, fantastic kid will never be able to reason and understand and see the world except as a five-year-old. That was the biggest lie told in this courtroom, and there were a lot.

Of course, I pointed out to Dr. Nass, "You're saying that a test done when Auggie was four years old dictates his IQ? Do you know the Bailey is a very poor indicator when it comes to motor-impaired children?" She admitted that. There are tests that are much better, and he's never had the benefit of them. He's never had a formal IQ test since he was four, and she nonetheless makes these predictions. And I said to her, "Are you saying if you had a private patient, treating him like Auggie Ballinas, that you would make predictions when he's ten based on a Bailey done when he was four"? And do you remember what she said? She said yes. That was Ruth Nass.

This is just one page of Auggie's rehabilitation record. He is now familiar with Reading Blaster Junior, in which he is touching the pictured object, which begins with the sound spoken and shown him by a friendly creature in the "game." He is touching the computer screen with his athetoid fingers. The report continues, "The touch window made by Edmark Corporation, which was initially installed on our classroom computer by Auggie's occupational therapist, has enabled him to reveal his learning in- and output on an independent level. Auggie has much learning inside him."

On his word board that he can point to—but not easily because, don't forget, he has athetoid cerebral palsy—he indicated, "I want the computer." He is trapped within his body. Locked in, as Dr. Kremenitzer says. Ruth Nass didn't even know that he could use a computer. And that is not hidden away on one page. That is on many pages.

They are not doing well by Auggie in the Board of Education. It is not a question of negligence. They are just not plumbing him. They are not getting what they should be, and they are not allowing him to grow.

When he was seven years old, September 23, 1997, Auggie took the Brigance Inventory of Basic Skills, a test that measures fundamental skills and lasts for several days. The defense would have you believe that this child, at ten years of age, has the intellectual ability of a five-year-old and will never be higher than a five-year-old. Look at this: "Color recognition: Kindergarten [level]." He was only seven years old at the time. "Identification of body parts: Kindergarten. Directional/positional skill: First grade. Matches uppercase letters: First grade. Matches numerals: Kindergarten." Figure it out.

This child trapped within that body was, at most, a year behind on the Brigance Inventory of Basic Skills. I knew it, and you knew it— to see that face light up in recognition, the way he reaches out, the way he relates. He's an intelligent child, and he'll be an intelligent adult if he gets intensive involvement.

I'm going to talk about the general damages we just alluded to. The economic damages pale by comparison to the enormity of the loss which must be given to this child if his condition is related to medical negligence. Bedlam, the Bastille, Alcatraz—you name some of the worst prisons ever known in the history of humankind. To be imprisoned in your own body—none of them could compare to that.

What amount do you award for pain and suffering and loss of enjoyment of life to the present? What sum of money would fairly compensate this child for the loss of a childhood?

"Pain and suffering" is the rubric the law uses to talk about the human loss. Enjoyment of life is everything that has been taken from him so that he's not what he would have been, could have been, and should have been.

Ladies and gentlemen, he strives, and he succeeds, and he fails. And he will succeed more and fail less, but they'll never, ever be close to a balance. I speak for this child who cannot speak for himself, and I am honored in that oration. But, ladies and gentlemen, your role is different. My obligation is to suggest; your role is to determine. I suggest, as the advocate for this child, $6 million, real, honest, present-day dollars, as just compensation, as a substitute in money, which is the only way the law has ever devised to compensate for the enormity of the loss to this point in his life. Is that fair? Is it too much? Is it too little? You, and only you, have the obligation and the authority to say.

What sum of money will compensate for future pain, suffering, permanence, and loss of enjoyment of life? Those are exactly the words taken from His Honor's question. Now we are talking again of the future, of sixty-four years. What will be just and fair in that time?

Can I suggest that before you decide on what this award should be, that you say to yourself, as follows: "We are going to finish this case Monday, and then we are going to go from this place and renew our lives. Everybody will be happy to have us back, and we'll be glad to be back." But you will never forget your experience here, as His Honor has promised you would not.

There will be a lot of other things going on in our lives. Let's say, a year from now, Augustin Ballinas will come into your mind and the days in Supreme Bronx as a juror. Think to yourselves, if and when we think of him in approximately a year, will we think that what we awarded him in May of 2001 was fair and just? Maybe, if it helps, think ten years from now. Augustin Ballinas and your days on this case may come to mind more fleetingly than a year from now. Nonetheless, in a quiet moment, will you think then that what you awarded in May of 2001 to this child was fair and just?

I'll go one more step—fifty years from now. Undoubtedly some of us, I'm speaking for myself, hopefully, will be in a better place. But will you think then of the strides that he hopefully will have made? Of the money that he has used to learn and grow over the course of a lifetime? Will you think of a man, loving though he is, never becoming a lover in a romantic way? Warm, though he is, and wanting to be held, not able to hold? Outgoing, as he is, and wanting to belong, yet many times not accepted? Will you think then that what you awarded in May of 2001, to that devastated human being, was fair and just?

Again, now, over the course of sixty-four years. I suggest and you will decide. [At this point Mr. Moore writes the figure $65 million on the oaktag.]

Ladies and gentlemen of the jury, *ne cede malis*. The Bronx is proud to say it, borrowing it from the Roman poet Virgil in his Aeneid. Virgil added, *Ne cede malis, sed contra audientior ito*. "Do not yield to evil, but fight daringly against it." Dare, dare to raise him up. Dare to point the way. Dare to smooth his path. And if you do, ladies and gentlemen, you will make this hallowed house, this sanctuary of justice, a more sacred place by your verdict.

POSTSCRIPT

Augustin Ballinas won a verdict of $107 million, the second-highest in the history of New York State. The amount of damages awarded in this personal-injury case tells us a great deal about the quality of advocacy that made it happen.

Presumable, any jury in the United States would be sympathetic to a child who suffered debilitating brain damage. However, the massive amount of this verdict could only be obtained in a highly sympathetic jurisdiction. For plaintiffs in New York City, the Bronx is considered a very friendly jurisdiction. Of course, on some level, if justice is truly blind, the verdict should not depend on the locale of the trial.

Considered "top-shelf" among his colleagues, Thomas Moore is unfortunately not a household name among non-lawyers. This is a fine illustration of his skills. Thomas Moore's double-barreled attack consisted of putting a good face on his case through his emphasis on the blameless victims—Auggie and his mother, Carmen—while putting a poor face on the hospital's case by hammering away at the various acts of ineptitude resulting in Augustin's contracting meningitis.

Lawyers tend to use the same type of argument repeatedly in different trials. It saves them time and the bother of being creative on every single case. Thomas Moore, however, came up with the phrase *ne cede malis*, "do not yield to evil," from a recent banner announcing Bronx Week. That theme in Mr. Moore's speech shows extraordinary creativity. Obviously, he cannot use this speech outside New York City or even outside the Bronx.

All terrific lawyers know how to turn a phrase. Mr. Moore is no exception. His ability to use the language ("a ripple of credibility in an ocean full of lies"), and his urging the jury to "make this hallowed house, this sanctuary of justice, a more sacred place by your verdict" maximized his other courtroom strategies.

Mr. Moore let the jury know in the most accessible way how Auggie Ballinas now lived as a result of this meningitis—beyond the mere numbers of life expectancy and cost of therapy: "Will you think of a man [Auggie Ballinas], loving though he is, never becoming a lover in a romantic way? Warm though he is, and wanting to be held, not able to hold? Outgoing as he is and wanting to belong, yet many times not accepted?"

Thomas Moore succeeded in putting it all together. This was more than an eloquent speech: Moore had the facts to convince the jury. Sometimes excellent lawyers can give good speeches, but their speeches, lack the facts that are necessary to carry the day. Moore did it all: He elicited the facts during trial, he drove them home during summation, He put a good face on his case through his poignant description of Carmen and Auggie Ballinas, and he attacked the hospital for its numerous misdeeds.

If Thomas Moore was right in claiming that the issue of negligence was clear-cut, then why include his speech in this book? Was his victory attainable by any average negligence lawyer? Perhaps. But an outstanding lawyer like Thomas Moore consistently wins cases that he should win, such as this one. And, no doubt, his brilliance contributed to the amount of the award.

15

HIGH TIMES AND NEPOTISM AT THE KOCH COURT

THE UNITED STATES OF AMERICA v. BESS MYERSON, ANDY CAPASSO AND HORTENSE GABEL

IF SOAP OPERA–STYLE drama is what you are after, you would be hard-pressed to find a trial more salacious than the Bess Myerson case. Dubbed the "Bess Mess," the case sent the media into a month-long frenzy, and for good reason; only a crazed circuit-board designer could make up the incestuous interconnections between all the players. Offering the public front-row seats for a Manhattan-style upper-crust free-for-all, the Bess Mess had a little bit of everything: sex (of the adulterous kind), fame (Myerson was Miss America 1945), family conflict (a mentally unstable daughter testified against her mother, who happened to be a judge) and politics (Rudy Giuliani, the prosecutor, was going after Bess Myerson, the Commissioner of the Department of Cultural Affairs under the Koch administration).

One afternoon as Nancy Herbert gazes out of her window, she spots a handsome younger man, Andy Capasso, working on the sewers. She invites him in for coffee, and shortly thereafter the two begin a torrid affair that resulted in her divorcing her husband and becoming Mrs. Capasso. But this marriage did not last. Eventually,

Bess Myerson, having traded her Miss America tiara for a highly visible position in the Koch administration, met Andy Capasso at a political fund-raiser. She, too, fell for the handsome younger man, and now these two began having an affair. When Mr. Capasso announced his plans to divorce his wife, Nancy, Myerson offered to help him win the suit.

The theory of the prosecution was really quite simple. They accused Bess Myerson of hiring Sukhreet Gabel, thirty-four years old, as a way of bribing her mother (already an acquaintance of Myerson's), Judge Hortense Gabel—who happened to be the judge ruling on Andy and Nancy Capasso's pretrial motions. (It so happened that Judge Gabel also secured Sukhreet an apartment through Nancy's divorce lawyer, Raoul Felder, that June.)[1] Judge Gabel's first key decision in the Capasso divorce proceedings awarded Nancy Capasso $1,500 per week temporary maintenance. That decision was made on June 23, 1983. In September 1983—one month after Sukhreet started her new job—Andy Capasso's lawyer, Samuel Fredman, requested that she revise her decision. Judge Gabel lowered the temporary maintenance that Andy had to pay Nancy from $1,500 to $500 per week. This $1,000 deduction would be heavily cited by the prosecution in their claim that Bess Myerson and Andy Capasso, acting together, bribed Judge Gabel by hiring her daughter, Sukhreet.

Nancy Capasso felt that of the seventeen pretrial rulings made by Judge Gabel, all except the first ruling granting her $1,500 per week temporary maintenance favored her husband. Some of these rulings were subsequently reversed on appeal by the appellate division.

The defense, led by Jay Goldberg, had material aplenty to refute the prosecution's allegations. For starters, though Judge Gabel decreased Nancy's monthly disbursement—which was taxable—she increased Andy's tax-free child-support payments. The difference in benefit to the family as a whole was $500 per year,

---

[1] According to Shana Alexander in *When She Was Bad*, Judge Gabel reached out to a judge, who reached out to Felder. Id. At 257.

so said the defense, which was hardly a significant enough sum to be the basis of a court case. In addition, Judge Gabel had ultimately ordered Andy to pay Nancy $358,000 in alimony and child support—$26,000 a year more than he had. Goldberg argued that this was hardly a decision evidencing a bribe.

The prosecution featured a number of witnesses, the star being Sukhreet Gabel, who had received fifteen electroshock treatments in 1985 and had a love-hate relationship with her parents. At the request of the prosecution, Sukhreet had taped conversations with her parents and provided the prosecution with some of her mother's files. There was also Shirley Harrod, a housekeeper at the Capassos' $1.9 million Westhampton beach home, who claimed that Andy said to Bess regarding his divorce litigation, "Bess, can't you do something about this?" (It seemed that she had also photographed one of Andy's two Mercedeses, though she vehemently denied doing so, at Nancy's request.)

Herbert Rickman, Mayor Koch's special assistant, also testified for the prosecution, denying the defense's claims that he had asked Bess Myerson to hire Sukhreet Gabel. He claimed to the FBI that he was in the beginning stages of Alzheimer's disease. Rickman also had stomach problems. It appeared at the trial that each time Bess Myerson's lawyer, Fred Hafetz, got up to cross-examine Rickman, he asked to be excused to go to the bathroom. Rickman claimed to have been with Judge Hortense Gabel at a reception in honor of Bess Myerson when Gabel said to him, "Is Whatshisname here?" The prosecution claimed that Andy Capasso was "Whatshisname." This reception took place prior to Judge Gabel's revised court decision in favor of Andy Capasso. This seemingly meaningless phrase became hotly contested as the prosecution and defense sparred endlessly over whether Hortense Gabel even knew that Andy Capasso was having an affair with Bess Myerson at the time she revised her ruling in favor of Andy Capasso. And, of course, Howard Leventhal, Judge Gabel's law clerk, along with other character witnesses, testified that the judge was very honest.

Nancy Capasso never testified at this trial.

Excerpts from the Summation of Defense Attorney Jay Goldberg

This is the only time that the law provides me an opportunity to share with you and reason together with you in the course of our analysis of the case. The law, in its wisdom, provides government counsel with an opportunity to speak with you two times.

If you search the record in this case, you will conclude that, despite the presence of a staff of three prosecutors and an investigation that commenced two and a half years ago, the prosecutors have failed in their obligation to present solid proof to a point beyond a reasonable doubt, and it matters then to me not one whit that they have two chances to speak to you, because two times zero will still turn out to be zero.

It has been said by a legal scholar that the most effective tool in the search for truth is cross-examination. It is so easy to prepare a witness for some forty-four working rehearsal sessions, another witness eighteen to twenty times, and then put them on as windup toys, asking them questions that have been rehearsed, but it's the art of cross-examination that's designed to search out the truth.

I stand here on behalf of one person, Andy Capasso. Stripped to its essentials, the charge in this case is that a scheme supposedly existed to victimize the City of New York of moneys that were paid to Sukhreet Gabel for her employment at the Department of Cultural Affairs [from] the period of August '83 to June of '84, and the second victim is claimed to be Nancy Capasso, who the proof will show, through the restructured order of Justice Gabel, lost $575 a year prior to city and state taxes.

I haven't picked this number out of the air. You will see that this million-dollar federal case involves a claim when reduced to its essentials that, through the restructured order of Justice Gabel in September of 1983, this supposed victim, Nancy Capasso, lost—and properly so, you will conclude—the grand sum, considering city, state, and federal taxes, of less than $500 a year.

The claim is that the city was victimized and Nancy Capasso was victimized because Justice Gabel, in rendering her decision of September 13, 1983, was corrupted because a job had been given to her daughter.

In our system we have two sets of judges. Judge John Keenan is supreme on the law. No one here may question it. When he rules, that is the law of this case. But just as he is supreme, so you as the jury are supreme within your sphere. You are what we call the "supreme judges of the facts."

When you think that you as a group exercise the power to decide the fate, the future of three people, that you hold that enormous power in your hands, you understand that it is no overstatement to say that for you this is an extraordinary occasion.

A doctor may operate on a patient. When you deliberate, you will be operating on the lives and future and fate of three people. That's the heavy responsibility that you have as the supreme judges of the facts.

When you analyze the thirty-four witnesses in this case, and the thirty-five trial days, you will be convinced that the government sought to divert your attention from their lack of proof. They gave you so much smoke and dust that you have to ask yourself, Why was it necessary that we hear this proof? What desperation was there on the part of these adversaries that caused them to present this kind of material to us that has no real bearing on the issues in this case?

Was it important, for example, for you to know through the testimony of Sukhreet Gabel that Bess Myerson tried on Nancy Capasso's bathing suits? Or that Bess Myerson threw out Nancy Capasso's potted plants? That was some part of the proof in this case.

How important was it that you learned that for a time Bess Myerson didn't want people to know that she was sleeping—this is the eighties, now—she was sleeping with Andy Capasso, that she used to make it appear that she slept in Herbie's room [Herbert Rickman, a frequent visitor to Capasso's home], she ruffled his bed, and when guests came—remember that—she ran out the back door, and then came in the front door? What was the purpose that the government chose to bring it out?

Or that, over a lifetime of sixty-four years, she had accumulated enough jewelry to fill a box?

Well, aside from the proof being that she was a millionairess herself, that was the burden she carried from being selected Miss America forty years ago. The government felt that it might prejudice you, that it might divert your attention, and so they developed it for you.

Or that, through Sukhreet Gabel, Bess Myerson fell on a tennis court? He [the prosecutor] even has it on his chart: "Bess Myerson fell on the tennis court." Sukhreet Gabel says she witnessed it; she bruised her knee and she bruised her face. And he went to the trouble of making an entry to that effect on his chart, so important is it to the case.

Or that Andy Capasso gave gifts to Bess Myerson as he courted her. I would suspect, there being proof in this case that he is a terrific human being—a breath of fresh air, a witness said—that he gave the same gifts to Nancy Reese Herbert [Nancy Capasso was married to Mr. Howard Herbert before marrying Andy Capasso] after she spotted him the first time in the trench outside her house digging a sewer as she sipped her coffee after the children had gone off to school. Of what relevance was that?

Or was it really important to Mr. David Lawrence, [the prosecutor] that Ed Koch thought that Mr. Capasso's home was an estate? Do you remember that? He put the question to the honorable mayor: "Now, at the estate of Mr.—" That was the question, when the mayor interrupted him and said, "No, hold it." You see, the fatal flaw committed by Mr. Lawrence, if I may be so bold as to correct him on trial strategy, is that one question earlier he had said to the mayor, "Did you know the housekeepers?"—obviously the Harrods —and the mayor, obviously—I know his head—the mayor, obviously thinking back on the steady diet of hamburgers, remember, hot dogs, macaroni salad, that he had gotten at the hands of the Harrods, said to himself, "Listen, this was no estate. This was a home. I've gotten better meals at Popeye's, Forty-fourth Street and Eighth Avenue."

Throughout, there was a steady effort to divert you. We were locked in a pursuit of trivial matters in this federal court.

Why was it necessary? Because when you don't have proof of the charges, you have to rely on this smoke and dust, these diversionary issues. But you have to spot what the government is doing and realize the purpose.

You know, ladies and gentlemen, at least in Brooklyn, where I grew up, there was an expression: "Don't make a federal case out of it." It was meant to suggest, don't take something and turn it into some big deal, a federal case.

Nancy Capasso, through the structured order [Judge Gabel's revised order]—pity poor Nancy, having lived in a state of royalty, by her own declaration, she has suffered, for a justifiable reason, to the extent, after federal taxes, of reduction of $578 [per year], and we are here.

[The prosecutor asked] Mayor Koch, "Did Bess Myerson tell you that she was going to hire Sukhreet Gabel?" Was there any showing that any commissioner ever has to clear with Edward I. Koch before they hire some assistant? All this was asked, I suggest, in bad faith.

Aside from my observation that there is this smoke-and-dust diversionary material thrust at you, I make also the observation that this case had an inordinate amount of biased, disgruntled, disturbed people, who the government used to try to make up for its lack of proof, witnesses who—well, in the old vaudeville days when a person performed very badly from the side of the stage, there would be a hook, and the person would be whisked right off the stage.

I don't know if you people are this old, but there was *Amateur Hour* with Major Bowes, when a person would perform, and if the performance was utterly terrible, he would ring a bell, and off the person would go.

Then, in the seventies, you remember we had *The Gong Show*. When a person was on center stage and was really bad, Chuck Barris—remember?—gong, and that was the end of the performance.

This is the only new addition I can make to the court structure, that jurors should have at their chair a button that could sound the gong. I'm going to give you a few as we go along. You see if I overstate it.

You see, so much of this case, I told you thirty-four witnesses, had so little to do with Andy Capasso, I examined by my own count about five or six out of the thirty-four, and, quite frankly, I don't know whether I examined those witnesses because they were really relevant to Andy Capasso or [because] I wanted my picture drawn by the artists [i.e., courtroom sketch artists].

How and why were we here, and what were we doing? What TV or daytime serial could I put this case into?

The first one that came to my mind early in the trial was the dispute [concerning] Nancy's claim that her potted plants had been wrongly discarded and her bathing suit had been used. That was a perfect case for Judge Wapner. Any question about that? That was a *People's Court* case, clearly.

But with Shirley Harrod you had the PBS program, right? *Upstairs, Downstairs*. Look what Shirley Harrod told you. She was the first one for which the gong would be in order.

She would have you believe the following. She would have you believe that her husband, Ray Harrod, was fired because Barra Reilly, that's Bess Myerson's daughter, and Bess Myerson's son-in-law traveled six thousand miles—three thousand from California to Westhampton, three thousand back, six thousand miles—and rather than enjoy the sand and the surf at Mr. Capasso's home, rather than play tennis and enjoy the pool, the one pleasure that Barra Reilly had in life was that when Ray Harrod went into the kitchen to prepare his meal, the Reillys would come into the kitchen and stand there—this was their thrill—just to watch him masticate. Wait a minute. That's chew. That's chew.

That was the only reason, she says, that there was a dispute. After all, she says, "We are fascinating people."

Now, look, ladies and gentlemen, a little more on Shirley Harrod, a critical witness, appears on the chart [prepared by the prosecution], a number of entries. Exhibit 535 was [a photograph of] the rear end of a Mercedes automobile Shirley Harrod took. Do you remember that? She took a picture of the rear end of a Mercedes automobile.

Was that Mercedes automobile in some way helpful to Nancy Capasso?

She took this picture one month after she meets Nancy Capasso. Was that Mercedes important to Nancy Capasso? Let me read you what Mr. Leventhal, the judge's law clerk [Judge Gabel] says:

Q: By the way, did you ever make a statement that you believed that Nancy Capasso from the [court] papers that you read was more interested in getting a Mercedes for herself than support for the children? Did you ever say that?

A: Yes, sir.

Q: What did you mean by that?

This is what the law clerk says about this Mercedes that Shirley Harrod would have you believe she just took.

A: From the papers before me, I could think of at least three separate motions where she asks the court for exclusive use of a Mercedes vehicle which seemed to be a fixation with her.

Q: Fixation?

A: Yes, sir.

Shirley Harrod would have you believe that she took a picture of the rear end of a Mercedes, not at the urging of Nancy Capasso, who she secretly met a month before, and she kept this rear-end picture of a Mercedes for five years, and then turned it over to the government, because in her own words she is fascinated with tailpipes.

Now, tell me, you couldn't see a hook come right out, whisking her, poof, right off? She is hooked on tailpipes.

But then there was more. You heard about Sukhreet Gabel's hospitalization and her fifteen shock treatments and her care by a psychopharmacologist. And then you had that sterling special assistant Herbert Rickman's hypochondriasis, right? His fear, according to [FBI] Agent St. Germain, that he is in the beginning stages of Alzheimer's disease. And his obvious stomach cramps and frequent trips to the bathroom at the mere sight of Fred Hafetz [Bess Myerson's attorney]. I don't know if you remember that. As soon as he got up to cross-examine, he [Rickman] had to run to the toilet up and back.

That was only because Mr. Hafetz was trying to get the truth, but you remember what happened.

I said to myself that this took on shades of *General Hospital*, and the government didn't need a paralegal like Joan Alexander; it could have used a paramedic.

And even the defense was a part of it, too. Justice Gabel, unfortunately, there was proof had suffered a heart attack; she had been hospitalized for a stroke. Bess Myerson had endured ovarian cancer, chemotherapy, and a stroke herself.

What a tragedy that we are here because Nancy Capasso has sold the government on a bill of goods that just won't hold up once I analyze the nuts and bolts of the case.

And, finally, David Lawrence stood up here, my learned and esteemed adversary, and he had the mayor on the witness stand, and there had to be the consideration given by the government to the mayor for having made the walk over from City Hall [City Hall is a few blocks from the Foley Square courthouse], the mayor's political future hanging in the balance, the matter of his health somewhere looming largely. Do you remember David Lawrence standing here and saying, "Mayor, how is your health? And state to us, how you are feeling?"

That had to be the mayor's consideration for having walked over. I of course objected, concerned as I was that, desperate as the government is to bring Andy Capasso into this case, who the heck knew whether his elevated cholesterol and his stroke might somehow be related to the hamburgers, hot dogs, and macaroni salad. [Mayor Koch had had hamburgers, hot dogs and macaroni salad at Andy Capasso's Westhampton home].

Luckily for me, the judge sustained my objection.

That's where we were in this case. So before I get to the nuts and bolts, I make the following observation to you. Never has so much time—thirty-four days, thirty-five, thirty-six days—so much energy, and taxpayers' money, charts, agents, and the like been spent on such trivial pursuits, such diversionary issues, while bringing to you such little proof to support the government's case.

What I want to do with you now is get into the decision of Justice Gabel. I am not up here to give smoke and dust. I'm going to put this case on track. I'm going to discuss with you the critical issues in this case.

The backdrop of this case is the divorce between Nancy and Andy Capasso. Some jurors indicated they have been parties to a divorce. Not all divorces, obviously, are amicable. Some are bitterly contested. It is fair to assume that a bitter divorce affects family, husband, and wife. You don't have to be a great philosopher to know how easy love can turn to hate and how easy it is for some bitter, disgruntled spouse to make false charges against the other. That's life's experience.

But what is wrong about all of this is for the government of the United States of America not to recognize that fact of life, and so wrong was it to allow the bitter, disgruntled spouse to orchestrate witnesses who the government feels are key to this case.

During the examination of Sukhreet Gabel, Judge Keenan [the trial judge] instructed you that the government has two offices, one at 1 St. Andrew's Plaza and another at 26 Federal Plaza. No one ever mentioned that the government also had an annex in the living room of Nancy Capasso at 990 Fifth Avenue.

In 1986, Ray Harrod and Shirley Harrod were asked to come at night from Connecticut, bring documents, and come to the home of Nancy Capasso, where, in those evening hours, sitting in the living room —I think he just left—was Tony Lombardi, the government's investigator. And he took documents from the Harrods, documents which the Harrods said they viewed normally as confidential, without even a subpoena. And this occurred in Nancy's living room in the early stages of this investigation.

I said to you the government's case, which I likened to a ship, the government's ship was launched by Nancy Capasso. That's wrong. You will conclude from the things I say that the government's case, the government's ship, was built by Nancy Capasso. The government mistakenly bought that ship without inspecting it, without realizing that it had such gaping holes, such lack of evidence, such defects, that it failed to have solid underpinnings, that the government's case, its ship, not only was unseaworthy but it can't sail to a point beyond a reasonable doubt. It just can't.

The government took that complaint, launched or built by Nancy Capasso, and they mistakenly ran with the ball. The biased and bitter hand of this unseen, unconfronted manipulator runs throughout this entire case. [Mr. Goldberg is referring to the fact that Nancy Capassso did not testify at the trial.]

While Shirley Harrod worked for [Andy Capasso], Nancy Capasso arranged to secretly meet Shirley Harrod at the home of the Ponterellis. Shirley Harrod said it wasn't a prearrangement; she came to the Ponterellis, Nancy was there, and Nancy knew she worked for Mr. Capasso because her name was Shirley. Do you remember that?

And I said to her, "You mean the mere mention of your first name, there was something so distinctive about the name 'Shirley' that once Mrs. Capasso heard that you had the first name of Shirley, she knew that you were Andy's housekeeper?" And of course this woman said, "Yes."

That's baloney. That was a meeting arranged by Nancy Capasso while Shirley Harrod was working for Mr. Capasso. Mrs. Capasso called Shirley Harrod six times long-distance in Maryland, called her in Armonk, and Shirley Harrod says all they talked about was social things. Do you believe that?

We know of at least one meeting in the living room between the government investigator and Nancy Capasso at the beginning of this investigation. The claim that Shirley Harrod supposedly saw Mr. Capasso throw papers down and say, "Can't you do something about this, Bess?" is something that occurred only after Shirley Harrod had met numerous times, spoken numerous times, with Nancy Capasso.

You may conclude that since Shirley Harrod had been grilled intensively for two days by the Tyler Commission [Judge Harold "Ace" Tyler had been asked by Mayor Koch to prepare a confidential report regarding the incident. He did and concluded that Bess Myerson tried to bribe Judge Gabel] and never, ever said, in over twelve hours of interviews, that she ever saw Mr. Capasso throw down papers and say to Bess Myerson, "Can't you do something about this?"—you may conclude that that in-court testimony of Shirley Harrod was not based on what she saw or heard at the Capasso residence, because she never told that to the Tyler Commission, never told that to Tony Lombardi before she went to the Tyler Commission, never told that to the United States Attorney before she went to the Tyler Commission, but did say it only after she and Nancy had conferred over a half a dozen times.

I told you in my opening something which bears repeating. I

said there was no fury as intense and mean-spirited as [that of] Nancy Capasso. No rage as venomous as that of Nancy Capasso once her love for Andy Capasso turned to hate. Even at the expense of the two small children. Even if it meant destroying her husband, the father of her two children and the person who by all accounts was a wonderful father to the three stepchildren.

Why was it that there was such rage? It couldn't be because there was a $500 difference to her in the two orders out of which this whole case is fabricated and concocted. Well, Andy left her for an older woman. Nancy was rejected by her husband for an older woman. Andy and Bess did to Nancy what Nancy really did to Mr. Herbert when she left him [and] three children and ran off with Andy.

This is by no way justifying extramarital affairs, but please don't mistake Nancy Capasso for some virginal victim.

Secondly, remember that it wasn't Nancy who started the divorce action. Andy went to court on December 20, 1982, and he swore in a set of papers that she was guilty of such callous neglect of the children that he wanted a divorce. That had an effect on this unseen, unconfronted witness.

Then we learned Nancy was terribly angered because some court, not Justice Gabel, mind you, some court had only awarded her $2 million. Pity poor Nancy. She couldn't make ends meet with a piddling $2 million. She was angered.

The government claims she is the victim, having through the restructured order lost less than $500 or about $500 with city, state, and federal taxes because she only got $2 million. Pity poor Nancy.

No, ladies and gentlemen, properly analyzed, Nancy Capasso is not the victim. They, the three of them, they [the defendants] are the victims of the rage. They are the victims of the venom and the bitterness, and the government wrongly fails to recognize a simple fact of life: that a rejected and bitter spouse can carry a false tale.

As we go through Justice Gabel's decision making, after a lifetime of service, with a record that gives you, really, goose bumps, when you hear people testify with respect to her reputation, you may conclude that a person can reach such a point of reverence, such a point of esteem that even if she asked you for a favor, you wouldn't have the audacity to suggest to her or intimate to her that she change or modify her decision making.

No more did Raoul Felder's having secured an apartment for Sukhreet Gabel, on June 1, 1983—that was Nancy's lawyer—influence Justice Gabel's award on June 23, 1983, than did Bess Myerson having secured a job at the urging of Herbert Rickman for Justice Gabel affect her consideration of the motion that she decided on September 23, 1983.

There are people in our society who have the esteem and standing that they can reach out, but you wouldn't have the guts, the audacity, the gall, the chutzpah to say to the judge, "I got an apartment for your daughter. I'm Raoul Felder. Now, do something for Nancy." Or "I got a job for your daughter. Now do something for Andy."

In life there are judges and judges, but they are human beings, but this particular justice of the Supreme Court stood tall and taller, perhaps, among her equals on the bench. She was a heroine.

If this were a judge that was corrupted or bribed, it would be improper to require Mr. Capasso to pay a sum of money greater than the net amount of income that he had available to him, and, giving credit to the expenses that Mr. Capasso had to pay—his interest payments, the lawyer—Mr. Capasso swore under oath that all he had was $332,000 available to support his wife and children.

In the September papers, if bribery was afoot, ladies and gentlemen, wouldn't it be contrary to the notion that there was bribery if you learned that this justice of the Supreme Court on September 14, 1983, in her decision rejected Mr. Capasso's plea and required him to pay—see that $332,000?—she required him to pay $358,000 in payments—isn't that wholly contrary to the notion of what we call in the law a quid pro quo? That he got something from Justice Gabel? He got a free ride from Justice Gabel. He went before Justice Gabel and said, "I only have $332,000 to pay. That's my plea to you, Judge." And if this judge were fixed—that's the street word— wouldn't she take that into account and justify some massive reduction, pointing to the fact that he only had $332,000, and say, "He now has to pay $200,000." She rejected it in its entirety for the benefit of the children, who came first in her mind.

[Mr. Goldberg is using a pointer to point to a chart] New kind of pointer. I don't want you to think I got it from a Chevrolet. It looks like an antenna.

Why could not a judge, concerned about the welfare of the children, with a law clerk who believed that the wife was more interested in an automobile than in the welfare of the children, with papers submitted by Mr. Capasso detailing his wife's neglect of these two children, why could not a judge, concerned about infant children, restructure an award without some bitter, disgruntled spouse coming in and calling her, after forty-five years of service, a bribe taker, a graft taker, a person who was corrupted? For what? To vent her anger and spleen and subject these people to the worst tragedy that a human being can endure, to suffer a trial where your life hangs in the balance in the hands of twelve strangers?

At the same time, Nancy is so complaining about the job being offered to Sukhreet, she obviously keeps from Mr. Lombardi, who sits in her living room, the fact that Nancy's lawyer has gotten an apartment for Sukhreet.

While the government is not under an obligation to call a witness, not only don't they call Nancy Capasso to explain her actions in the case, but they don't dare call Mr. Felder to explain the efforts he made to get Justice Gabel's daughter an apartment.

The man who knew Justice Gabel best, Mr. Howard Leventhal, and Brenda Shrobe [Judge Gabel's legal secretary], tell you that it mattered not one whit whether people had been asked by her for a favor. She is a human being, but she is a professional as a justice of the Supreme Court. You take the word of the people who work with you eyeball to eyeball for six and eight years, and they told you that she had reached a level of such prominence, respect, and reverence. Brenda Shrobe said she belongs to a dying generation of people dedicated to honesty and truth. Mayor Koch told you that in words or substance. Mayor [Robert] Wagner told you that.

She had reached such a point of personal prestige that she could ask Raoul Felder to help her daughter get an apartment, but you didn't see Andy Capasso run to them and say, "Listen, lock up Felder and Nancy." Nancy, because she didn't get her Mercedes and she only got $2 million, poor Nancy, she runs to this office and never tells them the role of Raoul Felder.

The government wants you to believe that Justice Gabel knew Andy Capasso was going with Bess Myerson as early as May 1983. Well, that, ladies and gentlemen, you will conclude is just false. What does the government do? They call Herbert Rickman.

We know that he lied before you when he said that he didn't tell [FBI] Agent St. Germain that he was concerned about the fact that he was in the beginning stages of Alzheimer's disease. He falsely told you that he never raised the prospect of a job with Sukhreet Gabel in the eight weekends he spent with Bess Myerson. That's just not believable. Think about it.

Hortense Gabel meets him every six weeks, has lunch with him at the Hunan Garden, talks to him about a job for Sukhreet Gabel. Bess Myerson is now new to the administration. [Rickman] is a special assistant to the mayor and a freeloader, and he's living in "Herbie's room" [the room at Capasso's Westhampton home was nicknamed, since he was such a frequent visitor] out in the Capasso home, and he never even raised the issue of a job with Bess Myerson, because to him work at the DCA [Department of Cultural Affairs] pasting pictures of museums on a map, the DCA, was just too taxing for Sukhreet Gabel.

[Rickman] tries to make you believe that the DCA is the CIA. It is just too hard. He would never think of suggesting that she should work in this agency probably three-quarters of you jurors never even heard of, and it seems to be the most perfect spot for her, with all due respect.

He said that he was livid when he found out that Bess Myerson had hired Sukhreet Gabel, so he immediately ran in and spoke to Patrick Mulhearn [counsel to Mayor Ed Koch]. He lied.

You saw that witness, Patrick Mulhearn. Never happened. It just didn't happen. Did Herbie Rickman look like the kind of self-restrained, self-contained person who could keep a secret? Forget it. Let me tell you what he really did. We know that he was interviewed by the government. I don't know whether it was twenty-eight times, eighteen times—it was a lot of times—and never once did he ever say that more than five years ago he remembered that on May 23, 1983,

Hortense Gabel said at the Bess Myerson reception [a reception thrown by Mayor Koch at Gracie Mansion in honor of Bess Myerson's appointment as DCA Commissioner], "Is Whatshisname here?" or something like that, "Whatchamacallit," which Mr. Abrams puts on his chart as May 23.

But now, for the first time, he supposedly remembers Hortense Gabel saying to him more than five years ago, this man in the beginning stages of Alzheimer's disease, "Is Whatshisname here?"

Let me run through very quickly with you how this vision came to him. How, Herbie, did you suddenly remember more than five years ago, despite your twenty-eight other contrary statements, that Hortense Gabel ever said that to you in May? Well, he says —this is a few months ago—"I went to a reception. I sat on the bench that I sat on when I sat there with Hortense Gabel five years before, and that refreshed my recollection from sitting on the bench."

So my question to Herbie is, "I've heard of people who have had their recollection refreshed when an idea popped into their head, but I have never in my life heard of a man's recollection being refreshed through the seat of his pants."

But then there was a kicker to all of this. It was the judge who said this to him. It is like you want to know if somebody is hard of hearing, and you say, "Are you hard of hearing?" and the guy says, "What's that you said?" This is a question that was put by the learned court:

"Now, you say you remember something that occurred five and a half years ago?"

"Yes," says Herbie.

"You say this was at a recent reception that you went to just a month or two ago?"

"That's right."

"Well, if you can remember what you say happened five and a half years ago from sitting on that particular seat cushion, what reception was that that you went to just a couple of months ago?"

He said he couldn't remember.

Just think about it, ladies and gentlemen. This man occupies a position of prominence in the Koch administration. If the mayor wants to run for office again, the suggestion is that he ought to call up the talent bank; he's the one who can do better with his special assistants. Let him post a vacancy notice.

Herbie Rickman was a gofer with half a brain, someone to whom the oath meant very little. The preservation of his job—it is not civil service—was all-important, and he was intent on preserving that job. There was no proof in this case that Bess Myerson ever asked or suggested that Justice Gabel should compromise her decision, and she never did with her $358,000 award. There is no proof that prior to September 14 this justice of the Supreme Court knew of Bess Myerson's relationship with Andy Capasso.

Bess Myerson operated ethically in not mentioning that relationship to Justice Gabel. There is not one single person after two and a half years of investigation that can say that Bess Myerson ever said anything to Justice Gabel to compromise her decision making, and for sure Andy Capasso got neither a free ride or played any part in this whatsoever.

Do you know what Andy Capasso's position was as to whether Sukhreet Gabel should be hired or not? Do you know if Andy Capasso felt at the time, even assuming he knew it, that it was a decision that would not look good and should not be done? Do you know that either way?

This is the extent of the proof: zero. There is no proof in this case on how Mr. Capasso stood on the issue of whether, for appearance's sake, Bess Myerson should hire Sukhreet Gabel at all.

There was no proof that Andy Capasso, except on one occasion in his lifetime, was ever at the DCA. There is no proof that he controlled the staff of Bess Myerson any more than she picked the construction foreman on the sewers in Queens for him.

I challenge my friends [the prosecutors]. I don't want them to sit here, their pens . . . in their hands; I want them to work. Don't give me editorializing. Read one piece of testimony which you say reflects Andy Capasso's attitude one way or another, Mr. Abrams [the prosecutor]— let the chips fall where they may—one way or another on the issue of whether Bess Myerson should or should not hire Sukhreet Gabel.

We had no chance to confront Nancy Capasso. Of course, I have subpoena power; the government will come back and say I could have called her, but who wants her? Lucky Mr. Herbert. Unlucky Mr. Capasso. What could have set her off to cause her to orchestrate this case? This gives you some idea of it. Let me read you what she says:

> Over the years the children and I have had unlimited charges and credit-card privileges with American Express, two cards, Visa, Diners Club, Hertz, Avis, gasoline charges, Bergdorf Goodman, Bonwit Teller, Martha's, Henri Bendel, Bloomingdale's, Tiffany, Saks, Altman's, Paul Stuart, Balducci—food got in there—David Webb Jewelers, the Palm Restaurant. We also for the past eight years had two full-time live-in maids and part-time help once a week when we went to Westhampton or Florida. We purchased numerous works of art, just one recently at Sotheby's for $192,000. When I say that our entire family lived in a style of royalty ["This is the victim," interjects Goldberg], I am also including my three children from my prior marriage.

This is what Capasso said about himself, and [Nancy] agrees with it:

> I took over the expenses as well as the parental responsibility of raising all three of those children through their minority and acted in the capacity of their father. So far as almost every aspect of their upbringing was concerned, I fed, I clothed, housed, educated, and loved those children in every way a father could do and then some.

I remember there was testimony that he participated and learned the Jewish prayers for the bar mitzvah of Nancy and Herbert's child, the eldest boy, but he is to be destroyed on a complaint which she falsely makes. Because of $500. This princess. Denied royalty. She didn't learn the lessons that the Revolutionary War was fought for, so there would be no royalty. What arrogance.

Nancy Capasso had lived in a style of royalty. She couldn't get along on $2 million and $358,000 a year. Poor, poor Nancy. What a victim.

When the justice of the Supreme Court issued her decision on June 23, Nancy liked that one because it gave her control of the money. Remember, the September award is virtually the same in dollars and cents after taxes, only the kids get the benefit —the first one Nancy liked, but it was the largest award ever granted by this justice in over thirty-seven hundred cases.

Now Fredman comes in with a set of papers that you will read in which he says that she missed the boat. It happens to judges. Judges are human beings. He says that the justice made a mistake and she failed to recognize that Nancy had lied in material respects. She failed to recognize that Nancy had disregarded her obligations to the children, and so the justice of the Supreme Court has two oral conferences to reexamine her situation.

What did the judge do, this judge who Nancy would have you believe was fixed? Not only did she reject Capasso's claim that he only had $332,000 available, but—this priceless possession, that Fifth Avenue home that you heard so much about, his pride and joy—she still kicked him out of the house.

Where was there a quid pro quo? Let's suppose somebody is in the 50 percent tax bracket, okay, because the judge assumed when she made her decision that the people were in the 50 percent tax bracket. Now, which gives a family more money, $100 of alimony or $60 of child support? Who comes out better when an award like that is contrasted?

Here is $100 of alimony. Here is $60 of child support. If you didn't pay any attention to taxes, you would say this decision is much better. Here somebody is getting $100. Here they are only getting $60. But you would be wrong.

Because if, as the judge believed, there was a 50 percent tax bracket, the alimony is taxed at 50 percent to the wife. She only keeps for her family $50.

If she is in the 50 percent tax bracket, and it is structured so that she gets $60 child support, that's better than $100 because there is no tax, and she keeps the $60. So tax and the impact of taxes is critical to an understanding of what this judge did. This judge had a purpose. She discussed it with Mr. Leventhal, [and] she made her decision accordingly.

The government claims there was a bribery scheme from April of 1983 on. Why would a man pay more than he is required to pay if he's got the judge in his pocket since April? Why would he incur—and you have the bills before you; I put them in evidence, the computer printout from this fancy firm, Fink, Weinberger, Fredman [Andy Capasso's law firm that represented him during the divorce suit], a detailed billing report in which Capasso spent—he didn't pay the whole bill yet—$465,000 in legal fees? If the judge was in his pocket, he could have picked up the [New York] Post any day of the week, and in the back you'll find that for $250 you can get a divorce special. You don't have to pay $465,000 if you've got the judge in your pocket.

The benefit to the children is enormous, because all of this money is now directed by that decision which has the force of law, as the judge told you, to be paid by Mr. Capasso directly for the children's benefit and not to get into the hands of a woman who is clearly more interested in benefits for herself than in the welfare of her own children.

[T]hat decision [Judge Gabel's first decision of June 23, 1983] itself was unique. It was the highest ever made by the justice of the court.

This judge, past the age of seventy, with failing eyesight, handled all of the motions during the period June to September of 1983, whereas today we learn the work that she and she alone did in 1983 is now done by five judges.

Isn't that extraordinary? She did all of that during the period 1983, and Mr. Leventhal tells us he couldn't be sure, with the volume of work that she had in June of 1983, she even read the papers before that decision was granted in June of 1983 that Mrs. Capasso liked so much and seeks to embrace.

These things, quite frankly, since they are temporary orders, are handled on a virtual conveyor belt. They just come in by the thousands, and they are pushed out. They are not final orders. They are not permanent decisions made by a judge with careful consideration.

Justice Gabel was presented with papers by Samuel Fredman, a leader of the bar, who said that the judge had erred, that she had overlooked facts, that there were misstatements made by Nancy Capasso, that there was a wrongful decision by the judge.

There was clear testimony that Justice Gabel from the outset felt that she had granted Nancy Capasso too much money based on these papers. By early to mid-August, well before Sukhreet Gabel was hired, the judge had drafted at least four decisions, drafts of decisions, in which she had decided to restructure the award for the benefit of the children.

So it wasn't, as the government says, a quid pro quo, a job to the daughter on August 29, the reduction on September 14. The judge, according to Leventhal, by mid-August had gone through four drafts in this monumental, unique case.

For Andy Capasso to be found guilty of these substantive counts, you would have to conclude that Andy Capasso counseled, advised, directed, the hiring of Sukhreet Gabel. Strong words. A very simple challenge: Don't come back with charts, Mr. Prosecutor. [The prosecutor presented various charts in his summation.] Tell these jurors, read them a page reference, where this jury can glean for itself that Andy Capasso ever knew of or, if he knew of, that he didn't say, "Bess, I think you and Rickman . . . I think it is a stupid thing to do."

If Mr. Abrams had to list on a chart the references on the record that he says show that Andy Capasso advised, counseled, commanded, the hiring of Sukhreet Gabel, it would be an empty chart.

I'm going to get to the statement that Mr. Capasso supposedly made to the fired, discharged maid, Shirley Harrod, or in her presence: "Bess, can't you do something?"

There were two mistakes in judgment. There was a mistake in judgment when Bess Myerson publicly hired Sukhreet Gabel and when she wrote her letter to the mayor when she realized there was an appearance of impropriety and she sought to cover it.

Editor's note: Myerson instructed her assistant, Richard Bruno, to write a letter to Mayor Koch falsely claiming that the hiring of Sukhreet Gabel was routine and was done after all the rulings were made in the Capasso divorce.

But we are not trying a case of appearances of impropriety, or misconduct, we are trying a case where you are going to have to decide whether the person who engaged in that conduct is one who acted with a corrupt criminal intent.

There is no proof whatsoever with respect to Andy Capasso. There is another mistake in judgment, and it rests with this table [the prosecution table]. They made a mistake in judgment because they bought the case from Nancy Capasso, and then they brought it but they didn't inspect the ship. They would have seen the holes in it. If they had examined Nancy and Felder, they would have realized that the judge had reached out perhaps for a favor, as she did with Felder, but that didn't mean she was corrupt when she made her June decision. They didn't adequately do their homework.

No one pays a bribe openly. Andy Capasso was a wealthy man dealing with many corporations. If there was a plan to confer some benefit upon Sukhreet Gabel, and he knew of it, Andy Capasso could have found a multitude of high-paying positions, $19,000 and more, in any one of the dozens of corporations that he is a successful man and does business with anywhere in this country.

Bess Myerson didn't put her on the public payroll, file a planned action report with Joe DiVincenzo, send to the Office of Management and Budget a notice containing her name, notify the Department of Personnel, put her on the public payroll under her own name, take her and introduce her openly around. If bribery was the scheme, Bess could have said to herself, "Listen, this is too conspicuous. There's got to be a better way. Andy Capasso has a lot of money. Let's do it another way." But that wasn't her program, that wasn't her plan, and it certainly wasn't her motive.

If one looked at it now with the benefit of hindsight, one would say, "Don't do it, don't do it, Bess. It wouldn't look good."

But, you see, Judge Gabel was not someone who was new to Bess Myerson. The proof is the opposite. Marcella Maxwell [Director of New York City Commission on Human Rights] says that they were friends for fifteen to twenty years.

The fact that Bess Myerson had secured a job that was very important to Hortense Gabel didn't stop Hortense Gabel from rendering that decision that required Capasso to pay $358,000.

Bess Myerson didn't hire Sukhreet Gabel when she wanted to if she were a bribe seeker herself. The agency decided to get rid of Bess's special assistant, Walter Kanter. Bess didn't. The agency [did].

In 1986 these gentlemen [the prosecutors], anxious to make a case—because the papers tell you this is a high-publicity case, there is a lot of gold, perhaps, emotionally at the end of the rainbow if they get a wrongful verdict, a lot of publicity—they take this disturbed girl in 1986 [Sukhreet Gabel], a girl who by 1986 has a self-confessed love-hatred relationship with her parents and Bess Myerson, a girl who has no friends, who uses the $1,800 a month allowance that her parents—her eighty-year-old father and her seventy-odd-year old mother—send her all for her medication, so she is on heavy medication, they take this woman, without the benefit of counsel, knowing that Hortense Gabel is impaired by having suffered a stroke and been hospitalized for weeks, and they put her up to tape her own parents; her mother, blind, ailing from a stroke, gives her daughter her papers. They know that she has in effect stolen them from her mother, because her mother entrusted them for her use. They voluntarily take the fruits of that misconduct of this girl who takes her mother's papers and tapes her mother after she has had a stroke.

There's got to be a level of decency below which even an advocate will not sink in a quest to make a case. It is ugly. And they knew what they were doing. One guy playing Mr. Good Guy, Tony Lombardi [government investigator], David Lawrence playing Mr. Tight-Ass—that's what she [Sukhreet Gabel] said. They knew they were doing the good guy/bad guy approach on this disturbed woman in 1986, without medication, without counsel, and they take her forty-four times, and they move her and manipulate her, take her to an empty courtroom and tell her how to dress, and put her on the witness stand for dry runs, and what are they doing? In effect giving her a forum for the unfair destruction of her parents.

Look what she said to Mr. Hafetz. She can't assure the jury that what she says today won't change in two weeks.

Ladies and gentlemen of the jury, you don't have those two weeks. You are going to have to make a decision. Suppose you don't hesitate to rely on the word of Sukhreet Gabel, and two weeks from now you find that she opened on Broadway at the Belasco taking over from Jackie Mason in *The World According to Sukhreet Gabel*. It could happen.

And you find out that everything she told [that] bunch of suckers was not true. It is too late for you. There is nothing you can do. She tells you, "I cannot assure you that what I say today wouldn't change in two weeks." That alone destroys her.

She says she sometimes mistakes what she thinks might have happened for what really happened. "Oh, dear, am I making this up?" She says that following shock treatment, she had memory derangement and that her mind and her memory [are] like Swiss cheese, full of holes.

Mr. Hafetz asks [Sukhreet Gabel], "It is correct, is it not, that from a deposition transcript of June 17, 1987, you acknowledge perjury in your grand-jury appearance?" "That is correct." Question: "No question about it?" "No question about it."

So this woman gave false testimony in the grand jury. Mr. Lawrence asks Sukhreet Gabel in the grand jury, "Is there anything you told us today or on prior occasions that is inaccurate or untruthful?" Now we know in this session she has lied. Look how she tells Mr. Lawrence, and the grand jury, something which we now know, through the benefit of the Hafetz examination, was a lie: "I want to answer you with the utmost seriousness. Never, on no occasions, have I either omitted information or confused information. I am conscious of the oath I took to tell the truth, and nothing but the truth, and the meaning of those words, and to the best of my knowledge, from the bottom of my heart, I told you every bit of truth that I know. I have never told you an inaccuracy or untruth on purpose."

She doesn't touch on Andy Capasso, but, by God, if the test of reasonable doubt is whether a prudent person would hesitate to act in matters of importance in their own lives, and the government comes to you and says, "Don't hesitate, rely on her word," how can you in good conscience do that?

I should say that desperate situations make for desperate people. The desperate people in this case were the prosecutors. The greed and the vengeance, the government has that on the wrong foot. That's an apt description of Nancy, not of Andy, who treated everyone with a state of royalty, Bess and his family, and paid $358,000 a year.

It was Nancy who should wear the shoe of greed and vengeance, and the prosecutors, in their quest to make a case, struck blows so low that they scuffed their knuckles on pavement. They weren't below the belt; they hit the floor.

It is an exceptional jury. I am not buttering you up, because that's the view of the government, I'm sure. Please understand, though, that you have the fate of three people in your hands. This is my last chance to speak to you about a person where I stand between him and the wrongful use and abuse of power by the government, so I have a heavy duty, just as you do.

They've got nothing in this case with respect to Andy Capasso except the vengeance of his wife because he left her, Nancy Capasso, for an older woman.

You know, with proof like that, it's time for the hook to come out this time for this table [the prosecutor's table]. If you seek a conviction with that kind of proof, it's time for the gong. But this time you people [the prosecutors] have to go. You have the burden. Don't tell this jury you recognize your burden. You know your responsibilities. You stand up here and you show us a page of this transcript reflecting Andy Capasso saying, "I think it's a good thing. I advise the hiring of Sukhreet Gabel," and then I'll give you anything you want.

Does the government gain one bit from showing that Andy Capasso was one of 249 guests at Bess Myerson's swearing-in? Because Hortense Gabel was there also. Is there any proof that the justice of the Supreme Court ever knew Andy? The government says, "Well, why would Andy be there? He's not from the cultural community." That's true. He's not a ballet dancer. He's not a part of the cultural motif here in New York.

But one thing we know: He is the lover of Bess Myerson, and one can assume that there is a reason for him being there. I mean, if he can send someone to fix her toilet, he has the right at least to go to her swearing-in. He's no stranger to her.

There is so much raw power at this front table. You have heard their use of FBI agents. You have seen an investigator, Mr. Lombardi. He looks pretty strong and hefty. Mr. Ford, Mr. Lawrence, Mr. Abrams, Ms. Alexander representing their one client with powers of subpoena, grand juries, the ability to fly witnesses in overnight.

What does it tell you that, after two and a half years, they have failed to present one item of proof that there was a scheme to corrupt somebody who earned a lifetime of respect and reverence, or any proof that Andy Capasso played one role in the hiring of Sukhreet Gabel? And that failure to offer such proof, ladies and gentlemen, is not chargeable to neglect on these people's part. They are energetic, hard-working, and able, but when the crime they charged was not committed, when the proof they seek is not there, no amount of FBI agents, their own investigators, even with the assistance of Nancy Capasso, can result in one credible witness coming to this court to support the allegations instigated by this wife.

This is not a civil case. This is a criminal case in which things much more important than money are at stake, and so the law imposes this enormous responsibility on these gentlemen and lady at the bar. They must prove their case to a point beyond a reasonable doubt, and if, after looking at this case, you say to yourself, "Well, I think this happened or maybe this happened or it might have happened, but there is no proof in this record beyond a reasonable doubt," your duty becomes crystal clear.

Knowing what you now know, if you find yourself hesitating to believe that the government has presented solid proof that a scheme existed to bribe Justice Gabel or that Andy Capasso sought to reduce the awards other than through lawful efforts; if you find yourself hesitating to believe that the government has proven beyond a reasonable doubt a plan to bribe Judge Gabel or that one would be envisaged, given her standing in the community, or that she would forsake a lifetime of dedicated service; if you find yourself hesitating to believe the group—I call it the bevy, the bunch of bitter, biased and disturbed and disgruntled people called by the prosecutor—that hesitation on your part will be the key to your finding of reasonable doubt and to the mandate of acquittal of these defendants.

Grieve not one moment for the fact that he spent a lot of money and time on his charts, five of them, or that every morning they wheel in their cart and all these exhibits. Grieve not one moment for them, because, you see, the local United States Attorney's office is part of a much bigger operation called the United States Department of Justice in Washington with its headquarters, and over the entrance to that building are the words that are at the heart of our system of justice, and those words are that "the government of the United States, the people of our country, never lose a case despite a not guilty verdict so long as justice is done."

Recognizing that our system is a unique contribution to the science of government, your careful scrutiny of this record, free of conjecture, surmise, prejudice, editorialized charts, will lead you to conclude that Andy Capasso and these defendants are entitled to an acquittal.

POSTSCRIPT

The defendants were acquitted of all charges. Had the jury believed Sukhreet Gabel's testimony, however, they could have convicted them easily. Separate to the trial, Mayor Koch had appointed former federal judge Harold Tyler, a onetime law partner and mentor of Giuliani, to take evidence under oath and provide a confidential report on the Bess Mess. Based on the sworn testimony of the key protagonists, the Tyler Report—leaked to the *Village Voice* on June 10, 1987—concluded that Bess Myerson "intended to and did improperly influence the Judge"[2] and was guilty of serious misconduct. In addition, it found Judge Gabel's testimony unbelievable.

In spite of Jay Goldberg's brilliant summation, some facts suggest that even if the portrait of Nancy Capasso as an evil, selfish spouse were true, Judge Tyler may have been right to conclude that Myerson had improperly influenced Judge Gabel. Andy Capasso was not a sympathetic character in reality. On one occasion, angry that Nancy had been indiscreet about a Capasso relative, Capasso became enraged and broke Nancy's thumb.[3] After all, it was Capasso who chose to have an affair with Bess

[2]*When She Was Bad*, by Shana Alexander, pages 205–7.
[3]*Ibid.*, page 69.

Myerson. While this may be a widespread practice in our times, and while Nancy had done the same thing, it hardly supports Mr. Goldberg's vision of Capasso as hero and Nancy as villain.

Jay Goldberg poked fun at Nancy's alleged obsession with the Mercedes. However, the Capassos had eight vehicles, including two limousines. Judge Gabel's order left Nancy with none of the vehicles.[4]

Shana Alexander, in her book *When She Was Bad*, opined that Goldberg's argument about the difference in Judge Gabel's rulings' amounting only to $500 per year was "an artful flimflam" and lamented that the prosecution had not "recalled the expert in matrimonial law to the stand so that he could have provided the jury with a true, complete, and accurate understanding of Justice Gabel's ruling and their major consequences to both parties in the dispute."[5]

Perhaps this verdict did not reflect the precise weight of guilt and innocence on both sides. Nonetheless, Goldberg's summation is a showcase in the use of humor for obtaining a favorable verdict. Humor is a great tool in argument if used properly and under the right circumstances. If you intend your argument to be funny and the jury laughs, you have hit a home run. If they don't laugh, it may be quite damaging. If you don't intend to be funny and they laugh, then you really have problems. Laughing jurors are acquitting jurors. Laughter shows that the matter is not serious. When you get the jurors laughing at the prosecution witnesses, you are well on your way to a successful result.

It is much more difficult for a prosecutor to use humor than for a defense attorney, since the prosecutor is trying to send someone to jail. The jury may be offended by a prosecutor's jokes in that context. Jay Goldberg's use of humor destroyed the credibility of key prosecution witnesses, thereby pulling the prosecution's story apart.

Every case has a feel to it, and the Myerson case is no exception. The cultural backdrop favored the defense. Is the case really

[4]*Ibid.*, page 209.
[5]*Ibid.*, page 282.

worth the effort, even if a technical crime was committed? Would any person with a job want to sit as a juror in a case where there may have been a crime but the smell to the case was bad? That is the reason the defense dwelled on Sukhreet Gabel's underhanded behavior when she took papers from her mother and secretly taped her parents. It made the prosecution smell bad. So did the fact that Raoul Felder helped Sukhreet Gabel get an apartment. In the end no one was killed, no one was injured. Possibly someone who was very rich lost some money. And you had to rely on Sukhreet to reach that conclusion. Ultimately, the prosecution's case rose and fell on the say-so of Sukhreet Gabel. Understandably, the jury gave the defendants the benefit of the doubt.

CONCLUSION

I HAVE CHOSEN TO conclude the book with some shorter extracts from memorable advocacy over the years—the poignant and absurd, comical and profound. In addition to being concentrated examples of oft-used rhetorical techniques, they have that transcendent "moment in history" quality that distinguishes them from the humdrum of everyday life.

Winning a Case by Shooting the Messenger

"The best defense is a good offense." Often, lawyers go on the attack, striking out at the witnesses who hurt their case the most. If they succeed, they may win the case. Contrary to popular belief, the public does not detest negative advertising; attacks on key witnesses score points.

THE UNITED STATES OF AMERICA V. JOSEPH GAMBINO

Jay Goldberg, well-known New York City defense attorney, cross-examined Sammy "The Bull" Gravano, the mobster primarily famous for his testimony that sent John Gotti to jail for life. In this case Gravano was a key witness against Joseph Gambino, who was charged with loan-sharking. Gravano testified for the government under a cooperation agreement and admitted to killing nineteen people. One of Gravano's victims, Mr. Frank Faila, had a contract to purchase a disco from Gravano. Gravano killed Faila and pocketed the deposit.

Excerpts from the Summation of Defense Attorney Jay Goldberg

What did Mr. Faila do to warrant his eradication from the face of the earth by this butcher? He walked in and gave him $650,000. Faila was hoping to buy a building and a discotheque, and for that he was murdered. What crime did Faila ever commit in his life? What mob connections did he have? These people were slaughtered by a person with no conscience or soul, and he said, "650,000 I gave back to the family." Perjury. [This refers to the deposit that Mr. Faila gave Gambino for the purchase of the disco.]

You have his tax returns. Remember what he said? He kept the money because Mr. Faila aborted the transaction. And I said to him, "Sir, isn't it more accurate that you aborted Mr. Faila?" He kept close to $400,000 of it, and Faila died because he wanted to buy a building and came innocently into the presence of this man.

This man tells you he had high hopes of rejoining our community, perhaps not by Christmas but maybe New Year's, certainly before Easter. What a wonderful thought for the people of your community who may have to buy double and triple locks on their doors to know that Salvatore Gravano, who admitted to at least nineteen murders, will one day be among us, because he knows from studying the careers of those people who have preceded him as government witnesses; he knows that by testifying for this table, he has every hope of being free.

When Gravano walked into the United States Attorney's office in 1991, acknowledged killing nineteen people, with a million dollars in property, and, knowing he got the money through labor racketeering, loan-sharking, and murder, [they] never said to him, "Listen, if you want to exchange a life sentence without parole for the possibility of a zero sentence, before you get our commitment to this plea agreement, we want that million dollars in property. You are not entitled to it. You didn't earn it through a day's legitimate work. At least the IRS is entitled to it."

What does the government do when they made a pact with the devil? They imposed no such obligation on him. He still to this day has given the government none of that million dollars.

Who was there at the time this deal was made with this person? What an atrocious, one-sided deal. Do you think for one solitary moment that Salvatore Gravano would hesitate [in] lying if he thought it would advance the government's cause?

You know, a trial doesn't really provide a perfect setting for jurors to analyze whether a witness is really truthful. You only see him for a couple of hours. He comes in with his little glasses; he is not in his work clothes; he is dressed immaculately, fancy suit, tie; he is rehearsed, schooled. He appears before you for two hours. The way he appeared on the witness stand—perfectly coifed, taking the glasses off like a professor—you have to look to the whole of his character and see what happened to other people who knew him far longer and better than you. Ask yourself what happened to other people who made the mistake of trusting him: Mr. Tommy Spinelli, Mr. Nicolas Mormando, Mr. Louis Molito trusted him, they relied on his word. And they no longer walk the face of the earth. They suffered the ultimate penalty from that mistake. Don't you be taken in by the fact that before the government put him on the stand, someone got him an Armani suit, a Sulka shirt, and beautiful tie to make a good appearance before you. Look to what this man has done in his lifetime, and you may conclude that people who spend a lifetime in deception, people who accumulate a horrendous list of violent and outrageous crimes, people who have entered into the jury box in other cases and physically bribed jurors to obstruct justice have in effect forfeited their right to be believed. That is Salvatore Gravano."

THE UNITED STATES OF AMERICA v. ETHEL ROSENBERG AND JULIUS ROSENBERG

Emanuel Bloch represented Ethel Rosenberg in the 1951 trial accusing Rosenberg and her husband, Julius, of giving the plans for the atom bomb to Soviet agents. David Greenglass, Ethel's brother, testified as a government witness against his sister and brother-in-law. Mr. Bloch went after him with no holds barred.

Excerpts from the Summation of Defense
Attorney Emanuel Bloch

Now, all of you are New Yorkers. We are a pretty sophisticated people. People can't put things over on us very easily. We are fairly wise in the ways of the world and the ways of people, and we all know that there is not a person in this world who hasn't some prejudice, and you would be inhuman if you didn't have some prejudice. Please don't decide this case because you may have some bias or some prejudice against some political philosophy.

If you want to convict these defendants because you think that they are Communists and you don't like communism and you don't like any member of the Communist Party, then, ladies and gentlemen, I can sit down now, and there is absolutely no use in my talking. There was no use in going through this whole rigmarole of a three weeks' trial. That is not the crime.

But believe me, ladies and gentlemen, I am not here as attorney for the Communist Party and as attorney for the Soviet Union. We are representing Julius and Ethel Rosenberg, two American citizens, who come to you as American citizens, charged with a specific crime, and ask you to judge them the way you would want to be judged if you were sitting over there before twelve other jurors.

Now, let us take Dave Greenglass. Is there any doubt in any of your minds that Dave Greenglass is a self-confessed espionage agent? He characterized himself that way. What did this man do? He took an oath when he entered the army of the United States. He didn't even remember what the oath was. That is how seriously he took it. But, in substance, he swore to support our country. Is there any doubt in your mind that he violated that oath? Is there any doubt in your mind that he disgraced the uniform of every soldier in the United States by his actions? Do you know what that man did? He was assigned to one of the most important secret projects in this country, and, by his own admissions, he told you that he stole information out of there and gave it to strangers, and that it was going to the Soviet government. Now, that is undisputed. I would like anybody who is going to sum up on the part of the government to refute that.

You know, before I summed up, I wanted to go to a dictionary, and I wanted to find a word that could describe a Dave Greenglass. I couldn't find it, because I don't think that there is a word in the English vocabulary or in the dictionary of any civilization which can describe a character like Dave Greenglass.

But one thing I think you do know: that any man who will testify against his own blood and flesh, his own sister, is repulsive, is revolting, [is a man] who violates every code that any civilization has ever lived by. He is the lowest of the lowest animals that I have ever seen, and if you are honest with yourself, you will admit that he is lower than the lowest animal that you have ever seen.

This is not a man; this is an animal. And how he got up there. Did you look at him? I know you did; you watched him; all your eyes were fastened on him, just as people are fascinated by horror; and he smirked, and he smiled, and I asked him a question so that it would be in the cold printed record: "Are you aware of your smile?" And do you know the answer I got? "Not very." Listen to that answer: "Not very."

Well, maybe some people enjoy funerals; maybe some people enjoy lynchings; but I wonder whether, in anything that you have read or in anything that you have experienced, you have ever come across a man who comes 'round to bury his own sister and smiles.

Tell me, is this the kind of a man you are going to believe? God Almighty, if ever a witness discredited himself on a stand, he did. What kind of a man can be disbelieved if we are going to believe Dave Greenglass? What is the sense of having witness chairs? What is the sense of having juries subject witnesses' testimony to scrutiny and analysis? Is that the kind of a man that you would believe in your own life, or would you punch him in the nose and throw him out and have nothing to do with him because he is a low rebel? Come on, be honest with yourselves, ladies and gentlemen, is that the kind of testimony that you are going to accept?

And he was arrogant. He felt he had the government of the United States behind him. He had a right to be arrogant, because the Greenglasses put it all over the FBI and put it all over Mr. Saypol's staff [Irving Saypol, US attorney and chief prosecutor of the

Rosenbergs], and I submit that they are smarter than the whole bunch. They sold them a bill of goods. Every man sitting over here is an honest man. The FBI representatives, Mr. Saypol and his staff, every man of them, they are doing their duty, but you know, even the smartest of us can be tricked, and do you want me to show you how they were tricked?

Sticks and Stones

Attacking a witness who has had a sordid past is certainly one effective technique an advocate has to advance his client's cause. Many murder cases, if not most, are drug-related. It therefore follows that many witnesses have a criminal history. As the messengers of the prosecution case, these witnesses are subject to attacks by the defense.

THE PEOPLE OF THE STATE OF NEW YORK v. ORLANDO RODRIGUEZ

Stephen Saracco, a former New York County prosecutor, demonstrates a prosecution response to attacks on its witnesses.

Excerpts from the Summation of Prosecutor Stephen Saracco

There is a general name-calling, attack on the witnesses we produced. I think jurors are savvy enough to know that this is not a game. We have a homicide here that took place in a drug location on 160th Street here in New York during a narcotics transaction.

We take the witnesses as we find them. We don't say, "We have a murder case here. Let me look through here and see what I can use. I hope the mayor was there or this businessman. I can use this nun."

Who do you expect the witnesses to be in a homicide with the circumstances such as this? Do you think you're going to find the living saints that walk around the streets of Manhattan? I make no apologies for any of my witnesses. I contend to you the three civilians that came in here comported themselves with dignity, with politeness; that they were frank and honest about their backgrounds

and did not try in any way to shade or minimize their drug addic-
tions and their criminal records in any way shape or form.

The Power of Analogy

If you're trying to persuade people, you certainly don't want to bore
them. Analogies and interesting stories serve the dual purpose of
entertaining and persuading the jury. The most compelling analogy
is the kind that fits the facts of a particular case effortlessly.

THE UNITED STATES OF AMERICA V. PETER GATIEN

Below, Benjamin Brafman, trying a case before New York jurors—
most of whom resided in apartment buildings—used the following analogy in attacking the prosecution's key witnesses.

Excerpts from the Summation of Defense
Attorney Benjamin Brafman

Assume you were going away on a trip and these guys lived on
your floor, in your apartment house. Would you leave them the key
to your apartment so they could water your plants? Nobody here
would do that. You would not give the key to these guys to water
your plants. They're asking you to let them hold the key on the rest
of Mr. Gatien's life.

THE UNITED STATES OF AMERICA V. MACK WILBOURN

Jerome Froelich, an Atlanta criminal defense attorney, was
defending Mack Wilbourn in a municipal-corruption trial in
Atlanta. The case against Mack Wilbourn was circumstantial, and
Mr. Froelich told the following story to show the limited value of
circumstantial evidence.

Excerpts from the Summation of Defense
Attorney Jerome Froelich

Now, [the government] talked about circumstantial evidence.
Let me give you an example that happened to me. I'm one of eight

kids. I have five brothers. It was a rough-and-tumble family, but there was one we did not fool with. I have a brother Brian who was a national heavyweight wrestling champion, and he played tackle at Boston College. He is as big an individual as you ever want to see, and he doesn't have an ounce of fat. He's been that way since he's sixteen years old. And he does not have a very nice disposition at times.

When we were kids, we would come home from our various practices and my mother would leave food for us. We would come home at different hours. I had a brother Larry. Larry was tough, but he wasn't as tough as Brian. I never thought Larry was very bright, but one day I learned he was. We came home, and we started eating dinner. We all had sandwiches, and we had a dish of pudding after dinner.

Brian was the last one home. He actually was running extra laps because of something he had done in practice. We had finished our pudding, and Larry decided he was going to have one extra pudding, and it was Brian's. He sat at the table, and he started to eat that pudding. I heard the door open, and I knew that Larry was one of the dumbest people on earth, and I was leaving that kitchen, because I wanted no part of when Brian got home to find that Larry had eaten that pudding.

Larry then proved to me how smart he was. We had a boxer, a dog. The boxer's name was Mo. Larry heard Brian coming through the door, too. Larry picked up Mo, picked up the side of the dish of pudding and stuck that dog's face in that pudding, and he put that dog back on the floor, and then he ran with me to our rooms to open books and start doing homework.

Why was Larry smart? Larry never got hurt on that. Mo had a tough week. He got kicked around, he didn't get fed real well for a while. But that's what circumstantial evidence can do to you, and that's what you got to be careful of. Don't let Mack Wilbourn wind up like Mo. That's what [prosecution key witness] Bernard Parks is trying to do to you. What my brother Larry did to that dog.

THE UNITED STATES OF AMERICA V. PETER GATIEN

In 1998, Ben Brafman told the following story to illustrate the weakness in the prosecution's evidence of corroboration.

Excerpts from the Summation of Defense Attorney Benjamin Brafman

This hysterical lady calls the police one day. Unbeknownst to the police, she's been in love with Robert Redford since she's a kid; she loves him so much. Robert Redford has ignored the five thousand letters she's written. One day she gets tired of this, calls the police, says, "Robert Redford came to my house, took me out into the backyard, beat me up, tied me to a tree." The cops come to the house. They say, "Lady, you mean Robert Redford the actor?" She said, "Yes, he tied me up, beat me up, stole my money, and tied me to a tree." They said, "Do you have any corroboration for this"? She says, "There's the tree."

In another instance from the same case, Brafman illustrates the importance of cross-examination.

Ladies and gentlemen, I've got to tell you a humorous story. Sometimes humor is the best way to make a point that you remember long into the night, long into your deliberations. The story is [in] an old town long ago. There's a busy intersection. The man is driving a horse-drawn wagon through the intersection. The dog runs out and scares the horse. The horse rears up, falls on the dog, turns over the wagon, and the wagon falls on the man. Ten years later there's a court case. The people who are being sued are trying to show that the wagon driver really wasn't injured. They call the policeman who is first on the scene. The lawyer gets up, says, "Sir, when you came on the scene, what did the wagon driver say to you?" and the police officer dutifully responds, "I'm okay, I'm okay."

Seems pretty solid evidence there's nothing wrong with that guy, right? Then I get up to do cross-examination, a search for the truth. I say, "Officer, tell this jury everything you saw and everything you did from the moment you came upon the scene." The cop says, "You know, I came there, it was terrible. The dog was howling in pain, had three broken legs. I took out my gun, I shot the dog. I went up to the horse; the horse had three broken legs, whining in pain. I took out the gun, shot the horse, I turned to the wagon driver; he said, 'I'm okay.'"

THE UNITED STATES OF AMERICA v. PATRICIA HEARST

Patricia Hearst was kidnapped by the Symbionese Liberation Army (SLA) and, in April 1974, took part in a bank robbery organized by the group. The issue at trial was whether she was coerced to participate in the robbery or did so of her own volition. The bank robbery was caught on videotape, and the jury ultimately convicted Hearst. Unfortunately, even if the analogy is entertaining, if the facts of the case do not match up for the jury, the analogy will not win the case for the advocate.

Excerpts from the Summation of Defense
Attorney F. Lee Bailey

This is not a case about a bank robbery. The crime could have been any one of a number. It is a case about dying or surviving; that is all Patricia Campbell Hearst thought about. And the question is, What is the right to live? How far can you go to survive? We all know that it is a generic, irresistible human impulse to survive. People eat each other in the Andes to survive. The big question is, Can you kill to survive? We do it in wartime, but that is a different set of rules. We allow ourselves all kinds of special privileges when we fight the enemy.

A novelist once wrote a most disturbing book. It was a best-seller and movie. A man who was condemned to hang for killing his wife killed his executioner to survive, and then it was determined that he had not killed his wife. A judge had to decide whether or not he could be tried for that second killing. Does one have an obligation at some point to die? It was called A Covenant with Death, and we all have a covenant with death. We're all going to die, and we know it. And we're all going to postpone that date as long as we can. Patty Hearst did that, and that is why she is here and you are here.

Inconsistencies

There is not a court case in the world without inconsistencies among the witnesses, and not necessarily because witnesses lie. People perceive and recall the same event differently, and everyone's memory fades with the passage of time. Besides, a skillful lawyer can create inconsistencies between witnesses on almost any case. The issue really facing the jury is whether these inconsistencies cut to the heart of the case.

THE PEOPLE OF THE STATE OF NEW YORK v. *ORLANDO RODRIGUEZ*

Prosecutor Steve Saracco told the following story to minimize the importance of inconsistencies among prosecution witnesses.

Excerpts from the Summation of Prosecutor Stephen Saracco

Ten individuals viewing a startling event will remember only the startling event, and the circumstances surrounding it, differently. Ten people are at a party, and there's a mother at the party holding a newborn, and something startles the woman, and she actually drops the baby.

Since I'm making up the story, I'll give it a happy ending. The baby is okay when they pick it up. A year or two later, the same ten people will be together again, and they are talking about the party, and someone will say, "Remember, her husband wasn't there?"

Someone else says, "He was standing next to you. You were there."

Then someone says, "Remember. she came out of the kitchen?"

"No. She came out of the bedroom."

"She was negligent holding the baby with one arm."

"No, no. She had both arms around the baby."

They may disagree with the certain aspects about the party, but they will all remember the one thing: The lady drops the baby. There were several inconsistencies here, but the one thing everyone remembers is, this defendant shot Irizarry in the head, and Mr. Hodge was shot in the back of the head by this defendant's partner.

Fighting the Current

In any case, the judge asks jurors to set aside everything that is going on in the world outside, the popular culture and current controversies. As Benjamin Brafman points out below, the advocate often must fight the popular current outside the courtroom to win a case.

THE UNITED STATES OF AMERICA v. PETER GATIEN

Excerpts from the Summation of Benjamin Brafman, February 1998

I was on the beach once, watching on a stormy day a lifeguard trying to save someone. The lifeguard was a tall, muscular young kid who was a brilliant swimmer, in great shape, cut through the water like a shark. He lost the person. The person drowned because of the current. The current was so strong that the lifeguard was not able to save that person. I'll never forget that. It was a horrifying scene. The lifeguard tried so hard.

I'm not concerned about the evidence. On the evidence in this case, I should be able to save Mr. Gatien without even breaking a sweat. For them to say they have proved his guilt beyond a reasonable doubt is the biggest lie of this case. The only concern I have is the current. We live in a time when everything is driven by the media, by television. Everything is a concern. There is a concern about drugs. There is a concern about regulating them, whether they should be legalized. That's a debate we can have until the cows come home. That's not what this trial is about. It's not a referendum. Don't let the current that's out there affect your decision. Without a current, on straight facts, straight law, I take a few easy strokes out, I grab Mr. Gatien around the chest, I save him from this case. I'm asking you to help me, because you heard the testimony and there isn't a juror here who I believe in honesty can go home tonight and say Brafman is wrong.

THE UNITED STATES OF AMERICA v.
BUTCHER AND STEINER

Bobbie Lee Cook spoke of fighting a different current in his summation in a bank fraud case in Chattanooga, Tennessee. A legitimate concern to any defense attorney is the fear that a jury will arrive at a "where there is smoke, there is fire" verdict (i.e., the police would not have arrested the defendant and the prosecutor would not have tried him if the charges weren't true). Below, Cook addresses the concern that perhaps jurors do not trust defense attorneys and presume a defendant guilty simply because he has been charged.

Excerpts from the Summation of Defense Attorney Bobbie Lee Cook, August 1986

I have a duty to perform which is just as significant and just as compelling as [that of] a soldier, a duty fixed by law, for which I offer no apologies and . . . which I am glad and proud to perform.

The philosophy of what I speak is equally as important to you and to your children in this country. Every man and every woman, irrespective of his race or creed or color, whether he is rich, whether he is poor, whether he is from Chattanooga or Maynardville or my little town of Summerville, is entitled to the same breath of fresh air in this country.

For over two hundred years ago, the founders of this Republic, meeting in Philadelphia, struck a Constitution which contained a Bill of Rights that has been with us for over two hundred years. And in that Bill of Rights, it says that in all criminal cases, the accused shall enjoy the right to a speedy and a public trial by an impartial jury, and to be informed of the charges, and to have the effective assistance of counsel for his defense, and the right to be confronted with the witnesses.

This jury under this system that was devised over two hundred years ago also has the duty and the responsibility to weigh the guilt or the innocence of two fellow citizens. It is not important that they may be Democrats or Republicans or independents, that they may be white, that they may be Baptist or Presbyterians; it is the fact that they are entitled to these rights.

The difference between the rights of Mr. Butcher and Mr. Steiner in this case and all other American citizens as how it would differ if they were in some Communist country, it would be the fact that for these two hundred years, thank God, that you cannot brand them as a felon or take away a penny of their money except by a unanimous verdict of twelve citizens such as you.

And it has been fought for and preserved in the jungles of Iwo Jima and Guadalcanal and the beaches of Omaha and Anzio-Nettuno, the Central Highlands and the delta of Vietnam and the Argonne, consecrated by the blood of patriots and ordinary citizens to preserve the rights of C. H. Butcher and Jim Steiner and all of us throughout this great land.

When each defendant comes into this court, he is cloaked with a presumption of innocence in his behalf that remains with him throughout the entire course of the trial until the Government establishes guilt beyond a reasonable doubt.

It is a strong burden. It is a necessary burden. It is a burden that is there because, when your Founding Fathers wrote the Constitution and took notice of the Bill of Rights, they understood more about liberty and justice and freedom than my generation or my children's generation, because these people had come here from England and France and Germany and the Highlands of Scotland and Ireland and the ghettos of Central Europe in order to escape the tyranny that they once had, the yoke of oppression that had been placed upon their heads and necks, and they understood it very well.

I speak to you of fairness, and I speak to you about justice. It is important that Mr. Butcher and Mr. Steiner get the same brand of justice that you would expect to receive. And it's necessary to speak up for what is right and what is decent, even though it might not be the popular thing to do.

The overwhelming evidence in this case does not establish beyond a reasonable doubt that C. H. Butcher possessed that requisite degree of specific intent to condemn him as a felon, and it's necessary for you to speak up, not only for his benefit but for your benefit and your children and their children.

It reminds me of something that was said by a German pastor after World War II, a Protestant pastor, a man by the name of Martin Niemoller. He said, "When they came for the Jews, I wasn't a Jew, and I didn't speak up.And then they came for the trade unionists and I wasn't a trade unionist, and I didn't speak up. Then they came for Catholics, and I wasn't a Catholic and I didn't speak up. And they came for me, and there wasn't anyone left to speak up."

I'm not asking you for any favors. I am not appealing for sympathy, I am appealing to you to do what is right and just.

Two hundred years ago, when these young men and women arrived at this great constitutional birth, this Bill of Rights, they emerged from the Constitution Hall, convention hall, and they were going down the steps. A young lady came up to Mr. [Benjamin] Franklin and said, "Mr. Franklin, what kind of government have you given us?" And he said, "We have given you a republic, if you can keep it."

This jury, you bring together all of you from all walks of life, from all strata of society; you bring here a wealth of experience, a great background, a diversity, in many things: at least one veteran of World War II, a Vietnam veteran, and others in many walks of life.

Use your common sense in this case. You don't have to throw your common sense out the window. Render a verdict in this case which speaks the truth of this transaction, and that is a verdict of not guilty.

THE PEOPLE OF THE STATE OF NEW YORK v. JON LESTER, SCOTT KERN, ET AL.

Charles Hynes was the lead prosecutor in the Howard Beach, New York, murder trial. In that case a group of young white men beat one black man and chased a second onto a busy highway, where he was run over and killed. The motive for the crime was racial hatred and territorialism. Below, Hynes addresses the possibility that racial loyalties exist in the hearts of the jurors.

Excerpts from the Summation of Prosecutor Charles Hynes

To breathe, to smile, to laugh, to cry, and to live—those are all gifts that we get when we come into this life. No one has the right to take those precious gifts away from us. The God that gave us these gifts, who gave us life, gave us liberty to come and go as we please. How different we are than those folks who are visiting from Soviet Russia. We can travel freely between continents on this planet, and there are no borders in this country that we can't cross freely.

Many years ago our nation established a principle that the color of a person's skin does not dictate where he goes to school, where they sit on the bus or what restaurant they can sit at. It also cannot determine where one travels or when a person's time to die is.

For centuries commentators have written about the sanctity of human life and the common interest we share in protecting it. No one has spoken more eloquently of the relationship between one life to another than the preacher-poet John Donne. More than 250 years ago, he wrote those words: "No man is an island, entire of itself; every man is a piece of the continent, a part of the main." Later on he said, "any man's death diminishes me, because I am involved in mankind." Finally he said, "Therefore, never send to know for whom the bell tolls; it tolls for thee."

Petrarch said, "A good death does honor to a whole life." He could have added that a bad death does dishonor to us all. The law and fundamental principles of life and human dignity say they (the victims) were entitled to walk the streets of Queens County without fear of violent attack, humiliation, or death.

In the Book of Ecclesiastes, we are told "To every thing there is a season, and a time for every purpose under heaven. A time to be born and a time to die." Who are these four defendants to decide it is his time to die?

As you look across the courtroom to where these four defendants sit, some of you have said, "My God, they're so young. How could they have done something so vicious? How could they have chased Michael Griffith to his death? And how could the three of them turn around and have beaten Cedric Sandiford until he appeared to be dead?" If you asked [those questions], do you recall how Theresa Fisher saw the attack on Cedric Sandiford and how she described the brutality? Listen to her voice paint a vivid picture of the beating he sustained. [911 tape played]

You see them now sitting over there. They can be attending a high-school graduation or waiting for a job interview. There isn't even a hint of anger now or hatred now or viciousness now. When you deliberate, think of them, not as they look now, but as they looked on the night of December 19, 1986.

The Human Prop

THE STATE OF WISCONSIN v. CHMURA

Gerry Boyle, a Milwaukee lawyer who successfully defended Green Bay Packers football player Mark Chmura against sexual-assault charges, uses his daughter as a human prop to minimize the harm caused by his having to cross-examine the alleged female victim, a seventeen-year-old high-school student, and her five friends.

Excerpts from the Summation of Defense
Attorney Gerry Boyle

I had the task of cross-examining some women up here, and I had asked them some hard questions. I worship women. They gave us life. They bring babies in the world. My daughter is my law partner, so I will never demean them, but my job here today is to point things out when somebody tries to say nobody would make something like that up, it's not possible, [that] a woman would never make a thing up.

I want to tell you about the story not too long ago where everybody in America had tears in their eyes watching a woman [referring to Susan Smith in North Carolina, who killed her children by driving her car into the river and then blamed a black man] talk about her children being kidnapped, praying that the person bring them back; [she] was crying uncontrollably on television cameras days at a time with the nation looking up to try and find these two youngsters, and some policeman said, "I don't know if I believe her. I don't buy the arguments some black man, an unknown black man, took these two children and ran off with her car." Then they found the car in the river with the two children in it, dead. She had killed them, and the reason was, the new boyfriend who she liked didn't like kids. Nobody is going to tell me that any of us have to take the position that because somebody said something that we have to believe them, because somebody wouldn't do that. Susan Smith fooled us all. And the reason that we knew she was lying is, eventually she said she was, but it was only after an investigation took place and [she was confronted with the fact that that happened.]

Humor

THE UNITED STATES OF AMERICA v. NELSON AND PRICE

> Although humor is usually a risky proposition for a prosecutor, federal prosecutor Alan Vinegrad, who tried Lemrick Nelson for the stabbing death of Yankel Rosenbaum in Crown Heights, Brooklyn, successfully used humor in his summation by mocking the O. J. Simpson trial. The defense claimed that the baggy pants containing Rosenbaum's blood that were introduced at the trial did not belong to Nelson because they did not fit him snugly, although he appeared in a photograph in *Newsday* wearing them.

Excerpts from the Summation of Prosecutor Alan Vinegrad

What [does the defense] resort to? The baggy-pants defense. Until today the fiascoes of the case on the West Coast—I won't mention the name—hadn't invaded this trial. But the defense in his desperation brought it into the courtroom and paraded it before you. It turned the courtroom into the theater of the absurd. Pants don't fit, you must acquit. That is what you would have heard from that table. You know what? They are wrong. They are baggy. Like it's a big surprise that teenagers in Brooklyn in the 1990s would walk around with big baggy pants on. I am sure that is a big shock to everybody here.

All that Lemrick Nelson's demonstration here proves is, he wears baggy pants. Over the last five and a half years, either these well-traveled pants have gotten stretched out a bit or he's gotten more slender or firmer or both. Who knows? Maybe that is why the police were able to catch him, because he couldn't run fast enough, because of holding on to these baggy pants. I guess what I am really saying, since that California case is in the courtroom now, "If the pants don't fit, I don't give a ———." You fill in the rest.

THE UNITED STATES OF AMERICA v. CONGRESSMAN JAMES TRAFICANT

In the case of Congressman Traficant, featured in Chapter 4, it seems that his outrageous oratory failed to prove his innocence but succeeded in establishing that reality is stranger than fiction. Here are some more of his most memorable one-liners:

Congressman Traficant spontaneously addresses the cameraman covering the hearing to expel Traficant from the House of Representatives: "If you don't get those cameras out of my face, I'm gonna go 8.6 on the Richter scale with gastric emissions that'll clear the room!"

Charged with selling an old boat in disrepair at an inflated price in return for political favors, Congressman Traficant explains to the Ethics Subcommittee why he kept the boat docked: "I wanted to have Playboy bunnies come on at night and meet with me. I wanted to be promiscuous with them."

Congressman Traficant speaks about the intestinal fortitude of the prosecutors at his trial: "The prosecutors have the testicles of an ant."

Congressman Traficant's eloquent summation to the Ethics Subcommittee: "I want you to disregard all the opposing counsel has said. I think they're delusionary [sic]. I think they've had something funny for lunch in their meal. I think they should be handcuffed, chained to a fence, and flogged, and all their hearsay evidence should be thrown the hell out. And if they lie again, I'm going to go over there and kick them in the crotch."

• • •

We are a society obsessed with lawyers and courtrooms. We may claim that we do not think much about lawyers, but a cursory glance at *TV Guide* demonstrates that lawyer shows with courtroom action dominate the airwaves. More often than not, we gain our knowledge about lawyers and law not from visiting the courtroom but from television, movies, and good fiction.

We all love watching the drama of courtroom action on film or TV, the witness who cries on the stand, the handsome young attorneys in Armani suits whose pearls of wisdom secure justice for their victimized clients. But real life is different, of course. In the movies the distinctions between right and wrong, victim and criminal, are always clear. In real cases, as we have seen, black and white give way to countless shades of gray. Evidence is limited or conflicting, arguments are complex and intricate, circumstances are inconvenient or misleading. It falls to the attorneys to sort things out for the judge and jury.

Having read through this book, you may have the impression of a society perpetually in conflict. Or, if you have an optimistic bent, you might see a gigantic machine in the process of resolving massive polarities peacefully. After working so many years in the halls of justice fighting the crime wars, I'm still not sure which picture is more accurate. It is the unfortunate truth that the justice system often works inadequately; sometimes, even the most brilliant lawyer cannot win a case when the cultural backdrop is against him. Indeed, the system has myriad flaws. It does not, for instance, always arrive at the absolute truth; often, it offers conflicting truths. And sometimes, as in the Karen Silkwood case, you're left with the uneasy feeling that the truth never came out at all. But fallibility is no reason to turn away from the legal system altogether. As with any intricate piece of machinery, the more attention it gets, the better it works. I hope we have shown you that, if our system is not always a thing of beauty, it is at least as funny and tragic, flawed and redeemable as people themselves are.

SOURCES

Books

Alexander, Shana. *When She Was Bad*. New York: Random House, 1990.

Baselt, Randall. *Disposition of Toxic Drugs and Chemicals in Man*. Foster City: Biomedical Publications, 2002.

Blackburn, James L. *Flame-Out*. Leslie Books, 2000.

Goldberg, Steven, H. *The First Trial*. St. Paul, Minn.: West Publishing Company. 1982.

Knappman, Edward. *Great American Trials*. Detroit: Visible Ink Press, 1994.

Kohn, Howard. *Who Killed Karen Silkwood?* New York: Summit Books, 1981.

McGinniss, Joe. *Fatal Vision*. New York: Penguin Putnam,1984.

Novak, William. *The Big Book of Jewish Humor*. New York: Perennial, 1981.

Rashke, Richard. *The Killing of Karen Silkwood*. Boston: Houghton Mifflin, 1981.

Segev, Tom. *The Seventh Million*. New York: Henry Holt, 1991.

Spence, Gerry. *With Justice for None*. New York: Times Books, 1989.

Articles

Bajker, D., and Diehaus, B. 2002. "Florida Laws May Shield Erpenbeck," *Kentucky Post Online Edition*, www.kypost.com/2002/aug/01/kerp080102. August 1.

BBC.com. "Karen Silkwood—Campaigner." www.bbc.co.uk/dna/h2g2/alabaster/A634213. Created January 8, 2002.

CBC News Online, "Lindh Sentenced to Twenty Years," July 15, 2002, www.cbc.ca/stories/2002/07/15/lindh020715.

Cher, Michael Moore and others, December 8, 1999. www1.columbia.edu/sec.bboard/ssw/suboard/archive/1999.

CNN Online, "Albert Spared Jail Time for Hotel Room Assault," www.cnn.com/US/9710/24/albertupdate/. October 24, 1997.

CNN Online, "I Plead Guilty, Taliban American Says," www.cnn.com/2002/LAW/07/15/walker.lindh.hearing/. July 17, 2002.

CNN Online, "John Walker Lindh Makes His First Court Appearance," www.cnn.com/2002/LAW/01/24/walker.court/. January 26, 2002.

CNN Online, "O. J. Simpson Ordered to Surrender Earnings," www.cnn.com/2004/LAW/02/23/simpson.lawsuit.ap/. February 23, 2004.

CNN Online, People in the News, "The Case of the Taliban American, John Walker Lindh Profile," www.cnn.com/CNN/Programs/people/shows/walker/profile.

Cornelius, R. M. "William Jennings Bryan and The Scopes Trial." Bryan College, Historical Resources, www. bryan.edu/historical/wjbryan-trial/.

The Daily Beacon, "John Walker Lindh's Attorney Seeks Release From Conspiracy Charges," Volume 89, No. 20, www.dailybeacon.utk.edu/article.php. February 6, 2002.

The Daily Business Journal, Transcripts from Traficant's Criminal Trial Available Online, www. business-journal.com /TraficantTrial/ethics website7–19.html. July 19, 2002.

Epstein, J., and Pierre, R. 2002. Traficant Is Found Guilty, www.washingtonpost.com. April 12.

Estate of Silkwood v. Kerr-McGee, 464 US 238 (1984).

Famous Trials: The Rosenberg Trial, Biographies of Trial Participants, Emanuel Hirsch Bloch, www.law.umkc.edu/faculty/projects/ftrials/rosenb/ROS_BBLO.HTM.

Fenner, A., and Lonbardi, F. 1999. "Jesse, Pols Blast Police Policy," The Daily News. February 20.

Fitz-Gibbon, Jorge. 1999. "Two Cops Offer to Talk, Say Diallo Protests Will Keep Them Away." The Daily News. March 3.

Fox News Online, "Moussaoui Arrest Stuns Flight School, Online" www.foxnews.com/story/0,2933,40630,00, December 12, 2001.

Fox News Online, "Traficant Trial Demonstrates Congressman's Idiosyncrasies," www.foxnews.com. February 28, 2002.

Free Traficant website, www.freetraficant.com/submittedquotes.php.

Hays, Tom. 2000. "Officers Cleared In Diallo Killing." SouthCoast Today. www.southcoasttoday.com/daily/ 02-00/02-26-00/a01wn009.htm. February 26.

Houston Chronicle.com, "Justice Department Probes Texas Tech Professor's Policy," January 29, 2003.

"Justice Department Closes Religious Descrimination Inquiry at Texas Tech University." Department of Justice Press Release, April 22, 2003, www.usdoj.gov/opu/pr/2003/April/03_crt_247.htm.

Kaufman, J., and McNeil, E. 1999. "Abandoned by Mom, Karen Silkwood's Children Struggle with a Complex Legacy," *People Magazine*. March 15–22. Volume 21, Issue 10.

Lawyers Weekly USA, "Med-Mal Lawyer Breaks Personal Record with $107M Verdict," by Amy Johnson Conner, as appearing in www.lawyersweeklyusa.com. January 7, 2002.

Los Alamos Science, "The Karen Silkwood Story," November 23, 1995, Volume XXIII, appearing at www.pbs.org.

Los Angeles Times, "Traficant Case Goes to Jury," April 9, 2002, Volume 122, Number 17.

MSNBC News, "Official Charged with Perjury in Stewart Case," www.msnbc.com/id/5031557/=%Marth+Stewart%22+%22Larry+Stewart%22h1=en, May 21, 2003.

NewsMax.com, "Police Officers in Amadou Diallo Case Not Guilty," www.newsmax.com/articles/?a=2000/2/26/70122. February 26, 2000.

The Nizkor Project, Adolf Eichmann, www.nizkor.org/hweb/people/e/eichmann-adolf/.

Noel, Peter. 2001. "O. J. Simpson Meets Puff Daddy," *Village Voice*. www.featurewell.com/?WID=525. January 30–February 6.

PBS.org. "John Walker Lindh's Attorney," www.socialconscience.com/articles/2002/walker. July 16, 2002.

People v. *Kevin Boss, Sean Carroll et al.*, 261 A.D. 2d 1 (1999).

Reutter, Mark. 2001. "Bankruptcy Loophole Lets Debtors Keep Mansions While Others Suffer." *University of Illinois at Urbana-Champaign News Bureau*, www.news.uiuc.edu/biztips/01/04bankrupt.html. April 1.

Ristich Gatts, Michele. 2002. "Traficant Trial Tracker: A Look Back on Eve of Sentencing," *The Daily Business Journal Online*. July 29.

Ryan, Joel. 1997. You Enjoy Rough Sex, Accuser Says Albert Told Her," E-Online, www.eonline.com/News/Items/0,1,1812,00. September 23.

Ryan, Joel.1997. "Marv Pulls Rug Out from Under Wig Story," E-Online, www.eonline.com/News/Items/0,1,2046,00. November 6.

The Sacramento Bee, "Quotes from Traficant's Corruption Trial," www.sacbee.com. April 1, 2002.

Smith, M., Snow, K., Yoon, R. 2002. "House Gives Traficant the Boot." *CNN.com*, www.cnn.com/2002/ALLPOLITICS/ 07/24/traficant.expulsion/. July 25.

VerdictSearch, "Medical Malpractice," www.verdictsearch.com/news/specials/0204verdicts-ballinas.jsp.

Warner, Margaret. 2002. "Plea Bargain, Interview of James Brosnahan," *PBS Online News Hour*. "Plea Bargain." www.pbs.org/newshour/bb/law/july-dec02/plea2_7-15. July 15.

Washington Post.com, "The Quotable James A. Traficant," www.washingtonpost.com. July 25, 2002.

Wood, Andrea. 2002. "Jurors Seek Closure as They Watch Traficant Sentenced, Taken Away in Handcuffs." *The Daily Business Journal Online*. www.business-journal.com/TraficantTrial/SentencingSummary7-31. July 31.

INDEX